Gordon Merrick and the Great Gay American Novel

Gordon Merrick and the Great Gay American Novel

Joseph M. Ortiz

LEXINGTON BOOKS
Lanham • Boulder • New York • London

Published by Lexington Books
An imprint of The Rowman & Littlefield Publishing Group, Inc.
4501 Forbes Boulevard, Suite 200, Lanham, Maryland 20706
www.rowman.com

86-90 Paul Street, London EC2A 4NE

Copyright © 2022 by The Rowman & Littlefield Publishing Group, Inc.

All rights reserved. No part of this book may be reproduced in any form or by any electronic or mechanical means, including information storage and retrieval systems, without written permission from the publisher, except by a reviewer who may quote passages in a review.

British Library Cataloguing in Publication Information Available

Library of Congress Cataloging-in-Publication Data

Names: Ortiz, Joseph M., 1972- author.
Title: Gordon Merrick and the great gay American novel / Joseph M. Ortiz.
Description: Lanham : Lexington Books, [2022] | Includes bibliographical references and index.
Identifiers: LCCN 2022011944 (print) | LCCN 2022011945 (ebook) |
    ISBN 9781793635648 (cloth) | ISBN 9781793635655 (ebook)
Subjects: LCSH: Merrick, Gordon. | Authors, American--20th century--Biography. |
    Gay authors--United States--Biography. | Gay men in literature. | Romance fiction, American--History and criticism. | LCGFT: Biographies.
LC record available at https://lccn.loc.gov/2022011944
LC ebook record available at https://lccn.loc.gov/2022011945

For Paul

Contents

List of Figures	ix
Acknowledgments	xi
Introduction	1
Chapter One: An American Dynasty	11
Chapter Two: Et Ego in Arcadia: Princeton	27
Chapter Three: The Great White Way	49
Chapter Four: The Spy	71
Chapter Five: The Postwar Novelist	87
Chapter Six: Connecting with Forster	101
Chapter Seven: The Protest Novelist	117
Chapter Eight: The Dancer from San Francisco	133
Chapter Nine: The Island of Dreams	151
Chapter Ten: The Great Gay American Novel	167
Chapter Eleven: Getting It Published	189
Chapter Twelve: The Irene Rockwood Phenomenon	201
Chapter Thirteen: Going Greek, or Making a Gay Mythology	217
Chapter Fourteen: A Return to the Stage	239
Chapter Fifteen: Adventures in the East	255
Chapter Sixteen: Rewriting the Past	271
Chapter Seventeen: Merrick vs. Kramer	289

Chapter Eighteen: Imperfect Freedom	305
Afterword	317
Bibliography	329
Index	343
About the Author	359

List of Figures

Figure 1.1: Rodney King Merrick, Gordon's father. 14

Figure 1.2: Mary Merrick, holding a copy of *The Strumpet Wind*, with portraits of her sons on the piano. The painting is of John Merrick, Gordon's great-great-great-grandfather. 15

Figure 1.3: Gordon in high school. 23

Figure 2.1: Gordon with Mel Ferrer and Richard Barr in *The Tempest*, April 1937. 32

Figure 2.2: Gordon in *An Undiscovered Country*, March 1938. 42

Figure 3.1: Otis Bigelow, professional head shot, c. 1938. 51

Figure 3.2: Otis Bigelow, Hamilton College Naval Reserve Officer Training, c. 1939. 52

Figure 3.3: Scene from *The Man Who Came to Dinner*, with Monty Woolley, Gordon Merrick, and Barbara Wooddell. 59

Figure 6.1: Robert Blaine Richardson. 105

Figure 6.2: Robert Blaine Richardson. 106

Figure 8.1: Gordon in his Paris apartment. 134

Figure 8.2: Charles Hulse's headshot for the Lido program. 138

Figure 8.3: Charles Hulse (far left) dancing in *Funny Face* (1957). 139

Figure 9.1: Charles Hulse with George Johnston, Melina Mercouri, and Morton Da Costa, Hydra c. 1962. 154

Figure 9.2: Gordon with Jules Dassin and Tony Randall, Hydra c. 1962. 155

Figure 9.3: Gordon as an extra in *Island of Love* (1963). 155

Figure 9.4: Gordon welcoming the First Lady to Hydra in 1961. 156

Figure 13.1: Original Avon paperback cover for *The Lord Won't Mind* (1970). 233

Figure 16.1: Gordon Merrick at a book-signing for the French translation of *The Lord Won't Mind*, Paris 1987. 276

Figure 16.2: Pages of *The Demon of Noon* (1955) being revised for *Perfect Freedom* (1982). Longer additions were interleaved in the book as inserts. 279

Figure 18.1: Charles Hulse being interviewed about Gordon Merrick by the author, Galle 2012. 314

Figure 18.2: Charles Hulse, March 2012. 314

Acknowledgments

Writing this book has been a labor of love. Over the very long course of its gestation I had the pleasure of meeting many smart and generous people, some of whom I now count among my friends. This book would not have happened without them.

My most inexpressible gratitude goes to the members of Merrick's family who helped me research his life and very graciously allowed me access to their letters, photographs, and memories. Charles Hulse made possible an archive in the first place, and I will be forever grateful for his hospitality and his support of this project. Lawrence Hulse cheered me on in the final stages, and his assistance at the end was critical for the project. I am incredibly thankful to Eleanor Perry Merrick and Rodney and Meg Merrick, whose generosity made a significant part of this book possible. Vaughan Merrick was a helpful and charming emissary along the way.

Many friends and associates of Gordon Merrick also shared their memories and wit, which were a constant source of pleasure and inspiration: Mitch Douglas, Jeannie Sakol, Elmer Luke, Gerard Raymond, Steven Jongeward, Victor Gadino, George McDonald, Robert Wyatt. Some of them are no longer with us, but they have all touched this project in a significant way.

One of the biggest joys of this project has been the opportunity to meet scholars and writers whom I greatly admire. Their encouragement of this book has been both humbling and ennobling. Chief among these is Ian Young, a friend and mentor who has been an unflagging advocate for this book. His gentle prodding and reminders are part of the reason why this book has finally seen the light of day. Drewey Wayne Gunn was also a selfless supporter of the project, and I regret that he could not see the final fruits of his contribution. Brandon Judell's heroic efforts in recovering his interview tapes of Merrick not only helped me fill in gaps in the biography but they also made it possible for me to hear Merrick's voice for the first time. For that I am deeply thankful. Jerry Rosco, in addition to providing the perfect model for a biography, happily alerted me to Merrick letters at Yale. Ann Scott's expert translations of French magazine articles helped me discover a previously unknown chapter of Merrick's career. Other people who graciously provided helpful information and support were Debra Bazarsky, Matthew Bell, Christopher Bram, John Champagne, Alexander Chee, Joe Cosentino, Jerry Goldberg, Rex Hatfield, Andrew Holleran, Daniel Jaffe, Dominic Janes, Richard Just, Charles Kaiser, Richard Labonte, Paul Lanner, Daniel Lazar, Michael Nava, Amit Paley, Anthony Guy Patricia, Felice Picano, Andrew Reynolds, Mark Ritter, Irene Rockwood, Howard Rosen, Nicholas Salvato, Richard Schneider, Bruce Smith, Clifford Sofield, Susan Stryker, Tim Teeman, and Edmund White.

This book had its origin in the Princeton University Library, and I cannot express enough my appreciation for the library's steady support of this project over many years. I want especially to thank AnnaLee Pauls, Margaret Rich, Rosalba Varallo Recchia, Valerie Stenner, and the other people in the Department of Special Collections who helped make my research in the library both pleasant and productive. Louis Aaron was helpful in securing a photograph from the *Daily Princetonian*. Finally, I want to express my gratitude to the Friends of the Princeton University Library and the Fund for Reunion at Princeton University, whose timely research grants at the early stages of my research were instrumental to my continuation of the project.

Several other libraries also provided valuable resources and assistance. Many of these libraries went above and beyond the call of duty during the Covid-19 pandemic, when physical travel to archives was impossible, and I am profoundly grateful for their commitment to research. A Zwickler Memorial Grant from the Cornell University Library Division of Rare and Manuscript Collections allowed me to research the early reception of Merrick's gay novels. Lauren Theodore at the National Archives in College Park, Maryland, was heroic in her efforts to get Merrick's OSS file to me in the midst of the pandemic shutdown. I was also aided in my research by the Beinecke Rare Book & Manuscript Library at Yale University, the Howard Gotlieb Archival Research Center at Boston University, the Alexander Turnbull Library in Wellington, New Zealand, and the Manuscripts and Archives Division at the New York Public Library.

At Lexington Books I have been fortunate to have as an editor Holly Buchanan, who has been encouraging and helpful throughout the process. I would also like to thank Megan White and Linda Kessler for their expert work in shepherding the book through production.

The University of Texas at El Paso has been an ideal place for my research and teaching, and I am deeply grateful for the students and faculty who continue to motivate me on a daily basis. Maryse Jayasuriya and Brian Yothers gave much helpful advice as I was preparing to travel to Sri Lanka to interview Charles Hulse. For their friendship and encouragement of my work I also wish to thank Ernie Chavez, Lucia Durá, Ruben Espinosa, Andy Fleck, Bruce Louden, Robert Gunn, Mimi Gladstein, Jonna Perrillo, Marion Rohrleitner, Tom Schmid, and Barbara Zimbalist. I particularly want to acknowledge a generous grant from the Mimi Reisel Gladstein Endowment in English Literature that will help this book reach a larger audience.

Living in El Paso these last nine years allowed me to be closer to my family, my parents George and Martha Ortiz, and my brothers George and Gabriel. They are a constant reminder of how blessed I have been.

Finally, I want to thank my husband, Paul S. Hinkle Jr. I cannot imagine a more unwavering champion of this book or a more perfect partner in life. I like to think that reading gay novels helped make me "husband material," but in truth it is Paul who taught me how to be *un buen esposo*. Between the two of us, he has always been the one for public declarations. I can't do better than this.

Introduction

AUTOBIOGRAPHY OF A GAY READER

Gordon Merrick was the most commercially successful writer of gay novels in the twentieth century. He wrote four postwar novels in the 1940s and '50s that occasionally included gay characters, and in 1967 he started writing explicitly gay-themed novels. The first of these, *The Lord Won't Mind*, was on the *New York Times* top ten bestseller list for sixteen weeks in 1970. It was followed by nine more gay novels, all of which remain in print. Despite the unprecedented popularity of Merrick's gay fiction and his reputation as the inventor of gay romance, he has largely been neglected in histories of gay literature. The story of how he came to write gay novels is virtually unknown.

I first encountered Gordon Merrick when I was fourteen years old, in the summer before I started the ninth grade. I had known for a while that I was gay, but, living in the small town of Las Cruces, New Mexico, I didn't know any other gay people and was starved for information. Precociously, I knew there *must* be books—histories, social studies, novels—that could teach me more about life as a gay man, if only I could find them. I had memorized the Library of Congress call number for gay books (HQ76), but the four books listed in the card catalogue at my local library were always missing from the shelves. "They must be very popular if they're checked out every week," I thought to myself. Years later, I would realize they probably had not been checked out. Most likely they had been taken by a gay reader who was too afraid to bring them to the library's circulation desk in person.

One day fortune struck. I was at the local Waldenbooks in my town's only shopping mall, where I spent much time that summer. I regularly checked the social sciences section for books on homosexuality, but the only relevant ones seemed to treat the subject in a clinical manner that was not especially useful. I also resented the fact that they were on the same shelf as sociological crime books. This time, however, something caught my eye in the fiction section—it must have been a flash of skin, a muscular neck. I pulled out two books with vaguely suggestive titles, *Perfect Freedom* and *The Lord Won't Mind*. Looking at their front covers, I could barely believe my eyes. One had an image of two shirtless, muscular men, one of them lying languorously on the other's shoulder. The other had two well-dressed men gazing into each other's eyes and nearly holding hands. I started reading *The Lord Won't Mind* right there in the bookstore, and I was ten pages in when I realized this was a story about a love affair between two men. After ten more pages, I realized these men were having sex. For a gay kid who had never even seen two men kiss, this was almost too much to handle. I could feel my face getting hot, and other parts of me were getting aroused as well. I quickly put the books back on the shelf, suddenly worried that someone would see me and figure out what was happening.

    This happened three or four more times. I would go to the Waldenbooks, discreetly grab *The Lord Won't Mind* and read it, twenty pages at a time, in another part of the store where there was less traffic, usually History or Religion. Eventually I decided this would not work. At this rate it would take me months to read the entire novel, and there was always the danger someone would buy the book before I could finish it. I needed to buy it. After all, I told myself, a couple minutes of embarrassment was well worth owning this glorious book forever. So I took both *Lord* and *Perfect Freedom*—buying both could not be much more embarrassing than buying one—and hid them under a third book: Joan Rivers' *Enter Talking*, which I had heard about on *The Tonight Show* and which sounded like a good book. I waited until no one else was in the checkout line and handed the books to the sales clerk, a tall, slender African-American man whose lips twitched in a faint smile as he rang up my purchase.

    There were several things that my inexperienced fourteen-year-old self did not know that day. First, I did not know the sales clerk was gay. I only found this out years later, when I ran into him at a gay bar in nearby El Paso. It was then that I realized how kind he had been that day at Waldenbooks, hiding his amusement at the nervous teenager who was trying to act like buying gay novels was the most normal thing in the world. Second, I did not know that a Joan Rivers book would actually *call attention* to the gay books. Looking back, it's hard to think of another book in that store that would have set off fewer gay alarms. Third, I did not know that similar versions of my bookstore adventure had played out hundreds, perhaps thousands, of times in the previous eighteen years, in towns and cities all over the country. It all started in 1970 when *The Lord Won't Mind* broke new ground by appearing on the *New York Times* bestseller list for sixteen weeks, an unheard-of achievement for an explicit gay novel published by a mainstream press. When I found Merrick's novels tucked away in the general paperback fiction shelves, I thought I had discovered a hidden treasure—when in fact I had been the target of a carefully planned marketing campaign.

There was one other thing I did not know that day. I did not know that Gordon Merrick, the author of those two books and several other gay novels, would die only a few months later, on the other side of the world in a hospital in Colombo, Sri Lanka. He would leave behind a surviving partner, Charles Hulse, with whom he had lived for thirty-two years.

Needless to say, Merrick's novels fueled my imagination and expectations of gay life. They moved to the background two years later, when I met actual gay men and women, and they receded even further when I went to college and met many more gay people. I was disappointed, but not surprised, to find that gay men did not fall into relationships as quickly as they do in Merrick's novels. I *was* surprised, however, to find that hardly anyone appeared to have heard of Merrick. My literature professors clearly knew a lot of gay authors, but the ones they taught seemed to come from a different era: James Baldwin, Tennessee Williams, Frank O'Hara, John Ashbery. For the first time I read academic books *about* gay literature, but these also had almost nothing to say about Merrick. I found Roger Austen's *The Homosexual Novel in America*, which had a single sentence about Merrick: "Gordon Merrick has made a splash with his glossy love stories...which are pleasant escape fiction for the Gay and Gray set."[1] This was puzzling, since I was gay but certainly not gray. And "escape fiction," which for me meant *Star Trek*, seemed a strange way to describe books about gay men living together in New York. Equally puzzling were the other histories of gay literature, more recent and voluminous than Austen's book, that did not mention Merrick at all.

This curious absence of Merrick was the result of several historical events that I also didn't know. I didn't know that in the 1970s and '80s, fierce debates had taken place about the future of gay literature. That, in gay magazines and conferences, gay writers and activists had argued about whether gay fiction should be more positive or more critical, more mainstream or more radical, more democratic or more elite, more explicit or more respectable. They argued over whether gay novels should be imaginative works of art or faithful chronicles of contemporary gay life. Merrick's novels were a casualty of these debates. In fact they *had* received a lot of attention in the 1970s—it would have been impossible for the novels *not* to be noticed—and had provoked varied and conflicting responses. In Brian Distelberg's words, Merrick's novels "were praised as ground-breaking and derided as formulaic, cheered for shattering stereotypes and jeered for failing to depict typical gay people, embraced as signs and potential agents of political progress and shunned as political threats."[2]

Eventually the negative views of Merrick won the day, and by the time I got to college the postmortem reports were already being written. In his introduction to *The Penguin Book of Gay Short Stories*, the writer David Leavitt begins with a story about his own teenage discovery of *The Lord Won't Mind*, one very similar to my own. While his initial reaction to the book was excitement, it ultimately disturbed him since it seemed to tell him that only beautiful gay men could lead happy, fulfilled lives. As an adult, he reasoned that Merrick had idealized his characters to overcompensate for gay oppression—that he had written the novel "energized by Stonewall and the evolving gay liberation movement." Nonetheless, he concludes, *Lord* did lasting "damage," which he might have avoided if there had been gay novels that "told the truth."[3] A year later, the critic Michael Schwartz wrote a smart response to Leavitt in the *Harvard Gay and Lesbian Review*, in which he argued that Leavitt was reading in the wrong genre. Merrick's novels do not "tell the truth," he noted, because that is not what romances do. Perhaps knowing that Leavitt had written his senior thesis at Yale on Spenser's *The Faerie Queene*, Schwartz took a broad view of "romance," which in Renaissance studies refers to poetry that is full of idealized and fantastical characters. As Schwartz put it, "if Leavitt couldn't see himself in the big-dicked gods, it was his own failure to keep his part of the romance contract." For Schwartz the *real* problem with *The Lord Won't Mind* was its heroes' apparent racism, a trait that he suspected came from their author.[4]

Had I followed these debates, I would have been less surprised by Merrick's exclusion from gay literary history. But I still would have had only half the story, since I also did not know what the *critics* did not know. First, contrary to popular belief, *The Lord Won't Mind* was not influenced by Stonewall. Merrick started writing the novel sometime in 1967, and he was already showing the manuscript to publishers in 1968. Moreover, when he wrote it, he was living on a Greek island where his literary influences were other expatriate writers from Australia and England, most of them straight. He didn't start to grasp the American gay liberation movement until 1971, when he was visiting the United States to promote the sequel to *Lord*.

Second, there is a lot more "truth-telling" in Merrick's novels than readers have realized. When Merrick wrote his first novel in 1947, it was a thinly fictionalized account of his experience as an OSS spy during World War II. Years later he admitted the novel's factuality, which was corroborated by declassified OSS and military records. Every novel he wrote afterward included autobiographical material of some kind. If anything, Merrick had a hard time manufacturing stories out of whole cloth. His normal method when beginning a novel was to take an event from his life and then interweave it with other persons, places, and events that he knew well.

Third, Merrick's career is more complicated, and more interesting, than the covers of his gay novels suggest. Although he became notorious as a writer of "pulpy gay paperbacks," he had started out decades earlier writing serious postwar hardback novels. These earlier novels explored homosexuality and race, and they offer an illuminating context for his gay fiction. For one thing, Schwartz could not have known, without doing extensive archival research, that Merrick had written a protest novel about racial prejudice back in 1949. It was never published in English because American publishers were scared to print a novel that sympathetically portrayed an interracial couple. Merrick managed to publish a French version of the novel, which made him a cause célèbre in Paris as an "authority" on racism in America. Schwartz also could not have known that the racial storyline in *The Lord Won't Mind* was a late addition that Merrick made to satisfy his publisher, who thought the novel needed a more provocative punch at the end. As someone who had campaigned for FDR in college and who "rabidly" hated Nixon and Reagan, Merrick had always thought of himself as an enlightened liberal, and so he would get defensive and pugnacious when interviewers and critics pointed out racist passages in his novels. Incredible as it seems, Merrick thought he was *good* at writing race, because a group of urbane French literary critics had told him so.

I only learned these things about Merrick years later when I was a graduate student living in London. By a lucky chance, I met Rick Garcia, a tall, wiry handsome journalist who was visiting London on vacation. Rick had seen my gay.com profile, which listed Gordon Merrick novels among my "Likes," and he asked me about my interest in Merrick. He then proceeded to tell me several interesting facts about Merrick—details that were not in any of the published sources. As it turned out, Rick had had telephone conversations with Merrick when he was alive, and he had even taken it upon himself to write Merrick's obituary for the *New York Times*. He had been an admirer of Merrick ever since he was a teenager, and he had chosen to attend Princeton largely because of its prominence in the novels. Rick also told me that the library at Princeton had some of Merrick's old papers in their collection of manuscripts.

When I returned to Princeton to finish my PhD, I decided to look up these manuscripts, partly out of curiosity and partly as a distraction from my dissertation on Shakespeare. I quickly discovered that Rick had vastly undersold the collection. These "old papers" were actually a substantial archive of twenty-three large boxes, containing multiple manuscript drafts of several novels, scrapbooks, photographs, news clippings, passports, diaries, and hundreds of letters—all of which had been donated to Princeton by Hulse, Merrick's partner.

Exploring the collection was a revelation. I had never seen a photo of Merrick before, and so when I opened his 1954 passport, I was struck by the image of a handsome, steely-eyed thirty-seven-year-old man in a black turtleneck and black sport coat. It was like seeing one of his characters come to life. As I delved further into the archive I found more things that reminded me of passages Merrick had written—pictures of Greece and France, unpublished stories about American expatriates, articles about an imperious Southern grandmother, a glossy publicity photo of a young, beguiling Broadway actor. I began to suspect that Merrick had written himself into in his novels, a fact that became clearer the more I learned about Merrick's life. Had I known French I would have realized this even sooner, since Merrick was more forthcoming about the autobiographical nature of his novels when he was interviewed by French magazines.

The other unexpected discovery in the collection was the box of letters—hundreds of them—sent to Merrick from his readers throughout the 1970s and '80s. These letters spoke of their admiration and love for Merrick's gay novels, while their writers revealed personal information about their lives and hopes. What I found especially remarkable was the sheer diversity of the writers. Some were "gay and gray," but many more of them were not. Some were not even gay. Most of the letters came from gay men of all ages, from all parts of the country and from other countries throughout the world. The style of writing in the letters revealed a range of educational backgrounds, though some writers were academics, including literature professors. Some were living openly as gay men, and some were still closeted. Some were in heterosexual marriages, in various stages of dealing with their homosexuality or bisexuality. Some were in committed gay relationships, and some had never met another gay person. I will never forget sitting in the Princeton library reading room, my eyes tearing up as I read a letter from a young Latino man in Florida, whose only access to gay life was novels. His favorite writers were Mary Renault, Christopher Isherwood, Patricia Nell Warren, J. R. R. Tolkien, Oscar Wilde, and most of all Gordon Merrick. He implored Merrick to keep writing novels "for us people who make our homes between your printed pages." As I read these, I kept thinking, why does no one know about these letters? Why has no one thought to write about them?[5] I determined that *I* would write a history of Merrick that better explained the peculiar nature of his novels and their unrivaled popularity.

This book is the result of that determination. Through my research in the archive, and through interviews with people who knew Gordon, I have attempted to piece together a narrative of his life. In this book, I refer to him as Gordon since there were always other Merricks in his life but also because I want to distinguish between Gordon Merrick the person and the "Gordon Merrick" that became a catchphrase in gay culture for something markedly different. (In this respect I follow the example of Imani Perry's brilliant biography of Lorraine Hansberry, another understudied queer American writer.[6]) I use the word "gay" when writing about Gordon, since the term, as it is generally used today, best describes what appears to have been his sexual orientation throughout his life. Gordon himself did not like labels, but when he did use words for his sexual orientation he preferred "queer" over "gay," which sounded strange and faddish to him. However, Gordon's sense of the meaning of "queer" was very different than how it is used now, and I've decided against it to avoid confusion.

The point of this book is not to argue that Gordon's novels are masterpieces that have been unjustly banned from the upper echelon of gay literature. I personally think they are pretty good and have moments of real power and insight, but I am unlikely to convince anyone whose tastes are different from mine. Rather, this book suggests that the novels are worth re-evaluating because they shed light on a fascinating figure in gay history. Even if Gordon had not translated his life into fiction, it would make a fascinating tale in its own right: Princeton student, Broadway actor, news reporter, World War II spy, American expatriate in France, Greece, and Sri Lanka, all while living openly as a gay man. Gordon's unique talents enabled him to befriend many illustrious writers and artists, including Mel Ferrer, Otis Bigelow, Glenway Wescott, Leonard Cohen, Monty Woolley, Moss Hart, Emlyn Williams, Arthur C. Clarke, Ian McKellen, and E. M. Forster—to say nothing of the countless luminaries he met (and sometimes fought with) throughout his life. Tracing the narrative of Gordon's life teaches us more about the possibilities for gay men in the twentieth century, and it expands our knowledge of the intricate professional and personal networks that these men formed with each other.

This book is also about the critical fortunes of Gordon's writing, which is not well understood. The flattening of Gordon into a "pulp" writer has all but obscured the vastly different reactions that his novels provoked—and the complex reasons for these reactions. The widespread popularity of Gordon's novels had a lot to do with the publishing and marketing developments that were changing the landscape of gay literature, but it had even more to do with the desires and attitudes of gay readers. Taking seriously their response to Gordon's novels helps us see more fully the diversity of gay readers whose experiences were not always reflected in *Christopher Street* or *The Advocate*. At the same time, Gordon's critics had their reasons as well, and examining closely the forms of their criticism reveals much about the tensions that subtended gay culture in America. Thus this book is the story of Gordon's adventures, but is also the story of the publishers, editors, agents, critics, and readers who made "Gordon Merrick" into an anomalous, contradictory poster boy for a certain facet of gay life.

What is not disputable is that Merrick's novels were a cultural phenomenon. His books—and references to his books—were ubiquitous in the 1970s and '80s, and ripples of his influence continued to spread for a long time afterward. In the 1995 film *To Wong Foo, Thanks for Everything! Julie Newmar*, the character Vida Boheme visits her childhood home in Bala Cynwyd, Pennsylvania—Gordon's hometown. Still later, in 2017, Alan Hollinghurst's novel *The Sparsholt Affair* surprised me when I realized I was reading an episode that was slyly imitating the initial seduction scene in *The Lord Won't Mind*.

As a gay man who was influenced by Gordon's novels at a young age, I acknowledge that this book is inevitably biased. That is probably all right. Plenty has been written about Gordon by hostile critics, some of whom never read his novels, and so a sympathetically slanted account may provide some balance. St. Augustine wrote that "one cannot know someone except through friendship," which is a good ethos for literary biographies. Likewise, I have tried not to whitewash or gloss over Gordon's flaws, and I have attempted to document my observations as fully as possible, relying on my training as a historicist literary critic. Even so, many sources require interpretation, and in these cases I have relied on my knowledge and experience to make sense of them. I do not doubt that I have sometimes made mistakes.

This book is also biased in that many sources of information were friends and family of Gordon's, who were available and willing to speak with me. This has been both the challenge and joy of writing this book. I will never forget the kindness of Eleanor Merrick, Gordon's sister-in-law, who diligently combed through boxes of family letters she had saved over the years to help me reconstruct Gordon's time in college and in the war. I will never forget traveling to Sri Lanka with my husband to visit Hulse, who was still living in a home in Galle full of Gordon's books and pictures. My husband and I sat for hours in Hulse's frangipani-scented courtyard, drinking his famous Bloody Marys and eating meatloaf and fried okra (which Hulse, a true Southerner, had taught his cook how to prepare), listening to his fascinating stories about Gordon and himself during their thirty-two years together. His memories filled in countless gaps in my research, and I can only wonder what gaps might have been filled had others still been alive and willing to talk to me. Any biography is necessarily incomplete.

I was reminded of this fact when reading *The Stranger's Child*, Alan Hollinghurst's devastating masterpiece about the evanescence of history. The novel ends with a cache of personal letters burning in a rubbish pile, minutes before a would-be biographer can get to them. I thought about Hollinghurst's book often while writing this book, partly because it stoked my biggest fears as a biographer but also because it reminded me of the other gay writers who have influenced me. Writing this book has sometimes felt like writing autobiography, insofar as it made me reflect on what I learned from gay writers. It was Hollinghurst who taught me that language, when wielded by a master, can be simultaneously cruelly scathing and sublimely beautiful. It was Andrew Holleran who taught me that I was nostalgic for a period that I had not lived through. It was Richard Amory who taught me, long before I saw *Brokeback Mountain*, that Westerns are really, really gay. It was Arturo Islas, with some help from Ronald Donaghe, who taught me there is a gay poetic beauty in the desert where I grew up. It was John Rechy who taught me that the same desert is not for everyone. It was E. M. Forster who taught me that social class has always been a formidable, but not insurmountable, barrier between gay men. It was Mary Renault who taught me it was OK to project gay desires onto the past, since it may help us hear *their* desires more clearly. It was Mel Keegan who taught me that pirates are the sexiest characters in all of literature. It was André Aciman who taught me that not all gay novelists are gay.

And it was Gordon Merrick who, before I had read any of these writers, taught me what it feels like when two men start to fall in love. It was Gordon who taught me how to swoon.

NOTES

1. Roger Austen, *Playing the Game: The Homosexual Novel in America* (Indianapolis: Bobbs-Merrill, 1977), 216.
2. Brian J. Distelberg, "Mainstream Fiction, Gay Reviewers, and Gay Male Cultural Politics in the 1970s," *GLQ* 16, no. 3 (2010): 389.
3. David Leavitt and Mark Mitchell, eds., *The Penguin Book of Gay Short Stories* (New York: Viking, 1994), xviii, xvi, xix, xxi.
4. Michael Schwartz, "David Leavitt's Inner Child," *Harvard Gay and Lesbian Review* 2, no. 1 (Winter 1995): 42–43.
5. Since then there have been a few excellent studies of readers' letters, including letters sent to Christopher Isherwood and to the homophile magazine *ONE*. See Jaime Harker, *Middlebrow Queer: Christopher Isherwood in America* (Minneapolis: University of Minnesota Press, 2013); Craig M. Loftin, *Masked Voices: Gay Men and Lesbians in Cold War America* (Albany: State University of New York Press, 2012).
6. Imani Perry, *Looking for Lorraine: The Radiant and Radical Life of Lorraine Hansberry* (Boston: Beacon Press, 2018).

Chapter One

An American Dynasty

Gordon Merrick was born into privilege, the product of two influential American families. He always knew this fact, even if at times he pretended to forget it. Often he represented the circumstances of his upbringing as a personal burden, as something that threatened his individual freedom. He was generally ambivalent about his family history and the expectations that came with it, and he regularly expressed this ambivalence in his writing. In many of his novels, the pressures of money and class are cast as a prison that the protagonist struggles to escape (often unsuccessfully) in order to live an honest, morally sound life. Yet, for all his literary philosophizing, Gordon rarely refused the benefits that came with his social and economic position. His personal and familial connections—and his conventional good looks—made life easier for him on a practical level. They made it possible for him to pursue a literary career and to live all over the world, including France, Greece, and Sri Lanka. And to a significant extent, they also made it possible for him to live most of his life as an openly gay man.

In forging a career as a peripatetic gay novelist, Gordon cut a very different path from the men in his family. His great-great-grandfather was Samuel Vaughan Merrick, best known to history as a founder of the Pennsylvania Railroad. Samuel was born on May 4, 1801, in Hallowell, Maine, the oldest son of John and Rebecca Merrick, who had married three years earlier. John came from a long line of English merchants who traced their genealogy back to the reign of Henry III and who had migrated to America in the early 1700s.[1] At the slender age of fifteen, Samuel was sent to Philadelphia to work in his uncle's wine business, and by the time he was twenty-one he had started his own company manufacturing hand fire engines.[2] His engineering acumen and natural leadership abilities quickly vaulted him to the upper echelon of the Philadelphia business community, and when the Pennsylvania Railroad Company was established in 1847, the other founders unanimously chose him as its first president.[3]

In addition to having a talent for business, Samuel Merrick was also a genuine philanthropist. When he was twenty-two, he co-founded the Franklin Institute in Philadelphia, an organization whose aim was to promote science education among the general public—and which is now one of the nation's leading science museums.[4] He later became an active member of the American Philosophical Society, the institution founded by Benjamin Franklin to advance the production and dissemination of scientific knowledge. The Society had distinctly liberal leanings, and when Samuel died in 1869 the Society publicly honored him for his logistical support of the Union during the Civil War and his subsequent commitment to the nation's Reconstruction efforts. The Society noted in particular that, after the war, Samuel had helped his brother and sister, both abolition advocates, establish one of the first schools in Virginia for black students. "Conservative as he was in principle and feeling," the Society wrote about Samuel in their published journal, he had a large capacity for "large and liberal views."[5] This combination of capitalist and progressive impulses became a patrilineal tradition in the Merrick family. Samuel's eldest son, John Vaughan Merrick, took over the family business when he came of age and later served as president of the Franklin Institute for a number of years. He also helped found the Philadelphia Zoological Society, often billed as the nation's first zoo.[6]

Samuel's younger son, William Henry Merrick, was less fortunate in his business and personal life. His business ventures sometimes failed, and his family life was shaped early on by two nearly simultaneous tragedies.[7] His second son (also named William Henry) died five months after being born, and only seven months later he lost his wife, Sarah Otis (the daughter of a U.S. congressman). William's eldest son, Samuel, was seven years old when his mother died. The trauma of such early losses may have impressed upon the younger Samuel the preciousness of family relationships and the relative unimportance of wealth and power. If so, it was a lesson he passed on to his only son, Rodney King Merrick. Born on October 14, 1886, Rodney grew up with an awareness that he came from the *less* illustrious side of the Merrick family, and perhaps for this reason he did not follow the same path as many of his eminent cousins. Although he attended the University of Pennsylvania (like many Merrick men), he did not pursue a career in business or politics, instead becoming a stockbroker. And instead of marrying a wealthy or politically well-connected woman, he married Mary Cartwright Gordon, a gentle, soft-spoken Catholic woman who had been born in Natchez, Mississippi, and whose family had deep roots in New Orleans. Shortly after getting married they had two sons, Samuel Vaughan Merrick III, born on March 24, 1914, and William Gordon Merrick, born on August 3, 1916. The younger son, called "Bud" by his parents and brother, would become known in literary history as simply Gordon Merrick.

From all appearances, Gordon's family was a conventional, upper-middle-class WASP family. They lived in Villanova, Pennsylvania, a quiet and affluent suburb of Philadelphia, in a comfortable home that was staffed by a live-in butler. Like their father, Samuel and Gordon could not avoid regular reminders of their dignified heritage. They lived only a few blocks away from Merrick Street, named after their illustrious ancestor, and they both attended the nearby Episcopal Academy, where their father's great-uncle had been a trustee and his cousin a member of the faculty.[8] Nonetheless, Rodney did not pressure his sons to live up to an idealized notion of "Merrick gentlemen." While it was clear that he expected his sons to go to college and get respectable jobs, he generally did not lecture them or try to impose his views on them. This was especially true in the area of politics. Unlike his wife and sons, Rodney was a lifelong Republican, and he managed this difference of political affiliation by avoiding political discussions at home. He made an exception during the presidential election campaign of 1936, proclaiming Roosevelt to be "the most discredited man in American history." He was so passionate about his distaste for Roosevelt that he made a ten-dollar bet with Gordon that Roosevelt would not win reelection.[9] He lost the bet, and when Roosevelt was reelected again four years later, he stopped talking politics with his family altogether.[10]

Mary Merrick, on the other hand, relished political conversations with her sons. Known as "Mimi" to the rest of her family, she was a college-educated woman who kept abreast of national and international news by listening to political commentaries on the radio and reading periodicals like the *New Republic*. She was a voracious reader of both fiction and nonfiction, to the extent that books were the default birthday present from Samuel and Gordon. Despite being naturally shy and reserved in public, Mimi had no inhibitions about sharing her thoughts about politics and books with her sons. In letters she wrote to them throughout their adult lives, she frequently discusses a current issue or a book she has just read, going into detail about the relevant political and philosophical themes. She found in Samuel and Gordon her most trusted intellectual sounding boards with whom she could speak freely—even when she disagreed with them, whether over the virtues of communist Russia or the symbolism in a Franz Werfel novel.[11]

Mimi's passion about ideas was grounded in her identity as a devoted Catholic. Although she had married into a family with deep Episcopalian roots, she maintained her Catholic beliefs throughout her life and regularly attended Catholic church services and events. She constantly reminded her sons to "keep strong" their Christian faith and "return always to the source . . . of Christ's teaching." At the same time, while Mimi adhered to the tenets of Catholic doctrine, she embraced a religious liberalism that allowed for differences in beliefs and practices. She was happy to argue about

Figure 1.1 Rodney King Merrick, Gordon's father.
Source: Estate of Samuel and Eleanor Merrick.

the spiritual importance of fast days, but she had little patience for those who used religion as a political weapon rather than as a basis for humane behavior—notably "Boston Catholics," as she called them.[12] As she put it in a letter to Samuel, "One must find one's own spiritual home, but for me 'the

Figure 1.2 Mary Merrick, holding a copy of *The Strumpet Wind*, with portraits of her sons on the piano. The painting is of John Merrick, Gordon's great-great-great-grandfather.
Source: Estate of Samuel and Eleanor Merrick.

keys of the kingdom' will always be the kindly heart radiating from the love in Christ's heart rather than any theologic hair-splitting over this and that doctrine."[13] This openness to individual difference would prove crucial for her relationship with her sons, who would eventually strike off on their own paths in different ways. As someone who was an outsider to the Merrick family in more ways than one, she understood the value of a "big tent" philosophy in familial relationships. When Samuel's wife, Eleanor Perry, herself joined the

Merrick family as an outsider, it was Mimi who warmly welcomed her and showed her special kindness.[14]

The differences between Rodney and Mimi were in many ways reflected in their two sons. Samuel had been named after his paternal grandfather, while Gordon was named after his maternal grandfather, William Cartwright Gordon, who died when Mary was fourteen years old. If names were destiny, then this pattern would have predicted much about the two boys. Samuel followed in his father's footsteps by attending the University of Pennsylvania and specializing in economics, and he especially inherited his father's love of sailing. He took up competitive sailing at a young age, often going on trips to sailing competitions with his father and collecting many medals along the way. In 1980 he became director of the U.S. Olympic yachting team, preparing the team for the Moscow Olympics before the United States boycotted the games.[15] Gordon also gained a love for sailing, but as a child he was far less hale than his older brother. He suffered from chronic back troubles from an early age and spent much of his childhood coping with mastoiditis and other ailments. At one point Rodney and Mimi became so concerned about Gordon's physical softness that, when he was twelve years old, they enrolled him in the nearby Valley Forge Military Academy to "toughen him up." The experiment was unsuccessful, and the one effect it did produce was far different than what Gordon's parents had intended. Upon seeing a large group of athletic, adolescent boys exercising in the academy's swimming pool, Gordon got his first inkling of his attraction to other boys. "It was the first time I ever saw a lot of kids swimming naked," he later recalled, "and I must say it left its mark."[16]

Gordon was a sensitive and passionate child—his family called him melodramatic—and he naturally gravitated to Mimi for emotional support. As a child, whenever he was away from home he would write Mimi almost daily, bemoaning the fact that he missed her "dreadfully." The same pattern would continue into adulthood, with Gordon writing to Mimi frequently from his room at Princeton and urging her to visit him. If Gordon fit the typical definition of a "mamma's boy," Mimi was a doting mother who would empathetically listen to Gordon's accounts of his life "crises." She also encouraged his "dramatic tendency," as she put it, by prompting him to join a local dramatical club when he was thirteen years old. Gordon developed an enthralling love for the theater, and he saw plays and films as often as he was allowed. He was especially enamored with Greta Garbo and Joan Crawford, whose films he faithfully followed throughout his teenage years.[17]

Gordon's passion for the theater flourished even more when he entered the Episcopal Academy at the age of fifteen. He immediately joined the school's dramatics club and from that point was constantly busy working on one theatrical production or another. By his senior year he was universally regarded by the faculty and students as the best actor in the school—arguably the best they had ever had. Greville Haslam, the school's headmaster, attributed Gordon's acting prowess to his "great poise and considerable personal charm" but also to his intellectual approach to the theater. As Haslam noted, it was Gordon's practice to interview professional actors and directors in the Philadelphia area, in order to understand better their craft.[18] (This particular skill would prove useful decades later when Gordon interviewed the actor Ian McKellen.) The Episcopal Academy also nourished Gordon's other youthful passion: literature, particularly contemporary British and American novels. He was the editor in chief of the school's weekly newspaper, for which he inaugurated a regular book review section. He wrote many of the reviews himself, which covered many of the decade's most modish writers. Although Gordon's reviews are often florid and sniffy, they are also authoritative and informed. They show an impressive knowledge of a broad range of writers and critics—one typical review makes astute comparisons to Ernest Hemingway, Sinclair Lewis, and Cervantes' *Don Quixote*. Gordon may have only been seventeen years old, but he was confident enough in his critical acuity to point out James Hilton's clumsy attempt at realism or Thornton Wilder's awkward handling of "the seamy side of modern life." His reviews focus almost exclusively on a novel's themes, characterization, and style, and the prose in the reviews is itself carefully measured and marked by elegant (sometimes grandiose) turns of phrase. In this respect Gordon's youthful reviews hint at the kind of novelist he would later become. They also hint at an affinity with the novelist who would loom largest over his literary life: E. M. Forster. In his review of J. B. Priestley's *English Journey*, for example, he uses (without knowing it at the time) Forsterian language to distinguish Priestley from the celebrated Carl Carmer, "a literary juggler striving for an effect . . . the whole thing is a hollow, pretentious muddle."[19]

The Episcopal Academy also provided the setting for Gordon's first same-sex experiences, which he recounted on multiple occasions as an adult. After Latin class one day, a fellow student grabbed Gordon and pulled him into a broom closet in the school's basement. The two of them did "the usual jerk-off bit," which showed Gordon for the first time the unique pleasure he could get from another boy. Soon afterward he learned that there was a "whole sort of vice ring" of Academy students who frequented the broom closet, and he became a very popular member of the group. "I was solicited quite often," as he later put it. Eventually, Gordon's basement meetings with one particular classmate became more meaningful. He was in the broom closet one day with a classmate, an unusually talkative kid who—after the usual business was finished—told Gordon that he "ought to do it with Eddie." Eddie Collins Jr. was the school's top athlete, and Gordon had already developed a crush on him. He was surprised to learn that Eddie was a member of the "vice ring," but before long the two were meeting regularly. Gordon became enamored with Eddie, and he was elated when he found out that Eddie had similar feelings. Unfortunately, this budding high school romance ended almost as soon as it began, since both boys were weeks away from graduation, with Gordon going to Princeton and Eddie headed for Yale.[20] Gordon fictionalized the event in *The Lord Won't Mind*, in a passage where Charlie talks about his high school crush:

> "Haven't you really ever been in love before?" Peter asked. . . .
> "Oh, I suppose once, long ago. The last year of [high] school. With the captain of the football team, of all people. We didn't discover it until Graduation Day. That is, I didn't discover he felt the same way, and then it was a bit late."[21]

The fictionalized episode includes many details about the actual Eddie that Gordon revealed in interviews given in the 1980s, including the fact that the two met in New York City after graduation. In these interviews Gordon also revealed that he had received a letter from Eddie, who was now married and a teacher at the Episcopal Academy. Although the two never reconnected, Gordon still retained fond memories of "his first great love," as he put it.[22]

Outside of school, it is unlikely that Gordon had any other same-sex experiences or knew any other gay men. He may, however, have known about an old family friend who didn't fit the model of a masculine, heterosexual man. His great-granduncle John Vaughan Merrick had written an illustrious memoir three decades earlier that circulated among the family, in which he recalls meeting a friend of his father's while on a trip in England. He described this friend, Jesse Hartley, as a "queer" widower who had taken care of him when he became ill for several days, during which time he had been able to observe the elder man's strange habits:

> [Hartley] was a widower with queer ways. I remember he had 31 pairs of shoes, and they stood in a row in his room, changed daily each month. He was also fond of music and, being alone and not himself a performer, had a large Orchestrion with many cylinders containing tunes.[23]

Although the word "queer" did not refer to sexuality in 1900, it could have been suggestive in the 1930s, when the term was starting to signal "aberrant" gender behavior—and very often applied to a man with unusually extravagant fashion tastes.[24] In this sense, another "queer" widower whom Gordon certainly knew was his older cousin, John Vaughan Merrick, who had moved to Philadelphia after the death of his wife. This John (not to be confused with the memoir writer) had taught Latin and English at the Episcopal Academy and was a voracious reader of literature. He was known in the family for his gourmet cookery and for his habit of declining dinner invitations from eligible, husband-seeking women. He was also known for his dandyish style, which usually featured an English bespoke suit, brightly polished brogues, elegant walking cane, and a gold pepper pot hanging from his watch chain.[25] None of this means he was gay, but it *does* mean that, as a boy, Gordon had *some* examples of fashionable, culturally refined single men who lived slightly aslant from the rest of the family. In many ways Gordon was already playing a similar role in his own family. Artistic, literary, and theatrical, he would have stood out from all the masculine, business-minded Merrick men who followed the pattern of his legendary great-great-grandfather.

Gordon bolstered his maverick status in the family when it came time to choose a college. The normal expectation was that he would attend the University of Pennsylvania, which had been a Merrick tradition for over a century. Not only had many Merrick men gone to Penn; Samuel Vaughan Merrick, the family's famous patriarch, had been good friends with Daniel Goodwin, the provost of the university, who esteemed Merrick so much that he wrote a memoir of him.[26] Other Merricks, like his great-granduncle, had served on the university's board of trustees.[27] Gordon's own father had gone to Penn, and his brother Samuel was already a sophomore there. Gordon thus surprised his family when he announced that *he* would be going to Princeton. The small, idyllic campus was only an hour's drive from their home in Villanova, but it seemed a world away compared to downtown Philadelphia. Gordon may have been attracted by Princeton's theatrical and literary scene or by its reputation as a well-dressed country club.[28] F. Scott Fitzgerald, a Princeton alumnus, had crystallized this image of Princeton as "the pleasantest country club in America" in *This Side of Paradise*.[29] Fitzgerald himself had a reputation as "the most fashion-conscious male writer of the early twentieth century," and his particular style of writing was often associated with Princeton's clubbishness and sartorial trendiness.[30] Jesse Lynch Williams, another alumnus and a Pulitzer Prize winner for drama, had painted a similar picture of the school in *Princeton Stories*, his collection of stories about Princeton undergraduate life. Gordon, who had read *This Side of Paradise*, would have surely noticed Fitzgerald's characterization of Princeton men as "slender and keen and romantic and the Yale men as brawny and brutal and powerful."[31] He would have read "slender and keen and romantic" as a perfect description of himself, and he would have seen Fitzgerald's description of Yale confirmed by the fact that Eddie Collins, the school's star football player, was going there. In any case, Gordon decided that Princeton was more suited to his personality than either Yale or Merrick-friendly Penn.

There was, however, a problem. Gordon did not fit the model of an ideal Princeton student, at least on paper. He had an IQ of 118, he was not particularly athletic, and his academic grades were middling at best. At the time of his initial application to Princeton, he ranked twentieth in his class of forty students, in part because of his weak grades in Latin courses. In his letter of recommendation, headmaster Haslam tried to explain Gordon's lackluster academic performance by citing his immersion in extracurricular activities, particularly the theater and newspaper. Beyond this he was able to give little assurance of Gordon's intellectual ability, instead emphasizing over and over again Gordon's "absolute integrity" and "sense of honor." Such language was not merely an exercise in platitudes—in all likelihood Haslam was appealing to what he knew were the interests of Princeton's admissions committee. As Jerome Karabel has shown in his meticulous study of the admissions processes of the Big Three universities, Princeton had at the time made a deliberate choice to admit students based on "character" and "manhood" rather than on purely academic qualifications. This shift in admissions criteria was partly a response to Princeton's interest in limiting the number of Jewish students in each class—a goal that was shared by Harvard and Yale.[32] Accordingly, Haslam peppered his recommendation with buzzwords that assured the admissions committee that Gordon was the "right" kind of student: "a fellow of discrimination and conviction," "an excellent citizen," "all the concomitants of a good background," "distinctly the type of boy who ought to go to Princeton, or a similar college."[33]

Yet, even if Gordon was the right "type of boy" (i.e., not Jewish), his application had multiple red flags. Haslam noted twice that Gordon was not particularly athletic, and he admitted that Gordon was "capable" of achieving good grades *if* placed "under guidance." Gordon's own application essay likely did not help his chances. He spent the first part of the essay explaining that he had chosen Princeton because it was closer to his home than other Ivy League universities and thus would save him transportation costs (a claim that must have raised eyebrows given that he lived "next door" to the University of Pennsylvania). In the rest of the essay, Gordon mentions having met some Princeton alumni, whom he deems to be "of the finest sort," and he sums up his reasons for applying to Princeton by claiming that its buildings are better looking than Yale's or Harvard's. The rest of the application gave little evidence of Gordon's intellectual promise. Gordon misread the application's instructions for designating a prospective course of study, and he carelessly had the College Board send his entrance examination scores to Harvard instead of Princeton. When Haslam sent his Final Report to the admissions office at the end of the spring semester (a standard form intended to show that a student had not slacked off in the final semester), Gordon ranked thirty-third in his class of forty students, having earned an especially dismal grade in Latin. Based on his application alone, Gordon's chances of getting into Princeton were incredibly slim.

Gordon, however, had one advantage over many of the other applicants. He had a powerful and influential family member who was happy to intervene on his behalf—though this was *not* someone from the Merrick side of the family. Gordon's maternal grandmother, Clarice Marston Billups, was an intimidating, genteel Southern woman who claimed to be a distant relative of Louise de La Vallière, Louis XIV's mistress in the seventeenth century. Billups traced another branch of her family to John Marston, a ship captain who traveled from England to Salem, Massachusetts, in 1634.[34] After her first husband (Mimi's father) died, she married Melvin P. Billups, an executive for the Southern Railway Company from Mobile, Alabama. They eventually moved from New Orleans to New York, settling in a lavish apartment in the Grosvenor Hotel on Fifth Avenue—at the same address where Willa Cather lived years later. As a child Gordon spent a great deal of time with his grandmother, affectionately called "Bon Bon" by her family. In countless interviews and conversations later in his life, Gordon explicitly admitted the fact that the character of C. B. in *The Lord Won't Mind* was a thinly veiled version of Bon Bon. At the beginning of the novel, he recalls the sense of enchantment that had accompanied his childhood visits to Bon Bon's New York home:

> His childhood impressions of her apartment in New York had endowed it forever with the vastness of Versailles. . . . He thought of his childhood visits to C. B. in the city, when he would find the closets piled high with gaily wrapped presents, impromptu Christmases whose memory still made him tingle with delight.[35]

The Billups' other home was a sprawling Victorian house in Bay Head, New Jersey, where Gordon would regularly stay during the summers. The Bay Head house figured even more prominently in *The Lord Won't Mind*, as the initial setting for Charlie and Peter's tumultuous love affair.

Although psychoanalyzing a historical figure is a risky business, it is possible to speculate on the influence of Gordon's mother and grandmother on his ideas about women. He had no sisters and no close female relatives in his life, and all of his formal education took place in male-only institutions. After college, his work in the theater and newspaper business was likewise in male-dominated spheres. Such limited experience may partly account for the portrayal of women in his novels, which were justly criticized for their one-dimensional and stereotypical female characters. At the same time, the two formative female figures in Gordon's life may very well have looked like a study in stereotypes: his tender, soft-spoken mother and his stentorian, imperious grandmother. When, as an older man, Gordon finally did develop close friendships with women, he did not change his views about women so much as he regionalized them. In an interview he gave to a French magazine when he was thirty-three years old, he used a combination of his mother and grandmother to characterize American women in general. Unlike European women, he claimed, American women "have too much material and romantic power. They typically guard the wealth and confuse prejudices for moral law. Starting in childhood, we learn to respect them and obey them. Their demands and self-assurance don't make marital relationships any easier."[36]

As he grew out of adolescence, Gordon gradually became more conflicted about Bon Bon. He had always admired her extravagance and grand manner, which he associated with a romanticized Southern gentility. As he described her in *Lord*, she belonged to a different place and time:

> She was the way everybody should be: money flowed from her effortlessly, without being mentioned. All his formative years had been lived in the gray shadow of the Depression; she was the only person he knew who continued to bask in the bright light of ease and prosperity. While his parents' friends were leaping out of high windows, she maintained her two imposing establishments . . . as if nothing had happened. Others grimly discussed Hitler and such uncongenial places as the Sudetenland; C. B. projected a vision of marching heroes and flashing banners when she referred to the impending war.[37]

Eventually Gordon came to see the darker side of this romanticized Southern heroinism. For one thing, Bon Bon held racist views which she was not afraid to share with the rest of her family. In one instance, she made a ruckus when Gordon's brother Samuel, who was working as an attorney for the National Labor Relations Board, represented a group of African-American workers in a racial discrimination case. Bon Bon was appalled that Samuel was (as she put it) "taking up for the Negroes" and tried unsuccessfully to enlist Mimi's help in directing him toward another course. As the self-appointed matriarch of the family, she was inclined to dictate how her children and grandchildren should behave, and she would stage melodramatic scenes of disapproval—ripping up family photographs, delivering tirades over the telephone—when one of them dared to defy her. Gordon often recoiled from such histrionics, perhaps in part because he saw in Bon Bon a lot of himself. Mimi herself liked to say that Gordon inherited his "Sarah Bernhardt-style theatrics" from his grandmother.[38]

Bon Bon's imposing demeanor nonetheless proved useful to Gordon in 1935, when he was trying to get into Princeton. Likely annoyed that her two

Figure 1.3 Gordon in high school.
Source: Estate of Gordon Merrick.

grandsons were constantly under the shadow of their father's side of the family, she relished the opportunity to show that her side had some clout of its own. She must have also enjoyed the idea that, while the Merrick influence had helped get Samuel into the University of Pennsylvania, *she* would help get Gordon (who bore her deceased husband's name) into Princeton. She swiftly contacted her husband's friend, Cortlandt Van Rensselaer Halsey, a wealthy New York investment banker who had graduated from Princeton in 1918 and was now the mayor of Rumson, New Jersey (where the Billups kept their summer home), and had him arrange a meeting for them with Radcliffe Heermance, the Princeton dean of admissions. In his letter to Heermance—whom he addressed as "Rad"—Halsey expressed confidence that the dean would give his "very dear friends" any help that they would like. A few days later, Clarice and Melvin Billups drove down to Princeton from New York City and met with Heermance in his office.

There is no record of what Bon Bon or her husband said during their half-hour-long meeting with Heermance, but it must have been persuasive. Gordon was accepted to Princeton as a member of the Class of 1939, and he matriculated later that fall. His admission to Princeton would prove to be an incredibly decisive event in his life, but it would also typify one of his traits. Although he would eventually write several novels decrying the shackles of privilege and the evils of a capitalist society, he was not above taking advantage of the opportunities that such a system presented to him.

NOTES

1. Mary Williams Brinton, *Their Lives and Mine* (Philadelphia: Mary Williams Brinton, 1972), 12.

2. *The National Cyclopædia of American Biography: Being the History of the United States* (New York: James T. White, 1906), s.vv. "Samuel Vaughan Merrick."

3. George H. Burgess and Miles C. Kennedy, *Centennial History of the Pennsylvania Railroad Company 1846–1946* (Philadelphia: Pennsylvania Railroad Company, 1949), 43–44.

4. "Mission & History," The Franklin Institute, accessed May 5, 2021, https://www.fi.edu/about-us/mission-history.

5. Daniel R. Goodwin, "Obituary Notice of Samuel Vaughan Merrick, Esq.," *Proceedings of the American Philosophical Society* 11, no. 81 (1869): 595–96.

6. John W. Jordan, *Colonial Families of Philadelphia*, vol. 2 (New York: Lewis Publishing, 1911), 1578.

7. Brinton, *Their Lives and Mine*, 43.

8. Brinton, *Their Lives and Mine*, 12; Jordan, *Colonial Families of Philadelphia*, 1578.

9. Gordon Merrick to Mary Merrick, 26 October 1936, 5 November 1936, private collection.

10. Mary Merrick to Samuel Merrick, n.d. [November 1940], private collection.

11. Mary Merrick to Samuel Merrick, 1 February 1943, 27 March 1943, private collection.

12. Mary Merrick to Samuel Merrick, 12 August 1943, 8 September 1944, private collection.

13. Mary Merrick to Samuel Merrick, 13 March 1945, private collection.

14. Eleanor Merrick, interview by the author.

15. Frank Litsky, "Samuel V. Merrick, 86, Director of U.S. Olympic Yachting Team Dies," *New York Times*, April 21, 2000.

16. Brandon Judell, "Orgasm and Organdy: Gordon Merrick, the Champion of Gay Romance," *The Advocate*, October 14, 1986.

17. Gordon Merrick to Mary Merrick, 3 and 5 December 1929, 29 June 1932, 5 July 1932, private collection.

18. Greville Haslam, Principal's Report on Applicant, March 12, 1935, Gordon Merrick student file, Princeton University Archives, Seeley G. Mudd Manuscript Library, Department of Special Collections, Princeton University Library.

19. Gordon Merrick, reviews of *Heaven's Destination*, *Lost Horizon*, and *English Journey*, n.d., GMP, box 20, folder 7.

20. Brandon Judell, "A Conversation With Gordon Merrick," *Stallion*, January 1987; Judell, "Orgasm and Organdy."

21. Gordon Merrick, *The Lord Won't Mind* (New York: Bernard Geis, 1970), 42.

22. Gordon Merrick, interview by Brandon Judell. For corroborating details about Edward T. (Eddie) Collins Jr.'s affiliation with the Episcopal Academy and Yale University, see Rick Huhn, *Eddie Collins: A Baseball Biography* (Jefferson, NC: McFarland, 2008), 270, 283.

23. Brinton, *Their Lives and Mine*, 31.

24. Siobhan Somerville, "Queer," in *Keywords for American Cultural Studies*, ed. Bruce Burgett and Glenn Hendler, 203–7 (New York: New York University Press, 2014).

25. Brinton, *Their Lives and Mine*, 276–78.

26. Thomas Coulson, "Some Prominent Members of the Franklin Institute: 1. Samuel Vaughan Merrick, 1801–1870," *Journal of the Franklin Institute* 258 (November 1954): 335.

27. Brinton, *Their Lives and Mine*, 42.

28. Deirdre Clemente, "Caps, Canes, and Coonskins: Princeton and the Evolution of Collegiate Clothing, 1900–1930," *Journal of American Culture* 31, no. 1 (2008): 20–33; James Axtell, *The Making of Princeton University* (Princeton: Princeton University Press, 2006), 311–22.

29. F. Scott Fitzgerald, *This Side of Paradise*, quoted in Jerome Karabel, *The Chosen: The Hidden History of Admission and Exclusion at Harvard, Yale, and Princeton* (Boston: Houghton Mifflin, 2005), 74.

30. Catherine Mintler, "From Aesthete to Gangster: The Dandy Figure in the Novels of F. Scott Fitzgerald," *F. Scott Fitzgerald Review* 8 (2010): 104–29.

31. Quoted in Karabel, *The Chosen*, 72.
32. Karabel, *The Chosen*, 121–23.
33. Haslam, Principal's Report.
34. "A Record of the Descendants of John Marston, Master Mariner," 1934, private collection.
35. Merrick, *The Lord Won't Mind*, 6–7.
36. Jeanine Delpech, "Gordon Merrick a choisi la Provence," *Les Nouvelles Littéraires*, March 2, 1950. Translation by Ann Scott.
37. Merrick, *The Lord Won't Mind*, 6.
38. Mary Merrick to Samuel Merrick, 20 March 1943, private collection.

Chapter Two

Et Ego in Arcadia: Princeton

The Princeton University that Gordon Merrick entered in September 1935 was a very different institution than the one that exists today. In February 2020 the university presented its prestigious Woodrow Wilson Award to Anthony Romero, the executive director of the American Civil Liberties Union (ACLU). The award, named after the Princeton University president who became the twenty-eighth U.S. president, is given annually to a Princeton alumna/us who has performed distinguished national service. In his acceptance speech, Romero quipped "there's a good chance that Woodrow Wilson is right now spinning in his grave like an Olympic figure skater." In saying this, he was pointing out the irony that an award commemorating Wilson, a "racist xenophobe" and segregationist who had worked to keep Princeton's student body white and American-born, was being given to a civil rights leader. Romero was also pointing out that a student like himself—a "working-class Puerto Rican kid from a vocational public high school" *and* an openly gay man—would not have been admitted to Princeton during Wilson's tenure, or for many decades afterward.[1] Gordon, by contrast, was a clear beneficiary of the exclusionary policies that characterized Princeton in the first half of the twentieth century.

Gordon had the opportunity to witness firsthand Princeton's discriminatory practices on his first day of college. When he showed up at McCosh Hall on the morning of September 23 to register as a freshman, he encountered no problems.[2] Another young man, Bruce Wright, was not as fortunate. Wright was a bright African-American student from New York City who had been admitted to Princeton with a full scholarship—the admissions office had not known that Wright was black when he applied. When he appeared on campus in person, an upperclassman assisting with registration pulled him from the line and escorted him to the admissions office.[3] April Armstrong gives a heartrending account of the circumstances surrounding Wright's ejection from the university by Dean Heermance:

Though many students stood in line with Wright to register for classes at the start of the academic year, Heermance refused to admit him. In a later interview, Wright recalled what Heermance had told him: "If you're trying to come here, you're going someplace where you're not wanted." With no other recourse he could see, Wright went outside, sat down on his suitcase, and waited for his father to drive down from New York to pick him up.

Wright later wrote Heermance demanding an explanation for his revoked admission, but Heermance was immovable, citing Princeton's "long standing tradition." Wright ended up attending Lincoln University, a historically black university in Pennsylvania. After college he was awarded a Bronze Star and Purple Heart for his service in World War II, and later in life he became a New York State Supreme Court judge.[4] The episode highlights Princeton's discriminatory practices as enforced by Heermance, who would be the longest-serving admissions dean in Princeton's history. Throughout his career Heermance worked vigorously to control the number of Jewish students at Princeton—the "Hebrew invasion" as he called it—and he was not about to open up the college to African Americans.[5] Sixty-five years later, in an attempt to atone partly for the university's egregious policies, the Class of 2001 made Wright an honorary member of their class.[6]

Another young man who registered at Princeton that day—without incident—was John F. Kennedy. Although his father had wanted him to go to Harvard, his alma mater, Kennedy chose Princeton so that he could be at the same college with his best friend from the Choate Academy, Kirk LeMoyne ("Lem") Billings. He and Billings shared a room in Reunion Hall with Rip Horton Jr., another Choate classmate who would later be part of Kennedy's presidential campaign staff.[7] Kennedy's stay at Princeton was considerably brief. In addition to spending most weekends gallivanting with Billings and Horton in New York City, he suffered from health problems that gradually worsened over the course of the fall semester. He finally withdrew from Princeton in December after being diagnosed with jaundice, transferring to Harvard the following year. Billings stayed, however, and graduated in 1939 with a degree in art and architecture. Although Gordon likely met Kennedy and Billings during his freshman here, there is no evidence that he and Billings were anything more than casual acquaintances—much less that he knew Billings was gay. Even though Billings had known since high school that he was attracted to men (Kennedy himself also knew this about Billings), he seems not to have acted on his feelings during his time at Princeton.[8]

Although not part of the Kennedy crowd, Gordon socialized with other sons of illustrious men. He hung around with a group of students that included Henry Morgenthau III, the son of the U.S. Treasury secretary who had been instrumental in implementing Roosevelt's New Deal. (Gordon, knowing his father's feelings about Roosevelt, relished the opportunity to tease him with his "New Deal" friendship with Morgenthau.)[9] Overall, however, Gordon thought that Princeton's elitist "country club" reputation was overstated. In a letter to his mother, he claimed, "As for snobbishness . . . I've seen none of it. As a matter of fact they all seem on the poor side more than anything else."[10] There was some truth to this, insofar as Princeton's president Harold Dodds had worked to expand the student body beyond its few "feeder" prep schools, and the incoming class of six hundred students was one of the largest that the university had ever seen.[11] But it was also the case that Gordon had simply gravitated toward students who were like himself: upper middle class, educated at private schools, and good-looking. If anything, *he* was the snobby one, especially around his roommate, Curtiss Cummings, a hard-working, academically minded student who was studying biology. Gordon constantly complained that Cummings was "uninteresting, appallingly serious-minded . . . and completely humorless."[12] (He later relented when Cummings treated him to some of his homemade potato salad.) In the circle of preppy, cultured young men, Gordon fit in perfectly. It was in this environment that he discovered his talent for making friends quickly and for adapting to the mores of a local, insular community.

    Princeton life was not all socializing, however. In addition to growing the student body, Dodds had continued the process—begun by Wilson in 1902—of putting academics at the center of the university's mission. At the turn of the century, Princeton had been notorious for its lax academic demands on students—"second to none in its lack of rigor," as the historian George Marsden put it.[13] By 1935 the college had mostly shed this image, and Dodds had been particularly successful in transforming the faculty into a distinguished group of research scholars.[14] For Gordon, this meant that his professors were demanding yet impressive, and he relished being around so many sophisticated minds. As he put it, Princeton was full of "literate, intelligent people, all of which makes life here so very stimulating." He went to numerous talks and academic teas, especially ones that featured prominent writers and journalists.[15] In his first semester he took classes in English, Latin, history, military science, and French. Gordon had initially tried to get out of French by passing an entrance test, but the beefed-up language requirement—another sign of the college's new rigor—demanded an unusually high level of proficiency.[16] This stringent requirement would prove to be a boon for Gordon. The method of language instruction at Princeton was far more immersive than anything he had experienced in high school, and his proficiency in the language grew rapidly. Years later, the fluency in French he acquired at Princeton would profoundly shape his life's direction. In the short term, his French classes would bring him to the attention of Maurice

Coindreau, a brilliant professor of French literature who would remain his friend and mentor long after Gordon left Princeton.

Gordon threw himself into Princeton life with enthusiasm. In his first month he joined the rowing team—an out-of-character move for someone who had shown little athletic interest in high school.[17] As a further test of his newfound vigor, he exerted himself in the annual Cane Spree, a brawny Princeton tradition in which the freshman and sophomore classes battled each other in a series of physical contests. The 1935 edition had been unusually raucous, ultimately devolving into a frenzied melee that left many sophomores standing naked on the Witherspoon Green.[18] For his efforts Gordon boasted a "battered" nose and clothes torn to shreds. As much as he enjoyed these hardy endeavors, Gordon's main extracurricular interests were the same ones he had in high school. He joined the *Nassau Literary Magazine* (the *Lit*), a venerable student publication that featured poetry, short stories, and essays on literature and culture.[19] After hearing a campus talk by Stanley Walker, an editor at the *New York Herald*, he was further inspired to sign up for the news board of the *Daily Princetonian*, the college's long-running student newspaper.[20] He also joined the Theatre Intime, a fifteen-year-old dramatic club that had grown from humble origins in a dormitory room to a full-fledged theater company that staged both canonical warhorses and original, student-written plays.

Without question the Theatre Intime became Gordon's passion at Princeton. He started off in the lower rungs of the company, working as an usher for a production of Edwin Justus Mayer's *Children of Darkness*. The group's directors soon noticed Gordon's acting abilities, and in February 1936 he was cast in the role of Eliphaz in *The Book of Job*, a one-act play written by a Princeton senior. The play was staged for a private audience that included theater scouts and other theater professionals—a situation that was not unusual for Intime performances.[21] One of these audience members was the playwright Sidney Howard, who had scored a huge Broadway hit with *Dodsworth* and who would later write the screenplay for *Gone with the Wind*.[22] Also in attendance was Percival Wilde, the experimental American playwright and theater critic who had written a manual on acting. In a published review, Wilde commended the actors (including Gordon) for their fine intonation and stylized performances.[23] This would be the first published testimonial to one of Gordon's greatest assets: his voice, which was notable for its articulateness and warm sonority.

Following his success in *Job*, Gordon got his first big "break" a few weeks later when he was cast as a last-minute replacement for Intime's production of *The Talk of the Town*, a satirical comedy about Princeton college life co-written by three undergraduates. Tom Wolf, a Princeton junior who would later become an NBC news correspondent, was originally slated to star in the play. Wolf became seriously ill at the start of rehearsals, and Gordon was tapped to fill in. Although Gordon was excited about the opportunity, the play was hardly a vehicle for his serious acting talents. Written for Junior Prom weekend, the play was a farcical, buffoonish send-up of Princeton's eating clubs that featured a cameo appearance by Haile Selassie, the emperor of Ethiopia—performed in full blackface by a Princeton junior. Afterward, one of the play's writers, George Cooke, perhaps worried about his association with such questionable fare, asked that his name be removed from all future credits for the play. Nonetheless, despite the show's scurrilous humor (or perhaps because of it), it was a campus sensation, selling out all performances and held over for two nights.[24] Thus hundreds of Princeton students saw Gordon's high-profile performance. Only six months into his freshman year, he was already becoming known as one of Princeton's top theatrical talents.

From that point Gordon was a regular star in Theatre Intime productions. A few weeks after *Talk of the Town* he was cast in a small role in Ibsen's *Peer Gynt*. The play was directed by Lemuel ("Lem") Ayers, a Princeton senior and close friend of Gordon's who would eventually be an extremely successful Broadway producer and set designer. The play had two performances in New York City, one of which was seen by Gordon's mother. A few months later, when the company opened its new season in the fall of 1936, he was cast as Lane in Oscar Wilde's *The Importance of Being Earnest*.[25] Gordon's boyish good looks and genial charm made him a natural choice for roles that called for a male ingenue—someone who could exude both innocent vulnerability and seductive physicality. Hence, when the company put on Shakespeare's *The Tempest* the following spring, he was a shoo-in for the role of Ferdinand, the young Neapolitan prince marooned on a Mediterranean island. He beat out dozens of other Princeton men who auditioned for the role, and his subsequent performance was a dazzling success. The reviewer for the *Daily Princetonian* hailed the production as the best he had ever seen at Princeton, singling out Gordon for special praise: "[Merrick] did an intelligent thing in recognizing the part for the bloodless, *papier-mache* role that it is and being content with making it merely decorative, reading his speeches with a glowing tone and attempting little more." Another reviewer found Gordon's acting to be flawless. As it turned out, this was the perfect time to make a splash. The show's preview performance at the McCarter Theatre in Princeton was attended by several prominent theater critics from New York City, including Brooks Atkinson, the Pulitzer Prize-winning drama critic for the *New York Times*, and John Anderson, the president of the New York Drama Critics Circle. Another performance was seen by a group of Broadway producers and directors, including John Houseman, who at the time was collaborating with Orson Welles to found the Mercury Theatre in New York. If photographs of the production are any indication, Gordon must have made a strong impression with his beguiling looks. In a half-page photograph published in the *Herald Tribune*, Gordon is the clear center of attention: decked in Renaissance grab, brandishing a devilish smile, and showing off a pair of shapely legs in snugly fitting tights.[26]

It was during the *Peer Gynt*, *Earnest*, and *Tempest* productions that Gordon became good friends with two other Princeton undergraduates who would go on to illustrious theatrical careers. The first of these was Richard Barr (originally Baer), a Jewish student from Washington, DC, who was in the class above Gordon despite being more than a year younger. Barr was a theatrical wunderkind who excelled at all facets of drama. As a freshman he had impressed the Intime leadership when he stepped in as a late replacement in Patrick Hamilton's *Rope's End*, and over the next two years he directed and starred in a number of Intime productions, including starring as Prospero (alongside Gordon's Ferdinand) in *The Tempest*. Barr was a shrewd networker who took advantage of the Princeton shows to make connections that would lead to valuable professional opportunities. His *Tempest* turn had been seen by John Houseman, who later helped him get a job working for

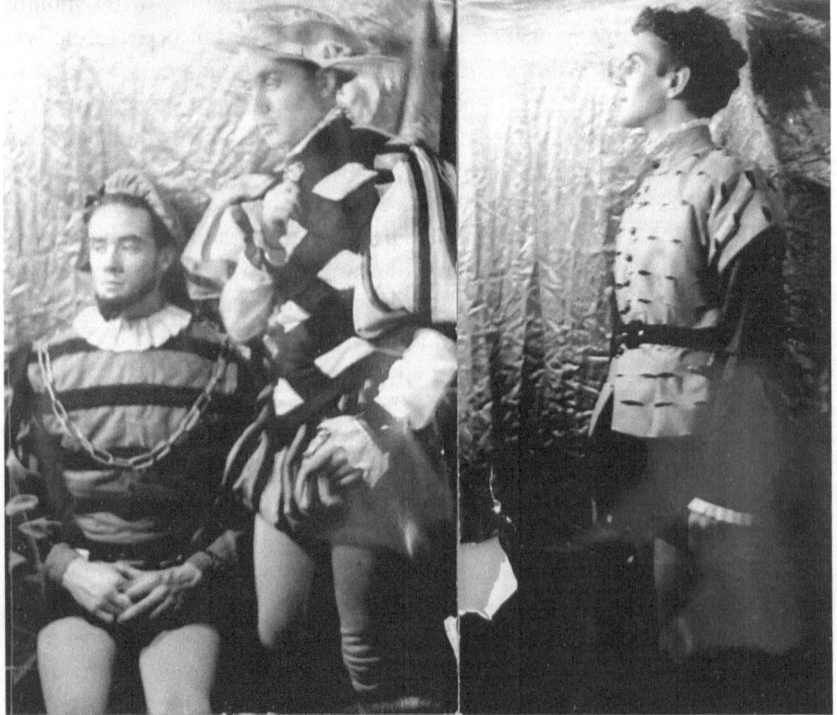

Figure 2.1 Gordon with Mel Ferrer and Richard Barr in The *Tempest,* April 1937.
Source: Estate of Gordon Merrick.

Orson Welles at the Mercury Theatre. After a performance of *Falstaff*, he met a seventeen-year-old Clinton Wilder, his future longtime business partner.

Barr also distinguished himself at the Intime with his adventurous programming. For the company's 1937 spring production, he had planned the American premiere of W. H. Auden and Christopher Isherwood's *The Dog beneath the Skin*, an experimental satire on German Nazism. Although the project fell through because of "production difficulties," it foreshadowed the role that Barr would have as one of the most important Broadway producers of the twentieth century, particularly his work on plays written by gay men.[27] He later produced the plays of Edward Albee, including *Who's Afraid of Virginia Woolf?*, and other landmark shows such as Adrienne Kennedy's *Funnyhouse of a Negro* and Stephen Sondheim's *Sweeney Todd*. One of his uniquely significant productions was Mart Crowley's *The Boys in the Band*, the groundbreaking 1968 play about a group of gay friends that was made into a 1970 film directed by William Friedkin. Barr was himself an openly gay man, though he never spoke publicly about his romantic relationships.[28]

The other Intime connection was Mel Ferrer, who became one of Gordon's closest college friends. Ferrer (born Melchor Gastón Ferrer), the son of a Cuban doctor, had gone to preparatory school in Connecticut before Princeton. A tall, lanky young man with wavy dark brown hair and large, melancholy blue eyes, he would be a Broadway actor before enjoying a successful career as a Hollywood star. Among his many film credits was the 1956 film *War and Peace*, in which he starred opposite Audrey Hepburn, his wife at the time.[29] Ferrer was almost the exact same age as Gordon and had joined the Theatre Intime at the same time. Like Gordon, he was quickly recognized as a promising talent, and the two performed together in several Intime productions, usually one of them playing the lead.[30] By the end of freshman year they were inseparable. Gordon was clearly enamored with Mel, whom he described to his mother as "unusually intelligent, amusing, etc. and thoroughly nice." Mel appears in Gordon's letters to his mother with increasing frequency, usually in gushing accounts about Mel's performances or stories about their trips to see theater in New York City. In one poignant letter, Gordon reveals how much Mel has become part of his idyllic view of Princeton:

> Out my window, I can see pink magnolias against a gorgeous blue sky, while the background is the yellow of the forsythia on the grey walls of the building. . . . The dogwood is beginning to bloom, and so is the laurel which, also, has been trained against some of the walls. When they all come out, this place is going to be indescribable . . . the afternoon has come and gone. Instead of canoeing, Mel & I took a long walk, found a nice stream with picturesque banks and sunned ourself [sic] for hours.[31]

Gordon's description here is reminiscent of a scene in Evelyn Waugh's *Brideshead Revisited* (in the chapter "Et in Arcadia Ego") that romanticizes the homoerotic relationship between Charles Ryder and Sebastian Flyte. Whether or not Gordon had read Waugh by this time, there are glimmers of the literary style that would characterize his novels—the musically turned phrases, the alternation between florid and simple language. The memory of the afternoon with Ferrer must have stayed in Gordon's mind, consciously or subconsciously, since he wrote a version of it in one of the final scenes in *The Lord Won't Mind*.

Although Gordon was clearly infatuated with Ferrer, there is no evidence that their relationship was anything other than chaste. But this raises a big question: *Did* Gordon have any same-sex relationships at Princeton? In interviews that he gave late in his life, Gordon admitted that he did have sexual experiences at Princeton, but he gives very few details about them—and he never names names.[32] When it came to his Princeton classmates Gordon generally followed a "gentleman's" code of conduct, never publicly outing a classmate he knew to be gay. In his novels, he wrote a few scenes that were likely based on his college experiences, but it's hard to tell how much is fact or fiction. For example, in a long flashback scene in *One for the Gods*, the protagonist Charlie (a fictionalized version of Gordon) recalls his freshman year at Princeton, where he was cruised by Hal, an upperclassman, in the college dorms. The two end up meeting regularly in the dorm for sex, which—in typical fashion for Gordon's gay novels—is described in graphic detail. While the episode includes many factual details from Gordon's life, the sexual fling between Charlie and Hal may itself be an exaggeration, if not actually an imaginative rewriting of Gordon's college experiences. Another, more verifiable, passage in *One for the Gods* is Charlie's recollection of the college theater group as a relatively hospitable environment for gay students:

> He never made a move to take what he wanted but somehow, perhaps because there was a circle here into which Hal had dropped his name, his conquests multiplied. When he became active in the undergraduate theater, the field widened, and this aspect of life became more overt. There were those who hinted at it quite openly. He received his first declaration of love, which stunned him and which he rejected as silly and exaggerated, but it unexpectedly set him to thinking about Eddy [his high school boyfriend].[33]

In his later interviews, Gordon says much the same thing about the Theatre Intime, though he suggests that the Triangle Club, the other dramatic group at Princeton, was an even livelier hotbed of same-sex activity. (He implies that part of the reason for this is that the Triangle Club, unlike the Theatre Intime, regularly cast men in female roles.) He also suggests that there were additional opportunities from the non-Princeton college men who came to the Intime shows because they knew the actresses involved. According to Gordon, the Intime shows attracted "some very likely lads [who] would come down presumably to be with their girls," but whose true interests were directed elsewhere. However, he gives no information about how these "likely lads" made themselves known to Gordon or other gay Princeton students, or what actually happened when they did.[34]

Although Gordon's account of Princeton gay life is vague and incomplete, it is remarkable for the fact that it exists at all. Unsurprisingly, there are no other extant accounts of same-sex activity at Princeton in the 1930s. The proscriptions against homosexual conduct at Ivy League universities during this period made it unlikely that any such accounts would survive, and the little evidence that does exist has come from disciplinary records. For example, in 1920 a group of Harvard students were victims of a covert "homosexual witch hunt" by the university's administration, a campaign that resulted in several student expulsions and some suicides.[35] The incident was not publicized for more than eighty years, when a Harvard sophomore accidentally discovered a secret file in the university archives. If there are any similar disciplinary files at Princeton, they have not yet come to light. When Richard Just, a Princeton alumnus and editor of *The Washington Post Magazine*, wrote a groundbreaking article on Princeton's gay history, he was unable to find any sources earlier than the 1950s.[36] In fact, the closest thing to a direct account from the 1930s complains about the *lack* of gay life at Princeton. Alan Turing, the English mathematician who "invented" the computer, was a graduate student at Princeton's Institute for Advanced Study from 1936 to 1938. Turing, who knew he was gay, was constantly frustrated by his inability to find other gay men in the small New Jersey town.[37] Given the fact that Princeton undergraduate and graduate students inhabited different worlds—a pattern that continues to this day—it is unlikely that Gordon ever met Turing, though he may very well have passed him on the street.

Like Turing, Gordon found more opportunities to meet gay men in nearby New York City, and in later interviews he was more explicit about his activities there. During his freshman year he took the hourlong train ride to New York to meet with Eddie, his high school crush who was coming down from Yale (Gordon included this detail in *The Lord Won't Mind*). The two rented a hotel room in the city, where they planned to resume their heady romance. According to Gordon, "it was a disaster." In the few months that he had been at Yale, Eddie had developed an appetite for sexual activities beyond those that he and Gordon had performed in their high school broom closet—most likely anal intercourse. Gordon, by contrast, had not advanced as quickly. As he later put it, "[Eddie] was much more sophisticated sexually [and] physically than I was, and he wanted things I didn't." This new incompatibility proved to be insurmountable for the two men, and the romantic reunion ended almost as soon as it began. In Gordon's words, "that was the end of Eddie."

It was not, however, the end of Gordon's trips to New York. The city gave him an opportunity to visit his grandmother Bon Bon and, more importantly, to visit the theater. In his sophomore year he landed a job as theater critic for the *Daily Princetonian*, giving him more reason to see new Broadway plays. He saw two productions of *Hamlet* whose coincidental timing had ignited a media circus by effectively setting up a competition between their respective leads, John Gielgud and Leslie Howard. Gordon differed from most New York critics by judging Howard's performance to be the better one, arguing in his review that Howard "has not been slavishly bound by scholarly tradition but has sought rather to make the play exciting to modern audiences without tampering with the general outline of the manuscript or in any sense 'modernizing' it." He may have been only twenty years old, but he was not afraid to criticize Gielgud for his "inconsistencies of characterization" or to dismiss the critical preference for Gielgud as "pure tosh."[38]

Gordon also took advantage of the opportunity to see some of the latest films when he was in New York. He raved to his mother about Frank Borzage's *Desire* (1936), which starred Gary Cooper and Marlene Dietrich (whom he would meet in person years later). "You must see it!" he urged his mother.[39] There is a hint of the future writer in the films that fired Gordon's imagination as a young man. Borzage's film is a classic jewelry heist caper in the grand international tradition, shot in Paris and Spain. One of Gordon's novels (which was never published) would feature a similar plot, though with paintings instead of jewels. He was even more effusive about Walt Disney's *Snow White and the Seven Dwarfs* (1937): "Magnificent! The first legitimate example of the cinema as an art."[40] The film had certainly been praised for its innovativeness at the time, but Gordon's enthusiasm shows already a predilection for lavish backgrounds and gothic figures.

He did not restrict himself to theater and film while in New York. During one visit he saw a performance by Josephine Baker, the African-American entertainer who had become a household name with her wildly successful revues in Paris. Baker had returned to America to star in a Broadway revival of *Ziegfeld Follies*, and while in New York she set up a Parisian-style nightclub in midtown where she performed with two white male dancers. Gordon was mesmerized. "She's really marvelous," he wrote his mother, "I can easily see why she was such a favorite in Paris."[41] The experience was memorable enough that Gordon later fictionalized it in *The Lord Won't Mind*, using Baker as the model for a character, Sapphire Hall, a singer who has a large gay following. Indeed, Gordon's attendance at the Baker shows indicates that he had found a gay scene in New York. Baker's nightclub was in fact very popular with gay men (Baker herself was either lesbian or bisexual), a fact which the perceptive Gordon would surely have noticed.[42] Gordon also found his way to another New York performer with a gay audience: Dwight Fiske, a gay nightclub entertainer who was notorious for his risqué monologues and gay in-jokes.[43] Fiske's reputation as an "edgy" burlesque performer was well known enough that a minor scandal erupted when a friend of the family spotted Gordon at Fiske's nightclub and reported the incident to his grandmother, who in turn reported it to his mother. For the next several weeks he tried to reassure his mother that Fiske's shows were not the "dens of iniquity" that Bon Bon had proclaimed.[44] It is unclear how Gordon found his way into such places. He may have learned about them from his theater friends at Princeton, or he may have fallen in with a crowd during one of his many theatrical outings. In any case, it would not have been difficult for Gordon to find his way into this "gay circuit." As the historian George Chauncey has shown, the distance between the city's "serious" theater scene and its "gay circuit" of burlesque theaters was remarkably small.[45]

Gordon's trips to New York became more frequent in his sophomore and junior years. This was mostly due to the city's charms, but also to the fact that he was growing more restive at Princeton. As much as he was stimulated by the college's theatrical and academic offerings, he was increasingly irritated by the social hierarchy that subtended the undergraduate student body in subtle and overt ways. Gordon felt the effects of this hierarchy most keenly at the end of his sophomore year, when it came time to join the Princeton eating clubs. Although not officially part of the university, these private eating clubs had been an integral aspect of Princeton undergraduate life since the beginning of the century, and the annual competition to get into the clubs—known as "bickering"—inevitably intensified the social pressures already felt by Princeton students. According to the historian Jerome Karabel, the eating clubs were "a veritable obsession among freshmen and sophomores . . . the failure to get into the right eating club could be devastating." This outsized significance of the clubs had impelled Woodrow Wilson to wage an unsuccessful campaign to abolish them when he was university president, and debates over the clubs were still raging in the 1930s. During Gordon's freshman year, the *Daily Princetonian* and the *Nassau Literary Review* printed several editorials arguing for the dissolution or reformation of the clubs.[46]

Given the clubs' inherent elitism, Gordon was well positioned for a prestigious club. He was a good-looking man from a prominent family who had come from a private school and was now star of the college theater scene. He had a good chance at Ivy, an especially status-conscious club that would not admit a public school graduate until the 1950s, or Cottage, the club to which F. Scott Fitzgerald had belonged. In the end, however, Gordon did not join one of the prestigious clubs. Instead, he settled on Terrace, which was known as one of the friendlier—and less illustrious—options. (Years later Terrace would enjoy a reputation as the most gay-friendly eating club.[47]) When he broke the news to his mother over the telephone, she immediately responded by saying she was "sorry [he] hadn't joined a good club." Gordon erupted in fury. With his trademark melodrama, he castigated his mother for her "tactlessness" and slammed down the phone. Later, when he had calmed down, he wrote her a long letter explaining that the bicker process had been emotionally draining and had forced him to confront the uglier side of Princeton's social scene:

> When I called I was as near to a complete collapse as I have been for I have been thru an experience as wearing, as disgusting and terrible as any I have known. It is all too close and too complicated to begin to tell you about now, but I have the consolation that, at a time when the worst in everybody was showing, I did as fine and strong a thing as I have ever done in my life. . . . As for the whole club question I feel really ashamed and disgusted for undergraduate standards and mentality. And I am very pleased that in the midst of the ruthlessness of it all, I was able to do something that was really fine.[48]

Gordon did not specify the "ruthless" incident in his letter, but it likely concerned a student who was affected by the clubs' discriminatory practices. One possibility is Henry Morgenthau, one of Gordon's friends in the Theatre Intime whom he had known from his first few weeks at Princeton. Morgenthau may have been the son of a treasury secretary, but he was also Jewish—and thus almost guaranteed to be excluded from the eating clubs. In his own autobiography, Morgenthau characterized bicker week as the most traumatizing episode in his college career, calling it "an emasculating experience that left me feeling that I was something less than a Princeton man."[49] Another possibility is Mel Ferrer, who, despite coming from a private school, was a Cuban-American who *looked* Cuban—a trait that may have worked against him in the bicker process. Whether it was Morgenthau or Ferrer (or both) who had been marginalized by the clubs, it appears from Gordon's letter that he took some kind of moral stand against such discriminatory practices. His decision to join Terrace, which he resolutely defended, was part of this stand: "Terrace, *which Mel and I joined*, has the best general sophomore group this year of any of these clubs."[50] The incident may have been important only to Princeton students who cared about the clubs, but it illustrates an aspect of Gordon's character that would show itself at various times throughout his life. When forced to choose between social prestige and loyalty to a close friend, he would almost always choose his friend.

If Gordon's reason for choosing Terrace was to be with Ferrer, then he was likely disappointed when Ferrer dropped out of Princeton only a few months later to pursue a stage career. After landing an acting job in a summer stock company, Ferrer felt he was ready to try for Broadway. He had a couple of tentative starts, working as a chorus dancer in two Cole Porter musicals, but after two years of auditioning he finally got a big break with the role of Peter Santard in Edward Chodorov's *Kind Lady*.[51] Ferrer's other reason for leaving Princeton was Frances Pilchard, a "titian-haired" drama student from New York who had starred in a play that Ferrer had written and directed for the Theatre Intime in the spring of 1937.[52] The two were married in late 1937, shortly after Ferrer left Princeton. Between his new wife and his struggling career, Ferrer had little time for Gordon. For his part, Gordon distracted himself that summer by traveling to Europe with his mother and brother. He fell in love with Paris immediately. He found that his French was serviceable, and Coindreau had given him useful tips to help him experience the city more intimately than a typical tourist.[53]

Gordon arrived back from France in September, just in time to start the fall semester. With Ferrer gone, Gordon and Barr were now the undisputed titans of the Princeton theater scene. Gordon confirmed his status by winning a lead role in the Intime's season opener, a revival of *Time of Their Lives*, a play about Princeton undergraduate life by Richard Nail, class of '33 and a former Intime member. The play had been a huge hit when it premiered on campus four years earlier, and it was expected to be just as popular again—as with *Talk of the Town*, Princeton students loved seeing themselves portrayed on stage. Unlike *Talk*, however, *Time of Their Lives* was a serious play that took a critical view of Princeton's social hierarchy. Gordon was cast in the role of Austin Clement, a freshman with a "hypersensitive" personality and "superfine sensibilities" who regularly goes to New York on the weekends to see theater.[54] He has a flair for histrionics and a piercingly sardonic wit, as well as a tendency to philosophize on the banality of college life. In short, the character of Austin bore a striking resemblance to Gordon himself.

Austin is also probably gay, although the play does not say so explicitly. When Ken, a fellow student, attempts to befriend him, Ken's friends harangue him with insinuations about Austin's sexuality:

KEN. What did [Austin] want?

WILLIE. To see you.

JOHN. He's having a little tea party tomorrow—bought some special paper-lace doilies and some little French cakes, and pistachio nuts, and thought you might want to come. . . . You're an ass to run around with him, Ken.

KEN. Why?

JOHN. Look at the guys he goes with—that senior for instance; why don't you wake up and . . . [*There is a timid knock at the door.*]

Arguably, this is one of the earliest depictions of a gay college student in American literature. The play develops Austin's marginal status by making him a critic of conformity. In one of the play's climactic moments, a somewhat drunk Austin delivers a stinging tirade on the shallowness of Princeton masculinity:

> Shut up, shut up, you bawling imbeciles. . . . Yes, don't dress differently. Be like everybody else. . . . They're just animals beneath. . . . And each one of those boys has a mother at home who likes to brag that her son is a Princeton man—a gentleman above the common run. . . . They want us all to think as they think, act as they do. And look at them. . . . And they'll all go on, stumbling around in their surity, and they'll all have big funerals and a solid steel coffin to keep out the worms—and lots of flowers to hide the reality.[55]

After the bicker ordeal of the previous spring, the act of saying these words to an auditorium full of Princeton undergraduates must have been cathartic for Gordon. He certainly remembered this speech, since versions of it appear in nearly all his novels. At the end of the play, Austin attempts suicide—another way in which the play "codes" him as gay. Gordon may also have remembered this two years later, when one of his cousins, Clement Kite, a twenty-one-year-old Yale University hockey player, committed suicide on Christmas Eve. The event was all the more disturbing since it occurred at Gordon's family home, Kite's body having been discovered by his mother. There is no reason to think that Kite was gay—one newspaper speculated that he was "worried about his schoolwork"—but it is not unreasonable to assume that the earlier experience of acting in *Time of Their Lives* would have raised the idea as a possibility in Gordon's mind.[56] In any case, whatever he may have thought at the time, Gordon would eventually decide that the conventional, stereotypical treatment of Austin in *Time of Their Lives*—a gay character who attempts suicide at the end—was a highly unsatisfactory one.

The play itself was a smash. It proved even more popular than when it premiered four years earlier, this time selling out all performances and adding two extra shows because of student demand. The production was lauded in the college and local newspapers, which singled out Gordon for special praise. Writing for the *Daily Princetonian*, assistant dean Peter Schwartz marveled at the "explosive dramatic effect" of Gordon's tirade at the end of the play, noting that "his violent denunciation of his fellow students and of all things collegiate makes one wonder for just a minute, whether or not it *is* worth while." Another review in the same newspaper extolled Gordon for his ability to wrest a "splendid performance" from the play's most "exacting role."[57] By all measures this was a turning point for Gordon, who was now the most popular and well-recognized actor on campus. His success in *Time of Their Lives* was followed by his role as Bonario in Ben Jonson's *Volpone*, which was seen by José Ferrer, a recent Princeton graduate who would later become the first Hispanic actor to win an Academy Award.[58]

Having attained considerable clout in the company, Gordon tried his hand at other theatrical jobs. He directed and starred in the Intime's production of William G. Robinson's *Undiscovered Country*, a student-written play that had won the Intime's annual playwriting award and that was well suited to Gordon's literary interests. The *Daily Princetonian* described the play as a story about "the struggles of a young man against frustration and convention," a summary that could easily apply to many of Gordon's later novels. As director, Gordon took an experimental approach to the play's staging. He thought up the idea for a two-tiered stage, in which lighting and gauze curtains would be strategically used to create the effect of a fantastical, dream-like vision. The advance news of this innovative approach generated a lot of buzz for the play, including an article in the *New York Times*. Other advance articles capitalized on Gordon's boyish good looks, such as an article in the *Daily Princetonian* that featured a photograph of Gordon acting in one of the play's scenes. When the play finally premiered, it was an unmitigated triumph. It received glowing reviews from the local press, which praised Gordon's acting and directing. Coindreau, Gordon's devoted mentor, was quoted as saying that the play, under Gordon's direction, was even better than *Time of Their Lives*. The *Daily Princetonian* confidently proclaimed that "Gordon Merrick gives one of the best performances of his career."[59]

However, Gordon's dramatic laurels came at a price. The theater was consuming his college life, and his academics were suffering even more than usual. His course grades had been consistently mediocre (even in French, which was one of his strongest subjects), but the fall semester had been especially unimpressive. He had received a 6 in English Renaissance Literature, which was a mark of near failure (Princeton grades ranged from 1 to 7, with 1 being the highest grade). The situation was serious enough that Robert Albion, the dean of the faculty, wrote Gordon's parents about their son's unsatisfactory progress. The news came as a bit of a shock, since Gordon had told them three weeks earlier that his grades were "quite satisfactory." Nonetheless they admitted that they had suspected Gordon was too involved in the Intime, and they promised to have a serious talk with him to put him back on track.

Gordon's parents did not know he had different ideas about his future. For months he had been mulling the possibility of dropping out of Princeton and moving to New York to pursue acting—very much like what his friend Ferrer had done the previous year. Gordon had already been cultivating his New York theater contacts in the hopes of getting a job. He had managed to get

Figure 2.2 Gordon in *An Undiscovered Country*, March 1938.
Source: This photograph was originally published by the *Daily Princetonian* and is republished here with the *Daily Princetonian*'s permission.

Carl Reed, a former Broadway actor turned agent, to see him in *Undiscovered Country*. Reed was highly impressed with Gordon's acting, and he agreed to meet with him in New York and introduce him to people involved in summer stock theaters. Gordon likewise made arrangements to meet Maurice Evans, the famous English stage actor who had just lit up Broadway with his performances of Richard II and Hamlet.[60] While in New York he also made a regular point of visiting Orson Welles and John Houseman's Mercury Theatre. Thanks to Richard Barr, Houseman had already seen Gordon perform with the Theatre Intime, and one of Gordon's family friends, Charles "Chizzie" Mayon, was working at the Mercury.

Gordon may have had additional reasons for leaving Princeton, besides poor grades and theatrical ambitions. On March 20, 1938, he was involved in a disciplinary incident that resulted in him being officially reprimanded by the dean of the college. According to Gordon's academic record, he committed a serious infraction of the university code while at a cast party in Murray Theater following an Intime performance of *The Life and Death of Sir John Falstaff*. Gordon had not acted in the production, but he was always involved in all Intime activities, especially their parties. The record does not specify what Gordon did to merit an official reprimand, indicating only that the infraction occurred at 2:15 a.m. and had been reported by another student.[61] Although a beer party is mentioned, it is unlikely that he was reprimanded for drunkenness. Drinking was a regular weekend activity for many Princeton students, and this particular weekend would have seen even more student drinking than usual since it coincided with the annual campus prom.[62] Years later, in *The Quirk*, Gordon gave a hint as to what *might* have happened that night. In the novel, the protagonist, an ostensibly straight man, recalls an incident in college when he almost reported a fellow student for making a sexual advance at him at a beer party:

> It had been almost ten years ago, when he had been a freshman at Yale. There had been a big night of drinking and he had awakened to find a senior performing this service for him. He had screamed the place down and threatened to report the aggressor to the dean.[63]

Although there is no mention of sexual misconduct in the academic record, such a scenario would explain many of the strange details of the incident. If something like this took place that night in Murray Theater, it would have likely further encouraged Gordon to leave Princeton for the less insular atmosphere of New York City.

Gordon received mixed reactions to his New York plan. His parents were remarkably coolheaded about the prospect of Gordon leaving college without a degree, especially after the considerable expense his three years at Princeton had cost them. Most likely they knew that loud objections would only stiffen his resolve. By contrast, Gordon's friend Lem Ayers, who had already graduated from Princeton and was doing technical work on Broadway, vehemently implored him not to give up his senior year. Surprisingly, the person who most encouraged him to drop out was Gordon's faculty advisor, who told Gordon that he could not "honestly advise [him] to graduate."[64] It is unclear whether the advisor was making an honest assessment of Gordon's career plans or whether there was something about the Murray Theater incident that was motivating his advice. By April, in any case, Gordon had settled on leaving Princeton. Before leaving, however, he was determined to have one last *coup de grâce* to crown his undergraduate acting career. He got a leading role in the Intime production of George Farquhar's eighteenth-century comedy *The Beaux' Stratagem*, acting alongside Barr and Richard Niehoff. The show was billed as "the largest production in Intime history" and was slated for the McCarter Theater, the professional theater in Princeton, rather than one of the student venues.[65] Thus there would be important press in the audience. Gordon's role as the seducer Aimwell would be a perfect vehicle for his particular talents, since, in addition to requiring him to faint on stage, it would give him one more opportunity to wear tights.

As the date of the performance grew closer, the production seemed headed for disaster. Because of the large number of female roles in the play, nearly half of the cast had to travel from Finch College in Manhattan, making rehearsals exceedingly difficult. Moreover, the timing of the play meant that rehearsals and set construction were scheduled when students were most distracted by end-of-semester coursework and parties. *The Daily Princetonian*, which got wind of unfinished sets and constant fighting among the crew, predicted a shipwreck. They were wrong. Perhaps spurred by the alarmist previews, the company rallied and put on a spectacular performance on opening night. The show received rave reviews from a number of New York newspapers, all of which mentioned Merrick in glowing terms. The *New York Journal-American* had a front page article on the production, with a large photograph of Gordon at the center, and the *New York Herald Tribune* likewise published a very flattering photo of Gordon. Perhaps the most meaningful review came from Coindreau himself, Gordon's one true friend among the faculty. He praised the production in superlative terms, proclaiming it as one that could "easily compare with the finest productions of Broadway." He tried to be more objectively critical of Gordon's performance, but his affection and pride in his young protégé was unmistakable: "Merrick, a little stiff at times, plays like a born actor and will always be served by the splendid quality of his voice."[66]

At this point Gordon's only aspirations were for the theater. He made little effort to pass his spring courses (which he didn't) and officially withdrew from the university on May 26. He gave one more campus performance, reprising his role as Austin in *Time of Their Lives* for Reunion Day—an appropriate encore to cap off his Princeton career. While in the play the character of Austin leaves Princeton in a tragic fashion, Gordon's exit was far more auspicious. Princeton had taught and shaped him in profound ways, but it could do no more for him now. He was ready to start the next chapter of his life on a much bigger stage.

NOTES

1. Anthony D. Romero, "Public Service in a Self-Interested Age," *Princeton Alumni Weekly*, April 8, 2020.
2. "Freshman Class Will Register in McCosh Hall September 23," *Daily Princetonian*, September 7, 1935.
3. Jerome Karabel, *The Chosen: The Hidden History of Admission and Exclusion at Harvard, Yale, and Princeton* (Boston: Houghton Mifflin, 2005), 232.
4. April C. Armstrong, "Bruce Wright's Exclusion from Princeton University," Princeton & Slavery, Princeton University, accessed June 1, 2020, https://slavery.princeton.edu/stories/bruce-wrights-exclusion-from-princeton-university; Karabel, *The Chosen*, 233.
5. Karabel, *The Chosen*, 123.
6. Karen W. Arenson, "Princeton Honors Ex-Judge Once Turned Away for Race," *New York Times*, June 5, 2001.
7. "Exhibition Showcases JFK's Brief Time at Princeton," Princeton University News, August 26, 2010, http://www.princeton.edu/news/2010/08/26/exhibition-showcases-jfks-brief-time-princeton.
8. David Pitts, *Jack & Lem: John F. Kennedy and Lem Billings: The Untold Story of an Extraordinary Friendship* (New York: Carroll & Graf, 2007), 22–25, 44, 49.
9. Gordon Merrick to Mary Merrick, 12 October 1935, private collection.
10. Gordon Merrick to Mary Merrick, 29 September 1935, private collection.
11. Karabel, *The Chosen*, 228–32.
12. Gordon Merrick to Mary Merrick, 29 September 1935, private collection.
13. George M. Marsden, *The Soul of the American University* (Oxford: Oxford University Press, 1996), 223.
14. James Axtell, *The Making of Princeton University: From Woodrow Wilson to the Present* (Princeton: Princeton University Press, 2006), 85–89.
15. Gordon Merrick to Mary Merrick, 23 February 1936, 8 November 1935, private collection.
16. Gordon Merrick, application, May 7, 1935, Gordon Merrick student file.
17. Gordon Merrick to Mary Merrick, 26 September 1935, private collection.
18. "Class of 1939 Takes Annual Cane Spree," *Daily Princetonian*, November 7, 1935.
19. Gordon Merrick to Mary Merrick, 8 and 17 November 1935, private collection.
20. J. D. Burke, "'Princetonian' Host to 1939, as Speakers Discuss Journalism," *Daily Princetonian*, November 6, 1935.
21. See Edward W. Borgers, "The Significance of Princeton's Theatre Intime," *Educational Theatre Journal* 4, no. 4 (1952): 308–14.
22. Gordon Merrick to Mary Merrick, 2 March 1936, private collection.
23. "Roles Partly Cast for Intime Dramas," *Daily Princetonian*, February 14, 1936; "Intime to Present Bill March 4 and 5," *Daily Princetonian*, February 28, 1936; Percival Wilde, "Intime's Three One-Act Plays Provided Charming Entertainment, Says Reviewer," *Daily Princetonian*, March 5, 1936.

24. "Intime Bill Scheduled to Open at 8:40 Tonight," *Daily Princetonian*, March 18, 1936; "Intime Declares Sell Out of Seats for Friday Show," *Daily Princetonian*, March 13, 1935; F. W. Rounds Jr., "'Talk of Town' Scores Heavily Against Clubs as 'Laugh-Happy Fans' Quake at Intime Farce," *Daily Princetonian*, March 19, 1936; George R. Cooke Jr., "Senior Refuses Intime Play Credit," *Daily Princetonian*, March 20, 1936; "'Talk of the Town' Held Over for Final Performance Tonight," *Daily Princetonian*, March 23, 1936.

25. "Intime Makes Final Selection of Male Actors for Forthcoming Production of 'Peer Gynt,'" *Daily Princetonian*, April 7, 1936; Gordon Merrick to Mary Merrick, 2 May 1936, private collection; Sturgis Hedrick, "Intime Announces Plans for 1936–37," *Daily Princetonian*, October 7, 1936.

26. "50 Undergraduates Compete for Roles in New Intime Play," *Daily Princetonian*, February 18, 1937; "From the Pit: The Houseparty 'Tempest,'" *Daily Princetonian*, May 7, 1937; Edward Hubler, "'Tempest' Reviewer Praises Intime Production as Having Caught Spirit of Shakespeare's Play," *Daily Princetonian*, May 1, 1937; A. C. Ulmer Jr., "Broadway Critics to Preview 'Tempest' at Private McCarter Showing Tonight," *Daily Princetonian*, April 29, 1937.

27. Theatre Intime minutes, February 26, 1937, Theatre Intime Archives, box 2.

28. David A. Crespy, *Richard Barr: The Playwright's Producer* (Carbondale: Southern Illinois University Press, 2013), 2, 9–10, 11, 13.

29. "Mel Ferrer, Versatile Actor, Dies at 90," *Los Angeles Times*, June 4, 2008.

30. "Cast Chosen by Intime for Second Production," *Daily Princetonian*, November 15, 1935.

31. Gordon Merrick to Mary Merrick, 25 April 1936, private collection.

32. Gordon Merrick, interview by Brandon Judell.

33. Gordon Merrick, *One for the Gods* (New York: Bernard Geis, 1971), 56.

34. Although evidence from this period is scant, historians have noted that theatrical clubs at Ivy League and Oxbridge universities frequently provided opportunities for gay male students to meet each other. See for example Dominic Janes, "The 'Curious Effects' of Acting: Homosexuality, Theatre and Female Impersonation at the University of Cambridge, 1900–1939," *Twentieth Century British History* 33, no. 1 (2022): 1–34.

35. William Wright, *Harvard's Secret Court: The Savage 1920 Purge of Campus Homosexuals* (New York: St. Martin's Press, 2005).

36. Richard Just, "Hidden Lives," *Princeton Alumni Weekly*, April 3, 2013; Richard Just to Joseph M. Ortiz, email, June 15, 2020.

37. Andrew Hodges, *Alan Turing: The Enigma* (Princeton: Princeton University Press, 1983), 161–64.

38. Gordon Merrick, "From the Pit," *Daily Princetonian*, December 5, 1936.

39. Gordon Merrick to Mary Merrick, 5 May 1936, private collection.

40. Gordon Merrick to Mary Merrick, 28 January 1938, private collection.

41. Brooks Atkinson, "Fannie Brice in the 1936 Edition of the 'Follies' under Shubert Management," *New York Times*, January 31, 1936; "New Josephine Baker Club Opens," *Daily News*, February 29, 1936; Gordon Merrick to Mary Merrick, 7 March, 1936, private collection.

42. Lester Q. Strong, "Josephine Baker's Hungry Heart," *Gay & Lesbian Review*, September/October 2006.

43. On the connections between New York's gay scene and burlesque shows, see George Chauncey, *Gay New York: Gender, Urban Culture, and the Making of the Gay Male World, 1890–1940* (New York: Basic Books, 1994), 194.

44. Gordon Merrick to Mary Merrick, 14 January 1936, 18 February 1936; Gordon Merrick to Samuel Merrick, 18 January 1936, private collection.

45. Chauncey, *Gay New York*, 194.

46. Krabel, *The Chosen*, 59, 64–68; Axtell, *The Making of Princeton University*, 291–309.

47. Luc Cohen, "Clubs Stand Up to LGBT Discrimination," *Daily Princetonian*, April 11, 2011; Princeton Terrace Club Alumni Newsletter, Spring 2017; Krabel, *The Chosen*, 301–2.

48. Gordon Merrick to Mary Merrick, 27 February 1937, private collection.

49. Axtell, *The Making of Princeton University*, 136–38; Henry Morgenthau III, *Mostly Morgenthaus: A Family History* (New York: Ticknor & Fields, 1991), 280.

50. Gordon Merrick to Mary Merrick, 27 February 1937, private collection; "Prospect St. Clubs Enlist 429 Members From Class of 1939," *Daily Princetonian*, March 1, 1937.

51. "Mel Ferrer: Dashing Actor-Director Disgruntled to Become Known as 'Mr. Hepburn,'" *The Independent*, October 23, 2011.

52. "Theatre Intime Announces Cast for 'Awhile to Work,'" *Daily Princetonian*, March 2, 1937; "Frances Pilchard, Titian-Haired Intime Star, Admits Nervousness as Opening Night Looms," *Daily Princetonian*, March 17, 1937.

53. Michel Mabille, "Ceylon to Tricqueville: The Restless Life of an American Author," *L'Éveil de Pont-Audemer*, August 27, 1981.

54. A. C. Ulmer Jr., "Intime Will Launch Season's First Play This Evening at 8:30," *Daily Princetonian*, October 25, 1937.

55. Robert Nail, *Time of Their Lives*, in *The Nassau Literary Magazine* 91, no. 5 (May 1933), 17, 68, 28–29, 85–87.

56. "Probe Shooting of Yale Hockey Player," *Lincoln Journal Star*, December 25, 1939; "Yale Youth's Death Recorded as Suicide," *New York Daily News*, December 26, 1939.

57. "Intime Play Held Over Through Monday Night," *Daily Princetonian*, October 10, 1937; P. A. Schwartz, "Schwartz Lauds 'Time of Their Lives' as of 'Suitable Brilliance' for Opener," *Daily Princetonian*, October 26, 1937; "From the Pit," *Daily Princetonian*, October 29, 1937.

58. "Intime to Present Jonson's 'Volpone,'" *Daily Princetonian*, November 3, 1937; "Jonson's 'Volpone,' Aged for 330 Years, to Open in Murray Theatre on Monday," *Daily Princetonian*, November 9, 1937; Crespy, *Richard Barr*, 10–11.

59. "Three Shows Ahead for Theatre Intime During Rest of Year," *Daily Princetonian*, February 9, 1938; "Cast For New Play Released By Intime," *Daily Princetonian*, February 16, 1938; "Prize Play to Open in Murray Theatre," *Daily Princetonian*, February 28, 1938; "Princeton to Give Drama by Student," *New York Times*, February 27, 1938; "Intime Thespians in Action on Murray Stage," *Daily Princetonian*,

March 3, 1938; Advertisement for *The Undiscovered Country*, *Daily Princetonian*, March 4, 1938.

60. Gordon Merrick to Mary Merrick, 2 February 1938, 10 March 1938, private collection; Rodney Merrick to Robert G. Albion, 25 February 1938, Gordon Merrick student file.

61. William Gordon Merrick academic record, Gordon Merrick student file.

62. "Intime Play to Star Baer in Leading Role of Raucus Falstaff," *Daily Princetonian*, March 4, 1938.

63. Gordon Merrick, *The Quirk* (New York: Avon Books, 1978), 33.

64. Gordon Merrick to Mary Merrick, 10 March 1938, private collection.

65. "Intime Announces Cast of New Play," *Daily Princetonian*, March 3, 1936.

66. "Final Preparations Launched by Intime for McCarter Show," *Daily Princetonian*, April 26, 1938; Review of *The Beaux Stratagem*, *New York Journal-American*, April 25, 1938; review of *The Beaux Stratagem*, *New York Herald Tribune*, May 8, 1938; Maurice E. Coindreau, "Coindreau Says Intime's 'Beaux Stratagem' Compares with Finest Broadway Productions," *Daily Princetonian*, May 7, 1938.

Chapter Three

The Great White Way

Gordon was now officially an aspiring actor. The summer after dropping out of Princeton, he secured an apprenticeship at the Farragut Playhouse, a summer stock theater in Rye Beach, New Hampshire. Summer stock theaters were professional companies that gave young actors a valuable opportunity to learn the nuts and bolts of theatrical production, from constructing stage sets to taking voice lessons. Gordon already knew much about stagecraft from his work in the Intime, but now he had the chance to learn from bona fide professionals. Many Broadway actors and directors worked in these regional theaters during the summer, and some of the most successful summer stock plays eventually transferred to Broadway.[1] One of the founders of the Farragut Playhouse had herself been "discovered" by a Columbia Studios talent scout during a summer performance and had gone on to a long film and television career.

At first Gordon was less than impressed with the Farragut operation. His romantic view of professional theaters had led him to expect something more glamorous than the Intime, yet he found himself doing much of the same laborious tasks he had done in college. The operation was, as he put it, "a bit on the amateur side."[2] His attitude changed, however, when dress rehearsals began, and he realized that the quality of the performances would be well beyond anything he had done at Princeton. He described this aspect of his summer stock experience years later in *An Idol for Others*:

> A few days later, the actors arrived; the opening night went off smoothly and the theater took over their lives even more completely than before. Everything they had been doing acquired an importance that lifted it above drudgery. There were rehearsals all day and performances at night.[3]

Life became even more exciting when Gordon was given the chance to perform. His good looks and talent made him an obvious choice for roles that couldn't be filled by older veteran actors, and by the second play of the season he had a featured role as the suicidal Henry in Sutton Vane's psychological fantasy *Outward Bound*. Gordon was a dazzling as a young, sensitive ingenue. The reviewer for the *Portsmouth Herald* singled out Gordon for the "highest praise," proclaiming that he had stolen the play's final scene and "held the audience tense throughout the entire scene up to its dramatic climax." He had another role later in the season in George Kaufman and Edna Ferber's *Stage Door*.[4] Although this was only a supporting part, it gave him the experience of acting in Kaufman's style of intelligent comedy—a skill that would later help him get his first big break on Broadway.

The role in *Stage Door* had another unanticipated consequence. It put Gordon in constant proximity with another young, gay actor: Otis Bigelow, a dark-eyed, furry-browed beauty who had just graduated from Phillips Exeter Academy. The two had a lot in common—both handsome prep school kids who had given up college plans in the fall to pursue an acting career on Broadway. Not surprisingly, the two were immediately drawn to each other, and before long they found themselves in the heady throes of a passionate affair. Although only eighteen, Bigelow was sexually experienced, and Gordon for his part was now more sexually adventurous than he had been during his freshman year at Princeton. By the end of the summer, Gordon and Otis were still madly in love, so much so that they decided to move in together in New York. Gordon had previously made arrangements to share an apartment with Richard Barr and Lem Ayers, his two friends from Princeton who were also pursuing theatrical careers in New York. Instead of scrapping this plan, it was decided that all four men would live together. Thus in August 1938, Gordon, Otis, Richard, and Lem moved into a small apartment on East 54th Street next to El Morocco, the glitzy nightclub famous for its café society clientele.[5] (Gordon would later re-create this apartment as the setting for the middle section of *The Lord Won't Mind*.)

Living in midtown Manhattan meant that Gordon had opportunities to meet other gay men in a way he never had in provincial Princeton. As George Chauncey has shown in his landmark study of New York's prewar gay subculture, the city offered an astonishingly widespread and variegated landscape in which gays and lesbians could live and socialize:

> That world included several neighborhood enclaves, widely publicized dances and other social events, and a host of commercial establishments where gay men gathered, ranging from saloons, speakeasies, and bars to cheap cafeterias and elegant restaurants. . . . [Gay men] organized male beauty contests at Coney Island and drag balls in Harlem; they performed at gay clubs in the Village and at tourist traps in Times Square. Gay writers and performers produced a flurry of gay literature and theater in the 1920s and early 1930s; gay impresarios organized cultural events that sustained and enhanced gay men's communal ties

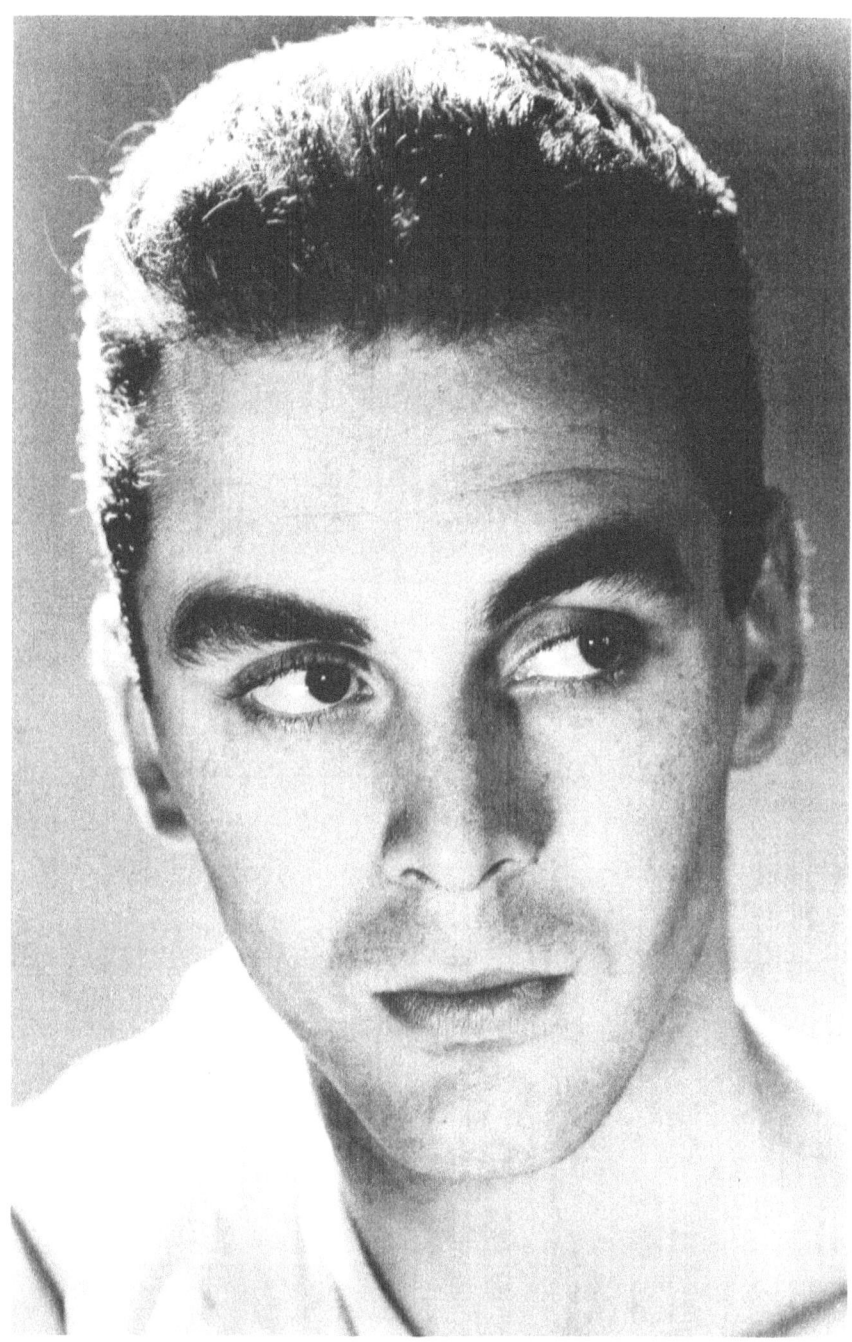
Figure 3.1 Otis Bigelow, professional head shot, c. 1938.
Source: Estate of Gordon Merrick.

Figure 3.2 Otis Bigelow, Hamilton College Naval Reserve Officer Training, c. 1939.
Source: New York Public Library.

and group identity. Some gay men were involved in long-term monogamous relationships they called marriages; others participated in an extensive sexual underground that by the beginning of the century included well-known cruising areas in the city's parks and streets, gay bathhouses, and saloons with back rooms where men met for sex.[6]

Gordon did not frequent most of the city's gay meeting places, though he certainly knew about them. His regular stomping grounds were the theaters and posh nightclubs near Times Square, whose terrain he had learned as a college student. This part of gay New York, which was steps away from most Broadway theaters, was known by the city's gay men as the denizen of "middle class queers"—gay men who distinguished themselves from the more flamboyant "fairies" of the West Village and Harlem.[7] In the midst of all these men, Gordon felt he was in his true element. As he wrote his brother Samuel, he was finally realizing a dream he had harbored since childhood: "It's a singularly exciting feeling—to be at last embarked on something that I've been looking forward to for about fifteen years."[8]

The gay scene in New York was exciting, but it was not conducive to Gordon's fledgling romance with Bigelow. Their living situation had already been awkward from the start, in part because of the cramped quarters. The apartment had a small alcove with a bed that was Barr's area, while the other three shared a daybed in the main room. "So as you can imagine," Gordon later said, "the activities [between Otis and I] were restrained." A further complication was the fact that Ayers was "probably in love" with Gordon and may have intensified the awkward tensions already inherent in such an arrangement. Gordon didn't realize the nature of Lem's feelings until later, though he recalled that at the time, Lem "used to kiss [him] goodnight very chastely every night."[9] Gordon had himself been attracted to Lem back at Princeton, but he hadn't realized his feelings were reciprocated. "We were obviously in love with each other without knowing it," Gordon later told an interviewer. Bad timing was a factor, but so was Ayers' conflict about his sexuality. He had once warned Gordon against getting in a relationship with a man—"Don't let it happen to you," he said—and he seems to have followed his own advice.[10] After graduating from Princeton, Ayers pursued a master's degree in theater arts at the University of Iowa, where he met a twenty-six-year-old Tennessee Williams. In his published memoirs, Williams recalled multiple flirtations with Ayers, first at Iowa and then years later in Hollywood. Though the two were clearly attracted to each other, their mutual reticence ensured that nothing came of it:

> Once during the rehearsals for *Richard of Bordeaux*, Lemuel Ayers . . . was walking around the men's locker room quite naked before a performance. He was like a young saint out of Italian renaissance painting—darkly gleaming curls, and a perfectly formed body.

> Once we had met at dusk in a tiny zoo on a hill. No one was around. . . . We lingered a while, which I would have liked to prolong, but Lem, I suspect was accustomed to more aggressive types, and he smiled and he drifted away.[11]

When Gordon later read Williams' memoirs, he scoffed at the great playwright's presumptuousness in thinking he could have seduced Ayers if he had only been more "aggressive." Gordon believed that Ayers, whom he considered to be bisexual, was far too inhibited to act on his attraction to men in any significant way. Consequently, when the opportunity arose for Ayers to get married, Gordon actively supported the idea. And so, in May 1939, less than a year after he had moved to New York, Ayers married Shirley Osborn, the daughter of the president of the New York Zoological Society.[12]

While Gordon was quietly being adored by Ayers, Bigelow was getting his share of attention from other men in New York. According to the historian Charles Kaiser, the eighteen-year-old Bigelow made a big splash when he came onto the city's gay scene: "Among gay men in New York [Bigelow] was a legend: a great many considered him the best-looking man in Manhattan." Bigelow quickly found that his good looks gave him entry into the well-heeled corner of New York gay society, and, as he later explained in an interview with Kaiser, he had no problem receiving the attentions of older, wealthy gay men:

> There were a number of places where wealthy, youngish men had duplex apartments on Park Avenue, and pretty much any day if you dropped by at five o'clock there would be people there for cocktails and, more often than not, somebody would say, "Well, I have tickets to the ballet and we can drop in on Tony's later." I was polite and gorgeous, and I was always jumping up to get drinks for people. I had social graces.[13]

Bigelow's popularity was a thorn in his relationship with Gordon, who was discomfited by the ease with which Bigelow fit into gay circles. Although he had been venturing into New York since his freshman year at Princeton, Gordon did not flock to gay hangouts and parties with the same alacrity as Bigelow. As Bigelow later told Kaiser, Gordon was "very into *not* being gay."[14] On rare occasions he would go with friends to gay spots in Brooklyn—"slumming [in] sailors' hangouts around the Navy yard" as he put it—but more often he went with Otis to private house parties: "mostly involved with rich men who gave fancy parties and everybody vied for the beauties of the season."[15] More often it was Bigelow who won the honor of being the "beauty of the season."

Things between the two became even further strained one day when Otis revealed to Gordon's grandmother the truth about their relationship. The details of the event are vague, but Gordon later revealed that he used it as the basis for an episode in *The Lord Won't Mind*. In the novel, Charlie's grandmother suspects something between him and Peter, and she slyly tricks Peter into confessing their affair. The fallout from the revelation is too much for Charlie, who promptly breaks up with Peter and throws him out of the apartment. Gordon admitted that the same thing happened with him and Bigelow, meaning that the romance with "dream-boy" (Gordon's term for Bigelow) was over within months of their move to New York.[16] Bigelow rebounded by taking up with a thirty-year-old printing mogul before matriculating at Hamilton College in the fall of 1939.

The blowup with Bigelow reminded Gordon that he had come to New York to act, not to be in love. He was now even more determined to get an acting job, especially since his Princeton friends were already working in the theater. Barr had landed an apprenticeship at the Mercury Theatre, the new venture headed by Orson Welles and John Houseman, and Mel Ferrer (now "Melchor Ferrer") had just gotten two Broadway gigs as a chorus dancer, in Cole Porter's *You Never Know* and Sundgaard and Connelly's *Everywhere I Roam*.[17] After a few months of trying, Gordon finally got a small part in the ensemble for George Kaufman and Moss Hart's *The American Way*. The part was a nonspeaking role in an unusually large ensemble (over two hundred people), but it brought him to the attention of Hart, the celebrated playwright who had recently won (with Kaufman) the Pulitzer Prize for Drama for *You Can't Take It with You*. It also gave him the opportunity to meet more actors, including a ten-year-old child actor named "Dickie" Van Patten, who would go on to become a successful television star as an adult. When the play opened on January 21, 1939, Gordon's dream of acting on a Broadway stage had finally come true, if only in a tiny way. The play ran for 164 performances and was favorably reviewed by Brooks Atkinson, the legendary theater critic at the *New York Times*.[18]

Gordon's *big* break came a few months later. Kaufman and Hart were already at work on their new play, *The Man Who Came to Dinner*, a witty comedy about an insufferable radio star who is compelled to stay with an upper middle-class family for several weeks after falling and breaking his hip on their house steps. The play was being produced by Sam Harris, arguably the most influential Broadway producer at the time, and starring roles had been given to Edith Atwater, Carol Goodner, John Hoysradt (later Hoyt), David Burns, and George Lessey—all established Broadway actors (Goodner and Lessey were even more well known for their film work). The marquis star was Monty Woolley, a larger-than-life actor and director who had just finished a two-year contract with Metro-Goldwyn-Mayer, during which time he had acted in fifteen films.[19] Woolley was cast in the role of Sheridan Whiteside, the radio star who terrorizes the Stanley family. Kaufman and Hart had based the role on Alexander Woollcott, the real-life radio personality who was known for his witty barbs and imposing personality. They had originally asked Woollcott to play the role of Whiteside—in essence, to play himself—and when he turned it down they offered it to Woolley, whose looks and demeanor were similar to Woollcott's.[20] At this point there was only one role that needed to be filled: Richard Stanley, the college-age son who dutifully tries to appease the cantankerous Whiteside. It was an ideal role for a young, handsome actor who was adept at delivering lines but still too inexperienced to carry the weight of a more pivotal character. It was thus the perfect role for Gordon, who had just finished his second season of summer stock theater and was desperately in need of a new gig to get him through the fall. He auditioned for the role and got the part.

Gordon never wrote a detailed account of the circumstances by which he was cast in *The Man Who Came to Dinner*, but he fictionalized his audition experiences in *The Lord Won't Mind*. In the novel, Charlie finds himself delivering lines on a stage under the hot glare of a spotlight, while an invisible director barks out orders from the middle of the auditorium. The total effect on him is overwhelming:

> Charlie was accustomed to walking onto stages. He moved well and with authority. He could have been back at Princeton. Except this was Broadway. This was the way the big hits and the big stars were born. A chill ran down his spine, and his knees began to tremble.[21]

The trauma of such an experience must have impressed itself on Gordon's mind, since he included a similar passage in *The Vallency Tradition*, a novel written twenty years before *Lord*. In both novels, the protagonist senses that he is being treated differently by some directors and producers, who seem to be more interested in his looks than in his acting ability.[22] In *Lord*, however, the playwright, an imposing figure named Meyer Rapper, takes things further. While the casting decision is still in flux, Rapper invites Charlie to his apartment—ostensibly to discuss the role and read scenes from the play. It soon becomes clear that the exercise is merely a pretense for seduction:

> Charlie stood with the typescript in his hand. When ordered to, he read. Meyer Rapper fed him cues from memory. He went all the way through the scene this time, and when he was finished Meyer Rapper nodded. "You could do it. It needs work, of course, but Hank was right. You have a lovely quality." Meyer Rapper paused and his satanic features sharpened as he went on, "Now Charles, I'm afraid you'll have to learn right from the start what a sordid business the theater is. I want to go to bed with you."[23]

Charlie is taken aback by Rapper's advance and promptly rejects him, thus losing the part in the play. Afterward he begins to doubt his hasty decision to run out of the playwright's apartment, and he convinces himself that he might have acquiesced if Rapper had been more artful in his attempt at seduction.

Many readers of *The Lord Won't Mind*, including Moss Hart's biographer Stephen Bach, believe that the Rapper episode is based on Gordon's actual experience in *The Man Who Came to Dinner*. Gordon later admitted that Meyer Rapper was a "fair" representation of Hart, and Bach shows that the character is a remarkably accurate study of the real-life Hart, capturing the minutest details of Hart's physical features and habits of speech.[24] Bach surmises that Hart likely made a sexual advance on Gordon, who at the time was known as "the handsomest young man on Broadway," which then likely led to some kind of sexual relationship. Hart was not openly gay—a few years later he married and had children—but he had already had a number of sexual affairs with other men when Gordon met him in 1939. His initiation into a certain segment of gay culture had taken a quantum leap a few years earlier through his friendship with Cole Porter, who was well known in the theater world for his ravenous pursuit of other men. Bach concludes that "it is unlikely Moss was ever as coolly manipulative as Merrick's fictional version of him," but he points to other instances where Moss struggled with his attraction to actors working for him.[25] There can be little question that Hart was attracted to Gordon, who fit to a tee the "idealized juvenile" type that was his perennial weakness. Likewise, Gordon often described Charlie as a more inhibited and prudish version of himself, suggesting that he himself would not have been as shocked by the idea of a casting couch. The notion that some kind of sexual arrangement was involved in Gordon's attainment of the role of Richard Stanley was indirectly corroborated by Otis Bigelow, who was still in New York when auditions for the play had started. When asked in an interview about Gordon's relationship with Hart at the time, Bigelow had a succinct answer: "We wanted work and we weren't naïve or unavailable."[26] A few years later Bigelow also got a role in a play that Hart was directing.

If the audition process for *Dinner* taught Gordon something about the sexual politics of Broadway, then he learned a very different lesson about the gay theater world from his costar Monty Woolley. Woolley was also gay, but he wasn't conflicted and secretive about his sexuality. He was close friends with Cole Porter, and like Porter he pursued other gay men and relationships relatively openly throughout his life. During production of *Dinner*, Woolley lived in the Astor Hotel with his longtime romantic partner, Cary Abbott (his "courier-secretary-traveling companion," as the newspapers put it). The two would be together until Abbott's death in 1948. Like Gordon, Woolley was an Ivy-educated man (Yale) who had done a lot of theater in college, an activity that had likewise led to many same-sex experiences.[27] Gordon and Woolley became instant friends. One sign of their friendship was their habit of pranking each other in the middle of a show. Woolley had long been a notorious prankster among his friends, and Gordon showed that he could come up with gags of his own. During one performance, in a scene where Sheridan Whiteside is looking through a set of photographs, Gordon replaced the usual prop photos with a bunch of "red hot 'feelthy pictures.'" The photos were raunchy enough to make Woolley blush on stage, but he kept his composure "and retaliated by making Merrick scrutinize each photo minutely as he criticised it."[28]

As Richard Stanley, Gordon was able to channel his affection for Woolley into his character, who responds to the sharp-tongued Whiteside with a combination of admiration and fear. In one scene Richard, an amateur photographer, works up the nerve to ask Whiteside if he can take a photo of him—a request that flatters the older man's vanity.[29] A photograph of this exact moment became one of the play's most frequently used publicity images, including a large-scale reproduction splashed across the *New York Times*.[30] In the photograph Woolley is sitting in a wheelchair with a smug, self-satisfied grin, and kneeling in front of him is Gordon, holding his camera in anticipation and looking as dashing and handsome as ever.

The Man Who Came to Dinner was an unqualified success. Following a nineteen-day period of rehearsals, the production had its first runthrough in Hartford on September 23, 1939. Two days later the show moved to Boston, where it had previews for two weeks.[31] Finally, the play officially premiered at the Music Box Theatre in New York on October 16, 1939, where it was met with a buoyant audience "dressed up to the nines."[32] In his review of the play Brooks Atkinson heralded it as "the funniest comedy of this season" and "a fantastic piece of nonsense" that appealed to everyone.[33] In a second review published less than a week later, he called the play an "explosion of wit" with an "ingenious" plot and "dialogue as devastating as any Mr. Hart and Mr. Kaufman have ever written."[34] *Time* called the play a "smash hit" that "hilariously held the mirror up to ill-nature."[35] As expected, the reviewers gave special praise to Woolley, whose resemblance to Alexander Woollcott was frequently noted. Cole Porter, who had contributed a song to the play, was also occasionally mentioned.[36] Gordon was not singled out by name in the major reviews, but his name regularly appeared in the list of supporting cast. His former classmates at Princeton took note of his success, and articles about his appearance in the play appeared in the *Daily Princetonian* and the *Princeton Alumni Weekly*. In the short autobiography that Gordon wrote for the show's Playbill program, he wittily described himself as having "a theatrical career which extends as far back as two years, during most of which time he was consigned to anonymity." With his name now splashed across

Figure 3.3 Scene from *The Man Who Came to Dinner*, with Monty Woolley, Gordon Merrick, and Barbara Wooddell.
Source: Estate of Gordon Merrick.

the Playbill title page, Gordon could relish the fact that he was no longer anonymous.

Despite this auspicious beginning, *The Man Who Came to Dinner* would be Gordon's last Broadway appearance. In fact, it would be one of his last acting jobs of any kind. For reasons that are not fully clear, he quit the play sometime in October 1940, several months before the production run ended. He later explained his decision as the result of the tedium of performing the same show night after night. It was one thing to do summer stock theater, where he might perform the same show five or six times at the most, but Broadway was a much different beast. He articulated this sense of ennui most fully in *The Great Urge Downward*, when the novel's protagonist Lance Vanderholden—another handsome, Ivy-educated kid who gets a big break on Broadway—grows weary of the monotony of a Broadway play:

> The working part, the part he was paid for, became pure drudgery within weeks. He liked having to report for work daily at the same place and hour, and he liked payday, because all that proved that he was a working man like everybody

else, but when he found himself on stage repeating words and gestures that had ceased to have any meaning for him, he was depressed by the monotony of it.[37]

There may also have been other reasons for Gordon's disenchantment with the theater. He may have come to resent the sexual politics of the theater, either because of Hart or because of other people involved in the production. In another novel featuring the character of Lance Vanderholden, Gordon described this seamier side of the theater:

> All the crap I have to go through now, being nice to people I don't like and fighting with people I don't think are worth fighting and. . . . Old Fineman making a pass at you and your not knowing what to do because he's a big producer. I hate all that.[38]

In an interview that Gordon gave near the end of his life, he revealed that he had also been influenced by someone who told him at the time that he "shouldn't be an actor."[39] He did not reveal who this advice came from. One possibility is the actor Clifton Webb, who Gordon became friends with around this time. Gordon looked up to the forty-year-old Webb and trusted him (two years later he used Webb as a reference on his OSS application[40]). By most accounts Webb was gay, though he never acknowledged it publicly.[41] If Gordon had been struggling with the difficulties of working in the theater as a gay man himself, Webb may have gently advised him to get out. Whatever the advice—and whoever it came from—it was persuasive enough to convince Gordon to quit the play.

From a professional standpoint, Gordon's early departure from *Dinner* represented a big missed opportunity. When the show's Broadway run ended in July 1941, it was quickly made into a highly successful film by Warner Brothers, with many of the original theatrical cast members reprising their roles on screen. (Gordon's part ended up going to Russell Arms, an up-and-comer who was already contracted with Warner Brothers.) However, Gordon was resolute in his break from acting, and he now turned to his other passion. He was eager to write again, and his experience suggested that journalism was the most viable option. He soon found that getting a journalist job was far more difficult in New York City than it had been in Princeton, and he spent months looking for a regular job with little success.[42] The lack of job prospects prompted him to apply for the American Field Service, the volunteer ambulance organization that had been reactivated in 1939 to support the Allied war effort in Europe. Many AFS volunteers were being sent to France, and Gordon thought his skills in French would make him a desirable candidate. When his mother and brother tried to dissuade him, worried about his safety, his resolve only stiffened. He applied for a post in France, and he was quickly rejected. Apparently, the AFS required its volunteers to be in "strong, robust physical health" and have "a certain ability to repair motors"—neither of which Gordon could claim. The AFS also indicated that "those with poor nerves are not wanted." Gordon's family thought (and hoped) that this would ultimately disqualify him. They were right.[43]

Gordon spent the next two years in a professional and personal slump. After quitting the play he spent a few months giving lectures for the Americana Corporation, the company that produced the Encyclopedia Americana. When the next summer came around he still didn't have a full-time job, so he got another summer stock job at Guy Palmerton's playhouse in Lake Whalom, Massachusetts. The experience only confirmed for him that he was done with the theater, and so at the end of the summer he tried looking for a job that would make use of his journalism skills. He found that breaking into the newspaper industry was much harder than he thought, and he spent the next six months unemployed. During a trip back home he finally got a job as a copy boy for the Philadelphia *Evening Bulletin*. It was regular work, but the salary was a measly fifteen dollars a week, and he was missing New York. After a few months he was able to land another copy job at a radio news station in Brooklyn. The commute to Brooklyn from his room on East 76th Street in Manhattan was arduous, and the graveyard shift hours were even worse. His chronic back problems started acting up again, making his daily routine even more painful. His family began to worry about his health, noting with concern his "very thin and so spiritless" appearance.[44]

Gordon's grueling job was clearly taking a toll on him, but he was likely also suffering from loneliness. His graveyard hours were not conducive to a social life, and the friends with whom he had moved to New York were all gone now. Bigelow was in college in upstate New York, Barr had gone to Hollywood to assist Orson Welles with several RKO films, and Ayers was married with children on the way. When his roommates left the 54th Street apartment, Gordon had initially moved into a place in Greenwich Village (riling his grandmother, who considered the neighborhood a "den of iniquity"[45]). He had a hard time fitting into the neighborhood gay scene. When he first moved to New York he had not thought of himself as leading a "gay" lifestyle, and he had instinctively recoiled from the flamboyant and effeminate gay men who lived in the city—the "gays" or "fairies" as they were called by both straight and gay men. Following the lexicon used by gay men in New York at the time, he thought of himself as "queer"—i.e., someone who was homosexual but who otherwise fit into "normal" society.[46]

As time went on, however, living in New York accelerated an identity crisis that he had tried to ignore. He found it increasingly difficult to distinguish himself from the "gays" and "fairies" he was constantly meeting. He met lots of other gay men who looked and talked like him, with similar upbringings, but who had no intention of getting into a heterosexual marriage. Many of these men had little problem interacting with less "straight-acting" gays, especially in Greenwich Village.[47] Gay bars were a particular problem for Gordon, since they stoked his internalized homophobia. In his mind gay bars were full of predatory and emasculated men—exactly what he feared becoming. In an early draft of *One for the Gods*, he could still vividly recall the distaste he had felt when walking into a gay bar in the 1940s:

> He knew of bars which catered to a special clientéle; Peter had taken him to one once and he had been appalled, but perhaps that had been because Peter was with him. . . . When he finally decided to [go back], he was appalled again. He found the older men disgusting, with their simpering effeminate ways. The younger ones, the prey, preened too self-consciously, were too arrogantly aware that they had favors to bestow. As for himself, he couldn't speak to anyone without its becoming a sexual engagement. If he had been seeking reaffirmation of his attractions it would have been highly gratifying, but as it was, it was only a bore.[48]

He later deleted this section from the novel, perhaps because he thought it might make Charlie *too* unsympathetic for his gay readers. Yet this was a prejudice he never completely got over, even after he became more comfortable in gay venues. It is one of the ironies in Gordon's life that, despite his lifelong ability to adapt to many different environments, a gay bar was the one place where he never knew how to act.

Things started to look up near the end of 1942, both professionally and personally. He got a job with the Washington *Evening Star* that paid more than his Brooklyn gig, and it gave him the opportunity to do actual reporting and writing of his own. He'd hardly had time to explore Washington, DC, before he moved to Baltimore for a reporting job with the Baltimore *Evening Sun*. Finally, after almost two years of struggling to get a foothold in the industry, he was rapidly gaining experience and building his skills. His peripatetic job-hopping paid off in October 1942, when he got a permanent job as a reporter for the *New York Post*. His salary of fifty dollars per week was higher than what he made starring on Broadway.[49]

The *Post*, which would later become notorious for its sensationalist headlines and right-wing propaganda, was in 1942 a respected, liberal-leaning paper. Gordon was hired to help build the newspaper's radio department, a task for which he turned out to be well suited. After only a few weeks on the job he received a raise of ten dollars more per week and was given the responsibility of training and managing a team of assistants—"none of whom know how to read or write," he lamented. Unlike the literary, culturally minded journalism he had produced at Princeton, his work for the *Post* required facility with several different types of news sources and an ability to respond quickly to late-breaking stories. The United States was now fully engaged in the war, and Gordon's managers expected him to be available whenever a new development was reported.[50] While the job did not give him fame—his name was not appearing on newspaper bylines—it did give him a lot of experience. He learned how to produce copy at a moment's notice, with a consistent style and with little need of correction or editing. This ability would be greatly appreciated by Gordon's future literary editors, who came to rely on his polished style and adherence to deadlines, and Gordon would often characterize his job at the *Post* as the ideal training for his novel writing.

At the same time that his career was looking brighter, his prospects for making gay friends also dramatically improved. Shortly after returning to New York for the *Post* job, Gordon moved back to Greenwich Village (to the consternation of his grandmother), this time into a small apartment of his own.[51] He was again encountering flocks of gay writers and artists on a regular basis but without the same level of anxiety and self-loathing as before. It was in this setting that he met one of the most important friends he would have in his life: Glenway Wescott, a forty-two-year-old writer whose recent novel *The Pilgrim Hawk* had been a huge critical success. Wescott was living with Monroe Wheeler, his longtime partner and a director at New York's Museum of Modern Art. They had been together for over twelve years, and they would remain a couple until Wescott's death in 1987. As Wescott's biographer Jerry Rosco puts it, theirs was "one of the great relationships of the century."[52] When Gordon met the pair, they had just gotten out of a complicated, ten-year-relationship with the talented photographer George Platt Lynes. The breakup had been harder for Wheeler, who had been more romantically attached to Lynes, but it had also deeply affected Wescott.[53] The pair rebounded by moving into an apartment at 812 Park Avenue, where they made a habit of giving parties attended by a glittering set of New York artists, writers, actors, and other cultural elites—most of them gay. Among the many illustrious figures who passed through Wescott and Wheeler's Park Avenue apartments in the 1940s were Paul Cadmus, Jared French, Virgil Thomson, Marsden Hartley, Alexander Calder, Pavel Tchelitchew, Charles Henri Ford, Paul Bowles, Cecil Beaton, Christopher Isherwood, Yul Brynner, Somerset Maugham, and Marlene Dietrich.[54] It was into this circle that Gordon was admitted. Wescott was impressed by Gordon's intelligence and cultural tastes, but he was also taken by his good looks—this "amiable, baby-faced, Priapus-bodied friend with whom I flirted unavailingly," as he put it in his journal.[55] For Wescott, the handsome, twenty-six-year-old Gordon must have been especially appealing after the recent breakup with Lynes.

Gordon does not appear to have been sexually attracted to Wescott, but he was deeply drawn to the older man's literary talent. He was extremely impressed by the fact that Wescott had known Gertrude Stein and F. Scott Fitzgerald (two of Gordon's literary idols) while living in France in the 1920s. He also enjoyed mingling with artists and writers who were more interested in his ideas about French literature than in his experiences as a Broadway actor. In many ways Gordon's initiation into Wescott's circle of friends resembled that of Paul Cadmus a few years earlier; Cadmus had been taken to a party at Wescott and Wheeler's home by Lincoln Kirstein, and afterward had become a regular in the group.[56] The Wescott-Wheeler crowd rekindled Gordon's literary aspirations and reminded him that his journalism work was only a temporary job. In many ways Wescott became an unofficial mentor for Gordon, and his influence on Gordon's literary development was profound. Gordon read Wescott's *The Apple of the Eye* and *Pilgrim Hawk*, which he thought remarkable and which inspired him to do more non-journalistic writing. After reading Wescott's novels he started writing a play, with the hope of finding a theater company in New York who would perform it. Even more momentous was the introduction to the works of E. M. Forster. A devoted admirer of Forster, Wescott was alarmed when he learned that Gordon had not read any of Forster's novels—and he subsequently commanded him to do so. (In this way, Wescott did for Gordon what the writer Katherine Anne Porter had done for him years earlier when *she* learned that Wescott had not read Forster.[57]) Gordon promptly followed Wescott's advice and was blown away. After reading Forster's *The Longest Journey*, he wrote his mother about the novel in a state of awe: "I think it an extraordinary piece of work and am now going on to the next. You must read them." Forster would eventually become the most important literary model in his life.[58]

Not all of Wescott's introductions were received so warmly by Gordon. He met Christopher Isherwood and W. H. Auden at a house party in Greenwich Village. At some point Isherwood and Auden started giving an impromptu performance of their play, *The Ascent of F6*, in the living room. Gordon was somewhat bored by the modernist, allegorical style of the piece, and he was more confused by Isherwood's and Auden's personalities: "These two little Englishman—rather forlorn little Englishmen—had just arrived." He evidently did not hit it off with Isherwood, whom he found "curiously unsympathetic" and "scratchy." Later, Gordon would profess to always having admired Isherwood's work, but he had no interest in emulating him like he did with Forster and Fitzgerald.[59]

Socializing with Wescott's circle also affected Gordon's ideas about life as a gay man. Wescott, Wheeler, and their gay friends were generally more open about their sexuality than the Broadway theater crowd, which was full of gay men who knew about each other but who kept their sexuality out of view from their straight colleagues. Richard Barr, for example, who had regular flings with men after moving to New York, strictly cordoned off his romantic life from his professional life at the Mercury Theatre. Otis Bigelow, who came back to New York after graduating from Hamilton College, likewise associated with "discreet" gay men who, as Charles Kaiser puts it, "were honest about their homosexuality only among themselves."[60] (By early 1944 Bigelow was back on friendly terms with Gordon and even stayed at his apartment while on his breaks from the Navy.[61]) Wescott's crowd was different. They were not the "flamboyant homosexuals [with] long hair" who gave Greenwich Village its reputation, but they did not avoid them nor recoil from them. They were not scandalized—Wescott in particular—by the city's less "respectable" gay venues, such as the cruising spots in city parks or places where "workingmen" types could be picked up. More importantly, they dared to represent gay life in their work. Wescott had already written several short stories with explicitly homosexual themes that he likely shared with Gordon, even though he was unable to publish them.[62] Wescott's friend Paul Cadmus likewise included homosexual images in his art: his 1934 painting *The Fleet's In* was so explicit in its representation of a same-sex flirtation that it provoked the Navy Secretary to ban the work from Washington.[63]

These men were not only unconventional in their work but in their romantic lives as well. Wescott and Wheeler remained friends with Lynes even after their relationship ended, and Cadmus, who had painted a stunning triptych portrait of Wescott, Wheeler, and Lynes, was in the middle of an eight-year-long relationship with the painter Jared French and French's wife Margaret.[64] In essence, Gordon was learning from Wescott's circle that there was more than one way to live as a gay man. These were gay writers and artists who didn't feel the need to give up their middle-class upbringing, but who still managed to lead relatively open lives.

Wescott's friendship was an important factor in the third new development in Gordon's life in 1943: an intense, short-lived romance with an Air Force pilot. The specific details about this relationship are vague, but its effect on Gordon's romantic life were profound. He had met the pilot one weekend in New York and instantly "fell madly in love." The two spent the entire weekend together before the pilot had to return to his base, and afterward they wrote each other constantly. Such experiences for gay soldiers in New York during the war were more common than one might expect. As John D'Emilio and others have documented, thousands of gay soldiers traveled to New York at one point or another, a situation which gave many of them unprecedented opportunities to meet and socialize with other gay men. As D'Emilio puts it, "for many gay Americans, World War II created something of a nationwide coming out experience."[65] Gordon and the Air Force pilot made plans to meet again in New York at Christmastime and resume their heady affair. Sadly, tragedy struck before the anticipated reunion could take place. The pilot, whose job was to help train the thousands of newly recruited Air Force pilots desperately needed for the war, had died in a plane crash during a training exercise. The pilot's body was sent to his parents in Richmond, and Gordon was asked to go to Richmond to identify the body. It's unclear why Gordon, and not the pilot's family, was asked to perform this somber task; the body was likely burned beyond recognition, and the pilot may have been wearing something (a watch, a bracelet) with Gordon's name on it. At any rate, Gordon took the train down to Richmond, identified his lover's body, met his family, and watched as the body was escorted by a retinue of Air Force lieutenants.[66]

Gordon was devastated. He had only known the pilot for a short while, but he had already been imagining a future with the man. He had learned of the pilot's death by chance, through a wire report that appeared on the evening news.[67] He didn't tell his family about the ordeal, but they could tell that something was wrong. Even his grandmother Bon Bon noticed a drastic change in his demeanor and was certain he was going through "some sort of crisis."[68] Gordon was unable or unwilling to turn to his family for support, but he did turn to Wescott, whose friendship and advice were an invaluable source of comfort. Years later Gordon was still thanking Wescott for the "kindness" he had shown him during this difficult time.[69] Another person who helped Gordon through the tragedy was less expected. One of the lieutenants who was responsible for escorting the pilot's body, a handsome twenty-three-year-old Air Force pilot from Topeka, had introduced himself to Gordon in Richmond—and revealed that he too had been romantically involved with the pilot. Gordon might have reacted angrily, but instead he found comfort in being able to speak honestly with another gay man who was grieving in much the same way as he was. He also found himself undeniably attracted to the slim, blond, blue-eyed lieutenant.[70]

The man's name was Robert Blaine Richardson, and he would become one of the great loves of Gordon's life. Before that could happen, however, the war would intervene. Gordon had all but given up hope of aiding the American war effort after being rejected by both the army and the American Field Service. However, he was about to get tapped by another military agency—an agency which a few months earlier he had not even known existed. The assignment would take him to Europe, to the Mediterranean coast, and the experiences it would give him would change his life in the most profound way.

NOTES

1. "Various Types of Summer Dramatic Activities Busied Several Members of Community Players," *Princeton Herald*, October 7, 1938; Martha Schmoyer

Lomonaco, *Summer Stock!: An American Theatrical Phenomenon* (New York: Palgrave Macmillan, 2004), 3–4.

2. Mary Merrick to Samuel Merrick, 24 August 1938, private collection.

3. Gordon Merrick, *An Idol for Others* (New York: Avon Books, 1977), 46.

4. "'Outward Bound' Opens Tuesday at Farragut," *Portsmouth Herald*, July 11, 1938; "Farragut Players in Outward Bound," *Portsmouth Herald*, July 13, 1938; "Farragut Players Give 'Stage Door,'" *Portsmouth Herald*, August 3, 1938.

5. Charles Kaiser, *The Gay Metropolis: The Landmark History of Gay Life in America* (New York: Grove Press, 1997), 6–7; Gordon Merrick, interview by Brandon Judell. In his interview with Kaiser, Bigelow was vague about the extent of his romantic involvement with Gordon, though he admitted that *The Lord Won't Mind* had been partly based on their relationship.

6. George Chauncey, *Gay New York: Gender, Urban Culture, and the Making of the Gay Male World, 1890–1940* (New York: Basic Books, 1994), 1.

7. Chauncey, *Gay New York*, 105.

8. Gordon Merrick to Samuel Merrick, 21 August 1938, private collection.

9. Keith Howes, "Once A Spy . . . ," *Gay News*, August 24, 1978; Merrick, interview by Judell.

10. Howes, "Once A Spy."

11. Tennessee Williams, *Memoirs* (1972; New York: New Directions Books, 2006), 47.

12. Merrick, interview by Judell; "Lemuel Ayers, 40, Scenic Designer," *New York Times*, August 16, 1955.

13. Kaiser, *Gay Metropolis*, 7–8.

14. Kaiser, *Gay Metropolis*, 6.

15. Bjorn Rye, "Idylls for Others," *The Advocate*, April 4, 1979.

16. Merrick, interview by Judell; "An Exclusive Interview with Gordon Merrick," *Michael's Thing* 1, no. 30 (1971): 13.

17. David A. Crespy, *Richard Barr: The Playwright's Producer* (Carbondale: Southern Illinois University Press, 2013), 13; Helen Colton, "Reluctant Star," *New York Times*, September 4, 1949; "Mel Ferrer: Dashing Actor-Director Disgruntled to Become Known as 'Mr. Hepburn,'" *Independent*, June 5, 2008.

18. Brooks Atkinson, "Fable for Our Times," *New York Times*, January 29, 1939.

19. Billy J. Harbin, "Monty Woolley," in *The Gay & Lesbian Theatrical Legacy: A Biographical Dictionary of Major Figures in American Stage History in the Pre-Stonewall Era*, eds. Billy J. Harbin, Kim Maara, and Robert A. Schanke, 392–95 (Ann Arbor: University of Michigan Press, 2007), 393.

20. Moss Hart, "How A. W. Came to Dinner, and Other Stories," *New York Times*, October 29, 1939.

21. Gordon Merrick, *The Lord Won't Mind* (New York: Bernard Geis, 1970), 114.

22. Gordon Merrick, *The Vallency Tradition* (New York: Julian Messner, 1955), 86.

23. Merrick, *The Lord Won't Mind*, 118.

24. Steven Bach, *Dazzler: The Life and Times of Moss Hart* (New York: Da Capo Press, 2001), 134–35, 157–59.

25. Bach, *Dazzler*, 159.

26. Bach, *Dazzler*, 159.

27. Harbin, "Monty Woolley," 392–93; Billy J. Harbin, "Monty Woolley: The Public and Private Man from Saratoga Springs," in *Passing Performances: Queer Readings of Leading Players in American Theater History*, ed. Robert A. Schanke and Kim Marra, 262–79 (Ann Arbor: University of Michigan Press, 1998), 267.

28. Lucius Beebe, "Blowing Cold on 'Gone with the Wind,'" *St. Louis Post-Dispatch*, December 31, 1939.

29. Moss Hart and George S. Kaufman, *The Man Who Came to Dinner* (Bristol, RI: Hildreth Press, 1939), 27.

30. "Other News of the Theatre," *New York Times*, January 7, 1940.

31. "Aperitif to a Dinner," *New York Times*, September 17, 1939.

32. Harbin, "Monty Woolley: The Public and Private Man," 271.

33. Brooks Atkinson, "Moss Hart and George S. Kaufman Discuss 'The Man Who Came to Dinner,'" *New York Times*, October 17, 1939.

34. Brooks Atkinson, "White Owl of Lake Bomoseen," *New York Times*, October 22, 1939.

35. "Harts & Flowers," *Time*, October 30, 1939, 48.

36. "Aperitif to a Dinner."

37. Gordon Merrick, *The Great Urge Downward* (New York: Avon Books, 1984), 43–44.

38. Merrick, *The Vallency Tradition*, 119.

39. Merrick, interview by Judell.

40. Investigation Report for Gordon Merrick, Security Office, Office of Strategic Services, 24 November 1943, OSS file for Gordon Merrick, RG 226, Entry A1 224, Personnel Files of the Office of Strategic Services, Joint Chiefs of Staff, Office of Strategic Services, National Archives (hereafter OSS).

41. Leonard Leff, "Becoming Clifton Webb: A Queer Star in Mid-Century Hollywood," *Cinema Journal* 47, no. 3 (Spring 2008): 3–28.

42. Mary Merrick to Samuel Merrick, n.d., private collection.

43. Augustus Ernest D'Ambly Jr. to Samuel Merrick, 13 June 1940, private collection.

44. Clarice Billups to Samuel Merrick, 14 May 1942, private collection.

45. Mary Merrick to Samuel Merrick, 20 March 1943, private collection.

46. Keith Howes, "Once A Spy"; Chauncey, *Gay New York*, 15–16.

47. See Chauncey, *Gay New York*, 237–44.

48. Gordon Merrick, draft of *One for the Gods*, 72, GMP, box 10, folder 2.

49. The timeline of Gordon's work assignments from 1940–43 has mostly been reconstructed from his OSS application. Investigation Report for Gordon Merrick.

50. Mary Merrick to Samuel Merrick, 20 March 1943; Gordon Merrick to Mary Merrick, 22 October 1943, 11 February 1943, private collection.

51. Mary Merrick to Samuel Merrick, 20 March 1943, private collection.

52. Jerry Rosco, *Glenway Wescott Personally: A Biography* (Madison: University of Wisconsin Press, 2002), 18.

53. Allen Ellenzweig, *George Platt Lynes: The Daring Eye* (Oxford: Oxford University Press, 2021), 336–38.

54. Rosco, *Glenway Wescott*, 105, 116; Gregory Woods, *Homintern: How Gay Culture Liberated the Modern World* (New Haven: Yale University Press, 2016), 279; Martin Duberman, *The Worlds of Lincoln Kirstein* (New York: Alfred A. Knopf, 2007), 450.

55. Glenway Wescott, *Continual Lessons: The Journals of Glenway Wescott 1937–1955*, ed. Robert Phelps and Jerry Rosco (New York: Farrar Straus Giroux, 1990), 239.

56. Rosco, *Glenway Wescott*, 69.

57. Rosco, *Glenway Wescott*, 70.

58. Gordon Merrick to Mary Merrick, 22 and 7 October 1943, private collection.

59. Rye, "Idylls for Others."

60. Crespy, *Richard Barr*, 20; Kaiser, *Gay Metropolis*, 13–14.

61. Clarice Billips to Samuel Merrick, 2 February 1944, private collection.

62. Chauncey, *Gay New York*, 244, 108, 181; Glenway Wescott, *"A Visit to Priapus" and Other Stories*, ed. Jerry Rosco (Madison: University of Wisconsin Press, 2013), xiii.

63. "'Fleet's In' Artist to Eschew Navy," *New York Times*, May 31, 1934.

64. David Leddick, *Intimate Companions: A Triography of George Platt Lynes, Paul Cadmus, Lincoln Kirstein, and Their Circle* (Miami Beach: White Lake Press, 2020), 128–31.

65. John D'Emilio, *Sexual Politics, Sexual Communities: The Making of a Homosexual Minority in the United States 1940–1970*, 2nd ed. (Chicago: University of Chicago Press, 1998), 23. See also Allan Bérubé, *Coming Out Under Fire: The History of Gay Men and Women in World War Two* (New York: The Free Press, 1990), 106–20; Kaiser, *Gay Metropolis*, 38–46; Chauncey, *Gay New York*, 10–11.

66. Merrick, interview by Judell.

67. Merrick, interview by Judell.

68. Clarice Billups to Samuel Merrick, 1 February 1944, private collection.

69. Gordon Merrick to Glenway Wescott, 31 January 1946, Glenway Wescott Papers, box 76, folder 1139.

70. Merrick, interview by Judell.

Chapter Four

The Spy

In February 1943, Gordon wrote his mother about his disappointment over being rejected by the American Field Service a second time: "I'm restless. I can't imagine how anybody could be anything else at times like these. And I'm curious. I crave some first-hand knowledge. . . . Almost everything we do is motivated more or less by restlessness and dissatisfaction. . . . And right becomes hopelessly involved in contingency."[1] Gordon's habit of framing personal problems in terms of larger philosophical issues would become a regular feature in his novels, but he was genuinely frustrated over his apparent uselessness in the war effort. Hunt Brown, his Princeton friend who had rowed with him on the crew team, was already flying a Hellcat fighter in the South Pacific (a few months later he would survive an aerial attack by Japanese forces), and many of his other Princeton classmates were also performing important military missions.[2]

The whirlwind romance with the Air Force pilot only exacerbated Gordon's sense of uselessness, and the memory of this feeling stayed with him for a very long time. In an early draft of *One for the Gods*, Gordon describes the experience of being stranded in New York while his lover is fighting overseas:

> It had been strange being so alone in the wartime city, an apparently sturdy specimen rejected by the Army because of   . When Peter was drafted just after Pearl Harbor, they had been living together for less than two years. . . . Supreme happiness and then total solitude. He had been so desperately alone when Peter was gone. Their commitment was too great; it enclosed him and cut him off from the world around him. He envied Peter the simplicity of his enforced military life, when he wasn't gnawed by worry about him.[3]

Gordon later deleted this passage from the manuscript, perhaps because he felt it was too autobiographical and inconsistent with the rest of the novel. The blank space in the passage indicates he had not figured out how to fictionalize the reason for his own military rejection. In actuality, Gordon's chronic health problems had disqualified him from military service—but Charlie Mills, his fictional avatar, was a paragon of health and fitness.

Gordon's disappointment over his American Field Service rejection also had to do with his literary aspirations. The AFS had a reputation for attracting writers who had stagnated in America and who wanted fresh inspiration. Arthur Howe, an AFS ambulance driver who would later become the organization's vice president, described the typical AFS volunteers as "people who have been unable to get in to other services because of minor physical defects and who are anxious to do something, people who have never been happy and here find an opportunity to try something new, and finally several who want to get material with which to write books, newspaper articles, plays, etc."[4] This description fit Gordon to a tee, and so it came as a heavy blow when even this opportunity fell through. As much as he appreciated his new job at the *New York Post*, he still held out hope of becoming a serious writer one day.

The solution to both dilemmas—his military uselessness and professional stagnation—came unexpectedly in the fall of 1943. In this case it was Gordon's Princeton connections, not his friends in the New York literary or theater worlds, that were instrumental. By chance Gordon learned from a family friend (and fellow Princeton alum) about a government agency that had recently been created to aid the American war effort.[5] This new agency was independent of both the armed services and FBI and was being run by William "Wild Bill" Donovan, a Republican, Columbia-educated lawyer who had once run an unsuccessful campaign for governor of New York. Donovan had been appointed by President Roosevelt as an unofficial envoy to Britain in the lead-up to America's entrance into the war, and by the end of 1941 Donovan had convinced Roosevelt of the need for a new intelligence service. This became the Office of Strategic Services (OSS), which would be later known as the precursor to the CIA. By 1943 the OSS was already running missions in the Pacific and Europe, with operations ranging from the dissemination of propaganda in Axis-controlled territories to true cloak-and-dagger espionage missions throughout Europe. Most important from Gordon's perspective, the people recruited by the agency were not subject to the rigorous physical requirements imposed on military soldiers and ambulance drivers.[6]

Under Donovan's leadership, the OSS had ruffled feathers in Washington with its unconventional tactics. J. Edgar Hoover, the director of the FBI, was especially hostile toward Donovan and constantly worked to undermine him. Yet it was precisely Donovan's maverick approach to warfare that Roosevelt liked, despite the fact that the two would have been political opponents in peacetime conditions. Roosevelt was dissatisfied with intelligence operations in the armed services and FBI, which he thought "primitive and parochial," and had even assembled his own private group of spies.[7] Donovan's unconventional methods included the type of people he brought to the OSS. Among his recruits were powerful businessmen and influential cultural figures, such as the Wall Street banker Junius Morgan (a Princeton alum who later donated a collection of early Virgil editions to the university) and the film director John Ford. Many OSS agents were smart, privileged men who had not found a place in the American military machine:

> Donovan's "league of gentlemen," as he liked to call them, also included a healthy share of social misfits, spoiled rich kids, and military castoffs ... many the Army had rejected as physically unfit. ... His headquarters soon earned the nickname "bad eyes brigade" because so many wore glasses. Society WASPs who were fit for combat but hoped to stay out of it also gravitated to Donovan. Reporters began to call the agency a "draft dodger haven." Generals called them the "East Coast faggots."

While the branding of OSS recruits as "East Coast faggots" was mostly meant as a general pejorative, it is likely that Donovan did knowingly recruit men who were known or suspected of being gay—and that he did not care as long as they were useful. He did knowingly hire "men with prison records who could be useful as burglars, and occasionally Mafia thugs for paramilitary operations." In addition to such "social misfits," Donovan also recruited "respectable" people who would have been relegated to menial positions in other military outfits—particularly women. Julia Child, the most famous female OSS agent, started out as a file clerk in Donovan's office before being sent to the agency's China headquarters in Chungking to carry out top-secret research. Over the course of its operations, the OSS enlisted nearly 4,500 agents, 900 of whom were assigned to missions overseas in Europe, North Africa, and Asia.[8]

It is unclear who brought Gordon to the attention of the OSS. Most likely he was recruited by Archibald MacLeish, the distinguished poet who was selected by Roosevelt as the ninth Librarian of Congress. Gordon had met MacLeish during his sophomore year at Princeton, at a Terrace Club forum that featured MacLeish, the French writer André Malraux, and the popular detective novelist Dashiell Hammett. MacLeish had dazzled the undergraduates by trouncing Hammett in a debate over the Spanish Civil War. He especially charmed Gordon, who sat next to him and made a point of speaking to him during the breaks. MacLeish was likewise impressed by Gordon and invited him to meet with him the following week.[9] Later, when America entered the war, Donovan called on MacLeish to help build the OSS's Research and Analysis Branch. MacLeish sent Donovan a number of researchers from the Library of Congress, and he scouted around for other linguistic specialists who could help the OSS. It is possible that MacLeish reached out to Maurice

Coindreau, Gordon's French professor at Princeton; Coindreau had organized the Terrace Club event, and so the two already knew each other. If so, then it is also possible that Coindreau mentioned Gordon's name. Coindreau had always had a high opinion of Gordon's abilities and had been an unofficial mentor to him at Princeton. If MacLeish and Coindreau were in fact involved with the OSS's interest in Gordon, it would explain the agency's speedy response. Soon after receiving Gordon's application in September, the OSS initiated a rigorous background investigation—a crucial part of the agency's recruitment process after its early days, when it had inadvertently allowed in a number of communist and Nazi sympathizers.[10] The resulting report was only three sentences long and unequivocal in its assessment of Gordon's suitability for the OSS: "Confidential informants recommend the Subject as to loyalty, ability and personal character."[11]

In his OSS application Gordon had emphasized his journalism work, which he thought would be of most interest to the agency.[12] This was a reasonable assumption, since the OSS had just formed a new branch, called Morale Operations, that ran propaganda operations in Europe as part of its psychological warfare program. The branch was comprised mostly of "decidedly unmilitary journalists and artists" whose activities included the creation of fake leaflets and letters intended to spread disinformation and conspiracy theories among German soldiers.[13] Gordon's newspaper training would have served him well in such a role, but the OSS realized that he had other desirable talents. He had an impressive command of French—largely thanks to Coindreau—and was an experienced actor. He was also adept at fitting into different groups and making people feel comfortable around him—so comfortable that they would start talking to him and reveal information about themselves. MacLeish had firsthand knowledge of this. He would have remembered the disarming Princeton undergraduate who had charmed him into a private meeting. In any case, the OSS ultimately decided that Gordon could be more useful than a mere producer of propaganda. They would make him a spy.

Given the extensive background investigations performed by the OSS on prospective agents, they also likely knew that Gordon was gay and had gay friends. In his application he mostly listed married couples as references—including his old Princeton friend Lem Ayers, who was now living with his wife in California—though he also listed the Broadway actor Clifton Webb, a lifelong "confirmed bachelor" who in theatrical circles was known to be gay.[14] In a series of interviews that he gave in the 1970s and '80s, Gordon claimed that he actually "came out" at a later stage of the OSS screening process. When an OSS psychiatrist asked him, "Have you had homosexual experiences?," Gordon decided to tell the truth:

I thought for a moment—what the hell!—then answered, "Yes!" He said, "Well, you mean when you were in school." "Yes . . . " and I was ready to go on, but he was so flabbergasted. Honest to God, he didn't know what was happening to him. Obviously no one had ever said yes. Fumbling with his papers and dropping his pen, he said, "Well that's fine."

Gordon assumed that it was his candor about his sexuality that reassured the OSS: "I guess they figured that if I was going to be that relaxed about it, then it couldn't be a very serious problem." He also claimed that the OSS then tried to use him to try to ferret out other gays: "Apparently on the basis of [my admission] I became an expert on getting the queers out. They kept coming to me: 'Do you think he's queer?'" In 1986 Gordon told an interviewer, Brandon Judell, that he did *not* out other gays when asked.[15] He often joked afterward that he was recruited *because* he was gay. In *An Idol for Others*, one of his characters quips that being gay is "excellent training for secret agents. You know, working up a cover and sticking to it so you're never caught being who you really are."[16]

In actuality an admission of homosexuality was not unusual in the military screening process. As the historian Allan Bérubé documented in his landmark study of gay soldiers in World War II, the army had actually developed a protocol for dealing with male recruits who declared themselves homosexual (the concern was that some men would falsely claim being gay in order to get out of military service).[17] Most likely the OSS simply did not care about Gordon being gay. They were more concerned with weeding out Nazi sympathizers and double agents. Donovan himself did not seem to have a problem with gay men at the OSS, even at high levels of administration. Donald Downes, an eccentric Yale-educated classics scholar who had worked as a spy for Britain's MI6, was recruited by Donovan to come up with new ideas for covert operations. Donovan knew that Downes, who had been identified by the FBI as a "sex-deviate," was gay.[18] If anything, Donovan might have appreciated the unique skills possessed by Downes and other gay men who had spent years learning how to "switch codes" in different social settings.

In spring 1944 Gordon traveled to Washington, DC, for training in the agency's "spy camp." Here he learned the OSS protocols for communications and operations, as well as skills needed by OSS agents—like parachuting, a common method for sneaking agents into occupied territories. From his room at the Hotel Statler, he wrote his mother telling her that he would be shipping off soon to Algiers or Naples, depending on where the OSS had decided to base its operations. He also told her not to expect to hear from him for at least a month, owing to the difficulty of sending letters from the European stations. Knowing how worried she must have been, Gordon reassured her with cheery words of optimism. "I'll be back before you know it," he promised.[19] On July

6, 1944, Gordon took a train from Washington to Lee Hall, Virginia, where he would then be put on a flight to Algiers.[20] On his way to Lee Hall he changed trains in Richmond, which must have brought back painful memories. The last time he had been in Richmond was less than a year earlier, when he had gone to identify the body of his fallen Air Force pilot.

Although Gordon fictionalized much of his OSS experience in *The Strumpet Wind*, his first novel, he never wrote directly about the specific details of his assignment. (As always he was extremely disciplined when it came to sensitive information.) Nonetheless much can be inferred from details he did provide in his writings and interviews, as well as by collating the information in his OSS file in the National Archives with other documented histories of the OSS operations in Europe. From this it is clear that Gordon was part of Operation Dragoon (previously known as Operation Anvil), the name given to the Allied campaign to liberate southern France from German forces and eventually merge with Operation Overlord, the campaign that had overseen the D-Day landings in Normandy. Although Dragoon had initially lagged behind Overlord because of supply problems and other logistical issues, in August and September 1944 it succeeded in securing a number of French Mediterranean ports. Chief among the Allied forces in Dragoon was the American Seventh Army, which was headed by General Alexander Patch. The army had been assisted by naval and French resistance forces, and it had been especially helped by the OSS, which for months had been busy setting up agent networks throughout southern France to collect information on German troop movements and fortifications. Over a period of five months these networks produced over eight thousand reports on the German operations in the region, a trove of information that proved pivotal for the Dragoon campaign. Colonel William Quinn, the head of intelligence for the Seventh Army, later credited the OSS's work for the success of the invasion, particularly the relatively small number of Allied casualties. "We knew everything about that [Mediterranean] beach and where every German was," he is reputed to have said, "and we clobbered them."[21]

Even with control of several southern cities, the movement northward for Dragoon was a treacherous affair. German forces remained scattered throughout the region, along with German intelligence (Abwehr) agents who still had the ability to transmit radio information about Allied movements to German control. Again, the OSS networks in France proved useful. Agents assigned to Allied regiments as detachments could connect with other spies in the area and retrieve intelligence about any German military activity in the vicinity. In addition, the OSS had managed to identify and locate many of the Abwehr agents still working in France. In some cases, this information was used to help the Allied forces arrest Abwehr agents and render them inactive. In other cases, however, the OSS used Abwehr agents as part of a deliberate counterintelligence scheme. They convinced (or compelled) them to switch sides and transmit false information, typically through radio communication channels, about Allied movements to the Germans.[22] Gordon would participate in all of these OSS activities once he got to France.

In July 1944, after a terrifying twelve-day boat trip, Gordon arrived in Naples, now the hub of OSS operations in Europe.[23] While waiting to be deployed to France, the OSS put him up in a luxurious seaside villa on the nearby island of Capri. It was common practice for Allied forces to commandeer private homes for officers and agents, and they did not aim for humble accommodations. Gordon's residence was the magnificent Il Fortino, the mansion villa owned by Countess Mona von Bismarck, the "queen of Capri" as she was dubbed by the local authorities. In a letter to his mother, Gordon described his splendid new digs:

> [The] villa [is] a breathtaking and luxurious pink confection set in riotous gardens and magical terraces hanging over the Mediterranean. It's been several days of complete bliss—swimming, lots of sun, unbelievable food and liquers served under a star-filled sky. Quite a war. All of Capri is a dream—so fantastically picturesque that you are torn between roaring with laughter and weeping with joy. All of Italy is crowded into it—fine tall cypresses against startlingly white houses with the sparkling blue Mediterranean serving as a backdrop. And creeping over everything brilliant vines and tropical flowering shrubs and trees. It's all untouched of course.[24]

Book reviewers would later criticize Gordon for similarly florid passages in his novels, but here he was simply trying to capture what he saw in front of him and the sensations they provoked. The villa came staffed with Italian servants who served extravagant meals with exquisite wines, all of which Gordon devoured. He may have been officially on a top-secret military mission, but he was more than happy to enjoy this Mediterranean holiday while it lasted.

The idyll soon came to an end. He was parachuted into southern France, where he joined one of the regiments in Patch's Seventh Army. In order to explain his presence, the OSS disguised him as an army officer. Gordon was forced to get rid of all his civilian clothes—most of which he sold at a profit—and don a regular military uniform, complete with boots, field jacket, and equipment pack. For Gordon, this was simply a costume change in another acting gig. He took to the role with gusto, quickly learning the soldier's routine: brushing his teeth in a tin helmet, sleeping on slats, and learning how to make a "very passable salute." As part of his "officer" duties, he was responsible for provisioning the soldiers in his unit with food, clothing, and other supplies, as well as performing other tasks to ensure that they could move at a moment's notice when necessary—all done under the threat of occasional shell fire and other hazards. Despite the challenges of the job, Gordon found to his surprise that he was rather good at it. It turned out there was not much difference between playing as an army officer and being one. At one point, the senior officers in the regiment (who knew that Gordon was really an OSS agent and not an actual officer) suggested making him a commissioned officer. Gordon considered the offer before turning it down, and he was thoroughly amused. "It's funny, isn't it," he joked with his mother, "that I should finally become a military man?"[25] The sensitive pretty boy who had been rejected by the army and the American Field Service because of a wonky mastoid was now in France leading a military unit through enemy-infested territories.

In a letter to his mother, Gordon explained that the army had offered to make him a real officer because of a "specialty in this service that is rather in demand and fairly interesting." He did not explain what this "specialty" was, though it may have been related to his skill with languages. In addition to the challenge of occupying French towns with few English speakers, the army itself was comprised of English, French, and Italian speakers. Gordon had come to Europe with excellent French, but being in southern France gave him the opportunity to learn colloquial, "fast slangy" and "often racy" French—"the sort of thing my classic education left out of account," he told his mother. His command of colloquial French increased dramatically, so much so that he sometimes found it difficult to switch back to English. Such fluency was indeed valuable in the army, but so was his evident ability to lift morale among his men. On one occasion he jokingly addressed his unit as The Lost Battalion. The soldiers liked the pithy epithet and started using it for themselves, in turn referring to Gordon as "Major Merrick."[26] He was eminently companionable, often drinking, singing, and playing cards with the soldiers. He also had a popular habit of making the troop movements seem like sightseeing tours, pointing out historical and architectural details whenever they passed by an interesting site. George Patton, the commander of the Seventh Army, had in fact complained about such cavalier behavior in the OSS agents embedded in his ranks, but in Gordon's case it gave the other soldiers a much-needed sense of normalcy.[27] One anecdote about Gordon that became popular in his unit was a story that, when he first parachuted into France, he landed wearing a white dinner jacket, black patent leather shoes, and a martini glass in his hand.[28] Of course this was impossible, but it shows the reputation Gordon had among his men as an unruffled, sanguine leader. The anecdote may also have been understood, at least by some soldiers, as a genial, winking acknowledgment of Gordon's sexuality.

The fictional anecdote about a dandyish Gordon raises the question of how many people among his military and OSS groups knew he was gay. That *some* people knew is beyond question. Besides the nameless OSS psychiatrist who had been supposedly shocked by Gordon's openness about his sexuality, other people involved in the French campaign clearly knew that Gordon was gay—including some who were gay themselves. In his interview with Judell, Gordon admitted that there were a few sexual diversions during his OSS assignment—"a couple of nice commissions," as he put it. He didn't specify the circumstances of these short affairs, other than to mention they were with "very nice French officers and so forth."[29] Thaddeus Holt, whose book *The Deceivers* is one of the most comprehensive, well-researched accounts of the OSS missions, indicates that Gordon's sexuality was known by his commanding officer, Arne Ekstrom, a married, Swedish-born American who enjoyed reading Proust in the original French and who had quickly moved up the ranks in the OSS. After the war ended, Ekstrom spent a few days celebrating with Gordon and another OSS agent, Humphrey Hare, who was also gay: "Ekstrom did not share their interests [i.e., he was not gay] but it was a luxurious way to end the war." Hare, a Welshman and an aspiring poet, would go on to have a prolific career as a translator of French biographies and romances. Ekstrom clearly knew that both men were gay, but he did not see this as an impediment to working with them or socializing with them. His working relationship with Gordon had in fact gotten off to a rocky start, though not because Gordon was gay. As Holt (who had interviewed Ekstrom) describes the situation, Gordon "at first resisted taking direction from Ekstrom; but Ekstrom laid down the law and Merrick became his faithful follower."[30] Gordon, the well-bred product of all-male schools, responded well to masculine discipline, and he quickly became one of Ekstrom's most loyal friends.

Gordon had not been sent to France to make friends, however. His mission was to turn double agents, and so he focused most of his attention on the Abwehr operatives that the OSS had assigned to him. He managed this job by splitting his location—and identity—on a daily basis. He was set up by the army in a magnificent villa in Cannes, which came equipped with a maid, a cook, and a fully stocked wine cellar (as usual the army found the best residences for commandeering). From the villa he maintained contact with the nearest OSS field office and kept tabs on the various agents he was monitoring. When he needed to visit an agent in person, he would put on civilian clothes and drive to the agent's house in his personal appointed car. Each afternoon he would change to his military uniform and rejoin his unit, where he would carry out his officer duties and spend time "drinking cocktails at the Carlton."[31] This was exhausting work, both physically and mentally. It kept him occupied all day long and required him to shift constantly between roles. This was a high-stakes acting gig, though with none of the monotony of Broadway.

The double agent work itself was grueling, since it demanded extreme alertness and attention to detail. Whenever the OSS identified an Abwehr agent they thought could be turned, it became the case officer's job to manage agent and get them to transmit counterintelligence to the Germans without arousing suspicion. This was incredibly tricky. In addition to convincing the agent that cooperation was in their best interest, the case officer had to ensure that the agent did not make the slightest deviation from protocol when making transmissions. Holt gives a rich account of the daunting responsibilities of a case officer:

> The case officer for a double agent is his hand-holder, guru, rabbi, therapist, shoulder to cry on, taskmaster, Dutch uncle, guard, and parole officer, in a foreign country and a strange world. . . . He has to know details of his agent's background and personal history, has to understand his psychology, has to sorrow with him in his failures and rejoice with him in his successes, watch him for any sign of treachery or instability, and keep him worried, if necessary, about what will happen if he does not deliver. He keeps meticulous records of everything his man does, cross-indexed against what others have done; for any tiny inconsistency can raise a suspicion in the opposition's mind. And he must understand the psychology not only of his agent but of the officer in the opposing service who thinks he is the agent's control; must know what will appeal to him and what will not, how to arouse his sympathy when that is needed, what excuses for nonperformance he will accept.

Gordon included every one of these duties when he fictionalized his OSS work in *The Strumpet Wind*. He also based the novel's Abwehr agent on one of his actual agents, a forty-four-year-old Frenchman named Lucian Herviou whose OSS codename was Forest. Herviou lived on a farm in Draguignan, a small town in the Provence region of southeastern France. After agreeing to act as a double agent, Herviou's job was to respond to questions from the German intelligence office with information that was carefully tailored by Ekstrom, all while pretending to be hiding from the Allied forces.[32] Herviou was unquestionably Gordon's most important agent as a case officer, though he managed other agents as well—all of whom presented challenges of their own. On one occasion, Gordon arrived at the home of one of his Abwehr agents at the same time that the agent's German intermediary was in the house delivering a payment. Gordon quickly took out his gun, a Colt 45, arrested the intermediary and proceeded to take her in his car to the nearest OSS station. He was so nervous, however, that he failed to put the safety on before putting the gun back in his pocket. The gun went off, barely missing his body. "I nearly blew myself to smithereens," he later said.[33]

As demanding as the logistics of the job were, for Gordon the psychological stress was even greater. For one thing, he may have witnessed one of the

Abwehr agents being tortured during an OSS interrogation. He included such a scene in *The Strumpet Wind*, which many newspapers at the time interpreted as confirmation of their theories about American espionage tactics.[34] He certainly was aware that he was exploiting and lying to the agents, promising them leniency or immunity if they agreed to cooperate, even though he knew they would be imprisoned (or worse) once they had ceased to become useful. Such knowledge took a heavy toll. What bothered Gordon was not only the realities of the work, but the fact that he was *good* at it. He was able to play the "warm and loving" collaborator with his agents while remaining "totally detached" internally. For a man who had been known as effusive and sensitive for most of his life, this talent for emotional detachment was a side of himself he didn't know he had—and which stayed with him in one form or another. In a letter to his mother, he bemoaned the pressures of his job, without divulging any information about what he was doing: "Much of the work is intensely interesting . . . but much of it is extremely unpleasant and my spirit constantly revolts at the necessities I'm involved in. I get so soul-sick of it that I always feel that I've reached the limit, that I must get away from it all, but then I snatch at a little pleasantness and am able to plod on."[35]

Gordon's mother Mimi was one of the people who helped him "plod on." He wrote her several long letters from France, always being careful not to give specific information about what he was doing or where he was stationed. He tried to assuage her concerns over him by writing mostly about cheery mundane matters, like how well he was eating and how much he loved the French countryside. He also implored her to send him books and cigarettes. It was all but impossible to find the latest novels in southern France, and so he depended crucially on Mimi for literature to read. She gladly complied, sending him as many recent novels as she could find, including works by Robert Nathan, Lion Feuchtwanger, and Somerset Maugham. She also sent him contemporary war novels, perhaps thinking that Gordon would enjoy reading books by other people who were also experiencing the war firsthand. One novel, H. E. Bates' *Fair Stood the Wind for France*, about an English bomber pilot who gets stranded in German-occupied France, was likely a model for *The Strumpet Wind*. Another book, Ben Hecht's *Miracle in the Rain*, centers on a soldier who leaves his lover to fight in the war; although killed in battle, his spirit returns to his lover as a beatific vision in St. Patrick's Cathedral.[36] Mimi, a devout Catholic, enjoyed the novel's Catholic overtones and spirituality, but more importantly she relished the chance to discuss literature with Gordon as she had when he was in college. For Gordon, the letters and packages from Mimi, along with the letters from his brother Sam, were a dear reminder of his loving family back home.

Gordon found other things to cheer him while in France. He managed on occasion to have a semblance of a social life, mostly with people he met who knew his friends back home. Through these circles he met Maurice Chevalier, the French cabaret singer, who was performing in a casino in Cannes.[37] A former prisoner in World War I, Chevalier had been a target of both Allied and Nazi propaganda efforts, resulting in the widespread (and inaccurate) rumors that he had collaborated with the Germans and later been killed by French Resistance fighters.[38] Gordon also made another friend—a poodle who had been given to him as a puppy when he first got to Cannes. By the time the war ended and he was preparing to leave, the poodle had become a full-grown dog. Gordon often talked about losing all sense of time during his OSS assignment, and it was only this growing dog that reminded him of the passing of weeks and months. By the end of his assignment he had grown very attached to the dog—whom he affectionately called "his little Frenchman"—and swore that he would leave the dog behind in France "over my dead body."[39] Unfortunately, there is no evidence that Gordon's "little Frenchman" ever made it to America.

Gordon later claimed that, after the war, he didn't suffer from post-traumatic stress disorder—"sediment or residue," in his words—because he didn't repress his feelings of grief and guilt at the time.[40] Whether or not this is true, he did sometimes break down when the pressures of work and separation from family and friends became too much to bear. One of these times was on December 24, 1944. He was feeling especially lonely after getting a letter from his mother that day, and so he decided to attend a midnight mass in a local church. He had never been particularly religious (an issue that he and his mother had argued about when he was at Princeton), but this time he thought going to church might help his mood. To his surprise the experience was epiphanic:

> On Christmas Eve I went to Midnight Mass here in a fine vast old church. It was very moving—the first midnight mass that had been held since the war started, packed back to the great doors with people who wanted to laugh and cry at the same time. I quite shamelessly cried, tears streaming down my face, but nobody paid any attention.[41]

Mimi must have loved reading this, believing that God had somehow gotten through to her agnostic son—and in a French church, no less. For Gordon, the opportunity to show his emotions and vent his grief in the presence of others was cathartic. The experience of seeing other people—French, American, English, Italian—in a similar state reaffirmed his faith in humanity and reminded him of what was truly important to him.

A few months later, when the war in Europe officially ended on May 7, 1945, Gordon went up to Paris to participate in the Victory Day celebrations. Afterward he collapsed from exhaustion, partly from the two-day-long festivities but even more so from the yearlong ordeal he had just endured. A few weeks later he officially resigned from the OSS. Before he returned to America he spent a few weeks roaming all over France, taking in the sights in Paris, Marseille, Cannes, Nice, and elsewhere. As he traveled throughout the country, he was struck by the transformation he saw in the French people:

> The background against which I've been working is profoundly discouraging—a nation completely deranged, discouraged, hurt, disillusioned, wondering rather forlornly what happened to the spirit and the hope that animated them through the long years of war. Still mildly drunk on the trumped-up propaganda out of which resistance was born, the French are cross and bewildered to find that they don't really count in terms of the final peace settlements. They are beginning to hate now, the British, the Americans, even the Russians, and possibly on the basis of that hate some sort of nation will be recreated.[42]

Gordon was witnessing the ravaging effects of a brutal occupation and war, but he was also seeing the country through a different perspective. The man who would be going back to America in August was not the same man who had come to Europe more than a year earlier. His experience in the war had compelled him to discover strengths and abilities he didn't know he had. This new, emboldened self-awareness would partly explain why, when he returned home, he would lead his life more openly and fearlessly than he had before.

NOTES

1. Gordon Merrick to Mary Merrick, 11 February 1943, private collection.
2. Gordon Merrick to Mary Merrick, 9 October 1935, private collection; "Ann and Hunt Brown," obituary, *The Wilton Bulletin*, November 20, 2012, http://wiltonbulletin.com.
3. Gordon Merrick, draft of *One for the Gods*, 69, GMP, box 10, folder 1.
4. Arthur Howe Jr. to Margaret Mayo Burke, 21 January 1942, Arthur Howe Jr. Collection, 1914–2014, Archives of the American Field Service and AFS Intercultural Programs, http://archon.afs.org.
5. Gordon Merrick to Mary Merrick, 14 September 1943, private collection.
6. Douglas Waller, *Wild Bill Donovan: The Spymaster Who Created the OSS and Modern American Espionage* (New York: Free Press, 2011).
7. Waller, *Wild Bill Donovan*, 70.
8. Waller, *Wild Bill Donovan*, 93, 98, 79.
9. Gordon Merrick to Mary Merrick, 15 March 1937, private collection.
10. Waller, *Wild Bill Donovan*, 73, 94. In a similar fashion MacLeish had recruited Wilmarth Sheldon Lewis, a former Yale student who eventually became chief of the

OSS's Central Information Division. Robin W. Winks, *Cloak & Gown: Scholars in the Secret War 1939–1961*, 2nd ed. (New Haven: Yale University Press, 1987), 96.

11. Investigation Report for Gordon Merrick, Security Office, Office of Strategic Services, 24 November 1943, OSS file for Gordon Merrick, RG 226, Entry A1 224, OSS.

12. Gordon Merrick to Mary Merrick, 14 September 1943, private collection.

13. Waller, *Wild Bill Donovan*, 150.

14. Leonard Leff, "Becoming Clifton Webb: A Queer Star in Mid-Century Hollywood," *Cinema Journal* 47, no. 3 (2008): 3–28.

15. Keith Howes, "Once A Spy . . . ," *Gay News*, August 24, 1978; Brandon Judell, "Orgasm and Organdy: Gordon Merrick, the Champion of Gay Romance," *The Advocate*, October 14, 1986.

16. Gordon Merrick, *An Idol for Others* (New York: Avon Books, 1977), 319.

17. Allan Bérubé, *Coming Out Under Fire: The History of Gay Men and Women in World War Two* (New York: The Free Press, 1990), 20.

18. Waller, *Wild Bill Donovan*, 123–24.

19. Gordon Merrick to Mary Merrick, n.d., private collection.

20. Memorandum, Thomas Damberg to William Sherwood, 4 July 1944, OSS.

21. Waller, *Wild Bill Donovan*, 264–65.

22. Waller, *Wild Bill Donovan*, 270–71.

23. Gordon Merrick to Mary Merrick, 12 May 1945, private collection.

24. Gordon Merrick to Mary Merrick, 24 July 1944, private collection.

25. Gordon Merrick to Mary Merrick, 31 July 1944, 9 August 1944, 22 October 1944, private collection.

26. Gordon Merrick to Mary Merrick, 22 October 1944, 9 August 1944, 13 December 1944, private collection.

27. Waller, *Wild Bill Donovan*, 270.

28. Ricardo Hunter Garcia, "Gordon Merrick, Journalist, Actor and Popular Novelist, Dies at 71 in Sri Lanka," press release, 1988, Gordon Merrick student file.

29. Gordon Merrick, interview by Brandon Judell.

30. Thaddeus Holt, *The Deceivers: Allied Military Deception in the Second World War* (New York: Scribner, 2004), 663, 652.

31. Howes, "Once A Spy"; Gordon Merrick to Mary Merrick, 5 September 1944, private collection.

32. Holt, *The Deceivers*, 139, 651–52.

33. Howes, "Once A Spy."

34. See, for example, the connection made in the *Austin American-Statesman* between *The Strumpet Wind* and reports that Abwehr agents had been beaten by American soldiers during interrogations. Leonard Lyons, "Coalition of Liberals in Congress Forms," *Austin American-Statesman*, January 29, 1947.

35. Howes, "Once A Spy"; Gordon Merrick to Mary Merrick, 14 October 1944, private collection.

36. Gordon Merrick to Mary Merrick, 9 August 1944, 13 December 1944, 19 February 1945, private collection.

37. Gordon Merrick to Mary Merrick, 19 February 1945, private collection.

38. Alan Riding, *And the Show Went On: Cultural Life in Nazi-Occupied Paris* (New York: Vintage Books, 2010), 94–99.

39. Gordon Merrick to Mary Merrick, 13 July 1945, private collection.

40. Howes, "Once A Spy."

41. Gordon Merrick to Mary Merrick, 19 February 1945, private collection.

42. Gordon Merrick to Mary Merrick, 12 and 30 May 1945, 13 July 1945, private collection.

Chapter Five

The Postwar Novelist

On June 1, 1945, only a few weeks after the war ended, Gordon tendered his resignation from the Office of Strategic Services. The OSS had been more than satisfied with him—William Donovan himself wrote a letter to Gordon expressing his "appreciation and gratitude" for the work he had done as an intelligence agent in France—but Gordon had no interest in staying on at the agency.[1] He spent three months touring France and England before boarding the RMS Queen Elizabeth in Southampton for the five-day journey back to America.[2] On August 31 he arrived in New York, which he had not seen in over a year. He took a few days to see his family, including his effusive and relieved mother, and then went down to Washington for a final exit interview.[3] Now back in America with no job and no obligations, Gordon had to figure out what to do with his life. There was no question of a return to the theater, which he had quit for good. He still harbored dreams of being a writer, and his OSS work had given him a wealth of material to write about—but the confidential nature of this work meant that a straightforward journalistic treatment was not a possibility. So he decided that the only logical thing to do was to write a novel about it.

In 1945 "postwar" novels were enjoying a vogue in America. Gordon's friend Glenway Wescott had just published *Apartment in Athens*, a novel about a Greek family living under the German occupation, which had received critical acclaim and had become an instant bestseller.[4] Gordon teased Wescott that he had "become a Macy's-window author," a quip that betrayed his intense admiration of his older mentor.[5] He had little experience writing fiction or memoirs, but he had read voraciously over the last several years and had imbibed the literary style of Forster, Maugham, Wescott, Hecht, and other novelists. He excitedly wrote Wescott about his plans for the project, which he described as "a novel with an espionage background. But not a spy story. Not a spy story at all."[6]

His first step was to get away from his family's home in Villanova, where he was staying. Since moving to New York he had felt more claustrophobic in his family's suburban home, and the year in Europe had only shortened his tolerance for family drama and social obligations. He sensed that his novel would be a critique of American bourgeois society, and he needed physical distance from his childhood home—with its grand paintings of Merrick ancestors on the walls—to give his subject the analytical perspective it required. An opportunity arose when a friend of the family, Louise Munson, invited Gordon to stay at her home in Mexico City. Munson had made a name for herself as a decorator for wealthy families on the Philadelphia Main Line, which led to her being tapped for the celebrated renovation of the Pennsylvania governor's mansion. She had recently married James B. Windham while visiting Mexico, and the two settled in Windham's home in Mexico City. She was a flamboyant, unconventional figure who later divorced Windham and absconded to Capri, where she died in 1949 after a reported suicide attempt.[7] Gordon would fictionalize her in *The Vallency Tradition* as the character Flip Rawls, an American emigré in Mexico who ingrains herself in the local expatriate community and surrounds herself with attractive young men. Gordon accepted the offer of an extended visit, and he was soon on his way to Mexico to write his book.

Gordon was not in Mexico alone. Waiting for him when he arrived was Bob Richardson, the Air Force lieutenant whom Gordon had met two years earlier in Richmond, where he had gone to identify the body of his fallen Air Force pilot. After getting over the initial surprise at the fact that they had been seeing the same man, Gordon and Richardson realized that they were attracted to each other. They had kept in touch after Gordon had returned to New York from Richmond, and they continued to write letters to each other while Gordon was in France carrying out his OSS mission. Now that both of them were free of their wartime obligations and could go wherever they wanted, they decided to make a go of a real relationship. They would be together for the next ten years.

Robert Blaine Richardson was born on April 3, 1920, almost four years younger than Gordon. He was born in Topeka, Kansas, the son of Newton L. Richardson, a clerk for the Santa Fe Railroad company, and Mary Hilburger Richardson. At some point he moved with his mother and grandmother to Denver, Colorado, where he attended college while working as a clerk at a bus station. By the time he was twenty-one, he was in El Paso, Texas, working at Fort Bliss as a clerk for the Quartermaster Corps, the division that handles supplies and equipment for the army. His goal was to join the navy as an aviator, so in the mornings he took classes at the nearby College of Mines and Metallurgy (now the University of Texas at El Paso) to get the required credits for his naval application. On July 1, 1941, he registered for the draft at the courthouse in El Paso, and seven months later he was accepted by the local navy recruiter as an aviation cadet, pending his performance on an examination. He did well on the examination, and so in March 1942 he was ordered to report for aviator training at Hensley Field in Grand Prairie, Texas.[8] He was tall with a slim but sturdy frame, six-foot-one and 150 pounds. He had blond hair and blue eyes and strong, angular features that were accentuated by his close-cropped hair. His only other identifying feature was a round scar on the inside of his left elbow. Pictures of him taken during the time he lived with Gordon show a dashing, unquestionably handsome man. According to Gordon, Richardson had a wife and child when they had first met in Richmond, but so far no records confirming this have come to light.[9]

Once in Mexico, Gordon and Richardson did little to hide the fact that they were a couple. They were nearly inseparable whenever they went out in Mexico City or the other Latin American cities they visited, and they soon became the subject of local society pages. A Havana-based newspaper hailed the arrival of "Gordon Merrick and Bob Richardson, two nice looking youngsters . . . from the States." The article noted that the two had traveled to Cuba from Mexico, where they had been living. It also noted that Gordon had just finished a novel—then titled *Practice to Deceive*—which chronicled "*their* past vicissitudes and learnings" (my emphasis).[10] When it came time for Gordon to return to America, the two of them traveled together on the RMS *Duc D'Aumale*, which left from Havana and arrived in New Orleans (the childhood home of Gordon's mother) on April 15, 1946.[11]

At the same time that Gordon was building a relationship with Richardson, he was writing as he never had before. He wrote the entire novel in less than five months, much of it based directly on his OSS mission in France—the memory of it still very fresh in mind. Eventually titled *The Strumpet Wind*, the novel is set in the south of France in 1944 after the Allied invasion at Normandy. At this point, the Vichy government has been overthrown and American and Free French forces are operating heavily in southern France. Roger Chandler, an OSS intelligence officer stationed in Marseilles, is part of a division trying to root out French agents who had worked for the Vichy and are possibly still cooperating with the Germans. The opening description of Chandler paints a portrait of an ideal American intelligence officer:

> Chandler had fallen into the work naturally because he spoke perfect French and pretty good Italian and German. His mother's family had been French, and he had gone to school for several years as a child in Chambery and Grenoble, and until just before the war had regularly spent his summers in the south of France and Italy. His father was a successful stock broker in New York and a member of a substantial New York family—not spectacular like the Vanderbilts or the Astors, but old and firmly rooted in New York social life. Young Chandler had been given a sensible education—Kent School in Connecticut after the brief period in France, and afterwards, Yale.[12]

Gordon modeled Chandler on himself with some modifications, like exchanging Philadelphia for New York and Princeton for Yale. He also made Chandler more masculine and athletic—a stereotypical image of American heroism—even though he kept the fact of his chronic back problems.

In the novel Chandler is assigned to Jean Louis Mercanton, a Frenchman who had earlier been recruited as a spy by the Vichy government. After the Allied invasion, Mercanton continued to send radio messages to the Germans before being caught by American intelligence officers. He is interrogated and tortured by the Americans, who ultimately enlist him in a counterespionage mission against the Germans. Under Chandler's supervision, Mercanton sends the Germans fake intelligence prepared by the Americans. The mission requires Chandler to live with Mercanton and his family in their rustic home in the Provençal countryside. As time passes, he becomes friends with Mercanton's family, and he comes to see Mercanton not as a cold-hearted Nazi supporter but as a decent man whose misguided patriotic duty put him on the wrong side of the war. As Chandler's sympathy for Mercanton grows so does his personal dilemma, since he knows that Mercanton will be executed by the Americans when the mission is over.

Chandler's conflicted feelings about his mission lead him to reflect on the complexities of war. He had joined the OSS as an idealist with a clear sense of right and wrong, but his realization of the Mercantons' basic humanity—and his witnessing of the brutality of American forces—persuades him that America's participation in the war is less principled than he had earlier believed. This view is articulated by the novel's narrator, an unnamed Frenchman who encounters Chandler at several moments in the novel and who lectures him on the messy politics of war:

> But when we say that we're fighting to destroy oppression, we're telling ourselves lies. And by lying to ourselves, we falsify everything we do. If we admitted that we're fighting to save our own skins, it'd be better. Hitler didn't happen in 1939. He was around a long time, and we looked the other way as long as it was convenient. As far as that goes, there's plenty of oppression being practiced right now by us and our allies, both at home and abroad. And we don't choose to do anything about it.[13]

Chandler's sense of the self-serving nature of the American government only intensifies as he develops a friendship with the Mercantons and learns more about the moral compromises made by his own commanders. Chandler devises a plan to save Mercanton from execution and expose other German agents in the region. His plan fails, however, and in a climactic scene Mercanton is shot in the back by Chandler as a kind of mercy killing. The novel ends with Chandler meandering around France, a broken and dejected man.

The novel was unquestionably a thinly fictionalized version of Gordon's OSS experience. Thaddeus Holt, arguably the best chronicler of the OSS missions, confirmed that the novel's account was a fairly close representation of the actual mission and that the character of Mercanton "was unmistakably FOREST [Lucian Herviou, Gordon's principal agent] for those in the know."[14] Gordon appended an Author's Note claiming that the events and characters in the novel were entirely fictional, but years later, after the need for secrecy had passed, he admitted the autobiographical nature of the novel: "The 'Author's Note' is utter nonsense. Of course I knew the people involved, lived with them, loved and hated them. I had barely extricated myself from the situation before I started writing it down. Only the ending is an invention. The real ending was much worse, and still haunts me."[15] He did not specify how Herviou's actual fate was "much worse" than Mercanton's, and Holt likewise does not reveal any details about the end of the mission. Given that Mercanton is killed while his family is spared, Gordon may have been implying that the real-life Herviou was not so lucky.

For a first novel, *The Strumpet Wind* is an impressive achievement. The writing is extremely polished and controlled, and Gordon's prose style has a concise elegance that shows him an admirer of Hemingway and Fitzgerald. The plot is tight and unified, with the exception of a romantic subplot that Gordon probably felt he was obligated to include. For a novel written in 1946, only months after the war had officially ended, the work is bold in its refusal to rehash the patriotic jingoism that had normally been used to frame America's role in the war. Instead, it shows that soldiers and agents experiencing the reality of the war learned a very different lesson—in Gordon's words, "that it wasn't all quite as simple as it seemed, that under certain circumstances values shifted and merged, clouding distinctions between right and wrong, that the conqueror wasn't any better off than the conquered."[16]

The novel was also bold in another way. Gordon created a gay character, George Meddling, Chandler's commanding officer in the OSS. Meddling oversees the military processes that lead to Mercanton's execution, and he derives a sadistic pleasure from torturing enemy prisoners during interrogation. (His "specialty" is whipping his subjects with a wet towel, a method that inflicts much pain but leaves few visible marks.) When Meddling first appears, he is every bit the image of American power and authority:

> a tall man with a superb physique and rather obvious good looks. He had a quality that was heavily male, overripe, decadent—a stifling quality compounded of the well-balanced characterless features, the full cruel mouth, the meticulous grooming of his whole body, the exquisitely tailored uniforms nicely calculated to reveal the broad shoulders, the full chest, the tapered symmetry of his waist and flanks.[17]

However, Meddling's meticulously groomed body and clothes are almost *too* perfect. The narrator makes a point of the fact that Meddling is attractive to *both* men and women—and that he had risen up the ranks by cultivating his attractiveness to men in particular: "His civilian career had been shaped by his willingness to use his body to attain his ambitions." These hints of Meddling's sexuality (and of the prevalence of gay men in the military) are confirmed later in the novel when Chandler accidentally runs into him in a gay bar in Nice. Chandler has come to the bar as part of an undercover mission to infiltrate the German underground, and he is caught off guard when Meddling shows up with a group of young gay soldiers. Meddling assumes that Chandler is gay and hits on him, though Chandler quickly rebuffs him. Later, when the two argue over the handling of the Mercanton case, Chandler threatens to "out" him to his superiors and get him discharged from the OSS. "I don't like to work with fairies," Chandler warns him. "A lot of people feel the same way."[18]

Gordon later said he regretted making the novel's gay character a villain, claiming he didn't think the novel would have been published otherwise. He may have been right, but in either case he managed to include a few tantalizing glimpses of gay life for the reader who was willing to look for them. His portrait of Meddling showed that, despite the official proscriptions against homosexual soldiers, there were gay men serving actively in the military—and not only in the lower ranks but in high-ranking leadership positions. Like Meddling, these gay soldiers were not the weak, effeminate stereotypical versions of gay men that appeared in newspaper cartoons or other mainstream venues. They were masculine, strong, and threatening to America's enemies. Moreover, Gordon's novel showed that these gay soldiers *knew about each other*. They socialized, went out together, got drunk together, and on occasion went to bed together. In the chapter where Meddling's sexuality is revealed, Gordon created one of the earliest representations of a gay bar to appear in a mainstream novel:

> [Chandler] found himself in a big, bare, brightly lighted room, with a bar at one end and tables placed along the walls. It took him an instant to realize that there were no women in the place, and that everybody at the bar had turned to look at him as he stood hesitating at the door. Music was coming from the next room and, looking in that direction, he saw several men dancing together. He turned back to the bar and found the row of eyes still on him—the eyes of boys with prettily waving hair and finely arched eyebrows.[19]

While Chandler is disquieted by the bar, he is not surprised by it. His contact explains to him that he chose a gay bar for their meeting since they would less likely be noticed by other agents, implying that there are a number of gay bars dotted throughout the south of France. In this case Gordon was likely writing from experience. As an OSS agent he had traveled throughout the region setting up meetings with double agents, and his ability to get information from French locals would have made possible his knowledge of gay meeting places.

With the manuscript for his first novel completed, Gordon now had to find a publisher. He asked Wescott for advice, wondering whether he should hire an agent or simply send the manuscript directly to publishers.[20] Some way or another, the manuscript—now bearing the title *The Web We Weave*—made it to the desk of an acquisitions editor at William Morrow, one of New York's top tier publishers. The editor was ecstatic. He knew there was a healthy market for a well-written war novel with a clear angle, and he believed he had found one. In his letter to Gordon, he made no effort to hide his enthusiasm:

> You are a born story-teller, and your narrative skill fills our heart with joy. In fact, you've told your story so well, that the reader doesn't come to until the last page is turned, and it is the next day that certain questions raise their deceptive heads. One more thing before passing on to them: this is not only a first-rate story well told, it is provocative. It is going to give some of your readers something to think about for a long time.[21]

The editor made a number of suggestions for fixing minor inconsistencies and ambiguities in the narrative, but his only significant criticism was about the novel's ending. In the original version, Chandler returns home to New York where he is consoled by his erstwhile fiancée. The editor thought this too uplifting, and he urged Gordon to give Chandler a more tragic ending. Gordon followed this advice without complaint. In the new ending, instead of returning to New York, Chandler finds himself huddled in a bar in Cannes, drinking himself numb and hearing a Charles Trenet song, *Vous Oubliez Votre Cheval* ("You're Forgetting Your Horse"), on the radio. It becomes a scene that Chandler replays over and over, wandering around Europe a broken man. This ending was a masterstroke that exemplified what would become one of Gordon's traits as a novelist: he could take an editor's criticism and, without sacrificing his vision, use it to improve his writing.

Another trait would be his struggle with titles. Nearly every title he initially proposed for a novel was rejected by his publisher, and his first novel was no exception. After some thought (and perhaps some review of his college reading list) he renamed *The Web We Weave* as *The Strumpet Wind*, taken from a line in Shakespeare's *The Merchant of Venice* in which Graziano mulls the idea that unsatisfied desires are more invigorating than satisfied ones: "How like a younker or a prodigal / The scarféd bark puts from her native bay, / Hugged and embraced by the strumpet wind!" (2.6.14–16). William Morrow loved the new title and splashed it in big, rough-hewn letters on the book's dust jacket. On the back was a photo of a Gordon, looking remarkably thin and casually brandishing a cigarette. Next to the photo was a short biography that detailed Gordon's professional background and explained his reason for writing the book in Mexico: "Back home in 1945, he had the choice of finding a job and getting married, or using his wartime savings to support himself while writing a book. Apparently the girl involved had some say in the matter, for he soon found himself on the way to Mexico to begin this book." It's unclear why the publisher felt the need to invent a "girl" for Gordon—perhaps to ward off any speculation that the novel was by a gay man. In any case, Gordon did not keep up this pretense on the dedication page, which he addressed solely to Richardson, "who contributed much more to this book than the author would like to admit."[22]

By any measure, *The Strumpet Wind* was a critical success. The novel was reviewed widely in newspapers and magazines across the country (and in several papers in England), of which most praised its careful delineation of the conflict between individual morality and civic duty. The *Hartford Courant* lauded Gordon's ability to be "sensitively aware of one of the great problems confronting many veterans . . . [he] has the courage to be articulate in dealing with the most delicately palpitating phases of real life." The *San Francisco Chronicle* was impressed with Gordon's craftmanship, proclaiming that "Mr. Merrick, who knows exactly what he is doing at every moment, conducts his story expertly, balancing suspense and physical action shrewdly against his development of character and situation." The *Philadelphia Inquirer* took great pride in its hometown boy, giving the novel a headline review and printing a large, handsome photo of Gordon. Ray Wilbur, the *Inquirer*'s book reviewer, called it "more than merely another story with a war-time setting . . . a novel you will not want to put down until you have finished the last page." Some reviews compared Gordon's prose style to Hemingway's, including one that complained that the novel's sex scenes were *too* like Hemingway's (i.e., too explicit). In general readers were less impressed with the romantic subplot, which seemed extraneous and unconvincing. Several critics admiringly pointed out that this was a *first* novel and raised high hopes for what might follow. The most in-depth, insightful review came from H. R. Pinckard, the editor of the *West Virginia Advertiser*. At the end of his essay-length analysis, he concluded that *The Strumpet Wind* is "a sound novel, though a disquieting one. It is not pleasant to consider the undeniable fact that we have killed a lot of people for doing almost precisely the same things that—at a slightly different level—we are doing ourselves."[23]

Not everyone wanted to be disquieted, however. One of the few negative reviews came from the venerable *New York Times*, which was offended by the novel's sympathetic treatment of Mercanton. The reviewer, C. V. Terry, accused Merrick of relying on the cliché of the noble underdog, claiming that it was "surprising to find a former OSS officer, now turned novelist, falling so promptly into the familiar groove." He went so far as to cite details about Gordon's own life as a snide explanation for this "unconvincing" portrayal of the war: "Mr. Merrick (who was a Princeton man before he became an actor, and a reporter before he turned to the cloak-and-dagger corps) is a scrupulous moralist who tries hard to see both sides." Calling Gordon a "scrupulous moralist" was not a compliment. By treating Mercanton's situation as a complex philosophical problem, Terry insinuated, Gordon had ignored the one salient fact: that Mercanton was a Vichy collaborator, and thus a Fascist, and thus not deserving of any pity. While he conceded Gordon's ability to create "pleasant word-painting" and "honest" pathos at times, he judged such sentimentality in this case to be profoundly naïve: "Roger's new world must still be free of such passive Fascists as the Mercantons if it is to endure." He emphasized this point in the title of his review, "The Passive Fascist." The *New York Post* made essentially the same criticism of the novel, though with more glibness: "The various degrees of treachery are a neat subject for psychological investigation—unless you happen to think that a traitor is a traitor and a bullet should always punctuate his career."[24]

When Gordon read the *New York Times* review a few months later, he quickly wrote an angry rebuttal. He accused Terry of "misrepresenting" his novel and of being too stupid to grasp its main message. In the letter Gordon argued that he had no real sympathy with Mercanton (or any "Vichyite" for that matter), but that he had intended the novel as a critique of a "basic contradiction" in American values: "We talk of human rights and yet we tolerate religious and racial prejudice of almost medieval fury. We talk of the dignity of the individual and yet our standards are almost entirely material."[25] This is a powerful argument, one that is still pertinent today. At the same time, in addition to mischaracterizing his own novel—no one who reads it can deny that it encourages the reader to sympathize with Mercanton—Gordon was missing the bigger picture. A review like Terry's would have bolstered his reputation in the long run. Gordon had not fully realized that even a negative review in the *New York Times* meant that he was being taken seriously as a novelist—something that would not always happen in the future.

In fact, *The Strumpet Wind* was soon overshadowed by two other "controversial" novels, both of which were published within months of *Strumpet* and both of which also featured groundbreaking representations of gay men. The first of these was *The City and the Pillar*, Gore Vidal's astonishing novel about a handsome gay man who falls in love with his best friend in high school. In his colorful biography of Vidal, Tim Teeman captures what was uniquely bold about *City* when it appeared in January 1948:

> *The City and the Pillar*, Vidal's third book and the first postwar American novel to feature explicit gay sex and gay characters . . . stands out as a coming out story—the protagonist Jim contemplates if he is gay and meets many different kinds of gay men—but also as an evocative portrayal of a number of gay worlds, from glossy Hollywood homes to dive-y hustler bars. It is also an intense love story.

In Vidal's first version of the novel, this love story ends with Jim murdering his high school love, thus reinforcing the idea that an explicitly gay novel necessarily had to end in tragedy. At the same time, Jim is not a pathological or sadistic character like Meddling in *The Strumpet Wind*. He is a strong, masculine "normal" man whose unhappiness is the result of a homophobic society rather than any inherent deformity. For this reason the novel was, as Teeman puts it, "a singularly radical act," and was perceived by many readers as such.[26]

The second novel that took the limelight was John Horne Burns' *The Gallery*, a 1947 chiaroscurist novel that takes as its setting the Galleria Umberto Primo, the famous indoor arcade in Naples where Italian people and Allied soldiers had come together in various (and often sordid) ways during the last years of the war. The novel is organized as a series of vignettes, the centerpiece of which is the chapter "Momma." "Momma" is the owner of the lone gay bar in the Galleria, and every night she plays host and witness to the sundry gay men who flock to her establishment:

> Her dreams were always the same, of the boys who came to her bar. There was a heterogeneous quality about them. They had an air of being tremendously wise, older than the human race. They understood one another, as though from France and New Zealand and America they all had membership cards in some occult freemasonry. And they had a refinement of manner, an intuitive appreciation of her as a woman. Their conversation was flashing, bitter, and lucid. More than other men they laughed much together, laughing at life itself perhaps. Momma'd never seen anything like her boys. Some were extraordinarily handsome, but not as other men were handsome. They had an acuteness in their eyes and a predatory richness of the mouth as though they'd bitten into a pomegranate. Momma dreamed that she was queen of some gay exclusive club.[27]

Although Gordon had been to gay bars in America and Europe, he could never have written something like this. In part this was because he never got over his instinctive aversion to gay bars, which he always saw as predatory spaces that reduced gay men to simple sexual drives. Burns, by contrast, was able to see the gay bar as a singular place where gay men could express their infinitely varied desires and histories. It was this insight that led the gay literary critic Roger Austen to call the "Momma" chapter in *The Gallery* "one of the most brilliant pieces of gay writing in English of [the twentieth] century," and contemporary critics likewise generally preferred Burns' depiction of the war in Europe to Gordon's.[28] *The Saturday Review of Literature* commended *The Strumpet Wind* as a "competent novel" but judged it too "sterile" and neatly packaged compared to Burns' gritty book—which was named by the *Review* as the "Best 1947 War Novel."[29]

In many ways *The Strumpet Wind* is closer to *The Gallery* than to *The City and the Pillar*. Both *Strumpet* and *Gallery* were based on firsthand experiences of the war in Europe, and both were written by Ivy-educated gay men who ended up as expatriates in Europe (Burns, who was only two months younger than Gordon, attended Harvard). At the same time, the similarities between Gordon and Burns also highlight their differences. Whereas Gordon's novel has a tightly controlled plot and theme, Burns' book is far more kaleidoscopic and shifting, and as a result its characters are more interesting and authentic. *The Strumpet Wind* likewise preserves its moral center in the character of Chandler, while *The Gallery* makes no such pretense. This contrast reflects a fundamental difference in the two men themselves. For all of his criticism of American bourgeois society, Gordon was still grounded in the refined, cosmopolitan circles that he had always known—he and Bob were appearing in society pages at the same time that *The Strumpet Wind* was being praised for its incisive depiction of Western values. Burns on the other hand followed up *The Gallery* with a putatively "libelous and obscene" novel that relentlessly satirized the preparatory school where he had taught for several years, doing very little to mask the identities of the people he was skewering. Later, while Gordon was building a following among the French literati, Burns was gradually deteriorating in a bar in Florence.[30]

There is no evidence that Gordon ever met Burns, though they were briefly in the same city a few times during their lives. There is the remote possibility that they traveled together in July 1944, when the Allied forces moved their headquarters from Algiers to Naples. If, after getting to Naples, Gordon had explored the city instead of retreating to his luxurious villa in Capri, he may very well have met Burns in one of the bars or opera houses that the restless soldier liked to frequent.[31] But, even if he had, it's not clear that these two future postwar novelists would have had much to talk about.

NOTES

1. William J. Donovan to Gordon Merrick, 26 September 1945, OSS.
2. List of United States Citizens, *RMS Queen Elizabeth*, departing Southampton on August 26, 1945.

3. Memorandum by F. M. Bishop to Special Funds Division, Finance Branch, Office of Strategic Services, 4 September 1945, OSS file for Gordon Merrick, RG 226, Entry A1 224, OSS.
4. Glenway Wescott, *Apartment in Athens*, introduction by David Leavitt (New York: New York Review of Books, 2004), vii.
5. Gordon Merrick to Glenway Wescott, 31 January 1946, Glenway Wescott Papers, box 76, folder 1139.
6. Ibid.
7. "Sally Harris' Letter," *Harrisburg Telegraph*, June 9, 1944; "Mansion Redecorator Dies on Isle of Capri," *Harrisburg Evening News*, January 27, 1949; "Louise Franchot Munson," Lycoming County Women's History Project, http://www.lycoming.edu/lcwhp/munson.html.
8. 1940 United States Federal Census, Denver, Colorado; 1950 United States Federal Census, Topeka, Kansas; Robert Richardson, U.S. World War II Draft Card, July 1, 1941; "E. P. Youth Works Hard, Gets in Navy," *El Paso Times*, February 4, 1942; "E. P. Youth Is Accepted as Air Cadet," *El Paso Times*, February 8, 1942; "Ordered to Training," *El Paso Herald Post*, March 2, 1942.
9. Gordon Merrick, interview by Brandon Judell.
10. Unidentified newspaper clipping, GMP, box 21.
11. Passenger list, *S. S. Duc D'Aumale*, Havana to New Orleans, April 12, 1946.
12. Gordon Merrick, *The Strumpet Wind* (New York: William Morrow, 1947), 7.
13. Merrick, *The Strumpet Wind*, 129–30.
14. Thaddeus Holt, *The Deceivers: Allied Military Deception in the Second World War* (New York: Scribner, 2004), 785–86.
15. Gordon Merrick, television adaptation of *The Strumpet Wind*, GMP, box 15, folder 13.
16. Ibid.
17. Merrick, *The Strumpet Wind*, 39.
18. Merrick, *The Strumpet Wind*, 39, 188–89.
19. Merrick, *The Strumpet Wind*, 180.
20. Merrick to Wescott.
21. William Morrow & Company to Gordon Merrick, 27 August 1946, GMP, box 21.
22. Gordon also incorporated a number of subtle details in the novel that indirectly point to Richardson. For example, he gives a minor character the name Hilburger, the maiden name of Richardson's mother.
23. Henrietta Hardman, "By Men, for Men, about Men," *Hartford Courant*, March 2, 1947; Joseph Henry Jackson, "A Bookman's Notebook," *San Francisco Chronicle*, January 30, 1947; Ray Wilbur, "Clash of Duty and Principle," *Philadelphia Inquirer*, February 23, 1947; Mary McGrory, "Tragic Wartime Dilemma Is Theme of Fine First Novel," *Boston Traveler*, February 26, 1947; H. R. Pinckard, "Lean, Rent and Beggar'd by *The Strumpet Wind* of Fate," *West Virginia Advertiser*, February 22, 1947.
24. C. V. Terry, "The Passive Fascist," *New York Times*, March 2, 1947; Clip Boutell, "Soup de Gaulle or Vichyssoise," *New York Post*, February 10, 1947.
25. Gordon Merrick to the *New York Times*, draft, GMP, box 21.

26. Tim Teeman, *In Bed with Gore Vidal: Hustlers, Hollywood, and the Private World of an American Master* (Bronx: Magnus Books, 2013), 152–53.
27. John Horne Burns, *The Gallery* (1947; New York: New York Review of Books, 2004), 130.
28. Roger Austen, *Playing the Game: The Homosexual Novel in America* (Indianapolis: Bobbs-Merrill, 1977), 107.
29. Arthur C. Fields, "The War, Bandaged and Sterile," *Saturday Review of Literature*, April 5, 1947.
30. David Margolick, *Dreadful: The Short Life and Gay Times of John Horne Burns* (New York: Other Press, 2013), 272.
31. Margolick, *Dreadful*, 113–15.

Chapter Six

Connecting with Forster

Gordon did not stay in America long enough to see the reviews of *The Strumpet Wind*. In fact he didn't even stay to see his novel on the bookstore shelves. By November 1946 he and Richardson were on a ship headed for Europe, stopping in Casablanca and Genoa before finally arriving in Marseille.[1] Since leaving France at the end of the war, Gordon had been eager to return—and he was weary of America, which had become too provincial and closed-minded for him, especially now that he was living openly with Richardson. He convinced Richardson that France would be an ideal place for the two of them, and so they agreed to make it their home for the foreseeable future.

The France that Gordon returned to was a different place than the one he had left. There were no more German military forces creeping through the country nor OSS offices running covert operations. Gordon had changed as well. He was no longer an OSS agent, an instrument of the vast American war machine. He was officially now an American novelist, and he began to act like one. Having a literary reputation, even a modest one, had both professional and social benefits in France, which was still a popular destination for American and European expatriates. Gordon used his charm and newly acquired credentials to establish himself in the local cultural and social circles—and he always included Richardson with him. In Cannes their arrival was heralded in the local society papers, which implied (without explicitly revealing) their status as a couple:

> Gordon Merrick, an American novelist of the rising school, has arrived in Cannes with his friend Bob Richardson, a famous chicken expert. They are living at Draguignan where Merrick, who was last year here with the American army, hopes to write his next novel, while Richardson tries to improve the daily egg out-put of Riviera hens.[2]

As with the Havana newspapers, the French papers did not try to hide Gordon's relationship with Richardson. There was clearly a big difference between Gordon's American publisher, who had felt the need to invent a "girl" for him, and the French journalists who used him to paint an idyllic picture of gay domestic life. For their part, Gordon and Richardson relished the attention—the idea of Richardson as a "famous chicken expert" soon became a running joke between the two of them.

Gordon's happiness about being back in France made it easier for him to cope with the challenges of life in Provence, which was still recovering from the devastating effects of the war. In his letters to his mother, he managed to make life in postwar France sound rustic and decadent at the same time:

> I'm leading an exemplary life. I've cut my cigarettes to ten a day in order to stay more or less within the ration and may, in time eliminate them entirely. I drink only wine, because that's all there is to be had, and only one bottle a day. The food is, of course, wonderful and I'm stuffing myself.[3]

He may have joked about the difficulty of finding cigarettes, but such scarcities were real and widespread. Rations were in effect throughout the country, which meant that many staples (such as sugar, soap, and gasoline) were very expensive and hard to find. In his grumpier letters, Gordon complained more earnestly about the region's food shortages and "primitive" hospitals. (His chronic back pain needed periodic attention, and Richardson had needed a foot operation after getting to France.) Ever the doting mother, Mimi responded by sending care packages stocked with food, including Gordon's favorite kind of jam—which in one instance arrived in France as a pile of broken glassware and fruit. "In the future, you'd best get tins," Gordon gently told his mother. The exorbitant French duty on cigarettes even made Gordon briefly consider quitting smoking—but only briefly. Instead he asked his mother Mimi whether she might "tuck a package or two" of cigarettes in her next care package.

More than jam or cigarettes, Gordon cherished the books that Mimi sent him from America. She had sent him books during his OSS period, and now, again, he depended on her to get his hands on contemporary books. He was thrilled one day when a package from Mimi arrived with a Gertrude Stein book—most likely *The Autobiography of Alice B. Toklas*, the notoriously popular novel that quickly cemented Stein's reputation as a leading American writer when it was published in 1933. Gordon had many reasons to take an interest in Stein, who had died only a few months before he returned to France. Like Gordon, Stein had lived in France during World War II, though her status as a Jew in a Nazi-occupied country had made her situation very different from Gordon's. Whereas Gordon had been in France as part of a mission to ferret out Vichy collaborators, Stein had earlier cooperated with the Vichy government, possibly as a way of inoculating herself from persecution. Gordon would not have known this, but if he had seen the October 1944 *Life* magazine article on the "liberation" of Stein, he would have picked up (as other discerning readers did) on the fact that Stein was living in a longtime relationship with Toklas, a "marriage" that is also suggested in the *Autobiography*.[4] Despite its overwhelming homoerotic content—Stein gives all of the signs of her romantic relationship with Toklas without naming it—the novel was an instant bestseller that reached a large, middle-class audience.[5] It was a model that Gordon would remember and imitate in many of his future novels.

In spite of the minor hardships of rationing and import taxes, Gordon managed to lead a very comfortable life in Provence. He learned how to cook French cuisine (he would later be known by his friends for his excellent French epicure cooking). Unlike Richardson, who had come to France without knowing French, Gordon could speak like a native, having learned the region's colloquialisms during his OSS days. His linguistic skills allowed him to navigate the intricacies of Provence culture better than most American emigrés. For instance, he found early on that he could get more money by trading a personal check on the black market in Provence than by converting a U.S. money order into French francs. "This may seem to you immoral," he told his mother when explaining why she should send checks rather than money orders, "but under current circumstances it's foolish to take a stand."[6] When royalties from *The Strumpet Wind* started to come in, Gordon splurged and bought a car—a "very pretty" Rolls Royce, as he giddily told his family. He briefly entertained the idea of naming it "The Strumpet Wind" or "Crowned Head," but he finally settled on "Gertrude."[7]

By most appearances, Gordon was living an idyllic life. At first he and Richardson stayed at a friend's villa in Draguignan, a small picturesque town in Provence about forty miles from Cannes. Gordon knew the area extremely well—Draguignan was only a few miles from the house where Lucien Herviou, his principal Abwehr agent during the war, had lived. Sometime afterward they found an old stone house in Gassin, an even smaller Provençal town about twenty miles away. The house, which had been part of an old cork factory, was run-down and desperately in need of renovation, which gave the two something to do together when Gordon wasn't writing or cooking. He described the house in an unpublished short story he wrote about life in Provence: "Bowing to economic necessity, we had abandoned our dream of rolling acres and had bought for practically nothing a dilapidated but still sound old stone house in a nearby hilltop village. The low purchase price left us enough over to take care of repairs, the installation of plumbing and the numerous modifications we had in mind."[8] He and Richardson bought bicycles which they rode from their country house to the center of town, saving the Rolls Royce for longer trips to Paris or Cannes. Gordon found a small artist's colony in Gassin, and he would occasionally venture to the nearby coastal town of Saint-Tropez, which had long been a regular destination for artists like Henri Matisse and Jean Cocteau. The glamorous city would later provide the setting for many of Gordon's trademark sun-bathed Mediterranean scenes in his novels.

Gordon and Richardson came to be known by the locals as "the Gassin boys"—the two handsome Americans who had restored a dilapidated house and roamed about in a Rolls Royce. Their friends in Provence would sometimes refer to them as "avowed Communists" when introducing them to others, a not-so-subtle way of saying they were gay.[9] Such relative openness was not confined to Provence. Gordon's letters to his mother during this period imply that she knows the nature of their relationship, and even Richardson's letters to Mimi have the tone of someone who is addressing a mother-in-law. In his letters, Richardson jokes with "Polly" (his nickname for her) about domestic life with her "famous son," asks about her own family issues, sends her a "firm handshake" for Gordon's father, and gives somewhat snippy advice on how to send care packages.[10]

Samuel Merrick also must have known about his brother's relationship, since he visited them in France on multiple occasions. In August 1947, Samuel married Eleanor Perry, a sharply intelligent woman from Boston who had graduated from Radcliffe College two years earlier. After getting married they settled in Philadelphia, where Samuel had moved his labor law practice from Baltimore.[11] The couple traveled to Europe for their honeymoon, spending a few days in Provence visiting Gordon and Richardson. Gordon was delighted to play host to the newlyweds, and he busied himself for weeks in preparation for their visit. He rented a house in Cannes for the occasion, thinking that the French Riviera would be more impressive than rustic Draguignan. He had also just learned about a new film festival happening in Cannes, which he thought might be "fun of a sort" for them. He had little idea that this local film festival would eventually come to be known as the Cannes Film Festival, the most prestigious and glamorous festival of its kind in the world.

The area around Cannes had already become a magnet for the elite set, and Gordon mingled with an unending parade of celebrities and fashionistas. He became close friends with Ginette Spanier, the director of the venerable Parisian fashion house House of Balmain. Spanier, who had likely met Gordon during the war when she was working as a clerk in the U.S. Army's Signal Service headquarters in Paris, was now regularly spending her summer holidays near Saint-Tropez. She had a knack for befriending internationally famous artists—many of them gay. One of her good friends was Maurice

Figure 6.1 Robert Blaine Richardson.
Source: Estate of Samuel and Eleanor Merrick.

Figure 6.2 Robert Blaine Richardson.
Source: Estate of Samuel and Eleanor Merrick.

Chevalier, the celebrated French singer who became friends with Gordon as well. Spanier and her husband threw glittering parties on the French Riviera, attended by luminaries like Noël Coward and Marlene Dietrich. (Gordon later fictionalized one of these parties, including a brief cameo by Coward and Dietrich, in *One for the Gods*.) Gordon likely also met two more of Spanier's friends, Victor Stiebel and Richard Addinsell, another gay male couple who were also living in Cannes. Stiebel was a celebrated London fashion designer and Addinsell was an English composer known for his many film scores.[12] In addition to the Spanier crowd, it was probably also in Cannes that Gordon met the French actor Jean-Pierre Aumont, whose romantic fling with Grace Kelly in Cannes had been the subject of much tabloid gossip. Gordon and Aumont were still friends many years later, when Aumont wrote a dust jacket blurb for a book written by Charles Hulse, Gordon's partner at the time.

Gordon had good reason to announce himself as a successful writer in such high-profile circles. Sales of *The Strumpet Wind* were already far better than he had ever expected. Paperback edition rights had been bought by the Dollar Book Club, which meant a sale of at least 400,000 copies. Shortly afterward, the American Army Service Editions series also picked up the novel, which guaranteed another 150,000 copies. By July there were already 600,000 copies of the novel in circulation, and arrangements were also being made for British, French, and Italian editions. Instead of resting on his laurels, however, Gordon was already at work on his second novel. As he explained to his mother, this new novel would be about "a very rich young man with a horrible mother and an urge to get out from under his family name."[13] Despite (or perhaps because of) the distractions of the French Riviera, he developed a disciplined work routine—one that he kept for the rest of his life—in which he spent the first few hours of each day at his typewriter until he had written at least two pages.

He was also thinking seriously about the kind of novelist he wanted to become. Although he professed to "care not a hoot" about what the critics thought of his work, he clearly read the published reviews of *The Strumpet Wind* and wrote multiple letters to the editor in response.[14] In fact, when he read the negative review of his novel in the *New York Times*, he wrote a long, angry letter to the editor in which he claimed that the reviewer had "completely misrepresented" the novel.[15] If he had read the reviews—both the positive and negative ones—more dispassionately, he would have noticed that they suggested a number of different directions he could take as a budding novelist. He could further ingrain himself in the group of "postwar novelists" who reflected on recent events and their effects on the modern world. Or he could sharpen his critique of American institutions and fashion himself as a progressive, anti-establishment writer—thus confirming the assessment of the jingoistic critics at the *New York Times*. Or he could take a cue from reviewers who praised the "psychological truth" of his characters and write stories that probed the inner conflicts of the human mind. Each of these options had a potential market in the 1940s and would have given him a niche in the publishing world.

Instead of taking advice from reviewers (a pattern that would continue for the rest of his life), Gordon turned to other novelists for ideas about how to write his next book. One novelist in particular was especially appealing to him as a literary model: E. M. Forster. By the time that Gordon settled in France, Forster was among the most acclaimed novelists in England, with a distinguished reputation throughout Europe and the United States. He had already been nominated twice for the Nobel Prize in Literature (in 1945 and 1946) despite the fact that his last novel, *A Passage to India*, had been published more than twenty years earlier. Although effectively retired as a novelist, Forster had remained in the English literary scene, acting as a BBC Radio commentator throughout the 1930s and 1940s. During this time he had become particularly well known for his political outspokenness and liberal views, many of which had been shaped by his firsthand experience with the British colonial occupation of India and the reality of racial injustice. Wendy Moffat, the most candid and straightforward of Forster's modern biographers, deftly sums up the extent of Forster's political activism in the 1940s:

> He protested against fascism, against censorship, against communism, against "Jew-Consciousness," against the British occupation of Egypt and India, against racism and jingoism and anything that smelled of John Bull. Morgan's public voice wasn't stentorian. He raised it, tremulously, often alone, against the edifice of conformity.[16]

Such a mixture of progressivism and philosophy immediately appealed to Gordon, whose first novel had been a scathing critique of jingoism and conformity.

There was also the fact (which Gordon knew) that Forster was gay. Although he never publicly acknowledged his attraction to men, Forster had no doubts about his homosexuality and he actively pursued romantic relationships with men throughout his adult life. Many of his close friends knew he was gay, including Virginia and Leonard Woolf, Lytton Strachey, and the archaeologist T. E. Lawrence, whose role as a British army officer during the Arab Revolt of World War I was later dramatized in the film *Lawrence of Arabia*. When Gordon met Forster in the 1940s, Forster was already in a longtime relationship with Bob Buckingham, a London policeman he had met at a Cambridge-Oxford boat race party in 1930. The relationship was at times difficult for Forster, in part because Buckingham was married to a woman, May Hockney. Despite the challenges of the situation, Forster more or less shared Buckingham with Hockney for the rest of his life. As Moffat puts it, Forster was enjoying "a kind of marriage of his own, outside of ordinary rules, a marriage composed of real patience and joy with an admixture of magical thinking."[17]

Although the circumstances are not clear, Gordon met Forster in person sometime in 1947 or 1948. Mostly likely he was introduced to Forster by way of Glenway Wescott, who was part of Forster's circle of gay male friends in America (many of whom who would go on to become iconic figures in the history of gay literature and art): Christopher Isherwood, W. H. Auden, J. R. Ackerley, Stephen Spender, John Lehmann, Paul Cadmus. Gordon knew most, if not all, of these men through his friendship with Wescott. Wescott had introduced Gordon to Forster's novels a few years earlier, and so it would have been especially fitting for him to facilitate an introduction to the man himself. Wescott himself had unsuccessfully tried to meet Forster during the Englishman's celebrated visit to America in the spring of 1947.[18] A bigger triumph for him came, however, in May 1949, when Wescott and his longtime partner Monroe Wheeler hosted a dinner party for both Forster and Buckingham at their apartment at 410 Park Avenue. Also invited to dinner were Joseph Campbell, the renowned mythology scholar, and Alfred C. Kinsey, the sexologist whose massive study *Sexual Behavior in the Human Male* had scandalized conservative America with its documentation of prevalent homosexual behavior.[19] Given that Wescott and Forster had been writing to each other this entire time, it would have been natural for Wescott to provide a letter of introduction for Gordon—his "Priapus-bodied friend," as he called him.[20]

Another possibility is that Gordon met Forster through William Roerick and Thomas Coley, two actors who had been in the original Broadway production of *Our Town* at the same time that Gordon was cast in *The Man Who Came to Dinner*. Roerick and Coley, a gay couple who had met while performing in *Our Town*, were good friends of Forster who hosted him during his first tour of America in 1947. They had treated Forster to the New York theater scene, including a performance of *Annie Get Your Gun* starring Ethel Merman, and they introduced him to many other gay artists and writers in New York. Both men remained lifelong devotees of Forster, and in 1970 they collaborated on an off-Broadway show, *A Passage to E. M. Forster*, based on Forster's writings.[21] Although there is no extant correspondence between Gordon and Roerick or Coley, it is clear that they had much in common—and in fact their relationship was remarkably similar to the one that Gordon would have with Charles Hulse. Coley, who had acted in the theater before serving as an army captain in the war, was the quiet and intellectual partner, while Roerick was the more extroverted and sociable one. Although they were never publicly demonstrative or active in the gay rights movement, their relationship was understood by their friends and colleagues. They remained together for over fifty years until Coley's death in 1989 (the year after Gordon died).

Like Wescott, Gordon had become an instant "disciple" of Forster after reading his novels, and, also like Wescott, he looked up to Forster as a sort of literary mentor.[22] After meeting Forster in person, Gordon would have realized even more how much the famous novelist had managed to incorporate subtle autobiographical details in his novels, and he was eager to learn from Forster more about the art of fictionalized autobiography. Thus in the summer of 1948, Gordon took the bold step of mailing Forster a copy of *The Strumpet Wind*—with a request for feedback. This was an unusual move for Gordon, who was typically reluctant to reach out to established writers for advice. Fortunately, the appeal was graciously rewarded. In an intimate, handwritten letter on Kings College stationery, Forster praised *The Strumpet Wind* as a thoughtful, respectable first attempt by a young novelist. He then went on, in his usual measured and objective style, to explain what he considered to be the thematic core of the novel:

> "Strumpet-Wind" duly arrived, and I found it very interesting. The official treachery in which the hero is involved rang painfully true. One of the appalling and corroding elements in the world today, is the secrecy. The dossiers, the black-lists, the ever longer grey-lists. The whole of our civilisation is corrupted by this element, nor do I see how it will ever be purged, for war and peace make no difference. All the individual can do is to feel shame. Too often he is like the Major.[23]

Forster's letter is perceptive on several counts. First, he is quick to recognize the political import of the novel. Like many reviewers, Forster sees the novel as a critique of American bureaucracy, though he expands this critique to a more global, Western phenomenon. In essence he reads *The Strumpet Wind* in alignment with his own political views, and his comments about the novel echo many of the points made in his radio broadcasts and pamphlets during the war—works that Gordon may have heard or read when he was stationed in France. In his 1939 pamphlet *What I Believe*, Forster had already complained about the secrecy underpinning modern governments, writing that "the men who are inside the Houses of Parliament—they cannot trust one another . . . still less can the Government they compose trust other governments. No caps upon the pavement here, but suspicion, treachery and armaments." Another line in the same pamphlet comes even closer to the theme of Gordon's novel: "If I had to choose between betraying my country and betraying my friend I hope I should have the guts to betray my country."[24]

Forster's second perception about *The Strumpet Wind* is more carefully stated. His seemingly incidental reference to the character of George Meddling ("the Major") acknowledges the novel's brief representation of gay culture. Unlike many of the novel's "straight" reviewers, Forster does not write off Meddling, a homosexual villain, as a stock literary convention. Instead he reads the character as an attempt to psychologize the deleterious effects of modern society on gay people. As Forster sees it, Meddling's sadism is not the result of his homosexuality but the result of being forced to *repress* his homosexuality. His condemnation of "dossiers, the black-lists, the ever longer grey-lists" was a not-so-thinly veiled reference to McCarthyism: the institutionalized persecution of gay people by both American and British governments, waged under the banner of anti-communism. Forster's characteristic cautiousness may have prevented him from explicitly naming homosexuality in the letter, but Gordon could not have missed the implication.

Forster's only criticism of *The Strumpet Wind* had to do with its romantic subplot. With his usual tact Forster pointed out the novel's flaws indirectly, through a series of reflections and hypothetical questions:

> Danielle (I think the girl's name was) struck me as insufficiently integrated into the main problem. Her suicide helps to upset the hero of course, but no more. I found myself wondering whether she *would* have killed herself, and, furthermore, reflecting that if she *hadn't* she would indeed have been integrated, and would have presented a fascinating and difficult situation for the novelist to cope with. Her reactions to the hapless Frenchman who was being destroyed by the man she loved—what would it have been? Would she have looked on complacently?[25]

Despite the technical nature of Forster's observations, the main gist of his criticism is simple: the novel's romance is unconvincing. Danielle's suicide may add some drama to the plot, but it too easily absolves Gordon of the task of developing fully her relationship with Chandler.

By identifying the heterosexual love plot as the part of the novel that fails, Forster confirmed what Gordon already suspected. On his copy of the *New York Times* review, Gordon had underlined the reviewer's claim that "Roger's sex-wallow in Cannes . . . rings as false" and had written next to it: "This is the only part of the *criticism* I agree with."[26] But Forster was also touching on his own struggles as a writer. Negative criticism of his novels had often singled out his depiction of romance, characterizing it as naïve and insipid. The eminent Cambridge literary critic F. R. Leavis famously demeaned Forster's novels by claiming that they demonstrate "a curious spinsterish inadequacy in the immediate presentation of love."[27] Leavis, well known for his belligerent sexism, knew about Forster's homosexuality and was hinting at it by repeatedly referring to his writing as "bent" and "spinsterly."[28] Yet even Forster's admirers recognized a sexual caginess in his novels. The American literary critic Lionel Trilling, who did much to establish Forster's place in the canon, did not refute Leavis's comments about Forster's depiction of love. Rather, he argued that the novels were concerned with universal and philosophical ideas—"about all of human life," as he said about *A Passage to India*.[29] Forster took a similar sublimating approach in his advice to Gordon. Instead of advising him to make the romance between Chandler and Danielle more realistic, his feedback suggests ways of making it more symbolic and philosophical. Forster knew that Gordon was gay, and he likely assumed that a realistic, believable representation of heterosexual love was too challenging.

Always sensitive to criticism, Gordon mulled over Forster's comments for a long time afterward. Over the next several years he continued to draw inspiration from his conversations with Forster and from his novels. *The Longest Journey*, Forster's novel about a struggling writer at Cambridge, was particularly meaningful for Gordon—so much so that he quoted from it for the epigraph to his 1954 novel *The Demon of Noon*: "Perhaps each of us would go to ruin if for one short hour we acted as we thought fit, and attempted the service of perfect freedom."[30]

This is an appropriate epigraph for the novel, but it also hints at Gordon and Forster's shared experience of living—somewhat openly—as gay men. (The novel itself featured a remarkably daring gay subplot.) Many years later, Gordon would use the same quotation from *The Longest Journey* for the title of *Perfect Freedom*, a novel that was essentially a large-scale revision of *Demon of Noon* and that makes the gay plot the main focus.

While *The Longest Journey* was an important model for Gordon, the Forster novel that would have the most profound influence was one that remained unpublished until 1971, the year after Forster's death. Sometime in 1913 Forster had started writing *Maurice*, a novel about Maurice Hill, a young gay man at Cambridge. In the course of the novel, Maurice falls in love twice, first with Clive Durham, his classmate at Cambridge, and then with Alec Scudder, a lower-class gamekeeper. Forster revised and worked on the novel over several years, but he refused to publish it, fearing that it would lead to public repercussions for his family and friends and possibly even criminal prosecution for himself. (In fact, when *Maurice* was finally published, it generated a backlash among literary critics, including some who subsequently "demoted" Forster from the ranks of leading British novelists.[31]) He did, however, show the manuscript to his close friends, such as D. H. Lawrence and Virginia Woolf.[32] He also showed it to his gay friends Isherwood, Cadmus, and Wescott. Isherwood's response to *Maurice* was rapturous. After reading the novel, he wrote a letter to Forster: "Have finished 'Maurice,' and am in a state of reverence which even my most irreverent moments of you do nothing to dispel. What a book! In some ways, your very best. . . . Maurice himself is a masterpiece—one of the few truly noble characters of fiction."[33] Wescott read the manuscript a decade later, during Forster's American visit in 1949. He had the same reaction as Isherwood and joined the chorus of friends who tried to persuade Forster to publish the novel. When Forster died in 1970, it was Isherwood and Wescott (along with Wheeler) who would be instrumental in getting the novel published and establishing Forster's reputation as one of the most important gay writers of the twentieth century.[34]

Sometime after their first meeting Forster showed Gordon his manuscript for *Maurice*. Like Isherwood and Wescott, Gordon thought that Forster should publish the novel "immediately," though it is not clear which version of the novel Gordon read.[35] In the first version, which Forster wrote in 1914, the protagonist is given a fairly elegiacal conclusion: Maurice is left alone pining for Alec, who has left for South America.[36] Over the following decades, Forster continually made revisions to the novel, struggling especially with the possibility of a happier ending for Maurice. Isherwood was a frequent sounding board on this subject, and Forster shared with him his various ideas for uniting Maurice and Alec at the end of the novel—a move that Isherwood enthusiastically supported.[37] When Forster finally settled on the ending, he did not refrain from showing the full emotional intensity of the lovers' reunion. Maurice and Alec find each other in a boathouse on Durham's estate, where they vow to leave the confines of London society and spend the rest of their lives together: "He had brought out the man in Alec, and now it was Alec's turn to bring out the hero in him. . . . They must live outside class, without relations or money; they must work and stick to each other till death. But England belonged to them. That, besides companionship, was their reward. Her air and sky were theirs, not the timorous millions' who own stuffy little boxes, but never their own souls."[38] If Gordon read this version of the ending—especially if he read it in 1949, the same time as Wescott—it would have been revelatory. To write explicitly about two men in love was daring enough, but to suggest that a gay couple could enjoy a lifetime of happiness was almost unthinkable.

Although Gordon continued to correspond with Forster through the 1950s, there is little evidence that Forster read any of Gordon's novels after *The Strumpet Wind*. Gordon sent him a French translation of his second novel in 1950 (for various reasons the English version of *The Vallency Tradition* was not published until years later), but Forster does not mention it in any of the extant subsequent letters.[39] Forster may simply have not read the novel, or he may have given his feedback to Gordon in person—his letter-writing in general had dropped off considerably in the 1950s, partly because of his health. In the letters to Gordon from this period that still exist, Forster mostly writes about his travels and about proposed plans to meet Gordon, either in England, France, or America. He touches on news about their mutual friends and their respective "Bobs"—Bob Buckingham and Bob Richardson. Knowing well that Gordon was a man of the theater, Forster also occasionally asks his thoughts about new plays, particularly those by Tennessee Williams, whom

Forster had met. Forster's letters suggest that he considered Gordon as part of a transatlantic network of gay writers and artists, even more than Gordon saw himself as part of such a group. They were drawn to the same people—and on occasion repelled by the same people. In a letter that Forster wrote to Isherwood around the same time that he met Gordon, he speaks ebulliently about Benjamin ("Ben") Britten while complaining about having to endure a meeting with Gore Vidal: "I disliked him a lot."[40]

Gradually Gordon realized that Forster would not be the mentor he had hoped for. Forster's worsening health made it increasingly difficult for him to respond to letters or meet with friends, and the overly sensitive Gordon may have taken Forster's silence personally. Many years later he claimed in a letter to the *Village Voice* that he did not consider *Maurice* a "very good novel."[41] This could hardly have been true. Most likely he was still smarting from the memory that Forster had lavished more attention on Wescott, Isherwood, and others besides himself. In either case, the example of *Maurice* always loomed large, and it would impel him eventually to write his own version of a gay novel with a happy ending. This novel would be criticized with the very same terms that hostile critics applied to *Maurice*—"fantasy," "escapist," "hysterical," "a fairy tale."[42] Unlike *Maurice*, however, Gordon's novel would be largely autobiographical. He would not need to invent an idyllic greenwood like the one that appears magically at the end of Forster's novel, since he had already lived in one.

NOTES

1. Gordon Merrick to Mary Merrick, 24 November 1946, private collection.
2. "British and American News," *L'Avenir de Cannes*, January 1947, GMP, box 21.
3. Gordon Merrick to Mary Merrick, December 16, 1946, private collection.
4. Barbara Will, *Unlikely Collaboration: Gertrude Stein, Bernard Faÿ, and the Vichy Dilemma* (New York: Columbia University Press, 2011), 126–28.
5. See Barbara Will, "The Strange Politics of Gertrude Stein," *Humanities* 33, no. 2 (2012): 25–49. On Stein's balancing of homosexual representation and public persona, see Jeff Solomon, *So Famous and So Gay: The Fabulous Potency of Truman Capote and Gertrude Stein* (Minneapolis: University of Minnesota Press, 2017), 83–114.
6. Gordon Merrick to Mary Merrick, 8 February 1947, private collection.
7. Gordon Merrick to Samuel Merrick, 3 March 1947, private collection.
8. Gordon Merrick, "The Leightons," unpublished short story, 5, GMP, box 15, folder 7.
9. L. J. Ludovici, *The Three of Us* (London: Marjay Books, 1993), 67.
10. Robert B. Richardson to Mary Merrick, 16 February 1947, private collection.

11. "Miss Eleanor Perry Married to Samuel Vaughan Merrick in Nahant," *Boston Globe*, August 24, 1947; "Along the Social Way," *Philadelphia Inquirer*, July 26, 1947.

12. Ginette Spanier, *It Isn't All Mink* (London: Collins, 1959), 35, 148–54, 167.

13. Gordon Merrick to Mary Merrick, 8 February 1947; Robert B. Richardson to Mary Merrick, 22 March 1947; Gordon Merrick to Mary Merrick, 18 July 1947, private collection.

14. Gordon Merrick to Mary Merrick, 21 April 1947, private collection.

15. Gordon Merrick to *The New York Times*, n.d., GMP, box 21.

16. Wendy Moffat, *A Great Unrecorded History: A New Life of E. M. Forster* (New York: Farrar, Straus and Giroux, 2010), 6.

17. Moffat, *A Great Unrecorded History*, 232.

18. Moffat, *A Great Unrecorded History*, 275.

19. Jerry Rosco, *Glenway Wescott Personally: A Biography* (Madison: University of Wisconsin Press, 2002), 123; Allen Ellenzweig, *George Platt Lynes: The Daring Eye* (Oxford: Oxford University Press, 2021), 337.

20. Glenway Wescott, *Continual Lessons: The Journals of Glenway Wescott 1937–1955*, ed. Robert Phelps and Jerry Rosco (New York: Farrar, Straus and Giroux, 1990), 249.

21. Moffat, *A Great Unrecorded History*, 259–61; Clive Barnes, review of "A Passage to E. M. Forster," *New York Times*, October 28, 1970.

22. This is Isherwood's term for himself in *Christopher and His Kind*. Quoted in Moffat, *A Great Unrecorded History*, 13.

23. E. M. Forster to Gordon Merrick, 7 July 1948, GMP, box 19, folder 3. See E. M. Forster, *Selected Letters of E. M. Forster*, eds. Mary Lago and P. N. Furbank (Cambridge, MA: Harvard University Press, 1985).

24. E. M. Forster, *What I Believe* (1939), in *Two Cheers for Democracy* (New York: Harcourt, 1951), 83, 78.

25. Forster to Merrick.

26. C. V. Terry, "The Passive Fascist," annotated copy, *New York Times*, March 2, 1947, GMP, box 20, folder 7.

27. F. R. Leavis, "E. M. Forster," *Scrutiny*, September 1938.

28. This is the view taken by Robert K. Martin and George Piggford, eds., *Queer Forster* (Chicago: University of Chicago Press, 1997), 15.

29. Lionel Trilling, *E. M. Forster* (1943; New York: Harcourt, 1964), 121.

30. Gordon Merrick, *The Demon of Noon* (New York: Julian Messner, 1954).

31. See Christopher Reed, "The Mouse That Roared: Creating a Queer Forster," Martin and Piggford, eds., in *Queer Forster*, 76–77.

32. Don Gorton, "*Maurice* and Gay Liberation," *Gay & Lesbian Review*, November–December 2009, 19.

33. E. M. Forster and Christopher Isherwood, *Letters between Forster and Isherwood on Homosexuality in Literature*, ed. Richard E. Zeikowitz (New York: Palgrave Macmillan, 2008), 74.

34. Rosco, *Glenway Wescott*, 124–25; Moffat, *A Great Unrecorded History*, 20.

35. Gordon Merrick, Letter to the Editor, *Village Voice*, July 11, 1974, 86. Merrick's letter is a response to an earlier *Village Voice* article by Vincent Cotugno, in which Cotugno criticizes *The Lord Won't Mind* and *One for the Gods*. In his letter Gordon defends his novels together with *Maurice*, arguing that explicit, positive representations of gay men are necessary "for a bulk of homosexual literature to develop."

36. Moffat, *A Great Unrecorded History*, 8.

37. Forster and Isherwood, *Letters*, 2–4, 12–13.

38. E. M. Forster, *Maurice* (1971; New York: W. W. Norton, 2005), 244.

39. E.M. Forster to Gordon Merrick, 20 February 1950, GMP, box 19, folder 3.

40. E. M. Forster to Christopher Isherwood, 25 June 1948, in *Letters*, 144.

41. Gordon Merrick, Letter to the Editor, *Village Voice*, July 11, 1974.

42. Martin and Piggford, eds., *Queer Forster*, 18–20.

Chapter Seven

The Protest Novelist

The *New York Times* may have intended "scrupulous moralist" as a pejorative, but Gordon quickly learned to embrace the moniker. For the next ten years after *The Strumpet Wind*, he persisted in writing novels that were critical of America. Fancying himself a progressive champion, he used his talent to rebel against the structures of American capitalism and class privilege that had shaped his upbringing. His time as an OSS agent in France, and afterward as an American emigré abroad, had given him a unique perspective from which to view American culture. He had always been a philosophically oriented literary critic, but now as a novelist he had a specific target for his ideas about humanity and morality. And as a gay man living openly in a committed relationship, he had grown less tolerant of American politics, which had become much more homophobic after the war. The House Un-American Activities Committee had grown more powerful, and by 1950 the armed forces were kicking out over a thousand people a year for homosexuality.[1] Gordon by contrast had come back from the war a changed man, determined to live according to his rules. He was well positioned to write the next "Cold War gay protest novel"—a genre that fought against the hypermasculinity and conservatism that had come to dominate American politics and fiction.[2]

Gordon had already conceived of a second novel when he was finishing *The Strumpet Wind*.[3] Inspired by his time living and writing in Mexico City, he got the idea for a story about a young man like himself—handsome, privileged, and Ivy-educated—who runs off to Mexico to escape a suffocating life in America. Lance Vallency, the novel's protagonist, is not gay, but he has reasons of his own for wanting to leave America. A celebrated scion of a wealthy New York family, he defies his domineering mother and asserts his independence by marrying a young woman while still in college. He infuriates his mother even more by quitting school to become an actor, which results in him being cut off financially. Although his controlling mother expects him to go into business, his true passion is for the theater. After toiling for months in a squalid New York apartment with his pregnant wife, he finally gets his big break on Broadway. His happiness soon fades, however, when he realizes that his job is contingent on his agreement to have sex with his co-star, an older, famous actress. Lance's mother finds about the affair and uses it to drive a wedge between him and his wife. The marriage deteriorates further when, weary of the theater, Lance decides to quit the theater and work for a civil liberties organization. There he meets Rose, a young black civil rights worker from Harlem, and the two become lovers. Although Rose fears the prejudice they will face as an interracial couple, Lance is adamant about being public and challenging racist society. One day he makes the bold act of taking Rose to an exclusive club in Manhattan, scandalizing the other guests. The incident sets off a tragic series of events that results in Rose's death that same night. Devastated and broken, Lance flees to Mexico to deal with his grief over Rose.

As he had done in *The Strumpet Wind*, Gordon included many details from his own life. He based Lance's theatrical experience on his own brief Broadway career—though Lance is more successful and is coerced into sex by a female actress instead of a male playwright. He winkingly set the premiere of Lance's big play in the same month that *The Man Who Came to Dinner* had premiered on Broadway. The storyline about the civil rights organization was an interesting twist, since it was based not on Gordon but on his brother Samuel, who had worked for the National Labor Relations Board as an advocate for African-American issues. Gordon used Louise Munson, his eccentric host in Mexico City, as the basis for the character of Flip Rawls, a similarly gregarious American expatriate (although he made Munson the designer for the governor's mansion in New York rather than Pennsylvania). He also gave the briefest of cameos in the novel to his old friend Lemuel Ayers, in this case without changing his name. Even Lance's surname was a subtle nod to his mother's side of the family, which claimed to have been descended from Louise de La Vallière, the famous mistress of Louis XIV of France.[4] This kind of fictionalized autobiography would remain a common feature in Gordon's novels.

Another common feature would be the character of an American emigré who fights to shake off the shackles of capitalism and social convention. In the Lance Vallency novel, Gordon portrayed this struggle as a futile one. Lance's new life in Mexico is initially an idyllic one. He buys a house near the beach and learns how to farm and make pottery for a living. He also falls into a relationship with his housemaid Louisa, a young, inexperienced Mexican woman who bears him two sons. For a few years Lance believes that his troubled American past is behind him, until the arrival of a vampish Hollywood actress. At this point the novel veers in the direction of melodrama. The actress turns up dead in her hotel room, and Lance is identified as the prime suspect. The corrupt Mexican authorities release Lance only after the intervention of his mother—who forces Lance to return to New York as a condition of his release. In effect, he trades one prison for another. The novel ends with Lance on an airplane headed to America, as he catches a fleeting glimpse of the rustic happy home that he will never see again.[5]

Gordon was proud of himself. He had finished his second novel, one that was longer and different from his first one. He had confronted the main problem of *The Strumpet Wind*—the portrayal of a heterosexual relationship—and, instead of avoiding the issue, he had structured the new novel around *three* heterosexual romances. And he had taken Forster's advice to heart. He had used heterosexual romance to make a point about social and political issues—not to produce an emotionally convincing love story. There could be no question about the political significance of the relationship between Lance and Rose, since it was part of the plot. Gordon had created a character, another version of himself, whose romantic life was in itself a bold challenge to American conservatism and bourgeois values.[6]

Unfortunately, this progressivism was too much for American publishers. When Gordon finished the manuscript in late 1948, he struggled to find a press that would take it. William Morrow, which had published *The Strumpet Wind*, declined its option to publish the new novel, despite the fact that *Strumpet* had sold extremely well—700,000 copies according to one source.[7] Morrow may have been wary of a continuing a relationship with a writer who had been branded "unpatriotic" by some reviewers. The publishing landscape had become more conservative in the last three years, in no small part because of the rise of McCarthyism and the censorship of books considered "un-American." Most likely Morrow was also afraid to promote a novel that had an explicit interracial romance at its center. Whatever the reason, it would take at least five more years—and some drastic changes to the manuscript—before Gordon was able to find an American press willing to put its imprimatur on the work.

Ironically, it was because of the "radical" nature of the novel that Gordon found a willing French publisher almost immediately. Flammarion, one of the oldest and largest publishing houses in France, published a French translation of the novel in February 1950. The translation was done by Therese Aubray, an accomplished poet who belonged to a literary salon that boasted Antonin Artaud and Gabriel Marcel among its members. The novel appeared in a plain, boldly lettered cover with the title *Lancelot 5ème Avenue* ("Lancelot of Fifth Avenue").

The French *Lancelot* was a critical and commercial success. It was proclaimed a bestseller in the press and was reviewed by some of the most prestigious French literary critics. The reviews were extremely positive, some of them drawing comparisons to Henry James, F. Scott Fitzgerald, D. H. Lawrence, and—to Gordon's immeasurable delight—E. M. Forster.

Most of the French critics loved the story of a good-looking, privileged American from New York who leads a "personal revolt against American society" (*une révolte individuelle contre la société américaine*).[8] They interpreted the fictional Vallencys as a stand-in for the Vanderbilts, and they understood the novel as a repudiation of American dynasties like the Rockefellers and the Carnegies. They also felt that the novel revealed the psychology of American males, namely the distinctive—and borderline pathological—relationship between American men and their mothers. Max-Pol Fouchet, the French poet who had been friends with Albert Camus, declared that *Lancelot* laid bare the intransigence of the American class system and "illustrate[d] the hegemony imposed by the mother on the American male" (*d'illustrer l'hégémonie de la mère sur le mâle américain*).[9] For Gilbert Guilleminault, the eminent Parisian journalist and literary critic, Lance Vallency was the right hero for the times, "a charming, candid Don Quixote who fights against money, racism, prejudice, and the false civilization of America" (*un charmant et ingénu Don Quichotte qui combat contre l'argent, le racisme, les préjugés, la civilisation fallacieuse de l'Amérique*).[10] Guilleminault was particularly impressed by the novel's engagement with race and racial prejudice—the "black problem" (*probléme noir*), as he put it.

The success of *Lancelot* convinced Flammarion to issue a French translation of *The Strumpet Wind* the following year. This version, titled *La Rafale Amoureuse* ("The Gust of Passion"), was translated by Denise Meunier, a promising writer who would later translate Aldous Huxley's *Brave New World Revisited*.[11] The French press again embraced Gordon's novel—and they fell in love with Gordon himself. Newspapers and magazines ran profiles of this American emigré who spoke French fluently and who had "saved" France from German operatives during the war. They also appreciated his handsome looks, describing him as someone with the "charm and beauty of a leading man out of Hollywood" (*le charme et la beauté de ces jeunes premiers auxquels Hollywood nous a habitués*).[12]

Some French reviewers, who knew something about Gordon's background, noticed the autobiographical elements in his novels, and they loved the idea of presenting Gordon as a real-life version of Lance Vallency or Roger Chandler. Some reviews of *Lancelot* even used a photo of Gordon to make him look like the subject of the novel. In her article on *Lancelot*, the journalist and novelist Jeanine Delpech actually seemed to confuse Gordon with his character. In her interview she asks Gordon questions about his romantic life, as though Lance's "woman problems" were his as well:

> Delpech: Did you decide to move to France so that you could escape American women?

Merrick: Certainly not. But I do have trouble tolerating the moral climate of America, the injustices that the Blacks and the Jews suffer.

Delpech: You present us with a 21-year-old student [Lance] lacking any experience with women. He seems to be in contradiction with the Kinsey Reports and with the liberated behavior that reigns, at least we believe over here, in your universities.

Merrick: I assure you that many 25-year-old boys enter marriage as virgins. Americans are afraid of their bodies, like they are afraid of nearly everything.[13]

Whether or not Delpech knew that Gordon was gay, she deftly allowed him to skirt the issue of his own sexual experience with women. It was precisely this kind of social suavity that Gordon appreciated, and it was a big reason why he felt more at home in France than in America. In actuality, most of Gordon's friends and associates in France knew perfectly well the truth of his relationship with Richardson, but they did not force him to make a grand proclamation about it—and they certainly did not put this information in print. More importantly, from Gordon's perspective, they admired his writing. As far as he was concerned, the French understood him and his novels far better than those repressed, "coarse" Americans.

Even though *Lancelot* was a hit in France, Gordon still could not find an American publisher for the original English version. He was too busy at work on a third novel to worry much about it, however. He had set this new novel in Saint-Tropez—half-disguised as the fictional town of St. Martin—just a few miles from Gassin where he and Richardson were living. His working title was *The Descent of the Pendulum*, though he was later persuaded to change it to *The Demon of Noon*.[14] Like his first two novels, *Demon* would be another "protest" novel that took a critical look at America from the perspective of an American emigré. But this one would not tackle the issue of race. Instead it would touch another civil rights issue—one that was even more controversial and risky in the 1950s.

The novel focuses on Stuart Cosling, a good-looking idealistic American who emigrates to the southern coast of France in 1927. The son of a wealthy (and mostly absent) father, Stuart is working as an editor for a New York publishing firm when he unexpectedly receives a large inheritance. He promptly quits his job and uses the money to move to France, taking with him his lover Marthe and their seven-year-old son Robbie. He and Marthe are not legally married, a distinction which he wears as a badge of progressive nonconformity. The unconventional arrangement is part of Stuart's attempt to reject society's expectations and the expectations of his wealthy family. He further asserts his independence by buying a dilapidated stone house on four hundred acres of land in the rural French countryside, with the intention of renovating the house and converting the land to a self-sustaining farm. (In this section of the novel Gordon drew directly from his experience renovating the cork factory home in Gassin.) For Stuart, this idyllic rustic life represents a triumphant break from the grubby capitalism of New York: "How good to be away from it all! How good to strip off the harness of city life, the ties and garters and heavy shoes and let in the sun and air. How good to be with people who couldn't even imagine such a world."[15] With his dogged habits of rationalization, Stuart tries to fit all the parts of his new life into this romantic vision of human freedom—including his affair with a local woman. Shortly after arriving in France he meets Odette, a poor, beautiful French girl, and within a few weeks the two are having sex in a remote cave near the beach. Although Stuart takes pains to hide the affair from Marthe, he convinces himself that it is not an act of infidelity but an enlightened embrace of the truth of human sexuality: "Perhaps someday, he thought, the world would accept the fact that there is enough love in a man to be given freely, not measured out in a dropper, each recipient determined by taboos arising out of a morbid shame of man's animal nature."[16]

As the novel progresses, Stuart finds it increasingly difficult to accommodate his liberal philosophy to the messy realities of life. His farm gets caught up in a property dispute that mires him in the byzantine French legal system. In order to keep his home, he is forced to sell most of his land to a corporate developer, who turns it into a luxury hotel strip. Stuart thus becomes responsible for the commercial exploitation of the land he had naïvely idealized. At home, his stubborn idealism creates a growing rift with Marthe, who tires of his isolationist fantasies and runs off with Carl von Eschenbach, a strapping blond German who is later revealed to be a Nazi agent. When Marthe is imprisoned by the French army for her association with Eschenbach, Stuart learns that his unconventional arrangement—i.e., the fact that he and Marthe are not legally married—makes it impossible for him to extricate Marthe from prison. At this point he realizes the flaws in his philosophy of "perfect freedom" with tragic poignancy: "The price that was being exacted for their offense to society was cruelly heavy."[17]

The Stuart Cosling storyline alone is enough to qualify *Demon of Noon* as a protest novel—a bitter critique of the corporatized, bureaucratic state. But Gordon went even further. He developed a substantial subplot around Stuart's son Robbie—who turns out to be gay. Robbie begins the novel as a sensitive, artistic child who becomes gradually aware of his homosexuality as a seventeen-year-old. Having lived a sheltered life with his parents in rural France, Robbie has no knowledge of homosexuality—much less any sexual experience with other men. He starts to get an inkling one day when he and his parents accidentally stumble into a gay bar in St. Martin (now a thriving tourist town). His parents awkwardly rush Robbie out of the bar, but the experience causes Robbie to feel a strange "excitement . . . beginning to stir in him."[18] Soon afterward he is compelled to admit to himself his indifference to women when a deckhand on his father's yacht tries to set him up with a female friend. His understanding of gay men grows when he meets Richard, an openly gay British man who surprises him by showing no shame about his homosexuality. Robbie senses an affinity with Richard, but he doesn't fully acknowledge the truth of his sexuality until he meets Toni, a beautiful French dancer staying with his family. Robbie is immediately infatuated, and after a few weeks of self-torment he confesses his feelings to Toni. Although Toni is heterosexual, his affection for Robbie leads him to overcome his initial aversion—and even to have sex with Robbie, his "silly little *pédé*." For Robbie, Toni's acknowledgment and acceptance of him as a *pédé* is both enlightening and ennobling: "The ugly word had been spoken and he didn't care, for Toni had said it as if he accepted him and for the first time he felt as if he were something. He had found his identity and discovered his world."[19]

Robbie's relationship comes to an end when Stuart one day discovers them having sex. He kicks Toni out of the house and confronts Robbie, who boldly admits to being gay and uses his father's own ideals to defend the naturalness of his sexuality: "You've always talked about acting the way you feel and how nature and being natural is right. Well, what's unnatural about it? I didn't ask to be that way. There're books about it. What about Gide? What about all the people here?" Stuart is not moved by his own arguments, and he proposes to "cure" Robbie with the help of psychiatrists. His belief that Robbie's homosexuality is an "illness" causes a years-long separation between them. When Stuart sees him again years later, he is stunned by Robbie's transformation: he is taller and filled out, sporting a beard and an expensive tweed suit. He is also living openly with an older man in Paris. Finally, Stuart starts to learn to accept Robbie's sexuality, and by the end of the novel he promises to help him live a happy life as a gay man. "Whatever you are," he tells Robbie, "you can make something good of it. It will never be easy for you. The world doesn't make any place for you. You must make your own place. You can do it only with self-discipline and a real belief in high principles, in decency, in love."[20]

Gordon was thinking of his own family when he wrote this tender exchange between Robbie and his father. His grandmother Clarice Marston Billups, who had been such a formative influence in his life, had just died on July 19, 1951. She was the first of Gordon's immediate family to pass away, and the loss reminded him that his family would not be around forever. He reflected on the fact that, for all his differences with his family, they had always supported him, even when it became clear that he was livingly openly in a romantic relationship with another man. And so while *Demon of Noon* is unquestionably a gay protest novel, Gordon preserved at the end the loving relationship between Robbie and his parents. In the novel's dedication page, Gordon acknowledged Richardson, as he had done in the previous two novels, but he saved pride of place for his parents and grandparents, using the intimate pet names he had always used for his mother and grandmother: "For Mimi, and for RKM and MPB, with love and gratitude, and for Bonbon with many memories."

Gordon did not publish *Demon* with William Morrow. He may have still been bitter about Morrow's refusal to publish the Vallency novel, or the press was too skittish about the new novel's gay themes. Instead, Gordon got a contract from Julian Messner, a firm that had stunned the publishing world when it appointed a woman, Kathryn Messner, as its president in 1948. Since then, Messner had earned a reputation for publishing unconventional novels that had been rejected by the other top presses.[21] *The Demon of Noon* appeared in print in October 1954, advertised incorrectly as "Gordon Merrick's second novel." Messner billed Gordon as "one of the truly talented young writers of our generation" and described the novel as one that captured the "bittersweet brilliance of Scott Fitzgerald's American expatriates." There was no mention of the novel's gay subplot in the dust jacket or promotional material, only a cryptic reference to Carl's "ambiguous, tantalizing looks at Robbie" and Robbie's untimely relationship with "Toni," whose gender is not clarified. Messner may have hoped that gay readers would pick up on the coded meaning of these terms. They certainly tried to catch the attention of gay male (and straight female) readers by plastering a full-size head shot of Gordon on the dust jacket. Unlike the rugged OSS photo of Gordon on the *Strumpet Wind* cover, this one looks like a Hollywood audition photo. Gordon's face is profiled from the side, accentuating his regal nose, strong cheekbones, and full lips. His thick, glossy hair is windswept and he is looking seductively at someone—a man? a woman?—outside the camera frame. The photo reveals just enough of his bare neck and shoulder to give the impression he is shirtless.

Gay readers noticed. The novel was reviewed in homophile publications, including the *Mattachine Review*, a monthly periodical published by the Los Angeles-based Mattachine Society, one of the earliest gay rights organizations in the United States. (The same issue also featured a review of Rodney Garland's *The Troubled Midnight*.) In his review, Robert Kirk called *Demon* a "well-written book" and "honestly observed," though he faulted the novel's occasional "melodramatic implausibility." He took a highly moralistic and psychological approach to the novel's depiction of homosexuality—a stance that was typical of the magazine:

> [Stuart Cosling] is shocked, of course, when he discovers his son's homosexuality, and in his shock and unbelief sends away Robbie's beloved, thus totally

alienating the boy and propelling him into a defiant life of reckless sexual amorality . . . the study which this novel offers of the mistakes of the father and their demoralizing effect upon his son does constitute a plausible comment on the genesis of homosexuality. In so many fictional case studies of the subject, the repressive, tyrannical father has been held up as the arch-villain. Now Gordon Merrick shows us that the opposite extreme of tolerance and permissiveness can lead in the same direction.[22]

The review echoes Stuart's speech about the necessity of "moral decency" for gay people, and in doing so it shows that *Demon* was very much in line with the prevailing arguments made by gay rights advocates in the 1950s. Writers like Edward Sagarin (Donald Webster Cory) had argued that gay people needed to be model citizens in order to "counteract the unfavorable propaganda to which homosexuals are subject," and Mattachine Society members had agreed.[23]

Strangely, Kirk did not point out what was highly unusual for a gay novel in the 1950s: the gay character does not end up dead, in prison, or alone. Instead, *Demon* ends with Robbie preparing to fight in the war on the side of the Allies—a plot point which Kirk called an "absurdity." He seems not to have known that the novel's author was both gay and *had* served in the Allied forces as an OSS agent. The novel's optimistic ending is all the more striking since it was published in 1954, when anti-gay sentiment in the American publishing scene was at its peak.[24] Other books like Gore Vidal's *City and the Pillar* (1948) and James Baldwin's *Giovanni's Room* (1956) had been more conspicuous as gay novels, but their gay protagonists ended tragically. Gordon's decision to write a heroic gay character—and Messner's willingness to publish it—was unquestionably a daring act.[25]

The Demon of Noon also caught the attention of George Sylvester Viereck, the German-American writer who had a lifelong fascination with theories of sexuality. Most likely gay or bisexual, Viereck had made a mark as a young man for his book of Uranian poetry—i.e., homoerotic poetry whose meaning is thinly veiled by Greco-Roman mythology. He later became a literary pariah after disseminating German propaganda during World War I and acting as an apologist for Hitler before World War II.[26] He wrote a long, five-page review of *Demon* for *Good Times*, an underground erotic magazine that regularly included nude photographs, sexually provocative fiction, and reviews of books considered controversial for their representation of taboo sexual topics.

At the start, Viereck pronounces *Demon* an "extraordinary novel." Far from considering Robbie a supporting character, he calls him "the astonishing young hero of Merrick's book." He notes that while there have been many books about the "untouchable theme" of homosexuality in England and the United States, *Demon of Noon* is among the best: "Merrick introduces certain novel nuances. His canvas is broad, he depicts complicated sex relations with delectable candor. He portrays realistically diverse personalities shifting through the divisions of Kinsey's sexual scale, from 90% 'normal' to 90% homosexual."[27] The entire review is a careful, detailed synopsis of the parts of the story that pertain to Robbie and his various relationships. For Viereck, Stuart's tragic flaw is his initial inability to accept his son's homosexuality—a failure that leads to the disintegration of his common-law marriage to Marthe, Robbie's chronic promiscuity, and (indirectly) the German invasion of France. Viereck, who had idealized the gay subculture of Berlin in the 1920s and who never fully admitted the Nazi persecution of homosexuals, reads *Demon* as an indictment of the sexual ignorance and prudishness of American men—which, as he frames it, contributed to the ascendancy of German Fascism.

The reviews in the *Mattachine Review* and *Good Times* show that at least some midcentury homophile readers recognized *Demon of Noon* as a significant contribution to gay literature. The mainstream "straight" press was a very different story, however. In his review for the *New York Times*, the poet and novelist Kenneth Fearing made no mention of the gay subplot in *Demon*, instead portraying the novel as a battle between naïve individualism and inexorable commercialism. He also made it clear that this was *not* an American problem, but the result of "franc-minded Frenchmen."[28] Fearing was a Leftist writer who had been called before the House Un-American Activities Committee for his associations with Marxist and Communist organizations, and so his anodyne reading of *Demon* may have been an attempt to ward off further scrutiny. Even so, nearly all of the other mainstream reviews also refrained from any mention of the novel's gay material. One outlier, the *St. Louis Post-Dispatch*, vaguely faulted the novel for its "several sordid scenes."[29] Perhaps the most insightful "straight" review came from a woman named Nancy Barr Mavity, a mystery novel writer who had studied philosophy at Cornell before becoming a career journalist at the *Oakland Tribune*. Although she too sidestepped the gay subplot, she had an incisive point about the myopic side of Stuart Cosling's philosophy: "There appears to be a lot more scope for 'living naturally' when you don't have to scrimp and sweat to meet the bills for bare existence."[30] If Gordon had read this review, two things likely would have happened. First, he would have been infuriated by the fact that the caption under his photograph read "Leonard Merrick"—apparently a photocopy editor's sloppy confusion of Gordon with the early twentieth-century British crime novelist. Second, he might have realized that Mavity's insight pertained to himself: a gay man "living naturally" with his male partner in France in large part because he had the economic means to do so.

Like Gordon's first two novels, *The Demon of Noon* was translated into French, as *L'amour est un commencement*, and was well received by the French critics.[31] The novelist Pierre Grenaud, writing for *L'Echo d'Alger*, praised the novel as a "quintessentially Mediterranean work" (*une œuvre typiquement méditerranénne*) and proclaimed Gordon "a psychologist and an animator of life and of landscapes" (*un psychologue et un animateur de vie et de paysages*). Unlike the American reviewers, he mentioned the storyline of Robbie's relationship with a man, though he took a morally conservative approach to it, referring to Robbie's homosexuality as his "irregularity" (*l'anomalie*) and comparing him to a youth who "gets mixed up in a bad crowd, not unlike the Teddy Boys or *zazous*" (*un milieu qui pourrait être celui des Teddy's boys aussi bien que des zazous*).[32] (Teddy Boys were the British equivalent of "greasers," while *zazous* refers to a French teen subculture whose flamboyant clothing was intended as a commentary on government rations.) He also warned "puritanical" readers that the novel contained scenes in which characters swim in the nude.

The success of *Demon* was enough to persuade Messner to publish the Vallency novel, whose English version had been languishing in a pile of unpublished work for more than six years. But Messner had one condition: the "race plot" would have to be removed. The publisher may have been known for taking risks, but it did not want to get embroiled in debates over interracial relationships—and it certainly did not want to appear to be valorizing an interracial couple. (Interracial sex and marriage were still felonies in some states, and *Loving v. Virginia*, the Supreme Court case that ruled anti-miscegenation laws unconstitutional, would not happen for twelve more years.) Gordon agreed to Messner's terms, convinced that the novel would never be published in America otherwise. It was better, he reasoned, to have the novel come out in *some* form rather than not at all. He excised entirely the section in which Lance works for a civil rights firm, and he changed the character of Rose to "Scot," a white divorcee. The novel appeared in October 1955 as *The Vallency Tradition*, advertised as a story about a young, rich man's difficult relationship with his mother. It received only a few reviews, which were generally mixed. The *Saturday Review* mocked the novel for its rehearsal of the cliché of the "poor little rich boy," lamenting that "Mr. Merrick . . . has shown himself capable of better work than this."[33] The *Wilmington News Journal* similarly dismissed it as "a series of tabloid tragedies involving a handsome young millionaire who is dissatisfied with his life."[34] By contrast, Nancy Mavity, who had earlier written a very sensitive review of *Demon of Noon*, thought that *Vallency* actually succeeded in breathing life into the old cliché. She acknowledged the difficulty of getting a reader to sympathize with a wealthy, over-privileged character, but she concluded that "Merrick turns the trick . . . [he] makes his point through action, not preachment, and he maintains a high level, both of suspense and of emotional sympathy with his hero."³⁵ More telling than the mixed reviews was the lack of *any* mention in most newspapers, including the *New York Times*, which for the first time decided not to review one of Gordon's novels. It is not difficult to see why they considered *Vallency* unremarkable. What had started out a trenchant protest novel—one that captivated the French literati with its critique of American racism—had been pared down to an anodyne drama about the burdens of class privilege.

However, the novel was not as anodyne as it might have appeared. Gordon had been compelled to expurgate the race plot in order to get the novel published in America, but in the process of revision he created a new, potentially controversial character. In *The Vallency Tradition*, Gordon added a minor character named Roddie Cameron, a young American who meets Lance at a party. Roddie, whose grandfather is an illustrious American businessman, is a talented painter who lost one of his arms in World War II. Though the novel never explicitly says so, Roddie is gay. Lance quickly becomes friends with Roddie, though he detects a hidden truth about him that he can't put his finger on. In a scene where Roddie is sketching a portrait of Lance, he comes close to revealing his homosexuality:

> "Why don't you get married and have kids?" Lance asked idly. There was a moment of silence and then Roddie spoke coldly from behind him.
> "I care about painting and not another damn thing in this world. And even that's not worth losing an arm over." Lance's throat tightened with sudden pity at the bleakness of the statement. . . .
> "Being creative must make a difference. You can do without other things."
> "You're the most creative person I know," Roddie declared with abrupt intensity. Lance turned with a smile and caught Roddie's eyes on him. For once they were unguarded and revealing and Lance's mouth dropped open at the depth of the hurt in them. They were like wells of tears. He averted his own, abashed at the intimacy of their revelation.

There are many other coded references to Roddie's sexuality in the novel that would have been understood by many gay readers. In one episode Lance notices a collection of Gertrude Stein books in Roddie's house—a seemingly pointless detail, except for the fact that Gordon had been assiduously reading Stein and reflecting on her method of writing a lesbian autobiographical character. In another scene Lance sees the portrait of himself that Roddie has painted, and he is struck by the sensuousness and explicitness with which Roddie captures his naked body: "There could be no doubt that the arms and legs and shoulders were his, the features his, even the sex was his."³⁶ In effect, Gordon compensated for the removal of the original novel's black character by adding a sympathetic gay character—hardly a safe choice in the mid-1950s.

The character of Roddie Cameron is completely extraneous to the novel's plot. But it offers a tantalizing key to the method by which Gordon would later insert himself—as a *gay* man—into his novels. There are many "clues" about Roddie that point to Gordon, from the illustrious grandfather to the World War II experience to the Gertrude Stein book. In his future gay novels, as in *The Vallency Tradition*, Gordon would again fictionalize himself as a painter rather than a writer. In the case of Roddie, moreover, the particular *style* of painting also hints at the kind of gay representation that Gordon would become famous for: sensuous, idealized, and sexually explicit.

NOTES

1. John D'Emilio, *Sexual Politics, Sexual Communities: The Making of a Homosexual Minority in the United States 1940–1970* (Chicago: University of Chicago Press, 1998), 44. See also David K. Johnson, *The Lavender Scare: The Cold War Persecution of Gays and Lesbians in the Federal Government* (Chicago: University of Chicago Press, 2006).
2. Jaime Harker, *Middlebrow Queer: Christopher Isherwood in America* (Minneapolis: University of Minnesota Press, 2013), 12–24.
3. Gordon Merrick to Glenway Wescott, 16 December 1946, Glenway Wescott Papers, box 76, folder 1139.
4. I am grateful to Ann Scott for this observation.
5. Gordon Merrick, *Lancelot 5ème Avenue*, translated by Therese Aubray (Paris: Flammarion, 1950): *Un instant il avait aperçu sa maison sur la colline* (305).
6. Gordon dedicated the novel to Elizabeth Adams Samuel ("Libsy"), a longtime family friend from Philadelphia who would regularly visit him in France. Her husband Snowden Samuel had also attended the Episcopal Academy (several years before Gordon) and had died at a relatively young age in 1939. When Gordon published the English version of the novel years later, he again dedicated it to Samuel.
7. Jeanine Delpech, "Gordon Merrick a choisi la Provence," *Les Nouvelles Littéraires*, March 2, 1950. Translation by Ann Scott.
8. Georges Roditi, "Gordon Merrick: Lancelot Cinquième Avenue," *Flammes: Bulletin D'Information des Éditions Flammarion*, February 1950. Translation by Ann Scott.
9. Max-Pol Fouchet, "Les Livres Etrangers," review of *Lancelot 5ème Avenue* from an unidentified French periodical, c. 1950, GMP, box 21. Translation by Ann Scott.
10. Gilbert Guilleminault, "On ne s'évade pas de la 5e Avenue," review of *Lancelot 5ème Avenue*, unidentified periodical, c. 1950, GMP, box 21. Translation by Ann Scott.

11. Gordon Merrick, *La Rafale Amoureuse*, translated by Denise Meunier (Paris: Flammarion, 1951).

12. "Gordon Merrick," anonymous review of *Lancelot 5ème Avenue*, *La Gazette*, c. 1950, GMP, box 21. My translation.

13. Delpech, "Gordon Merrick a choisi la Provence."

14. "Gordon Merrick," *La Gazette*.

15. Gordon Merrick, *The Demon of Noon* (New York: Julian Messner, 1954), 7–8.

16. Merrick, *Demon of Noon*, 28.

17. Merrick, *Demon of Noon*, 244.

18. Merrick, *Demon of Noon*, 126.

19. Merrick, *Demon of Noon*, 191.

20. Merrick, *Demon of Noon*, 208, 262.

21. "Mrs., Kathryn G. Messner, 61, Chief of Publishing House, Dies," *New York Times*, August 5, 1964.

22. Robert Kirk, "Irony Has a Field Day," *Mattachine Review*, May–June 1955.

23. Donald Webster Cory, *The Homosexual in America: A Subjective Approach*, 2nd ed. (New York: Greenberg, 1959), 157. On the politics of the Mattachine Society and other homophile organizations in the 1950s, see David Eisenbach, *Gay Power: An American Revolution* (New York: Carroll & Graf, 2006), 12–18; D'Emilio, *Sexual Politics, Sexual Communities*, 57–74; Martin Meeker, "Behind the Mask of Respectability: Reconsidering the Mattachine Society and Male Homophile Practice, 1950s and 1960s," *Journal of the History of Sexuality* 10, no. 1 (2001): 78–116.

24. See Christopher Bram, *Eminent Outlaws: The Gay Writers Who Changed America* (New York: Twelve, 2012), 47; Roger H. Tuller, "'A Subject of Absorbing Interest to Mankind': U.S. Supreme Court Obscenity Rulings, 1934–1977," in *The Golden Age of Gay Fiction*, ed. Drewey Wayne Gunn (Albion, NY: MLR Press, 2009), 135–40.

25. In his groundbreaking anthology of pre-Stonewall gay novels, the literary historian Michael Bronski includes *The Demon of Noon* in his list of mainstream American novels with gay subject matter. Michael Bronski, *Pulp Friction: Uncovering the Golden Age of Gay Male Pulps* (New York: St. Martin's Griffin, 2003), 352. Likewise, Roger Austen, in his capacious chapter on 1950s gay fiction, has only a single sentence on *Demon*, which he bafflingly describes as a "chichi" novel concerned with the "gay bohemian" set. Roger Austen, *Playing the Game: The Homosexual Novel in America* (Indianapolis: Bobbs-Merrill, 1977), 191. S. James Elliott, one of the few literary critics to include *Demon* in studies of gay literature, strangely misreads the novel. In addition to misremembering the characters' names and relationships, he seems not to notice that Robbie's character is gay. S. James Elliott, "Homosexuality in the Crucial Decade: Three Novelists' Views," in *The Gay Academic*, ed. Louie Crew, 164–77 (Palm Springs: ETC Publications, 1978).

26. Niel M. Johnson, "George Sylvester Viereck: Poet and Propagandist," *Books at Iowa*, November 1968; D. H. Mader, "The Greek Mirror: The Uranians and Their Use of Greece," *Journal of Homosexuality* 49, nos. 3–4 (2005): 377–420; James J. Gifford, *Glances Backward: An Anthology of American Homosexual Writing 1830–1920* (Peterborough, Ontario: Broadview Press, 2007), 162–74.

27. George Sylvester Viereck, "Sex Is a Demon," *Good Times* 2, no. 15 (1954): 56–64.

28. Kenneth Fearing, "St. Martin's Peninsula," *New York Times*, November 14, 1954.

29. Marion E. Weir, "Between Book Ends: Love Is the Beginning," *St. Louis Post-Dispatch*, February 10, 1955.

30. N. B. M. [Nancy Barr Mavity], "Freedom's Cost: Doing What Comes Naturally Is Not So Easy as It Sounds," *Oakland Tribune*, January 16, 1955.

31. Gordon Merrick, *L'amour est un commencement*, translated by Hélène Claireau (Flammarion, 1955).

32. Pierre Grenaud, "Aux Couleurs du Temps," *L'Echo d'Alger*, [1955], GMP, box 21. Translation by Ann Scott.

33. Jerome Stone, "Also Noted," *Saturday Review*, January 7, 1956.

34. "Fiction Shelf," *Wilmington News Journal*, October 17, 1955.

35. Nancy Barr Mavity, "Two Novels Defy Old Notions," *Oakland Tribune*, January 15, 1956.

36. Gordon Merrick, *The Vallency Tradition* (New York: Julian Messner, 1955), 174, 243. One of the unintended clues about Roddie's homosexuality is a typo on page 173 that has "Robbie" instead of "Roddie," suggesting that Gordon had absentmindedly used the name of the gay character in *Demon of Noon*.

Chapter Eight

The Dancer from San Francisco

By 1955 Gordon had found his stride as a novelist, though his personal life was in flux. Perhaps tired of chicken farming, Gordon and Richardson had moved to Paris, exchanging their rustic stone house in Provence for an urbane apartment at 1 Avenue de Tourville, near Napoleon's tomb in the 7th arrondissement. Gordon thought this a good move professionally, since it gave him more visibility among the French literati who had become his champions. A French magazine featured an article about him in his Parisian apartment, with a photograph of a serious-looking Gordon at work on a manuscript. A stunning view of the Musée de l'Armée appears in the background. Living in Paris also meant access to theater and friends, such as Ginette Spanier, whose apartment near the Champs-Élysées was a regular destination for celebrities like Laurence Olivier and Claudette Colbert. "More saloon than a salon," she liked to say about her home, which was covered with red carpet. Invigorated by the city's energy, Gordon started writing his fourth novel, a story inspired by a former French Resistance fighter he had recently met.[1]

Gordon was less sanguine about his relationship with Richardson. There had already been signs of trouble in Provence, where they had been drinking and fighting in public with increasing frequency. Ena Fitzpatrick and Alexander Hochberg later recalled that "the Gassin boys, while expressing all the devotion in the world for each other, were constantly quarrelling. Often these quarrels were provoked by over indulgence in drink and they would sometimes end in blows and black eyes."[2] A big source of contention was the issue of monogamy. Richardson was committed to Gordon, but he wanted to open up their relationship to allow affairs with other men. For Gordon, such an arrangement felt like a betrayal. He was instinctively possessive and distrustful in his relationships, and so any affairs would have been extremely threatening.[3] There had likely already been some incidents in Provence. At one point Gordon got rid of a beautiful local Frenchman, most likely because there was something going between him and Richardson, by "shipping" him to Glenway Wescott at his farm in New Jersey. The man was Henri de la

Figure 8.1 Gordon in his Paris apartment.
Source: Estate of Gordon Merrick.

Celle, a former French Resistance fighter—possibly the same one who had inspired the new novel—whom Wescott described as having "solemn, almost anguished good manners, château-style; and a certain antique beauty; very tall with elongated face, like Henri II, that is, like a stag." De la Celle briefly tempted Wescott, but Wescott quickly sent him away to live with his brother before anything could happen.[4]

In Paris there were inevitably many more distractions like Henri de la Celle. Gordon had been mulling the possibility of breaking up with Richardson, but he was hesitant to take such a big step after being together for more than ten years. The impetus for change finally came, unexpectedly, in the form of a young, ebullient dancer from San Francisco. In 1956 Gordon met Charles Gerald Hulse, a twenty-seven-year-old American who was working as a cabaret dancer at the Lido, the legendary nightclub on the Champs-Élysées in Paris. Although Gordon was still officially in a relationship with Richardson, he sensed immediately that this smiling, sparkly eyed man would change the course of his life. He was right.

Hulse, or "Charley" as his family called him, was born on March 26, 1929, in Berryville, a small town in northwest Arkansas that proudly advertises itself as the city "where history meets progress." His father, Clarence Hulse, worked variously as a steam fitter and air conditioner technician, while his mother May, who had always dreamed of being a teacher, taught regularly at public schools. At the time he had one brother, Clarence Jr., who was a year older than him. Because of the scarcity of jobs in the Midwest following the Depression, the family moved around frequently during Charles's childhood. In 1937, while living in Galena, Missouri, Clarence packed the family into their large Dodge sedan and moved them to Glendale, California, where he got a job working at one of the nearby farms. A few years later, Clarence Jr. suffered a sinus infection and died. As Hulse's younger brother Larry explained it, "these were the days before penicillin, and the only antibiotic was not a good one." The next year the family moved back to Arkansas. Such itinerancy left a lasting mark on Hulse, who for much of his life found it hard to stay in one place.[5]

From a relatively early age Hulse knew two things about himself. First, he was attracted to boys more than girls. Second, he wanted to be a dancer. He later wrote about both desires in *In Tall Cotton*, a fictionalized autobiography of his boyhood years. In the book he recalls being a five-year-old boy who was constantly teased by a neighbor for his love of dancing:

> "That silly kid's a dancer," Bonnie Lou's father said one day. . . . They moved away . . . leaving tingling memories in my loins and the ringing in my ears of "That silly kid's a dancer." I already knew I was going to be a dancer, but

Bonnie Lou's father was the first to recognize it. I'm going to be one day. One way or another.[6]

When he was sixteen years old, Hulse really did find a way. Determined to get out of Arkansas, he packed a bag one day and boarded a bus for San Francisco. He had paid for the bus ticket by borrowing money from his father, who gruffly told him this would be "the last he was getting from him." The sight of Hulse leaving on the bus was devastating for his four-year-old brother Larry, who idolized him and called him his "main buddy."

Once in San Francisco, Hulse quickly established himself in the city's entertainment culture. He enrolled in classes at a dance school on Haight Street, and before long he was getting dancing jobs at USO shows and nightclubs in the city—including the Copacabana, the glamorous nightclub on Fisherman's Wharf that was frequented by Hollywood stars and other celebrities. Legally, Hulse was too young to be hired as a dancer in some of these places, but the club owners were more than willing to overlook a minor technicality like his age. He was very talented *and* very attractive, and as such he was very good for business.

Hulse took advantage of the opportunities that San Francisco presented to a young, handsome gay man—and he had more than his share of admirers. When he was nineteen, he moved into the Sunset District neighborhood with a man who was twenty years his senior and who flew him to Hawaii on a privately chartered jet.[7] It's unclear whether the relationship was romantic in nature, but Hulse's undeniable charm surely had some influence over the situation. He also started to dabble in the theater, taking drama classes at San Francisco City College and joining a community theater that was known for its summer revues.[8] He might have continued as a local *belle of the ball* were it not for the outbreak of the Korean War in the summer of 1950. Hulse enlisted in the U.S. Air Force, where he served as a junior officer for three years during the war.[9] For much of this time he was stationed at Griffiss Air Force Base in Rome, New York, a town which he referred to as "a hell hole." Recognizing his stage talents, the Air Force conscripted him to perform in shows that toured other bases. One of these shows was a play about Air Force pilots written by one of the servicemen—"a perfectly dreadful little play," as Hulse later remembered it. The play was called *Flameout*, a title that was surely a source of amusement for Hulse and his fellow gay soldiers.[10]

As soon as his military service ended in September 1953, Hulse fled to New York City to pursue an acting career. He found a small apartment on West 50th Street, in Hell's Kitchen, and started auditioning for theater gigs. His combination of acting skills, dancing talent, and good looks soon landed him a role in the touring production of Rodgers and Hammerstein's *The King and I*, which was just ending its three-year run on Broadway. Yul Brynner, who had created the role of the King of Siam for the Broadway production, was staying on for the national tour. Hulse was cast as the Interpreter and Priest, effectively replacing Otis Bigelow—coincidentally, Gordon's former lover and roommate fifteen years earlier—who was leaving the show after its Broadway run in order to try his luck in Hollywood. (Bigelow's gambit turned out to be a flop, since he got only one movie gig—an uncredited, one-line part in a film called *Designing Woman*, which starred Gregory Peck and Lauren Bacall.) Since the tour began only three days after the Broadway run ended, Hulse was able to meet Bigelow and get advice about the role. The two men did not hit it off. As Hulse recounted in an interview decades later,

> I replaced a man called Otis Bigelow, who I thought was the most beautiful man I had ever seen in my life.... He was quite upset that I could fit into his costumes. He was quite the body man, you see. I couldn't fill out the chest like he could, but our waists were the same, and he was outraged. Quite a vain young man.[11]

Hulse may have been right about Bigelow (whose vanity is suggested in Charles Kaiser's *Gay Metropolis*), but he was also biased by his experience in the show. Throughout the tour he was constantly compared to Otis Bigelow by critics and audience members. "We saw *The King and I* on Broadway last year," one midwestern theatergoer told him after a performance, "and *you* were supposed to be Otis Bigelow."[12] After fifteen months on tour, Hulse quit the show, and, with the money he had saved, he boarded a ship to Europe—a childhood dream of his.[13] He was unpleasantly surprised to learn that, even in Europe, he could not escape Bigelow's shadow. "Everywhere I went, people would say, 'What do you do?,'" he recalled. "I'd say, 'I was in *The King and I*. They'd say, 'Ah, do you know Otis Bigelow?'"[14] Hulse detested the name.

Hulse's main passion remained dancing, and when he returned to America he got work doing burlesque shows in Hollywood. For a while he had a job as a backup dancer for two of the circuit's most popular strippers, Lotus Wing and Bobby "Bouncy" Bruce. This kept him busy, but he was not enamored with Hollywood. He longed to get back to San Francisco or even Europe, which he had found exciting. An opportunity arose when he learned that the famous Lido club in Paris was holding auditions for dancers. A famous cabaret that attracted a well-heeled clientele, the Lido was well known for its spectacular dinner shows featuring troupes of dancers. Hulse was offered a contract, and in a matter of days he was on his way back to Paris. He was one of four male dancers performing two shows a night, seven nights a week, and getting paid a "hot salary" of one hundred dollars per week.[15] He shared a "tiny, tiny house" in the 16th arrondissement near the Arc de Triomphe with one of the other dancers, Brad Cartwright, an older athletic man who

Figure 8.2 Charles Hulse's headshot for the Lido program.
Source: Estate of Charles Hulse.

had been at the Lido for a few years and who had danced on Broadway in the 1940s.

Working at the Lido gave Hulse another, more star-studded, opportunity. Stanley Donen and Leonard Gershe's *Funny Face*, a Hollywood musical starring Fred Astaire and Audrey Hepburn, was being shot on location in Paris, and male dancers were needed for the film's several musical numbers. Since the dance numbers were also being filmed in Paris, the production team held auditions locally, and Hulse won a coveted spot in the film's seven-man dance troupe. In the film, even though the dancers are always identically dressed and choreographed as a group, Hulse stands out with his trademark smile, devilish eyebrows, and sparkling eyes. A film still from one of the musical numbers shot on site at the Ritz Hotel shows Hulse tap-dancing next to the actress Kay Thompson—his facial expression and head position clearly setting him apart from the other dancers. At the time Hepburn was married to Mel Ferrer, Gordon's close friend at Princeton—another coincidence, though it's not clear if Hulse met Ferrer while performing in *Funny Face*.

Hulse finally met Gordon himself one night in March 1956. Since his shows at the Lido didn't begin until ten at night, he usually had time to socialize in the early evening with other gay men in Paris, typically at a gay bar or a pre-show cocktail party. Cartwright took him to one of these parties, and there was Gordon—alone, since Richardson was out of town that week. What followed could have been a scene from a film (or a Gordon Merrick novel). Hulse saw Gordon across the room and was instantly bewitched. Ever the uninhibited one, he walked straight up to Gordon and said, "You're the most attractive man I've ever seen." Gordon was nearly forty years old, thirteen years older than Hulse, but Hulse hardly noticed their difference in age. "He looked 24," he claimed afterward.[16]

The romance almost ended before it began. After chatting for a while, they discovered they shared a background in the theater. When Gordon asked what shows he had been in, Hulse mentioned *The King and I*. "Do you know Otis Bigelow?" was Gordon's immediate response. "Thank you very much," said an annoyed Hulse, "I don't need this Mr. Merrick." Fortunately, the two got past this initial awkwardness and made arrangements to meet later that night after Hulse had finished his shows at the Lido. They agreed to meet at 3:00

Figure 8.3 Charles Hulse (far left) dancing in *Funny Face* (1957).
Source: Paramount Pictures.

a.m. at Le Carrousel, a plush gay nightclub near the Champs-Élysées that was known for its drag performances. Hulse arrived at the club with a friend, but Gordon was nowhere to be found. He had a beer, and, concluding that Gordon had stood him up, decided to go with his friend to a "very grubby" gay bar in Montparnasse. He and his friend were outside Le Carrousel preparing to get inside their car—a "dirty little" Deux Chevaux—when he was spotted by Gordon, who had been running late and was hurrying up the street toward the club. At that moment Hulse had bent down to adjust his shoe while the car door was wide open. Before Hulse could see him, Gordon nimbly whisked himself behind Hulse into the passenger seat. Hulse got into car and sat down—right onto Gordon's lap. "We meet again," said a smiling Gordon. They drove to the gay bar in Montparnasse with Hulse sitting snugly on Gordon's lap the entire ride. Afterward Hulse went back to Gordon's small apartment near Napoleon's tomb and spent the night.[17]

The two saw each other constantly after that first night. Hulse would often come back to his house after work to find Gordon sitting on the steps outside the front gate, waiting for him. It was a dreamy romance but also a complicated one. Gordon was still living with Richardson, a fact he had disclosed to Hulse their first night together. Gordon intended to break things off with Richardson—indeed he had been considering it for months—but it would not be easy since Richardson had no desire to end the relationship. When Richardson returned to Paris, Gordon told him about Hulse—a bombshell that, as Hulse put it, "went down with the usual thud." Richardson refused to leave the apartment, convinced that Hulse was only a passing phase for Gordon. As Gordon and Richardson fought endlessly about their relationship, Hulse wondered if he had gotten himself into a quagmire. He had fallen hard for Gordon, but the drama with Richardson was giving him doubts. And his occasional run-ins with Richardson only made the situation more awkward, partly because Hulse made no attempt to hide his dislike. "I was not, as you say, particularly congenial to him," he admitted.[18]

Gordon realized that he and Hulse needed to get away from Paris, at least for a while. He had been traveling to Greece lately, and so he asked Hulse to come along with him for a two-week tour of the islands. Hulse was thrilled, but he didn't know how he could leave the Lido for two weeks. He asked his manager for a vacation and got a curt reply. "Sure, you can have two weeks off," said his manager, "*if* you can find a replacement who can fit your costume without any alterations, and *if* you can teach him all your routines so that he steps in without a hitch." "You've made it practically impossible," Hulse grumbled. But he did find a replacement: a handsome Dutch boy named Arthur who had been one of the other dancers in *Funny Face*. Hulse knew that Arthur learned routines quickly, and he also knew that they wore the same size. The *reason* he knew Arthur's size had to do with their earlier history. He had been attracted to Arthur when they first met and had invited him over to the house for a drink. In an attempt to break the ice, Hulse devised an elaborate ruse in which he "bet" that they were the same exact size—but in order to know for sure they would have to take each other's measurements. He proceeded to compare their height, shoulder width, arm length, waist, etc., giving him several opportunities to make body contact. Cartwright was at home witnessing the whole charade—"You're an embarrassment," he told Hulse disapprovingly. Hulse eventually told the story to Gordon, who later used it in the first love scene in *The Lord Won't Mind*—a scene that would be ridiculed by critics who thought it was too ridiculous to be believable.

Hulse flew to Athens, where Gordon was waiting for him. They hopped on a boat and headed to Mykonos, which Gordon had heard was one of the more touristy spots in the Mediterranean. It was an immediate disappointment. The island was unexpectedly plain looking, full of craggy steps and impossible walkways, and the strong winds were unbearable. Gordon apologized, and he proposed going to a nearby island called Hydra, which was his personal favorite. "Fine," said Hulse, "just get me the fuck out of here." Compared to Mykonos, Hydra was a revelation. Sailing into Hydra was itself a cinematic experience. The shape of the island makes it so that the harbor is not visible to boats until the moment they enter the port, at which point the entire harbor dramatically comes into view, a picturesque panorama of cascading white houses and rustic fishing boats. Hulse was awestruck, and he felt himself falling harder for Gordon.

When they got back to Paris, Gordon and Hulse started to discuss moving in together. Before any plans could be made, however, Gordon got the unexpected news from America that his father had died. Gordon was overwhelmed. He had lost his grandmother only five years earlier, and he had not expected to lose one of his parents so soon. Although he had always been closer to his mother, he knew that Rodney Merrick had loved him. Gordon had rarely been able to talk to his father, an investment broker, about his literary or theatrical passions, but he had always been able to count on him for support (and for financial advice). When *The Strumpet Wind* was published, it had been Rodney who had put pressure on William Morrow to make sure the publisher did not skimp on its contractual obligations.[19] Gordon was especially concerned about his mother, who was now alone for the first time in her life. He quickly made arrangements for a plane to America and arrived in New York on November 16, 1956, just in time for his father's burial service at the Greenwood Cemetery in Brielle, New Jersey.[20]

Around this same time Hulse's contract with the Lido was coming to an end, and he had no desire to renew it. Since Gordon was not ready to return to France so soon after his father's death, he suggested that Hulse simply come back to America and live with him. Hulse still had his Hell's Kitchen apartment from his *King and I* days, so they reasoned that they could live there, reassured by the fact that Gordon's family would be only a short train ride away. Hulse finished his Lido contract and got on a transatlantic steamliner from Calais to New York. His memory of arriving in New York would stay with him for the rest of his life: as he was getting off the boat he saw Gordon standing on the dock and waiting for him, looking more handsome than ever. Hulse had one word to describe the experience: "It was devastating." Gordon must have felt the significance of the moment also. Eleven years earlier *he* had been the one arriving in New York on a ship from France, with Richardson waiting for him. In a strange way his romantic life had come full circle. Gordon had planned a glittering night for Hulse's arrival, including dinner and a show. They went to the RKO Palace Theatre on Broadway and saw the opening performance of Judy Garland in concert. It would be hard to imagine a clearer sign from the universe that they were destined to be together.

They stayed in New York for a few months while Hulse looked for a theater job. None turned up, so Hulse "tossed in his jock strap" and suggested they leave. Instead of going back to France, however, they decided to go to San Francisco, Hulse's former stomping grounds. Gordon had never been farther west than Chicago, so it would be a new adventure for him. He made a quick trip back to Paris to pick up some of his belongings and take care of some business matters, and was back on a ship to New York in May 1957.[21] In the meantime Hulse had bought a car, a secondhand British Ford convertible—"a beautiful little pale blue job"—to take them across the country. They found an apartment in Sausalito, a few miles north of San Francisco near the Golden Gate Bridge. The city had been the site of a major shipyard during World War II, but now it was home to artists, writers, and hippies—all drawn to the woody environs and cheap rents.[22] Their apartment on Edwards Avenue was near the top of a narrow, sloping road with a stunning view of Richardson Bay on one side and Alcatraz on the other. Hulse reconnected with friends in San Francisco and quickly got a job teaching dance at a school for children.

Gordon had a harder time adjusting to their new home. Having lived his entire life in the northeastern United States and Europe, he found the bohemian culture of the Bay Area to be a foreign new world—one he didn't care for. He later recalled his sense of displacement in *An Idol for Others*, when Walter moves from New York to San Francisco to be with his lover Tom:

> They had been to some outrageous gay bars. They had seen some shows Walter found well-meaning, sometimes exuberant, but rarely professional. They had been to parties. He found the city—despite its vaunted cosmopolitanism, its exotic touches, the flamboyant drag prevalent in some of its streets, its

sumptuously decorated houses and apartments—as pleasantly provincial as he remembered it. The atmosphere was casual and diffuse.... It was a challenge.[23]

Because of finances, Gordon was not able to get back to New York until the following February, which meant Christmas in California. He found himself pining for his friends in New York and Europe, and so he was especially cheered when he got a letter from Glenway Wescott. "Apparently, Christmas *can* bring happy surprises," he wrote to Wescott, "your card has stirred up the few old dying embers of my faith in the institution."[24]

Still, he tried to make the best of things. He had just finished his fourth novel, *The Hot Season*—which he dedicated to Hulse, though he also thanked Richardson "for his many valuable editorial suggestions and his constant assistance in preparing this book." The book was published by William Morrow, which had published *The Strumpet Wind* but had rejected the subsequent novel. Since for the first time Gordon was in the United States at the same time one of his books was published, William Morrow urged him to do publicity with the American media. This was something he had managed to avoid with his first three novels, to his detriment. (Even prickly John Horne Burns, who had a somewhat antagonistic relationship with the press, had done publicity for *The Gallery*.) In any case, given the lukewarm American reception of his last two novels, it was a good idea to remind the literati who he was. He wrote a full-page article for the *San Francisco Chronicle* in which he talked about his inspiration for the new novel, and he did a feature article for the local Sausalito newspaper in which he pretended to enjoy California more than France or Greece.[25] He even did radio interviews, hoping his mellifluous voice would help book sales.

Unfortunately, the strategy did not work. When *The Hot Season* appeared in early 1958, it was virtually ignored by the critics. It received good reviews in the same Bay Area newspapers for which Gordon had done publicity, but nationally it got only a scattering of short, lukewarm reviews that pigeonholed it as "excitement-escape" fiction.[26] More disappointing, sales of the book were dismal. Even though William Morrow had been conservative in the size of the first printing run, it was unable to sell all its copies. The bleak sales figures meant that a paperback edition was out of the question. This would be the first—and only—published novel by Gordon that would not appear in paperback.

The failure of *The Hot Season* had much to do with the novel itself. Its plot centers on David Spofford, an American intelligence officer on assignment in an unnamed Mediterranean island nation during the Cold War. The island, whose proximity to Communist countries has made it an object of rivalry between the U.S. and Russia, is about to hold its first democratic presidential election. Spofford's mission is to protect Manoussein, the expected winner, from a preemptive coup d'état by the current regime. Spofford hides him in various places in the country, trying to evade the regime's mercenaries. Manoussein does not trust the Americans, however, and he has Spofford abducted and taken to a nearby island. Spofford manages to escape, only to find that his American supervisor is helping the regime, which has cancelled the elections and issued an arrest warrant for Manoussein. The American government had decided an alliance with a dictatorship would be more effective in fending off the Russians. At first Spofford refuses to give up Manoussein, effectively quitting his job. Meanwhile he discovers his wife is having an affair with a young American journalist who has been tracking Manoussein. In a final, desperate attempt to keep his family together, Spofford acquiesces and surrenders Manoussein. The novel ends with Spofford preparing to return to America, trying to convince himself that his betrayal of Manoussein, and of his own ethics, was in the interest of the greater good: "His betrayal of everything he believed in was as complete and abject as his betrayal of the old politician. And yet he had done his duty in his country's service . . . he had won the sanction and support of his community."[27]

Stylistically, *The Hot Season* is well written. By now Gordon had perfected a clear, Fitzgeraldesque style that he would use for the rest of his life. But it is also his least interesting and least engaging novel. By focusing so much on foreign intrigue and action sequences, Gordon left little room to create complex or sympathetic characters. The novel's only interpersonal plot—the extramarital affair—shows that Gordon still struggled with female characters. It is worth noting that this is also the only novel by Gordon that does not have a gay character (except for a brief paragraph in which Spofford is solicited by a male prostitute). Like the earlier novels, *The Hot Season* is undeniably a protest novel. Its main theme is the tyranny of powerful Western nations, whose hidden economic and political systems render the actions of the average individual irrelevant: "The source of power is far removed from the lives of the ordinary individual. . . . Political action as you conceive it, as an expression of individual will, no longer has any meaning."[28] Yet the political message feels sterile because of the novel's deliberate *vagueness*. There are almost no references to specific places, persons, or events in its 240 pages, producing a suspense thriller that seems contrived. Gordon eventually realized this, admitting afterward in an interview that *The Hot Season* was a "a great literary failure."[29]

Ironically, the vagueness that makes *The Hot Season* a failure may also be what makes it interesting from a historical perspective. It is possible that the novel is based on a mission that Gordon carried out—but never publicly disclosed—on behalf of the American government in the early 1950s. If so, the novel's vagueness is likely intended to protect classified information. Many details in the novel suggest the island of Cyprus, which had become a point of potential conflict between the U.S. and Russia. Gordon's passport from the 1950s shows that he took regular trips to Piraeus, one of the Greek ports by which Cyprus was directly accessible.[30] The reasons for these were never explained. In an interview given years later, Gordon admitted that, after the war, he had been approached by the French secret service and offered French citizenship "in return for more snooping." He turned down the offer, though he did not comment on whether he had been approached by the CIA, which regularly recruited former OSS agents.[31] In any case, it would have been extremely unusual for Gordon to devise a narrative out of whole cloth, and the novel's obsession with a specific aspect of Cold War politics is too arcane not to have come from somewhere. In the *San Francisco Chronicle* article, he claimed the novel was inspired by a French Resistance fighter he had met and an American intelligence officer he had known in the OSS. He did not identify either, but his description of the Frenchman sounds remarkably like himself: "a dashing figure, the offspring of an ancient and distinguished family, a man of taste and varied intellectual attainments. He was an idealist, a humanist, with passionate faith in the sanctity of the individual."[32]

Despite his disappointment over *The Hot Season*, Gordon continued writing, keeping to his disciplined routine while Hulse spent his days driving all over the Bay Area teaching dance classes. His next novel, which he wrote almost entirely in California, was yet another attempt to combine political intrigue, marriage drama, and a critique of American capitalism. The novel focuses on an American couple whose marriage is tested when they travel to the French Riviera and meet a group of glamorous tourists from America and Europe. A related plotline involves the discovery of a Nazi war profiteer who is living luxuriously under a false identity. In many ways, the novel is even worse than *The Hot Season*. The plot is labored and plodding, and the main characters are generally unsympathetic. And it further confirms Gordon's inability to write convincing female characters. Most of the women in the novel are either matriarchal gorgons or sexually submissive naïfs—the two types that Gordon perennially recycled. Unsurprisingly, the new novel was never published.

However, the novel did have one interesting feature: an openly gay character who has a substantial subplot and who is more explicitly autobiographical than anything Gordon had written before. William Marbury (a play on Gordon's full given name, William Gordon Merrick) is an American writer who worked for a New York newspaper before becoming a novelist. Now an expatriate in the south of France, he speaks flawless French and regularly turns his friends into characters in his novels. Marbury does not hide his sexuality from his friends and even brings his French boyfriend to their social gatherings. Such openness initially surprises the married Americans, who have only known gay men to be repressed or closeted.

In a long scene midway through the novel, Gordon writes the narrative from Marbury's perspective. He is drinking alone at a bar in Cannes, looking at the other patrons and pondering his place in society. He reflects on his married friends, with all their trials and tribulations, and wonders what it would be like if *he* could get married to another man:

> Christ on a cross, he'd like to get married, too. Who to, chum? Louis Bonchamps? Was there any spectacle more ludicrous than two graying and fortyish young men, so carefully young, wearing their youth like some carefully preserved garment, playing house together, with cats instead of children? No, there was no permanence for him, nothing stable, only a succession of doomed adventures, and fame was his only hope. Fame granted special dispensations. The whole thing would acquire a sort of literary unreality, like Gide.[33]

This fear—that an aging gay couple is inherently "ludicrous"—surfaces regularly in Gordon's later gay novels, usually in characters who are struggling to reconcile their sexuality with their preconceived notions of the world. At this point in the novel, Gordon could have explored Marbury's conflict further and suggested different possibilities than the ones Marbury imagines. Instead, he fell back onto stereotype. Marbury is approached by an attractive young French man in the bar and, thinking the guy is hitting on him, invites him to his hotel room. When Marbury makes a move in the hotel, the man recoils in disgust and beats him within an inch of his life. Marbury does not appear again in the novel, but we learn that he is in the hospital, barely alive and too ashamed to press charges against his assailant. His fate exemplifies the convention of representing gay characters as tragic, helpless figures—what Roger Austen calls the impossibility of the "happy homosexual" in midcentury American fiction.[34]

The "tragic gay" convention was a regression for Gordon, whose earlier *Demon of Noon* had suggested at least the possibility of a happy life for its gay character. Gordon was nearly forty-two when he wrote the unpublished novel, the same age as the "ludicrous . . . graying" gay man that haunts Marbury's imagination. Even though he was living happily with Hulse, he seems to have been wrestling with the same conflict as Marbury—the fear that there is a fundamental, fatal difference between him and his married, heterosexual friends. More signs of this struggle appeared in a review of Truman Capote's *Breakfast at Tiffany's* that Gordon wrote for the *New Republic* around the same time (incidentally, the only review of a prominent American gay writer that Gordon ever published). In the review he carps about Capote's Holly Golightly, who reminds him of a character in a Christopher Isherwood novel and who offends decorum by transgressing gender categories: "She has a streaky blond head like a boy's, she has a body like a boy's, she talks like a boy. . . . Having divested herself of desirability for the fastidious by her declared promiscuity, she can remain just a good chum as she strolls across the room stark naked. Capote writes of her with rapt admiration." There is a subtle, transphobic sneer here at Capote's sympathy for Golightly. As the review continues it grows yet more pharisaical, particularly when it gets to a passage by Capote that sounds like a defense of same-sex marriage:

> The point of Miss Golightly is that she believes in love. As one of the characters says of her, "She's a *real* phony." In the words of the young lady herself, "A person ought to be able to marry men or women or—listen, if you came to me and said you wanted to hitch up with Man o' War, I'd respect your feelings." She's obviously a comfortable girl to have around, if you're inclined to get a crush on a horse or some other eccentric love object.[35]

There are distinct echoes here of Gordon's Marbury, for whom the notion of two married men is nothing other than "ridiculous."

Clearly, living near San Francisco did not have a liberating effect on Gordon. If anything, the bohemian, queer cultures that permeated this "wide-open town" provoked his conservative impulses.[36] He and Hulse had moved out of the Sausalito apartment and bought a house in Mill Valley, using money that Gordon's mother had given them for a down payment. This put them a few miles farther away from the city, next to Cascade Falls and the slopes of Mount Tamalpais. Even with this natural splendor in his backyard, Gordon was starved for inspiration for a new novel. He continued to write book reviews for the *New Republic*, but at present he had no good prospects for another successful novel.[37] Perhaps if he had moved closer to San Francisco and explored its gay spaces—its gay bars, drag shows, homophile organizations—he would have gotten ideas for new characters and stories. He might have met members of the Mattachine Society (which had moved from Los Angeles to San Francisco) who had read *Demon of Noon* and were eager to talk about the future of gay literature. Instead, he stubbornly clung to his notion of the gay scene as an insular ghetto—a "half-world of exclusive homosexuality," as he later termed it.[38] In one of the few stories he set in San Francisco, Gordon described the city as visually attractive but spiritless: "San Francisco is beautiful if looked at from the right angles but much of it has the thrown-together, unadorned bleakness of a frontier town. . . . It could be almost anywhere."[39]

While Gordon was more than ready to leave San Francisco, Hulse needed more convincing. For one thing, his family was now living in the area. They had been living in Michigan when Gordon and Hulse drove from New York to California, and Hulse had suggested stopping in Michigan to introduce Gordon to his family. The meeting was far more awkward than Hulse had anticipated. He had planned to introduce Gordon first as a friend so that his family could get to know him before learning the full truth about their relationship. Hulse's sister however ruined his plans by "blurt[ing] the whole thing out to my father in the most unattractive way." Hulse's father was a very conservative Southern man—a "real redneck," as Hulse called him—and reacted with rage. Shortly afterward, Hulse's father wrote him a letter, railing about the situation and referring to Gordon as "a man who's lower than a snake's asshole." Eventually, however, Hulse's family—including his father—came around and accepted Gordon as Hulse's partner. Ever the itinerants, at some point in 1958 or 1959 Hulse's parents and brother moved to the Bay Area, so for a brief period his family was reunited. Even though Hulse himself wasn't feeling immensely "fulfilled" in California, it would take some persuasion to get him to pack up again and leave.

Such persuasion came in the form of Bob Richardson, who one day out of the blue showed up on their doorstep in Mill Valley. It was Hulse who answered the door. "Fuck," he said. He had long been in the habit of calling Richardson his "nemesis," and, true to form, here was the monster himself at his front door, sobbing and asking to see Gordon. Richardson slept on their couch that night, much to Hulse's annoyance. At that point, Hulse was "ready to go back to Paris and dance naked anywhere" if it meant getting away from the intolerable Richardson. As luck would have it, around the same time another person showed up at their house, asking if they were interested in selling it. Gordon looked at Hulse and asked, "Do you want to sell the house?" Hulse's answer was short and simple: "No, but I will."[40]

Within a couple of months they were back on the *Mauritania* headed to France, headed back to the Paris apartment. It was the same ship they had taken separately before on their transatlantic voyages. Now they were on it together. Richardson, for his part, stayed in the Bay Area, where he lived for the rest of his life.

NOTES

1. "Un écrivain dans le Quartier des Invalides," clipping from an unknown magazine, private collection; Ginette Spanier, *And Now It's Sables* (London: Robert Hale, 1970), 31–33; Gordon Merrick, "The Frenchman and the American Merged—And Merrick Had a Novel," *San Francisco Chronicle*, March 30, 1958.

2. L. J. Ludovici, *The Three of Us* (London: Marjay Books, 1993), 67.

3. Keith Howes, "Once A Spy . . . ", *Gay News*, August 24, 1978; Gordon Merrick, interview by Brandon Judell.

4. Glenway Wescott, *Continual Lessons: The Journals of Glenway Wescott, 1937–1955*, ed. Robert Phelps and Jerry Rosco (New York: Farrar, Straus and Giroux, 1990), 239–40.

5. Lawrence Hulse, interview by the author; 1940 Population Schedule, Los Angeles County, U.S. Census Bureau.

6. Charles Hulse, *In Tall Cotton* (Secaucus, NJ: Lyle Stuart, 1987), 29–30.

7. Passenger Manifest, Pan American Airways, Flight Number 80209, May 8, 1948.

8. David Perry, "A Gentleman from Another Country," *Bay Area Reporter*, June 30, 1988; Hortense Morton, "Theater School Planned by Straw Hat Group," *San Francisco Examiner*, August 15, 1954.

9. U.S. World War II draft registration card for Charles Gerald Hulse, serial no. W-317, order no. 11006, Draft Board 129, Kings County, California, March 26, 1947.

10. Perry, "A Gentleman from Another Country."

11. Perry, "A Gentleman from Another Country."

12. Charles Hulse, interview by the author.

13. Passenger list, USS *Liberté*, Le Havre, France to New York, July 8, 1955.

14. Perry, "A Gentleman from Another Country."

15. Perry, "A Gentleman from Another Country."

16. Perry, "A Gentleman from Another Country"; Charles Hulse, interview.

17. Perry, "A Gentleman from Another Country"; Charles Hulse, interview.

18. Charles Hulse, interview. The next five paragraphs are also based on this interview.

19. Gordon Merrick to Mary Merrick, 3 March 1947, private collection.

20. "Rodney K. Merrick Dies; Investment Broker Was 70," *Philadelphia Inquirer*, November 15, 1956.

21. U.S. Passport for William Gordon Merrick, issued January 21, 1954, GMP, box 19, folder 12.

22. Sausalito Historical Society, http://sausalitohistoricalsociety.com/sausalito-history.

23. Gordon Merrick, *An Idol for Others* (New York: Avon Books, 1977), 362.

24. Gordon Merrick to Glenway Wescott, 23 December 1957, Glenway Wescott Papers, box 76, folder 1139.

25. Merrick, "Frenchman and the American"; "Author Gordon Merrick Hops Atlantic to Exotic Locales," *Independent Journal*, April 26, 1958.

26. Joan Gill, "Merrick's New Novel Has Merit," *Miami News*, March 23, 1958.

27. Gordon Merrick, *The Hot Season* (New York: William Morrow, 1958), 242.

28. Merrick, *The Hot Season*, 84.

29. Michel Mabille, "De Ceylan à Tricqueville: La vie mouventée d'un écrivain américain," *L'éveil de Pont-Audemer*, August 27, 1981. Translation by Ann Scott.

30. U.S. Passport for Merrick.

31. Keith Howes, "Once A Spy." Gordon's passports in the 1950s and '60s also show a number of trips throughout the Mediterranean and central Europe that are not explained in any extant letter or diary. In a letter to Glenway Wescott written in January 1961, he mentions going to Rome for a few months "due to peculiar

circumstances," though this trip is also not explained. If Gordon was doing American intelligence during this period, I have yet to find conclusive evidence of it.

32. Gordon Merrick, "Frenchman and the American."

33. Gordon Merrick, unidentifed novel, 197, GMP, box 14, folder 16.

34. Roger Austen, *Playing the Game: The Homosexual Novel in America* (Indianapolis: Bobbs-Merrill, 1977), 143. Since Austen's study, some historians of gay literature, such as Michael Bronski and Christopher Bram, have shown that not all 1950s gay novels had tragic endings.

35. Gordon Merrick, "How to Write Lying Down," *New Republic*, December 8, 1958.

36. See Nan Alamilla Boyd, *Wide Open Town: A History of Queer San Francisco to 1965* (Berkeley: University of California Press, 2003).

37. Gordon Merrick, "The Home of the Phonus Balonus," *New Republic*, February 23, 1959; Gordon Merrick, "The Case for the Blob," *New Republic*, July 13, 1959; Gordon Merrick, "No Laughing Matter," *New Republic*, September 7, 1959.

38. Gordon Merrick, *The Day the Dog Talked*, unpublished manuscript, 278, GMP, box 1, folder 9.

39. Gordon Merrick, *The Pledge of Allegiance*, unpublished manuscript, 1, GMP, box 12, folder 2.

40. Hulse, interview by the author.

Chapter Nine

The Island of Dreams

In all the ways that Gordon was lucky in life, he was especially lucky in his good timing. This was certainly the case when he and Hulse moved to Hydra in the spring of 1960. After leaving San Francisco they had gone back to the Napoleon's Tomb apartment in Paris, but they had not given up their dream of a home in Greece. During one of their earlier visits to Hydra they had bought a small house, and they decided now was the time to establish themselves. Hydra was now on the cusp of becoming a trendy Mediterranean destination for celebrities and cosmopolitan elites, but—fortunately for Gordon—it was still "undiscovered" enough to be an economical haven for American expatriates who had some money in their pocket.

Hydra is a medium-sized island in the Aegean Sea on the southern end of Greece, a three-hour ferry ride from the mainland city of Piraeus. The port town of Hydra lies on the northern side of the island, with whitewashed houses and buildings built on top of hills that slope dramatically down toward a crescent-shaped harbor. Because of the island's unique history and topography, it was virtually ignored in the time of classical Greece and thus lacks the ruins that made other Greek islands important sites of archaeological study in the modern era. Although it was substantially developed in the first half of the nineteenth century, it managed to evade many of the modernization efforts of the twentieth century.[1] To this day it remains one of the few "wheel-free" islands in Europe.

James Burke, the photographer for *Life* magazine, made an extended visit to Hydra around the same time that Gordon and Hulse arrived. In a cable to his editor, he deftly sketched out the character of the island, which he hoped to use as the subject for a photojournalist series in the magazine:

> Island of Hydra, four hours slow ferryboat across Saronic gulf from Athens, is sort of minor key Greek Majorca still cheap and not yet famous. Its year around international colony of artists and writers (largely Scandinavian and Canadian at moment) is small but summer season now beginning brings visiting

stream ranging from fullbright [sic] scholars to beatniks like Gregory Corso. Atmosphere is fairly beat, with bearded barefoot types lounging about waterfront tables drinking oozo (strong Greek anisette) and talking about last nights party. Hydra islanders take them in stride and even join in—at least one local policeman is ardent poet himself. Only disharmony are American tourists who come on daily ferry from Athens to spend few hours gawking—but carefully keeping quay width distance from strange breed. Although surface atmosphere seems beat there are serious hardworking individuals in artist group.[2]

Burke, who had earlier profiled Beat poets like Corso, was predisposed to notice the "artist's colony" that was taking root in Hydra. Many of the hundreds of photographs he took in Hydra (which sadly were never published in the magazine) focus on these artists and writers, including those who became good friends with Gordon and who would exert a strong influence on his writing.

The small house that Gordon and Hulse bought in 1959 had cost them eight hundred dollars. (Had they waited another year or two the price would have easily doubled.) Their initial plan was to spend five months of each year in Hydra, from May to September, and then return to the Paris apartment. As they got more settled in their island home, however, their stays in Greece grew longer, until they were living in Hydra for eight months out of the year. The house alone was a full-time project. Like most buildings in Hydra, it had been built in the early nineteenth century by Venetian builders out of whitewashed stone. While this gave the house unparalleled charm, it also meant that constant upkeep and repairs were required as a defense against the cracking and crumbling stone.[3] Gordon and Hulse did most of this maintenance work themselves, and they started making renovations as soon as they moved in. At first the house was a fairly modest situation: "three tiny adjoining rooms, a bedroom, space to build a bathroom, a primitive kitchen and a donkey stable."[4] They tore down the walls between the adjoining rooms to make one large living room, and they converted the donkey stable into a study for Gordon's daily writing. They then added a small bathroom and modernized the kitchen, where Gordon continued in his role as the household chef. Even with these improvements, the living conditions were still very rustic for a while. There was no electricity, and the main source of water was the rainwater they periodically collected from the roof of the house.

As Hydra became more popular, the availability of modern amenities improved. The island's authorities approved measures to install electricity for residents, and they built a water reservoir that was filled each day by an incoming tanker. Gordon and Hulse had discovered they had a knack for renovation work, and they kept making improvements. They bought a garbage dump behind their house for one thousand dollars after hearing that it contained a buried water cistern, only to find that an entire house had been buried on the site—still virtually intact. They exhumed the building and restored it as an addition to their house. When the house next door went up for sale a few years later, they bought it (for five thousand dollars) and reconstructed it as an additional wing. By the time they were finished, their small rustic house had become a stunning, multi-tiered villa, with multiple terraces overlooking the port, a guest house, and a swimming pool. They decorated their home with furniture they had brought from San Francisco and Paris, along with antique pieces they found throughout Greece and France. Gordon's prize piece was a Louis XVI style dining table, which he complemented with French provincial chairs that he and Hulse had reupholstered with gleaming yellow fabric. Their villa was stunning enough to be featured by fashion journalist Barbara Taylor Bradford in one of her syndicated columns. In the article, Gordon described their home as "very authentic eclectic."[5]

Beginning in 1960, tourists descended on Hydra in increasing numbers. The expatriate artists who had "discovered" the island in the 1950s were now being overtaken by the jetsetters and celebrities who had heard about Hydra's trendy bohemian culture and its spectacularly picturesque port that provided the perfect backdrop for publicity photos. The list of luminaries who visited Hydra in the 1960s reads like a Who's Who list of artists and actors: Henry Fonda, Peter Ustinov, Jeanne Moreau, Douglas Fairbanks, Raf Vallone, Gregory Corso, Allen Ginsberg, Sidney Nolan, John Craxton, Norris Embry, Melina Mercouri, Peter Finch, Sophia Loren, Anthony Perkins, Maria Callas, Audrey Hepburn, Aristotle Onassis, and Elizabeth Taylor—who showed up in her yacht with her newest husband, Eddie Fisher.[6] The island was popularized on a truly international scale when it served as the location for two big Hollywood films: Jules Dassin's *Phaedra* (1962) and Morton Da Costa's *Island of Love* (1963). Hydra had earlier appeared in the films *A Girl in Black* (1956) and *Boy on a Dolphin* (1957, starring Sophia Loren and Alan Ladd), but the two newer films reached an even larger global audience. *Phaedra* brought Anthony Perkins, Melina Mercouri, and Raf Vallone, who (when they weren't filming) spent much time in Hydra's bars and cafés socializing with the local residents. The following year, *Island of Love*—whose theatrical trailer could have been mistaken for a tourist ad for Hydra—brought Tony Randall, Robert Preston, and Walter Matthau, who also took advantage of the island's bustling social scene.

The cinematic invasion of Hydra had a profound effect on the island's expatriate community. In her novel *Peel Me a Lotus,* the writer Charmian Clift vividly described the experience of being de facto extras in the Hollywood films. For Clift, the presence of film crews and movie cameras made the residents into "indigenous" figures, inducing them to adopt even more a kind of bohemian identity—"one finds oneself unprotestingly playing the assigned role," as Clift puts it.[7] Of course, Gordon and Hulse—who were good friends of Clift's—were at home in such a theatrical setting. Gordon was cast as an official extra in *Island of Love*, and a clip of him even made it into the movie's trailer. (This is the only extant video footage of Gordon that exists.) Gordon and Hulse also managed to insinuate themselves into the Hollywood set—not surprising, since they had at least one mutual acquaintance with most of the stars and directors who visited the island. Photographs taken at the time show them drinking and laughing with Melina Mercouri and Morton Da Costa at Douskos, one of Hydra's popular hot spots.[8] Another photograph taken at Katsikas, another expatriate hangout, shows Gordon casually socializing with Jules Dassin and Tony Randall. Although Gordon and Hulse had only lived in Hydra for two years, they were already fixtures of the expatriate community and gladly warmed up to their roles as island hosts.

Gordon's biggest triumph as unofficial host of Hydra came when they had been there only a year. On June 9, 1961, Jacqueline Kennedy visited Hydra as part of an Aegean yacht tour. The island officials made a huge commotion to welcome the First Lady, greeting her "with ringing church bells, a small festival and a clamour of school children and local dignitaries," and it was Gordon himself who was chosen to guide her through all these festivities.[9]

Figure 9.1 Charles Hulse with George Johnston, Melina Mercouri, and Morton Da Costa, Hydra c. 1962.
Source: Estate of Gordon Merrick.

The Island of Dreams 155

Figure 9.2 Gordon with Jules Dassin and Tony Randall, Hydra c. 1962.
Source: Estate of Gordon Merrick.

Figure 9.3 Gordon as an extra in *Island of Love* (1963).
Source: Warner Bros.

It is unclear how he got the honor, but it's likely he used the fact that he had been classmates with her husband at Princeton. As always, Gordon could be very persuasive when he wanted to be. A photograph of him and Kennedy shows him gallantly escorting her across the pier amid an entourage of officials, casually brandishing a cigarette and showing off his ability to look as fashionable in sandals as the style icon herself.

As the island's popularity as an international hot spot grew, more notables appeared, welcomed by an expatriate community that was increasingly prepared to fete them and share their spotlight. Two such residents were Patricia and Dale Keller, the interior design moguls who owned a huge seventeenth-century villa in Hydra where they threw extravagant parties for visiting celebrities. One of these, a masked ball that attracted people from Athens and nearby islands, was so ostentatious that it was covered by the New York newspapers—who mentioned Gordon's elaborate costume:

> Several hundred guests flew in from Athens, Lesbos, Skiathos, Scopelos, Samos and all the ships at sea. . . . Dale and Patricia were dressed as Captain Midnight and Lady Dazzle. Patricia's dark green dress with a pale green chiffon coat was by Giorgio di Sant'Angelo and with it she wore all her ruby and diamond jewelry from India. . . . Writer Gordon Merrick came dressed as a Carpathian prince, and singer Leonard Cohen arrived attired modestly as the sun.

Figure 9.4 Gordon welcoming the First Lady to Hydra in 1961.
Source: Estate of Gordon Merrick.

The festivities extended into the next day, when the composer John Cage arrived with his longtime romantic partner, the dancer Merce Cunningham. Reportedly, they were followed by twenty-five dancers, fresh from their performance at a festival in Athens and dressed in glittering attire.[10]

As much as Gordon enjoyed mingling with visiting celebrities and artists, the most important people on the island for him were the expatriate writers who were living in Hydra at the beginning of the 1960s. At the core of this group were Clift and her husband George Johnston, both Australian writers who had moved from London to Hydra with their two young children in 1955. Another married couple was Redmond and Robyn Wallis, who had come from New Zealand. Redmond was a journalist with novelistic aspirations, and Robyn was a devoted Hellenophile. The two had initially planned to move to London and make occasional visits to Greece, but they decided to settle in Hydra when they learned they could do so cheaply.[11] Other couples included the Norwegian writer Axel Jensen and Marianne Ihlen—whose relationship fell apart when Jensen left her for another lover in Athens—and David and Angela Goschen, two English artists who had also brought their children. The one person in the group who came to Hydra alone would prove to be the most famous: Leonard Cohen, a Canadian poet, composer, and singer. (He would also be the only one in the group to remain friends with Gordon until the latter's death in 1988.) Cohen became romantically involved with Ihlen after her breakup with Jensen, and the two stayed together for a few years—long enough for Cohen to write a song about Ihlen, "So Long, Marianne," which became an international hit. As Paul Genoni and Tanya Dalziell have shown in their meticulously researched account of Hydra's expatriate community in the 1960s, life on the island intensified and complicated the romantic lives of these writers and artists, but it also provided a spectacular backdrop for their personal dramas and fueled their creative energies in various and unexpected ways.

It was in the context of this small artistic community that Gordon and Hulse established the contours and rhythms of their relationship that would characterize the rest of their lives together. As usual, Gordon was the disciplined writer, working dutifully on his typewriter every morning. Hulse discovered that, in addition to all his other talents, he was handy with building projects and had an instinctive knack for design. When one day he painted their front door black on a whim, the local Greeks—whose architectural tastes were conservative—were annoyed, but the resident expatriates found it exciting.[12] As a team the couple had transformed their humble house into a magazine-worthy villa, and subsequently they were treated as authorities by other Hydra transplants adjusting to island life. Their combination of friendliness and perceptiveness made them unofficial "neighborhood association" leaders, so much so that the other residents would ask them to act as community spokespersons when matters of local government policies and regulations arose.

In social situations they formed a complementary pair. Gordon was the genteel one of the two—quieter and more reserved, though with occasional flashes of temper and a propensity for cutting remarks. Hulse was outgoing and endlessly amiable, with an ebullient sense of humor that was punctuated by his infectious smile and big dazzling eyes. At parties Hulse would typically entertain the crowd with a hilarious (and often off-color) joke, with Gordon standing nearby, looking askance. Jeannie Sakol, a writer from New York—a self-described "nice Jewish girl from Brooklyn"—had met the two while visiting Hydra with Patrick Harrington, an Irish poet she was seeing. Harrington had met Gordon before, through Ginette Spanier, and so he and Sakol were immediately welcomed to the island. Sakol quickly learned that Gordon and Hulse were the "movers and shakers" of the expatriate community, and acceptance by them meant admittance into the island's inner circle. She took an instant liking to them, and they became lifelong friends. She summed up their reputation on Hydra by citing the typical reaction she would get when mentioning the couple. "I admire Gordon," the person would say, "*mais j'adore Charley!*"[13]

And it was always Gordon *and* Charley. There was never any question among Hydra's residents and visitors that the two were a couple. In the various diaries and memoirs written by members of the Hydra crowd about this period, references to Gordon and Hulse always describe them as though they are a married pair, sometimes even confusing one for the other—"the American author Gordon Merrick and his partner Chuck Hulse," "Chuck and Gordon, dancers from New York," "C & G."[14] Axel Joachim, Ihlen's two-year-old son, simply called them "ChuckandGordon."[15] At a time when gay men in the United States were often compelled to be "invisible" in public, Gordon and Hulse had found a place where they could live openly. Of course, this is not to say homophobia did not exist in Hydra. When Redmond Wallis first got to Hydra, he identified the two in his diary as the "two US pansies" and the "two Yankee queens." As he got to know them better, he decided they were "very nice," "pleasant men," at which point he started referring to them simply as "C & G."[16] Others were not so willing to abandon their prejudice. One night at Katsikas a huge fight erupted when Goschen bellowed in front of everyone, "Thank God Angela and I always say our little prayer in the morning, 'God preserve us from all pansies.'"[17] His remark infuriated those who came to the gay men's defense (including Johnston and Clift), and soon everyone in the group was yelling at other in hysterics. Wallis later recalled his own part in the fight, which ended up with him barreling out of the bar screaming, "At least I don't shove my prick up other men's arseholes!"[18] Windows and furniture were broken, some ended up with black eyes, and aftershocks of the fight went on for days, resulting in some people deciding to leave the island altogether.

This argument over Hydra's two "pansies" had clearly blown the lid off a bunch of other conflicts that had been brewing. The incident exposed a fundamental irony in Goschen's bigoted remark. The fact was that he and his fellow straights needed "preserving" from each other—not from any gay men in Hydra. As they were suffering through their self-inflicted dramas of disintegrating marriages, extramarital affairs, paternity disputes, and alcohol-fueled rampages—many of which are detailed at length in different histories and memoirs—Gordon and Hulse were watching from the sidelines, essentially unscathed and in a relationship that was extremely stable compared to their straight counterparts. If anything, they were a calming influence on the group, and they spent many a morning helping their friends recuperate from the events of the night before. As one resident later recalled, "They served cocktails of Bloody Marys at their Sunday brunches. These were good for hang-overs from the previous night."[19]

It was in Hydra where members of Gordon and Hulse's families also got to know them as a couple. Gordon's nephews (his brother Samuel's sons), for example, visited the two when they were teenagers. They weren't particularly impressed by Hydra, and so they ended up going back to Athens, where there were more diversions for young American men.[20] Hulse's little brother Larry—now a grown man, who still looked up to Hulse as much as ever—came to Hydra frequently. He noticed the difference in Hulse's personality in this new setting, and he did not always approve. He thought Gordon a pompous "prick" at times, and it rankled him to see his brother taking on similar traits, especially when they were in groups of people. He observed the small community of expatriate writers, who seemed to do more "boozing" than writing, and it confused him to see Hulse at the center of this crowd.[21] Most likely Larry was witnessing a change from the struggling, tenacious older brother he had known in Arkansas, and he was not accustomed to the more urbane, confident figure that Hulse had become in Europe.

Since they were spending more time each year in Hydra, Gordon ultimately sold the Paris apartment sometime in the mid-1960s. He used the proceeds to buy a small yacht, which he christened *The Strumpet Wind*—a doubly appropriate name, since it comes from a passage in Shakespeare's *Merchant of Venice* about a "scarfed bark" that races through the sea. In actuality, the yacht's full name was *Strumpet Wind IV*—Gordon had bought a much smaller sailboat, the original *Strumpet Wind*, back in the 1950s. But he had never been as expert a sailor as his brother Samuel, a sailing champion and director of the U.S. Olympic yachting team, and the Mediterranean waters were notoriously unpredictable. On one occasion he got caught in a nasty sea storm that nearly capsized the boat (an episode which he later dramatized in *One for the Gods*). Afterward, Gordon blamed the Mediterranean for his brush with near death: "It killed Shelley, it almost killed me."[22]

One of the regular passengers on the larger, more stable *Strumpet Wind IV* was Ginette Spanier, Gordon's longtime friend from his early days in France. She often visited Gordon and Hulse in Hydra during the summers, and in her 1970 memoir she attributed her newfound love of sailing to her "two handsome hosts" who had put her straight to work on the yacht. For the refined English city girl, this was a new and exciting experience: "Pure exhilaration. Muscles were put to work that I did not know I possessed. It was exciting at my age to discover that I had a body, a body to which one gave orders, quite tough orders, which were carried out without too much difficulty. A body which became brown and lean from losing that beastly urban fat. A body which welcomed with gratitude the unaccustomed contact with the air and the sun and the sea."[23] Another regular on the yacht was Leonard Cohen, who often brought along Ihlen. A photograph now held in the Princeton University Library shows the three of them on the boat: a suntanned Gordon looking admiringly at a grinning Cohen, with Ihlen sunning herself langourously on the deck.

Hydra had a profound effect on Gordon's writing, which had stagnated in recent years. In San Francisco and Paris he had continued writing as he always had, but his new works were forced, poor replicas of earlier stuff he had written. In Paris, shortly before moving to Hydra, he had written most of a new novel called *Pledge of Allegiance*, about an American journalist in San Francisco who is assigned a story about a local wealthy French art collector. The writer recognizes the collector's paintings as stolen works he had helped smuggle in Europe years before. The rest of the novel is told as a flashback, alternating between art heist thriller and tragic heterosexual love drama. The work is hackneyed and melodramatic, and in many ways it reads more as a sketch for a television episode or second-rate suspense film rather than a literary novel. In fact, at one point a production company considered turning it into a film and bought an option, but nothing ever came of the manuscript, either in textual or cinematic form.[24]

By contrast, Hydra gave Gordon new material. The tumultuous dramas of his friends' relationships, the artists and writers (most of them alcoholics) struggling to make their mark on the world, the constant influx of celebrities, the clash between American and European cultures, all set against an obscenely picturesque backdrop—this was precisely the kind of environment that fueled Gordon's imagination. The new setting also prompted him to experiment with different forms. He started writing short stories, likely thinking of Truman Capote, whose short stories he had recently reviewed. One of his first short stories written in Hydra, "A Clear Conscience," was directly inspired by his experience of living on the island. The story's protagonist, Mr. Fuller, is an American businessman who settles with his wife on a Mediterranean island (clearly Hydra, though the island is not named) after realizing how cheaply he can live there:

> He felt a kiddish sort of elation simply at the thought of being able to buy a house, really buy it lock stock and barrel, for just about what he earned in a week. It would be all his, with no payments to meet, as nothing had ever been his before. It was so unlikely that when he thought about it he had this feeling, like a child playing house.[25]

Fuller then oversees the renovation of the house—much like Gordon and Hulse had done—and in the process his American business habits come into conflict with the island's culture. His renovation plans are changed by the workers without notice, his attempt to get running water is thwarted by the island's lack of civic authority, and—to his horror—ten-year-old children are allowed to perform dangerous construction work. At each turn Fuller tries to force the islanders to conform to his practices, priding himself on bringing American "standards" to what he sees as a backward culture. His attempt ultimately fails, and through a tragic series of events Fuller ends up running through the town completely engulfed in flames—a gruesome death partially caused by his (American) addiction to cigarettes.

"A Clear Conscience" is an interesting grotesque, but its heavy-handed message and stereotypical characters likely kept it from being published. Gordon's other short stories from this period are similarly problematic, and they show that Gordon needed more than a change of scenery to get out of his publishing rut. Fortunately, he found another, more transformative influence in his new friends, the other expatriate writers in Hydra who were living their personal dramas in front of his eyes but who were also writing and sharing their work with each other. The most important of these writers were developing a style of autobiographical memoir—a genre in which they narrativized an important period in their lives and thinly disguised it as novelistic fiction. Johnston had just published *Closer to the Sun*, a fictionalized version of his time in Hydra that included many details about his strained marriage with Clift. His later novel *Clean Straw for Nothing* would also dramatize material from this period in his life. When Gordon met him, he was beginning work on *My Brother Jack*, an account of his experiences as a young journalist in Melbourne during the Great Depression. Around the same time, Clift had also just published *Peel Me a Lotus*, vividly sketching the island's culture and the challenges it posed to her career and marriage. Clift was especially adept at drawing compelling portraits of her Hydra friends, easily recognized beneath the novel's pseudonyms. For his part Wallis also wrote an autobiographical novel using pseudonyms. *The Unyielding Memory* is probably the most faithful account of the Hydra group—many of the events in Wallis's novel correspond closely to the personal diary he kept at the time. While the novel was never published, it has been an important source for scholars tracing the history of Hydra's expatriate community.[26]

Gordon's novels had all included autobiographical material, and in fact the most successful parts of these novels had often been those that richly dramatized significant episodes in his life—his Broadway career, his work for the OSS. The novels being written by his Hydra friends, however, were more personal and revealing than anything he had attempted so far. Such an approach was a challenge for him. He had long taught himself to mask carefully the details he took from his personal life, in part because his first novel was based on confidential military information but even more because all his romantic and sexual experiences had been with men. With few exceptions he likewise refrained from producing authentic representations of himself or people he knew, instead reverting to character types and figures who are more mouthpieces for philosophical ideas than they are individual subjects. He was especially careful not to portray his close friends or the immediate members of his family, above all his parents. Notwithstanding how far he had moved from Villanova and Princeton, Gordon was still genteel to the core.

On December 4, 1964, Gordon received news that shook him from his gentility. His mother had unexpectedly died of a stroke in her home in Radnor, Pennsylvania. She was buried two days later in the Greenwood Cemetery in Brielle, New Jersey, next to her husband Rodney.[27] Gordon's brother Samuel, who was living in Alexandria, Virginia, at the time, was the first to be notified, and he promptly made the three-hour drive to Pennsylvania to handle the funeral. Gordon and Hulse were in France at the time and did not get the news until late. There was no time to make the transatlantic journey to attend the funeral, which was likely a small service at the cemetery. He had visited his mother in America six months earlier, not knowing it would be the last time he saw her.[28]

Gordon was devastated. All his life Mimi had been the person he could turn to for support and understanding. He had gotten his love of reading and theater from her, and from a young age he had depended on her as a sounding board for his opinions, disappointments, and successes. Her staunch Catholicism had likely created some difficulty when she learned that he was gay, but any conflict between them had long subsided. She had gotten to know both of Gordon's romantic partners, first Richardson and then Hulse. She was a doting mother even when Gordon was in his forties, tending to him when he got sick during a trip to Philadelphia and "bullying" him into recovery.[29] Afterward Gordon never mentioned his mother's death in any interview or in anything he published—a telling sign of the profundity of his sadness. His grief over Mimi was completely his own.

The loss of his mother spurred Gordon to begin work on a new novel, this time with fewer inhibitions than before. Without the fear of scandalizing or embarrassing his parents—and with a keener sense of his own mortality—he now had few reasons to hold back. His new project, titled *The Day the Dog Talked*, would be about an American family living in Hydra in the summer of 1960. Its characters would be closely based on the people he knew in Hydra, and it would include both himself and Hulse—with pseudonyms, but unmistakably as an openly gay couple.

The protagonist, George Leighton, is a famous American novelist who has moved his wife and son from New York to Greece to fix his splintering marriage and to break out of a creative rut. As Genoni and Dalziell have pointed out, Gordon's Hydra friends would have immediately recognized Leighton as George Johnston, who was notorious on the island for his excessive drinking and quarrelsome marriage:

> He stood for a long moment in front of the toilet, half-dozing and swaying slightly as the liquid absorbed the night before drained out of him. Then he braced himself to confront the ruin of his face. The mirror over the wash basin offered no pleasant surprises. The eyes were red and puffy, the deep tan looked gray and lifeless, a stubble of graying beard blurred the jaw line. The celebrated George Cosmo Leighton. Well, perhaps not quite . . . the *once* celebrated George Leighton? His flight from success had been perhaps more successful than he had intended.[30]

Other characters in the novel include Sid Coleman, a Canadian Jewish poet with "a smile of mad infectious glee"—a dead ringer for Leonard Cohen.[31] The main plot of the novel centers on Leighton's efforts to recover a large sum of money he lost while in a drunken rage. The primary suspect is Costa, a local Greek who had been friendly with Leighton's family. Although Leighton is not convinced of Costa's guilt, he pursues the case aggressively through the local authorities, not realizing that the Greek legal system works differently than the American one. In the end, Leighton's ignorance of both the island's culture and his own family problems results in the prosecution of an innocent man.

There is no evidence that an episode like the Costa plot occurred with Johnston or any others in the Hydra circle, though it is possible that something similar happened at some point. It seems just as likely that Gordon was consciously imitating Forster's *A Passage to India*, which similarly uses a clash of cultures to motivate a story about a wrongfully accused local man. Although Gordon had by now fallen out of touch with Forster, he still saw him as a model for his own work. He might have thought that a Mediterranean version of *A Passage to India* would be the perfect vehicle to revitalize his literary career. Unlike his last two attempts, *The Day the Dog Talked* gave him the opportunity to rediscover his inner Forster *and* include more of himself in his work.

In fact, many of the most interesting parts of the novel are its most explicitly autobiographical passages. In the story Leighton befriends a gay couple named Bob and Paul—clearly a fictionalized version of Hulse and himself. (Gordon's sense of humor prompted him here to use Bob Richardson's name as one of the pseudonyms.) Leighton respects and admires the couple, who have taught him that gay men can be upright, noble people. Their friendship becomes especially important when Leighton learns that his own son, Peter, is gay. The example of Bob and Paul assuages his fears that Peter will lead a difficult life, and he ultimately accepts his son's sexuality:

> There was Peter. If he was going through a homosexual phase, it would probably be better for him to work it out here, where it was understood and condoned, rather than to be plunged into an alien environment where he would be doomed to hostility or derision or the half-world of exclusive homosexuality. Should this be weighed in the balance? Perhaps he would remain a homosexual. The heavens wouldn't fall. Bob and Paul had managed. And damn nicely, too. If he was to be of any help to Peter in attaining and reconciling himself to his true nature, surely he could do so only if he remained true to himself.[32]

Johnston and Clift did have a teenage son, Martin, who was seventeen years old at the time Gordon was writing the novel. He did not turn out to be gay, but he was an introverted, artistic youth who was known for burying himself in his books and for his excellent Greek—at nine years old he had helped Sophia Loren with her Greek during the filming of *Boy on a Dolphin*.[33] In crafting the character of Peter, a gay American teenager, Gordon may have wondered what Martin's life on Hydra would have been like if he *had* been gay. And he may have wondered how he and Hulse would have responded.

Unfortunately the gay subplot in *The Day the Dog Talked* is only briefly sketched out, and the roles of Bob and Paul are hardly more than brief cameos. These episodes were more explicitly revealing of Gordon's sexuality than anything he had put in print so far, but he still kept himself (and Hulse) in the background. At one point in the novel, Leighton thinks to himself that, living in Hydra, he has found "a redefinition of freedom in his observations of a community released from all constraints, new judgments imposed by the clash of anarchy and order."[34] Like Leighton, Gordon also found new freedom in this small corner of the world, but it was not enough to put his own life, as a gay man, at the front and center of his writing.

This was about to change.

NOTES

1. Paul Genoni and Tanya Dalziell, *Half the Perfect World: Writers, Dreamers and Drifters on Hydra, 1955–1964* (Clayton, Australia: Monash University Publishing, 2018), 33–40.
2. Quoted in Genoni and Dalziell, *Half the Perfect World*, 17–18.
3. Genoni and Dalziell, *Half the Perfect World*, 124, 156, 43–44.
4. Barbara Taylor Bradford, "Gordon Merrick's Greek Home: Three Houses Turned into One," *Detroit Free Press*, August 14, 1971. A longer version of this article, "The House the Gods Built," is in GMP, box 7, folder 8.
5. Bradford, "Gordon Merrick's Greek Home."
6. Genoni and Dalziell, *Half the Perfect World*, 19, 29, 115, 240–41.
7. Quoted in Genoni and Dalziell, *Half the Perfect World*, 257.
8. Genoni and Dalziell, *Half the Perfect World*, 227–31.
9. Genoni and Dalziell, *Half the Perfect World*, 302.
10. "Ode to a Grecian Isle," *New York Daily News*, September 12, 1976.
11. Genoni and Dalziell, *Half the Perfect World*, 24.
12. Charlotte Mensforth, "Wine Dark Sea," in *When We Were Almost Young: Remembering Hydra through War and Bohemians*, ed. Helle V. Goldman (Tromsø, Norway: Tipota Press, 2018), 74.
13. Jeannie Sakol, interview by the author.
14. Genoni and Dalziell, *Half the Perfect World*, 303; Mensforth, "Wine Dark Sea," 74.
15. Kari Hesthamar, *So Long, Marianne: A Love Story*, translated by Helle V. Goodman (Toronto: ECW Press, 2014).
16. Redmond Wallis, Diary, 28–29, Redmond Frankton Wallis Papers, MSX-6716.
17. Wallis, Diary, 28. The episode is recounted at length in Wallis's unpublished memoir, *The Unyielding Memory*.
18. This is from Wallis's own version of the incident in *The Unyielding Memory*. Quoted in Genoni and Dalziell, *Half the Perfect World*, 124–25.
19. Valerie Lloyd Sidaway, "Hydra Reflections," in *When We Were Almost Young*, 134.
20. Charles Hulse, interview by the author.
21. Lawrence Hulse, interview by the author.
22. "Author Gordon Merrick Hops Atlantic to Exotic Locales," *Independent Journal*, April 26, 1958.
23. Ginette Spanier, *And Now It's Sables* (London: Robert Hale, 1970), 150.
24. Gordon Merrick, *Pledge of Allegiance*, unpublished manuscript, GMP, box 12, folders 2–5.
25. Gordon Merrick, "A Clear Conscience," unpublished manuscript, 2, GMP, box 15, folder 9.
26. Genoni and Dalziell, *Half the Perfect World*, 102–3, 364–65, 98–100.
27. Certificate of Death for Mary Merrick, Department of Health, Commonwealth of Pennsylvania, December 4, 1964, http://ancestry.com.

28. U.S. Passport for William Gordon Merrick, issued February 9, 1962, GMP, box 19, folder 12.

29. Gordon Merrick to Glenway Wescott, 1958, Glenway Wescott Papers, box 76, folder 1139.

30. Gordon Merrick, *Forth into Light* (New York: Avon Books, 1974), 13; Genoni and Dalziell, *Half the Perfect World*, 13.

31. Merrick, *Forth into Light*, 48.

32. Merrick, *The Day the Dog Talked*, unpublished manuscript, GMP, box 1, folder 7, 278.

33. Genoni and Dalziell, *Half the Perfect World*, 255–56.

34. Merrick, *Forth into Light*, 12–13.

Chapter Ten

The Great Gay American Novel

In 1967 Gordon was facing a midlife crisis. At fifty years old, he was still a good-looking man, but he was no longer the dashing young beauty who had turned heads in New York and Paris. His chronic back problems had returned with a vengeance, so much so that he decided to sell the *Strumpet Wind IV* and put an end to his sailing days.[1] He and Hulse had now been together for eleven years—the same amount of time he had been with Bob Richardson when they split up—and the thrill of the early years of their relationship had inevitably subsided. For a while there had been the excitement of Hydra and its illustrious crowds, but it was increasingly unclear where Gordon fit among the island's community of writers and artists. He busied himself as an amateur real estate developer, but this was never his goal. For two decades he had introduced himself to everyone as a novelist, but he hadn't published a book in nine years.

And the new novel was going nowhere. In late 1966 Gordon had finished the manuscript for *The Day the Dog Talked*, now titled *A Day with Leighton*, and sent it to his agent to shop around. Publisher after publisher turned it down. Many of them commended Gordon's skillful, elegant writing, but they couldn't see how the novel would sell in the current book market. Some rejection letters expressed confusion about whether it was meant to be a suspense thriller or a psychological character study.[2] One of the most prescient letters was also one of the shortest. In his two-sentence reply to Gordon's agent, the editor at New American Library remarked that the novel "seems to be a combination of fantasy and autobiography."[3] Gordon was demoralized by the stream of rejections. Later he would claim that he had stopped writing for ten years because of his debilitating back pain. The truth, however, was that he had written four novels and a bunch of short stories, all of which had been deemed unpublishable. He had even written a television adaptation of James Purdy's *The Nephew* for BBC Television, a project which never materialized.[4] It may have been around this same time that Gordon also wrote a television adaptation for *The Strumpet Wind*, which likewise went nowhere. For the

TV script, Gordon had completely cut out the romance storyline (following Forster's advice), but he retained, and even heightened, the scene in which Chandler runs into his commanding officer at a gay bar.[5] Despite the promise he had shown in his first novel, he was struggling more than the amateur writers in the Hydra colony. In a profound way, he was no longer the man that he imagined himself to be.

Strangely, or perhaps understandably, the crisis had a liberating effect. An idea for a new novel had been germinating in his mind—one that would be more explicitly autobiographical than his earlier works and that would not take place in France or Mexico or Greece or any other exotic place he had visited. It would be set on the New Jersey shore, where he had spent his youthful summers, and New York City, where he had worked before the war. Its principal characters would be an imperious, eccentric Southern matriarch and her grandson, a handsome *gay* Princeton man pursuing a career on Broadway. This time the gay character would not merely be a subplot that served to highlight the enlightened morality of a straight protagonist. His would be the *main* story.

Gordon's idea for a novel about a young gay man partly came from Forster's *Maurice*, which he had read years before. Although Forster had refused to publish *Maurice* during his lifetime because he feared it would scandalize his friends, Gordon now felt that there was no one he *could* scandalize, especially with his parents gone. Moreover, he finally admitted to himself what he had known for years—and what Forster himself had tried to tell him: he sucked at writing heterosexual relationships. "I was trying to write a heterosexual novel and couldn't," he later told an interviewer, "so I thought fuck this and wrote about a gay relationship."[6]

It would be an understatement to say that the prospects for a gay-themed mainstream novel in the 1960s were formidable. Gordon had been able to include gay subplots and minor gay characters in his earlier novels, but the most daring of these—the gay subplot in *The Demon of Noon*—had provoked negative reviews by most American critics. By this time only a handful of gay novels had been published by mainstream presses, and they had met with mixed reception. James Baldwin had struggled to find a publisher for *Giovanni's Room*, which then provoked a backlash in conservative circles when it appeared in 1956, at the height of McCarthyism and the "lavender scare." Even though the novel initially garnered positive reviews from literary critics, it became a regular punching bag for straight readers who masked their discomfort with Baldwin's sexuality with contrived statements about the novel's "many flaws."[7] John Rechy's *City of Night* (1963) had been surprisingly popular, but it had been issued by Grove Press, which had staked its reputation on publishing countercultural, potentially obscene works (its publication of an unexpurgated version of D. H. Lawrence's *Lady Chatterley's*

Lover in 1959 had embroiled the firm in a legal dispute).[8] Rechy's circuitous narrative style and gritty, violent portrayal of gay hustlers in California further confirmed its countercultural status outside of the mainstream.[9] Christopher Isherwood, who was the closest to Gordon in writing style and background, was able to get *A Single Man* published by Simon & Schuster in 1964. The novel was deservedly lauded by a few major publications (the *New York Herald Tribune* proclaimed it "a small masterpiece"), though its affirming, intelligent representation of gay men made it the obvious target of many homophobic reviewers in other newspapers and magazines.[10] Gordon had met Isherwood through Glenway Wescott back in the 1940s, and he knew his work well. If he had read *A Single Man*, then he would have known that there was at least some precedent for publishing a mainstream novel centered on a gay character.

The gradual relaxation of obscenity laws throughout the 1960s did much to facilitate the publication of books with homosexual content, but this growing permissiveness did not have an immediate impact on the number of gay novels put out by mainstream presses. The type of gay novels that did flourish in the 1960s were those published by small independent presses such as Greenleaf and Guild Press. These were operations that churned out dozens of titles each year, all in cheap, paperback editions and often sporting lurid or provocative covers.[11] Michael Bronski, who has done much to illuminate the prevalence of these paperbacks, notes that "many of these books—particularly those with more explicit sexual content—enjoyed large, but relatively clandestine, circulations. As paperback originals they were generally not sold in general-interest bookstores."[12] Even if Gordon had read some of these books, he would not have considered them "serious" novels. They were cheap paperback originals; they were not reviewed by the *New York Times*; they were not displayed in mainstream bookstores. They were not written by someone who had once been praised as a significant, if not major, postwar novelist.

Yet there *were* rumblings in some corners about the need for serious gay fiction. Many of Forster's friends, including Isherwood, had encouraged him to publish *Maurice*, and other writers also sounded the call for open, unapologetic gay literature. And it was not only gay people who were calling for change. In January 1966, an article titled "Homosexual Drama and Its Disguises" appeared in the *New York Times*. It was written by Stanley Kauffmann, the film and theater critic whose reviews had appeared alongside Gordon's book reviews in the *New Republic* in the 1950s. In the essay, Kauffmann criticizes gay American playwrights for masking homosexual plots and characters with heterosexual ones. (He had in mind plays like Edward Albee's *Who's Afraid of Virginia Woolf?*, which was often interpreted as a "cloaked" gay drama.) He admits that straight audiences and critics are to blame—"it is we who insist on it, not he"—but he concludes that the result was a distortion of both heterosexual and homosexual relationships. He thereby challenges the gay writer "to write truthfully of what he knows, rather than try to transform it to a life he does not know, to the detriment of his truth and ours." He ends the essay by praising Jean Genet, whose "greatness" he attributed to the playwright's refusal to hide or mask his gay characters.[13] Kauffmann's article did not go unnoticed. It prompted, at least in part, Mart Crowley to write *The Boys in the Band*, the groundbreaking off-Broadway play about a group of gay friends in New York City. As it turned out, the play, which premiered off-Broadway on April 14, 1968, was produced by Richard Barr, Gordon's friend and former theatrical collaborator at Princeton.[14]

At almost exactly the same time that Crowley was writing *Boys in the Band*, Gordon started writing his gay autobiographical novel. It was titled (appropriately) *Reflections in the Mirror*. The opening chapter begins in the middle of a conversation between Charlie Mills, a recent Princeton graduate, and his grandmother "C. B.," a genteel Southern dowager:

> "He's coming in a week," C. B. said, laying the letter down beside her breakfast coffee.
> "I suppose he's wildly good-looking," I said. No, not I. *He* said. He. I will not associate myself with the things I have to tell. If I must intrude occasionally, it will be from the distance of time and change. Charlie Mills has nothing to do with me.[15]

This oscillation between first- and third-person narrative was a new technique for Gordon. Its immediate effect is to make the reader feel like this is an autobiography, however veiled. Even without the first-person disclaimer, the personal details would have been recognized by anyone who knew Gordon reasonably well. Charlie is from a Philadelphia suburb with two parents and a brother. He went to Princeton as an undergraduate, where he devoted himself to acting and painting. He has a close relationship with his maternal grandmother, whom he visits at her grand apartment in Manhattan during the year and at her spacious Victorian house on the New Jersey shore during the summer. The novel is set in the summer of 1939, just after Charlie has graduated college and is preparing to move to New York City. This is a near replica of Gordon, except for the fact that Charlie finished college and is a painter rather than a writer—a change that Gordon had introduced earlier, when he created an autobiographical version of himself in *The Vallency Tradition*.

The character of C. B. is an even more accurate portrait. In letters and interviews, Gordon regularly admitted that C. B. was a fictionalization of his grandmother Clarice Billups (the initial letters staying the same). Gordon had earlier drawn inspiration from Billups when creating Gertrude Vallency, the controlling matriarch in *The Vallency Tradition*, but C. B. was an actual reconstruction. Gordon took special care to capture her mannerisms and appearance, even the subtle inflections of her faintly Southern accent:

> Again the roguish smile, a flirtatious tilt of the head. . . . Her accent was self-Anglicized with broadened *a*'s and well-shaped *u*'s from which emerged occasionally an unexpected echo of the South. She lifted a scrap of lace handkerchief and twirled it once in the air as if conjuring the future.[16]

By any measure, C. B. is an impressive creation; even critics who hated the novel would later praise its characterization here. Gordon had in fact originally intended her as the novel's main character, but "those boys keep taking over," as he told Hulse while writing the novel.[17] Still, the character provided him with a very convincing vehicle for the pressures of social status and heterosexual conformity that Charlie struggles against.

In the first few pages of the novel, C. B. sets the main plot in motion by introducing Charlie to Peter Martin, a distant cousin who is preparing to go to West Point. In her typical controlling fashion, C. B. proclaims she will "rescue" Peter from the military, and Charlie will be the principal agent in her plot:

> We must take him in hand. You're just what he needs at this stage—someone to look up to, someone who can offer him understanding. He gets none at home. Imagine being a general's son! Imagine being packed off to West Point! It won't do. His tastes are the same as ours. Books. The theater. You must take him under your wing for the summer.

Although Charlie is initially lukewarm about the scheme, his attitude quickly changes once he gets a good look at Peter for the first time. He is struck by Peter's physical features—eyes, nose, jawbone, hair, hands—which are unquestionably masculine but with a peculiar delicacy and sensitiveness: "Handsome was too strong a word. He was beautiful in a just barely formed way."[18] Charlie is mesmerized. He resolves to pursue Peter, and within hours of their first meeting he manages to get Peter into bed.

In an interview Gordon gave a few years later to *Michael's Thing*, a popular New York gay weekly, he claimed the character of Peter was "a total fabrication."[19] Like many of his other denials, this was inaccurate. In truth Peter is a combination of multiple people that Gordon had known, most of them romantically. He admitted in an interview (years after the *Michael's Thing* interview) that much of the Peter plot was based on his youthful affair with Otis Bigelow, though there are also details that came from Richardson and Hulse.[20] One interesting possible model is Robert Hardy Smith Jr., a blond, fair-skinned cousin of Gordon who actually did go to West Point. Like Peter, Smith came from a long line of military men, including his great-great-grandfather, who had also attended West Point. Gordon and Smith had been friends since childhood, and when they were older Smith would write Gordon from West Point, complaining about the "awful" life of a cadet. At one point he visited Gordon at Princeton, where he met Gordon's friends and attended some lectures.[21] In 1940 Smith was a patient in Highland Hospital in Asheville, North Carolina, a mental institution that specialized in the treatment of psychiatric disorders (Zelda Fitzgerald, the wife of F. Scott Fitzgerald, had also been a patient).[22] The reasons for his hospitalization are unknown, but it is plausible that Gordon, when hearing about his cousin, may have thought of homosexuality as a possible explanation. In any case, the elaborate backstory Gordon created for Peter in the novel suggests that he was imagining an alternate life for his cousin—had he been "rescued" from West Point.

The sexual pace of the novel moves at light-speed. Only twenty pages in, Charlie is fucking Peter, a virgin, an event that is described in graphic detail. The whole scene lasts about twenty pages, and there is never any vagueness about what exactly is happening. There are several other sex scenes in the novel, most of them just as graphic. Such quantity and quality of sexual explicitness would become a perennial lightning rod for Gordon's critics, who cited these episodes as evidence that the novel was essentially pornographic. For such readers, the frequency and graphic nature of the sex scenes were proof of its pulpy potboiler status, effectively disqualifying it as legitimate literature.

However, Gordon took his sex scenes seriously, even if his critics did not. The original working drafts of the novels—which are housed in the Princeton University Library—show that he spent an inordinate amount of time rewriting these scenes, far more than any other section in the novel. In these revisions, Gordon obsessively works over seemingly minor details, such as the placement of a hand or the words uttered during an orgasm. While the immediate impression on a jaded reader might be that the scene was meant only to titillate, the careful writerly revisions that Gordon made reveal that, for him, there was much more at stake in these scenes. In the novel, the mechanics of sex—what *exactly* happens—turn out to have profound effects on the characters themselves. Thus these episodes are crucial in establishing the emotional and psychical dynamics of their relationships. In other words, from Gordon's perspective, Charlie and Peter's sexual experiences are a meaningful part of their romance.

The challenge of representing sex in novels had been on Gordon's mind for a long time, long before writing *Reflections*. For one thing, many of his mentors and fellow writers had wrestled with the same problem. At a 1935 symposium with André Gide, Forster himself had argued for the importance of sex in fiction. "In England, more than anywhere else," he had claimed, "creative work is hampered because they can't write freely about sex, and I want it recognized that sex is a subject for serious treatment."[23] Glenway Wescott had likewise experimented with erotic writing, especially after being inspired by his collaboration with Alfred Kinsey, though he mostly kept this writing confined to his unpublished work. Gordon's writer friends in Hydra were also thinking about how to bring sex into mainstream writing, particularly Redmond Wallis, who in his diary wrote about his struggle to devise an appropriate style of "erotic realism."[24] For Gordon, the challenge had been compounded by the fact that, before *Reflections*, he was writing about something of which he had no direct knowledge. When he finally decided to represent gay relationships, the opportunity to write about sex *as he knew it* must have felt liberating. He was determined to get it right.

Gordon's meticulousness is very evident in the scene of Charlie and Peter's first coupling. At first, Charlie is attracted to Peter, but he doesn't know if the feeling is mutual. His first strategy is to use a "code" that would have been familiar to many gay men in the 1930s: eye signals. Charlie has already had experience cruising gay men in Princeton and New York, and so he tries to use the codes he has learned to communicate his sexual interest to Peter: "When he caught Peter's eye, he charged every look with significance without quite giving his hand away."[25] When this tactic fails to get an unambiguous response, Charlie spontaneously devises a ruse to get Peter out of his clothes. He makes a joke about them being mistaken for twins, and then he playfully proposes that they take each other's body measurements to see just how identical they are. What follows is a combination of strip tease and flirtation, as Charlie methodically applies a measuring tape to each part of Peter's body. (This part of the scene, which some readers found ridiculous, was actually based on one of Hulse's youthful experiences.) Charlie's efforts are finally rewarded when the "game" gives Peter a visible erection. Charlie continues to play along until Peter, no longer able to hide his feelings, collapses on the bed in the throes of an uncontrollable orgasm.

In the hands of a different writer, such an episode might come off as cheap porn. But Gordon carefully draws the scene, slowing the action and allowing the reader to inhabit Charlie's perspective. To achieve this effect, Gordon assiduously reworked and revised seemingly minor details, each time giving the reader more access to the complex emotions and sensations that Charlie is experiencing. A sample comparison of two versions of the manuscript is instructive:

> He smelled fresh and well scrubbed. He placed his head firmly against the jamb letting his hand linger on the thick silk of his hair.

> He inhaled the smell of him, fresh and scrubbed and faintly animal. He lifted his hands and straightened Peter's head, carefully avoiding his eyes but letting his fingers linger in the silk of his hair.[26]

In similar fashion, Gordon expands nearly every paragraph in the episode with nuanced detail. As a result, the narrative dramatizes and eroticizes the act of seduction itself. Charlie's game becomes a process of knowing for both men, simultaneously mystifying and revealing each part of their bodies. At times even the change of a single word gives access to the mental fantasizing that plays such an important role in a sexual experience. Thus Charlie's reaction to Peter taking off his sandals—"Charlie's heart accelerated as he watched this small *act of undressing*"—becomes "Charlie's heart accelerated as he watched this small *prelude to stripping*."[27]

Gordon worked hard to keep the sex scene from being too sappy. Instead of relying on conventional euphemisms for lovemaking, he allows the reader to see and understand all of the physical interactions between Charlie and Peter:

> He lowered his head and put his mouth on Peter's. He met with closed lips, but he ran his tongue along them, inviting entrance. Peter's mouth opened slightly, their tongues met, and then their mouths were devouring each other and they were seized by a storm of lust—legs thrashing, arms gripping, their bellies and chests writhing against each other, their sexes, hard columns of flesh, lifted in an insurmountable barrier between them. Charlie ran his hand down Peter's back encompassing the full smooth curve of buttocks. He slipped his hand between them. Peter's hips were agitated by brief thrusting spasms, and the muscles of his buttocks quivered in welcome of the invasion.[28]

This is extremely graphic, but it is also clearly specific. Gordon's approach was to treat the novel's action as though he were a choreographer, carefully directing the movements, positions, and rhythms of the performers from start to finish. At the same time, Gordon also tried to make Charlie and Peter's lovemaking seem spontaneous rather than scripted. In his revisions he continually removes lines that sound trite or conventional, consequently making the dialogue less "romantic" and more matter-of-fact:

> "I'm going to make love to you like this. You told me to teach you everything. Don't you want me inside you? . . . I'll stop if you don't like it."
>
> "No. I want it. I want everything. I don't care if it hurts. Don't stop no matter what."
>
> "I'm going to do it with you like this. You told me to teach you everything. . . . I'll stop if you don't like it."
>
> "No. I want everything. I don't care if it hurts."[29]

In the early versions of the episode, Gordon has Charlie and Peter say "love" often while having sex. He eventually decided this was unrealistic and removed all mentions of "love" from this part of the scene. Instead, the word is only spoken afterward, during their postcoital conversations. Gordon understood that the significance of a sexual event is not fully understood until afterward, when there is time to process it mentally. For this reason he deleted lines that overstated the momentousness of Peter's loss of virginity. Dozens of similar revisions had the cumulative effect of emphasizing the immediacy and practicality of the experience. Instead of recycling the language of heterosexual romance novels, Gordon routinely deleted sentences that evoked the genre, such as: "His dependence on it was a total submission and his hunger for it had become worship which wreathed Charlie in an intoxicating aura of adoration."[30]

The deliberate care which Gordon lavished on the novel's first sex scene was remarkable. In the *Michael's Thing* interview, he argued that it was important for straight people to know exactly what gay men *did*. Otherwise, he reasoned, straight people would fill in the gaps with their own distorted, horrifying, stereotypical fantasies:

> Merrick believes that the straightforward approach to writing about homosexuality in literature is best. In being explicit, the reader can understand more about this life style. "This is far better than descending to the lower depths which are terribly distorted as in 'Boys in the Band'," remarked Merrick. "The play was successful because of its presentation of the stereotype and the public accepts it."[31]

Gordon saw the London production of Mart Crowley's *The Boys in the Band* in February 1969, after he had already drafted *Reflections*. In the play Crowley puts gay sex offstage, in a way that makes it sordid and threatening for Alan, the nominally straight character. In this way the play confirmed for Gordon the choices he made in his novel. His point was precisely to *de*-mystify the specter of shadowy gay sex—to show that it did not transform these men into effeminate or grotesque stereotypes.

Hulse was the first person to read the sex scenes in *Reflections*. Being a better typist of the two, he was regularly tasked with making the typescripts of Gordon's drafts. "I was never a great typist, but I typed fucking well," he bluntly put it. When he got to the novel's first sex scene, he was shocked. "You can't put your name on this," he told Gordon. "They'll never print this."[32] Gordon's friend Ginette Spanier was another person who realized that something unusual was happening in the new novel. As usual she was visiting Gordon and Hulse in Hydra during the summer, and she was typically still asleep when Gordon started his morning writing routine. She had a favorite anecdote about her visit during the writing of *Reflections*: "There I was, in this dreamy house, on this steamy island of Hydra. The occasional donkey bray would sound in the distance, and buzz flies were all you could hear, until all of a sudden the beautiful silence was broken by the raucous voice of one of my hosts: 'Hey Gordon, is hard-on hyphenated?'"[33]

The novel's inaugural sex scene leads to a summer fling, which becomes a consuming romantic relationship. For a while the romance is idyllic, but problems arise when Charlie and Peter interact with other young people at a local country club. At the club's Saturday night dances, Charlie makes a regular habit of hitting on women, at one point going so far as to get mired in a sexual scandal with a young woman. Peter, on the other hand, befriends a young man, Jimmy Harvester, who is known as a "queer." Peter's friendliness with Jimmy makes Charlie jealous, but more significantly it stokes his internalized homophobia. Charlie does not think of himself as gay, despite the fact that he prefers men to women and has had many gay experiences. He tries to convince himself that his affair with Peter is merely a stage of masculine development that will eventually lead to a "normal" heterosexual lifestyle:

> He had never considered himself a fairy or a pansy or any of the other words bandied about contemptuously by his contemporaries and himself. His sexual activities with other boys were a natural extension of the play he had been introduced to at school. He had always assumed that in due course there would be a girl and marriage and the usual developments of adult life; it simply hadn't happened yet.[34]

Peter's attitude is starkly different. Despite being raised by a hypermasculine army general, he accepts his identity as a gay man after only one sexual experience with Charlie, and he sees no difference between himself and other "fairies" and "queers." He easily imagines a marriage-like life with Charlie, with the two of them as part of a healthy gay community: "Jimmy says there's lots of guys like us in New York, living together as if they were married. That'll be wonderful."[35]

In spite of their conflicting attitudes, Charlie and Peter attempt a life as a couple. Peter cancels his plans for West Point and moves into Charlie's small New York apartment next to El Morocco (the famed Manhattan nightclub by Gordon's actual apartment in the 1930s). He gets a job as a runner for a Wall Street firm while taking night classes at Columbia University. Charlie meanwhile starts a job at a publishing company, where he broadens his network of professional contacts, many of them fellow Princeton alumni. His real goal is to be a Broadway actor, and so he uses his connections to meet influential directors and producers. Charlie and Peter's domestic arrangement is "heavenly" at first, but living in New York soon takes a toll on their relationship.

Charlie insists on maintaining the pretense that they are merely "friends" in front of others—including C. B., who regularly invites them to her Manhattan apartment and introduces them to other New York socialites. Peter, however, becomes more aware of gay men in New York who live openly and happily, and he repeatedly asks Charlie why they can't do the same.

Charlie's theatrical pursuits put a further strain on their relationship. At one point he is offered a part in a Broadway play, only to learn that the playwright, a famous Broadway figure, expects sex in return. Charlie rejects the offer, but his self-confidence is deeply shaken. The situation is further complicated when he meets Hattie, an aspiring actress from a well-connected New York family. She suspects Charlie's involvement with Peter but pursues him anyway, and before long they are engaged in a very public affair. This becomes too much for Peter, who in a moment of vulnerability admits to C. B. his true feelings for Charlie. C. B. had already suspected something between them, and she deviously uses Peter's confession to force her grandson to break things off. In a long, heart-wrenching scene, Charlie and Peter have a huge fight about their relationship, which ends with Charlie throwing Peter out of the apartment. (As I noted in chapter 3, nearly all of this material, including the Broadway incident and the breakup, was closely based on Gordon's actual experiences in 1939.)

The second half of the novel traces Charlie and Peter's separate paths after their breakup. Charlie hastily marries Hattie, temporarily reassuring himself of his manhood and confirming his original plan to live a heterosexual life. Peter's reaction is very different. He drops out of Columbia and moves into the YMCA, where for the first time he has sex with men other than Charlie. He quickly becomes part of New York's gay subculture and gains a reputation as a highly desirable beauty, nicknamed "the Growler" by men who have been to bed with him. His popularity enables him to live comfortably, since many of his dates shower him with lavish gifts which he later sells for money.

After a while Charlie runs into Peter by chance on a Manhattan street. He is captivated by Peter's beauty but also repelled by his campy mannerisms and openness about his sexuality. Peter nonetheless convinces Charlie to accompany him to a party in Harlem. The party is being thrown for Sapphire Hall, an African-American opera singer who had been a maid in C. B.'s household before being discovered by Otto Kahn, the wealthy financier and president of the Metropolitan Opera. In a short, poignant passage, Sapphire gushes to Charlie about Peter:

> That's one lovely boy. He just dotes on you, Mr. Charlie. Of course, he has his ways that some folks don't understand, but I don't know. I say, if it's love, the Lord won't mind. There's enough hate in the world.[36]

Charlie, however, is discomfited by such casual acceptance of gay people—and by the easy mixing of black and white people at the party. At one point, a friend of Peter's, a young attractive black man, kisses Peter on the mouth, which causes Charlie to instinctively recoil. He stumbles away to the bar, where he strikes up a conversation with a handsome man who starts telling him stories about the legendary "Growler." At that point Charlie is overwhelmed and leaves the party in a rage, calling the man a "dirty faggot" and lashing out at Peter.

The Harlem party is an important scene for considering the novel's treatment of race. Beginning in the 1990s, a number of gay reviewers and literary critics upbraided the novel for its apparent racism.[37] Much of this criticism is warranted, but it also tends to overlook or oversimplify the way in which racism is represented in the novel. In general, most of the racist passages in the novel—particularly the ones that get cited by critics—are associated with Charlie or C. B. For example, when Charlie and Peter arrive at the Harlem party, the presence of black people is a fact that is registered specifically by Charlie: "'I've never been up here before,' Charlie said, feeling foreign and ill at ease among the milling black faces."[38] Likewise, the comfortable interactions between black and white people guests intensifies Charlie's *un*comfortableness, and it prompts him to recognize a deeply ingrained racism within *himself*:

> He had no taste for intimacy with Sapphire; the company made him sufficiently self-conscious. He had come persuaded that he had no racial feelings. Theory was no aid to practice. There was something about these whites and blacks sitting around together that made his skin crawl.[39]

Charlie's racial prejudice is undeniable, but it also sets him apart from the other people at the party—particularly Peter, who makes little distinction between his black and white friends, including those he goes to bed with.

The novel anticipates this difference early on, when Charlie and Peter have a short conversation about C. B.'s treatment of her black housekeeper:

> Later, when the boys were alone, Peter returned to the subject. "Darling, why does C. B. think it's so funny for Sapphire to be a singer?" he wondered out loud.
> "Oh, I suppose she knows it's all just a fake."
> "I don't see why it should be, necessarily. Lots of Negro singers have started out as somebody's cook. I don't think she should laugh at her."
> "Naturally, she doesn't laugh at her to her face," Charlie said with a dismissive tone. He didn't like criticism of C. B., and he was accustomed to Peter taking conversational directions from him. "You heard her. She said she treated the whole thing completely seriously."
> "Yes, but—well, I know Negroes too. They're not necessarily like children."

"Oh, come off it. She's letting her go, isn't she? Lots of people would've made a big stink about it."
"Yes, I suppose so."
The brief conversation left a little cloud between them that dinner at the club did nothing to dispel.[40]

The slight argument lasts only a few seconds, but it reveals the extent to which Charlie's racism is connected to his grandmother—and to his sense of masculinity. By contrast, Peter, who perceives and disapproves of such prejudice, is also the one who argues for living openly and honestly as a gay man. The intention here seems fairly clear: the same conservatism and bigotry that sustains racial prejudice is also what keeps gay men from self-acceptance. Gordon was not alone in making this connection in the 1960s—Crowley's *Boys in the Band* has a very similar point—even if he was clumsy about it.

Such clumsiness also helps to explain the character of Sapphire Hall, the most prominent black figure in the novel. Hall begins as a housekeeper in C. B.'s household before being discovered by Otto Kahn, the real-life president of the Metropolitan Opera, and becoming a famous opera singer. Unfortunately, Hall is at times redolent of a Mammy stereotype, in part because of Gordon's unskillfulness in representing African-American speech—the distinction between authenticity and mimicry is not always clear. Still, as with so much of Gordon's writing, biographical information reveals a more complex meaning. In this case, the seemingly fanciful detail about Otto Kahn and the Met Opera (an anachronism, since the actual Kahn died years before the novel's setting) derives from one of Gordon's early experiences. In the late 1930s when Gordon was pursuing an acting career, he worked briefly as a supernumerary at the Metropolitan Opera for a production of Verdi's *Aida*.[41] He would have noticed the regular practice of casting white singers as African characters (typically wearing blackface), and he likely heard about the public pressure to hire black singers in lead roles. He likely also heard about Otto Kahn's recent unsuccessful attempts to engage more black singers, including a production of Gershwin's *Porgy and Bess* with a predominantly black company of singers.[42] In this light, Gordon's historical rewriting of Kahn appears as an attempt, however unpersuasively, to revive the 1930s controversy over black artists and remind his reader of the racial prejudice that had permeated New York society, including himself.

Ironically, given the novel's reputation in the twenty-first century, Gordon likely thought he was being progressive with the Harlem episode. His original version of *The Vallency Tradition* had made him a liberal champion in Paris in the 1950s precisely because of its representation of racial issues, and he surely thought he was being even bolder here: the new novel not only had an interracial couple but a *gay* interracial couple. In addition to connecting the character of Sapphire Hall to the Metropolitan Opera and adding details recalling Josephine Baker (who Gordon *had* seen perform in New York in the 1930s), he also made her the novel's mouthpiece for gay acceptance.

After the Harlem party, Peter rebounds from Charlie's eruption and continues to socialize with his gay friends. At a party he meets Walter Pitney, a wealthy older man who offers to support him financially, asking only for his friendship and the opportunity to watch him masturbate from time to time. Editors and critics would later cite this storyline as an example of the novel's incredibility, though here again Gordon had a real-life model in mind: his ex-lover Otis Bigelow, the primary model for the character of Peter, who, after breaking up with Gordon, actually did get into a one-sided relationship with a rich older man who showered him with lavish gifts and money in exchange for the occasional opportunity to see him naked.[43] At the same party Peter meets Tim Thornton, a tall, blue-eyed lawyer who immediately sweeps him off his feet. The two move in together and settle into a passionate, committed relationship. Unlike Charlie, Tim approves of Peter's characterization of their relationship as a marriage. "I've got myself a husband," Peter tells him, "It's about time. I pronounce us man and something-or-other. We're married, big boy."[44]

Meanwhile Charlie devolves into a destructive cycle of self-pity. His marriage to Hattie becomes more strained. They both get parts in a small Broadway play, but the stress of the rehearsals only exacerbates their problems. Moreover, when C. B. learns that Charlie has quit his publishing job for the theater, she summarily disinherits him. Charlie starts drinking during rehearsals and arguing with the play's director, until one day when the director erupts at Charlie and calls him a "Park Avenue faggot." Charlie punches him and gets fired from the play. The incident unleashes a torrent from Hattie, who weaponizes her knowledge of Charlie's feelings for Peter: "You are a faggot. Not a plain, ordinary faggot, but a dedicated faggot. You can't have a roll in the hay for fun or profit. You've got to have the boy of your dreams."[45] The argument leads to a brutal fight, in which Hattie mutilates Charlie's penis with her teeth before being beaten unconscious. (Gordon got the idea for this violent episode from the 1940s news stories about Wayne Lonergan, whom he had known personally and who would later be the basis of another of Gordon's novels.) Charlie, barely able to walk and thinking he has killed Hattie, drags himself out of the apartment to a telephone booth and, broken and desperate, calls Peter for help.

The last forty pages of the novel sensitively detail Charlie and Peter's reconciliation. Peter gets medical help for Charlie and checks on Hattie (who is badly beaten but not dead). He patiently helps Charlie make sense of things, and in the process the two realize they still love each other. For Peter, the decision to leave Tim is a difficult but inevitable one. Charlie's path is more difficult, since reuniting with Peter requires a redefinition of his self-image. He is forced to recognize the depth of his internalized homophobia, and he is forced to be honest with himself and others, most notably C. B. In the first version of the novel, Charlie telephones C. B. to tell her the truth about his love for Peter, whereupon she brusquely hangs up. The novel ends with Charlie and Peter vowing themselves to each other and gazing into each other's eyes. Charlie's last words in the novel are effusive: "You're not true. I've measured everything, but there's so much more. You go on and on and on. I'll never get to the end of you. I'm going to try, darling. Just give me a lifetime to try."[46]

Gordon had never ended a work with such unrestrained sentimentality. His publisher would later claim that *no* writer had ended a novel in this way—with two gay men happily together. This was not entirely accurate, since there were a few earlier gay-themed novels with happy endings.[47] But it was true that no mainstream publisher had printed a gay novel as graphic and affirmative as this one. And it was true that the vast majority of gay novels *did* end in tragedy of one sort or another. Gordon at one point alludes to this convention in the middle of the novel, when Peter briefly contemplates suicide: "You're asking me to kill myself. I've been thinking about doing just that. I guess I'm not the type. It all seems all right up to the point where I pull the trigger or jump or whatever, and then I know I couldn't do it."[48] Before this, Gordon had always ended his novels with a tragic anagnorisis, a climactic self-discovery that leaves the protagonist broken and disillusioned. *Reflections* was a stark departure from his usual form.

Why did he do this? There are several possible reasons. The most obvious is E. M. Forster, whose influence always loomed large in Gordon's imagination. The last section of *Reflections* is replete with echoes of the end of *Maurice*, particularly the scene in which Maurice, thinking he has lost his lover Scudder, finds him in the boathouse and stays with him forever. It is possible that Gordon got his hands on one of the few gay paperback novels published in the 1960s that had dared to end with an affirmation of homosexuality—such as Richard Amory's *Loon* novels.[49] If Gordon had read these, he would have noticed their sexual explicitness, believing he could improve upon them with his elegant literary style. Indeed, in the novel's epilogue, Gordon roguishly identifies *Reflections* as a modern-day, gay-themed Jane Austen novel. (Strange as it may seem, there is a real similarity between the narrative arcs of *Reflections* and *Pride and Prejudice*.) The end of the epilogue, in which the narrator switches to first-person voice and appears to speak as Gordon himself, is an admirable attempt to imitate both Austen and Forster: "Always there would be Peter and Charlie, surviving the separation of war, against exotic backgrounds, passion intact if tempered by the years, experiencing daily happiness that plunges sometimes into despair, since it is man's nature to be easily surfeited with happiness. There would be very little new to record, for they have developed within the circle of their preoccupation with each other, a limitation that all intense relationships impose. Peter and Charlie. Peter has always been one for public declarations. I can't do better than this."[50]

One of the few critics who recognized the extent of Gordon's debt to Forster in *The Lord Won't Mind* was the writer and journalist Alexander Chee. He discussed the Forsterian origins of the novel first in a 1996 *Advocate* article on Gordon and more recently in a series of articles on Forster for the *New Republic*. Chee was also one of the very few readers who recognized that Gordon's novel contained a significant amount of autobiographical material, and so he was in a unique position to evaluate the influence of Forster on Gordon. As Chee put it, "two gay love stories, the one hidden by Forster and the other lived by Merrick, it seems, inspired the third, which, like *Maurice*, was meant to be purely a sympathetic tale of love between two men, a subversive act at the time." Not surprisingly, Chee also took the sex scenes in *Lord* seriously. Despite the critical tradition of ridiculing the novel's explicit sex scenes (usually by taking one or two lines out of context), Chee actually found them effective and integral to the novel. In this respect he further suggested the importance of Forster's literary model, which, above all, had been a novelistic manifesto of the importance of "flesh educating the spirit."[51]

The second reason for the happy ending is more political. At the same time he was making the final edits to his manuscript, Gordon read Donn Teal's landmark essay in the *New York Times* about the "tragic gay" convention. In the article, Teal (writing as Ronald Forsythe) decries the current state of gay-themed art, which invariably depicts gay people as doomed or pathetic. He cites the tentatively optimistic portrayals by writers like James Barr and Mary Renault, but for him these are overwhelmed by the tragic examples in novels by Radclyffe Hall, Gore Vidal, James Baldwin, Christopher Isherwood, and others. Moreover, Teal argues that this problem is not merely a matter of aesthetics, but of gay civil rights in general:

> At this point—if not long before—the heterosexual will insist: "How can you expect to see lasting love, marriage, the happy ending, in books and plays and music when these things don't exist for you in *life*?" We might counter in anger with, "For the most part, we did not make life as it is for us or the laws as they exist against us. . . . If our ultimate life goals have not yet been achieved, is this to prevent writers from fantasizing them? Haven't there always been artists who dreamed, who romanticized, who envisioned a better life—only to have some of those dreams come true?"[52]

In other words, gay people will be better equipped to achieve "a better life" if they can see it represented in art. Teal thus challenges gay writers to do just that, making the strategic objective as clear as possible: "Among the great modern creations, we still look in vain for the *happy ending*."

Gordon was moved enough by Teal's essay to write a reply to the *Times*, which the newspaper published. He wholeheartedly endorsed Teal's argument for the "happy ending," though he made one qualification:

> It strikes me, to dot Mr. Forsythe's i's for him, that the happy ending is essential to a serious and truthful treatment of homosexuality. The permissiveness that accepts it as a dirty joke or as simply dirty or, at best, as a tragic aberration leading conveniently to an early death, is another aspect of the sensationalism or voyeurism which pervades our fiction and drama. The happy ending attacks the roots of what is to me a social and moral error and brings the subject into the light of reason and love.[53]

Gordon's point was that some gay people *were* already living happily, and it was now the job of writers to document this reality. Whether he realized it or not, he was appropriating the "personal is political" dictum that was being used by second-wave feminists at the time. By faithfully representing his own happiness as a gay man, he was doing his part to correct the "social and moral error" that other writers had perpetuated.

The biggest reason for the happy ending may have been the most personal one. When the novel was finished, Gordon dedicated it to Didine Spanier, who had been his friend for over twenty years. She had been in France throughout Gordon's ten-year relationship with Richardson, and now she had seen Gordon's relationship with Hulse grow over the last fourteen years. He had her partly to thank for his ability to live openly in two long-term relationships with men while being surrounded by a circle of friends, and the novel's happy ending was a testament to that fact. The other woman that Gordon was likely thinking about when he wrote the novel was his mother, whose loss he still felt deeply after four years. Although his earlier novels had portrayed his upbringing in a negative light, the experience of writing about his experiences as a young man caused him to reflect on the unconditional love Mimi had always given him. He may have felt that an unapologetically optimistic novel was the most truthful one.

The evidence for this theory is a short, easily forgettable scene in the middle of the novel. Shortly after Charlie breaks up with Peter, he gets a call from his mother in Philadelphia inviting him to lunch. She had heard something from C. B. about a scandal involving Charlie and Peter, and so she takes a train to New York to check on her son. The ensuing meeting is awkward and uncomfortable. Charlie tells his mother that C. B.'s comments about Peter are hysterical exaggerations while at the same time trying hard not to betray his grief over the loss of Peter. He tries to dispel any questions about his sexuality by talking about Hattie, but it is clear that Charlie's mother suspects a more serious relationship between Charlie and Peter. Being a naturally shy and conciliatory person, however, she is too afraid to ask Charlie directly. Instead, she simply reminds Charlie of her love for him: "We love you very much, you know. We want you to know that if you're in any sort of trouble, we're prepared to stand by you."[54] Charlie is too flustered and panicked to listen to what his mother is trying to say, and he quickly changes the subject of the conversation.

The scene between Charlie and his mother is unique in Gordon's writing. It is the only moment in the novel where a member of Charlie's immediate family appears, and it is the only moment in *any* of Gordon's novels in which he fictionalized someone in his immediate family. The scene has no impact on the rest of the story; if anything it weakens the novel by introducing a character who is never developed. For these reasons it is all the more probable as a narrativization of an actual conversation Gordon had with his mother, Mimi. Charlie's mother uses the same language that Mimi used in her letters to Gordon, and her personality accords with descriptions of Mimi by Gordon and others. Gordon's motivation for writing the scene seems to have been a desire to commemorate his mother in his writing, however briefly. If so, then he chose a memory that was poignant but hardly sentimental—a moment in which he was too insecure and self-absorbed to recognize the fact of his mother's unflagging love. It would have been a difficult scene to write.

This may be the most personal scene that Gordon ever wrote. Without question, *Reflections in the Mirror* was the most personal novel Gordon had written so far. It had the same direct, Fitzgeraldesque prose as his previous novels, but its voice was more essentially his own. He had reconstructed the formative events of his heady youth as well as the emotional and physical thrills of his early romances. Yet he also framed these experiences from the perspective of a middle-aged man, one who knew firsthand what it was like to be in a long-term relationship with another man. Despite its undeniable "old-fashionedness," Gordon knew that it was different than anything he had read before. Perhaps it could even become the first Great Gay American Novel. *If* he could find someone to publish it.

NOTES

1. Gordon Merrick to Monica McCall, 18 May 1967, Monica McCall Collection, box 75, folder 41.

2. Ellis Amburn to Monica McCall, 23 October 1967, Monica McCall Collection, box 75, folder 41.

3. Robert A. Gutwillig to Monica McCall, 22 May 1967, Monica McCall Collection, box 75, folder 41.

4. Rainer J. Hanshe, "James Purdy: Bibliography," *Hyperion* 6, no. 1 (2011): 222–26.

5. Gordon Merrick, television adaptation of *The Strumpet Wind*, GMP, box 15, folder 12.

6. Keith Howes, "Once A Spy . . . ," *Gay News*, August 24, 1978.

7. Christopher Bram, *Eminent Outlaws: The Gay Writers Who Changed America* (New York: Twelve, 2012), 46–53.

8. Fred Kaplan, "The Day Obscenity Became Art," *New York Times*, July 20, 2009.

9. See Ricardo L. Ortiz, "L.A. Women: Jim Morrison with John Rechy," in *The Queer Sixties*, ed. Patricia Juliana Smith, 164–86 (New York: Routledge, 1999).

10. Bram, *Eminent Outlaws*, 114–15; Joseph Bristow, "'I Am with You, Little Minority Sister': Isherwood's Queer Sixties," in *The Queer Sixties*, 145–63; Claude J. Summers, *Gay Fictions: Wilde to Stonewall: Studies in a Male Homosexual Literary Tradition* (New York: Continuum, 1990), 199–214.

11. Drewey Wayne Gunn and Jaime Harker, eds., *1960s Gay Pulp Fiction* (Amherst: University of Massachusetts Press, 2013), 3–13; Philip Clark, "'Accept Your Essential Self': The Guild Press, Identity Formation, and Gay Male Community," in *1960s Gay Pulp Fiction*, 78–119; David Bergman, "The Cultural Work of Sixties Gay Pulp Fiction," in *The Queer Sixties*, 35–40; Susan Stryker, *Queer Pulp: Perverted Passions from the Golden Age of the Paperback* (San Francisco: Chronicle Books, 2001); Laurence Miller, "The 'Golden Age' of Gay and Lesbian Literature in Mainstream Mass-Market Paperbacks," *Paperback Parade* 47 (February 1997): 37–66; Tom Norman, *American Gay Erotic Paperbacks: A Bibliography* (Burbank: Tom Norman, 1994); Ian Young, *Out in Paperback: A Visual History of Gay Pulps* (Albion, NY: MLR Press, 2012); Ian Young, "The Paperback Explosion: How Gay Paperbacks Changed America," in *The Golden Age of Gay Fiction*, ed. Drewey Wayne Gunn, 3–12 (Albion, NY: MLR Press, 2009).

12. Michael Bronski, ed., *Pulp Friction: Uncovering the Golden Age of Gay Male Pulps* (New York: St. Martin's Griffin, 2003), 17.

13. Stanley Kauffmann, "Homosexual Drama and Its Disguises," *New York Times*, January 23, 1966. Some historians have criticized Kauffmann's essay as a disingenuous vehicle for homophobic bigotry (see Bram, *Eminent Outlaws*, 82–83). While his prejudice against "homosexual dramatists" is certainly evident in places, his main argument—that gay people should be represented explicitly—was taken seriously by many readers.

14. Matt Bell, ed., *The Boys in the Band: Flashpoints of Cinema, History, and Queer Politics* (Detroit: Wayne State University Press, 2016), 4, 27n3; Bram, *Eminent Outlaws*, 138–40; David A. Crespy, *Richard Barr: The Playwright's Producer* (Carbondale: Southern Illinois University Press, 2013), 150–57.

15. Gordon Merrick, *The Lord Won't Mind* (New York: Bernard Geis, 1970), 3.

16. Merrick, *The Lord Won't Mind*, 4.

17. David Perry, "A Gentleman from Another Country," *Bay Area Reporter*, June 30, 1988.

18. Merrick, *The Lord Won't Mind*, 4, 9.

19. "An Exclusive Interview with Gordon Merrick," *Michael's Thing* 1, no. 30 (1971): 13.

20. Gordon Merrick, interview by Brandon Judell.

21. Gordon Merrick to Mary Merrick, 2 July 1935, 18 February 1936, 3 December 1936, private collection.

22. U.S. World War II draft registration card for Robert Hardy Smith, serial no. 4717, order no. 4052, Asheville, NC, October 16, 1940.

23. Wendy Moffat, *A Great Unrecorded History: A New Life of E. M. Forster* (New York: Farrar, Straus and Giroux, 2010), 244.

24. Jerry Rosco, *Glenway Wescott Personally: A Biography* (Madison: University of Wisconsin Press, 2002), 139; Redmond Wallis, Diary, 28–29, Redmond Frankton Wallis Papers, MSX-6716.

25. Merrick, *The Lord Won't Mind*, 20.

26. Gordon Merrick, *Reflections in the Mirror*, manuscript, 13, Merrick Papers, box 13, folder 1; Merrick, *The Lord Won't Mind*, 15. A manuscript version with Merrick's final handwritten changes can be found in GMP, box 13, folder 14.

27. Merrick, *Reflections in the Mirror*, 13; Merrick, *The Lord Won't Mind*, 15, emphases mine.

28. Merrick, *The Lord Won't Mind*, 21–22.

29. Merrick, *Reflections in the Mirror*, 22; Merrick, *The Lord Won't Mind*, 22.

30. Merrick, *Reflections in the Mirror*, 24.

31. "An Exclusive Interview with Gordon Merrick."

32. Charles Hulse, interview by the author.

33. Charles Hulse, interview by the author.

34. Merrick, *The Lord Won't Mind*, 22.

35. Merrick, *The Lord Won't Mind*, 58.

36. Merrick, *The Lord Won't Mind*, 185.

37. Michael Schwartz, "David Leavitt's Inner Child," *Harvard Gay & Lesbian Review* 2, no. 1 (Winter 1995): 43; Charles Busch, "Guilty Pleasures," *The Advocate*, September 19, 1995.

38. Merrick, *The Lord Won't Mind*, 183.

39. Merrick, *The Lord Won't Mind*, 185.

40. Merrick, *The Lord Won't Mind*, 47–48.

41. Mitch Douglas, interview by the author.

42. Theresa M. Collins, *Otto Kahn: Art, Money, and Modern Time* (Chapel Hill: University of North Carolina Press, 2002), 256–57.

43. Charles Kaiser, *The Gay Metropolis: The Landmark History of Gay Life in America* (New York: Grove Press, 1997), 8–9.

44. Merrick, *The Lord Won't Mind*, 218.

45. Merrick, *The Lord Won't Mind*, 279.

46. Merrick, *The Lord Won't Mind*, 335.

47. James J. Gifford identifies Edward Prime-Stevenson's 1906 novel *Imre* as "the first great American gay novel" and "the first known American novel in which two men end up happily together." James J. Gifford, "Proem: How to Read Gay Pulp Fiction," Gunn and Harker, eds., in *1960s Gay Pulp Fiction*, 30–31. See also Victor J. Banis, "The Gay Publishing Revolution," in *The Golden Age of Gay Fiction*, ed. Drewey Wayne Gunn, 113–25 (Albion, NY: MLR Press, 2009), 117.

48. Merrick, *The Lord Won't Mind*, 141.

49. See Clark, "Accept Your Essential Self"; Whitney Strub, "Historicizing Pulp: Gay Male Pulp and the Narrativization of Queer Cultural History," Gunn and Harker, eds., in *1960s Gay Pulp Fiction*, 43–77.

50. Merrick, *The Lord Won't Mind*, 280.

51. Alexander Chee, "Paperback Writer," *The Advocate*, June 1996; Alexander Chee, "The Afterlives of E. M. Forster," *New Republic*, September 21, 2021. For a discussion of the importance of sex to Forster's novel, see Claude J. Summers, *Gay Fictions: Wilde to Stonewall: Studies in a Male Homosexual Literary Tradition* (New York: Continuum, 1990), 89–93.

52. Ronald Forsythe [Donn Teal], "Why Can't 'We' Live Happily Ever After, Too?," *New York Times*, February 23, 1969.

53. "Living Happily Ever After?," Letters to the Editor, *New York Times*, March 16, 1969.

54. Merrick, *The Lord Won't Mind*, 195.

Chapter Eleven

Getting It Published

Gordon's literary agent was a force of nature. When he hired Monica McCall to represent him in 1966, she was already a legend in the New York publishing world. She had been instrumental in establishing the careers of several writers, such as Richard Yates and David Martin, and had represented a long list of venerables, from Alice Walker to Graham Greene. People in the industry knew she only took on clients whose work she respected, and when she did, she was an unflagging advocate. Blake Bailey, in his biography of Yates, captures the combination of fierceness and geniality that made McCall such an effective agent:

> Often described as "a perfect English lady," sweet and devoted to her clients, she was also tough as nails and never to be trifled with. A grande dame who resembled "a pretty version of Margaret Rutherford." . . . McCall inherited the same quirky, determined nature that had spurred one of her sisters to leap off London's Waterloo Bridge after a failed love affair and another to become a nun who vanished at a tender age into a vow of silence.

She also had a droll wit to match her steely reputation. John D. Spooner, the investment advisor turned novelist, recalled her memorable quips about writers and agents. "All writers are children," she once said, "particularly the men. Novelists are the most interesting, and the neediest, because they almost never get what they think they deserve."[1]

McCall was also a lesbian, having lived for many years with her longtime partner Muriel Rukeyser, the provocative American poet. For all her primness and properness—she kept an embroidered footstool under her office desk— she was an ardent leftist. Rukeyser had been actively involved with a number of liberal causes, and McCall herself had once been arrested for protesting the Vietnam War in the U.S. Senate building.[2] Such political leanings may partly explain why McCall agreed to represent Gordon, who had established himself as a writer of protest novels. His openness about his own long-term, same-sex relationship may also have impressed her. Gordon originally hired her to place *The Day the Dog Talked*, now titled *A Day with Leighton*, and she dutifully used her connections to get the manuscript read by over a dozen editors in New York. When none of them accepted the novel, she encouraged Gordon to keep writing, assuring him that *Leighton* could be published later when the market was more favorable. When Gordon subsequently presented her with the manuscript for *Reflections in the Mirror*, she did not flinch. She promptly set the wheels in motion, making sure the novel would be seen by the city's top publishers.

Still, finding a publisher for an openly gay novel was a challenge, even for McCall. The normal course would have been to approach first William Morrow or Julian Messner, who had published Gordon's earlier novels. McCall refrained from this strategy, however, perhaps because she thought their highbrow reputations would make them wary of a book like *Reflections*. Instead, she sent the manuscript to Putnam, Delacorte-Dell, and David McKay, all established publishers of hardcover literary fiction but also known for taking risks and experimenting with edgier or more provocative books.³ Delacorte-Dell was then preparing to release Kurt Vonnegut's *Slaughterhouse 5*, and David McKay had just given the green light to David Reuben's *Everything You Always Wanted to Know about Sex* (*But Were Afraid to Ask)*. Putnam had already published Geoff Brown's *I Want What I Want* (1967), a novel about a male-to-female transsexual. Even so, all three firms quickly rejected *Reflections*. Most likely they felt that the novel's explicit sex scenes and unapologetic representation of gay themes were a bridge too far.

Shrewd agent that she was, McCall still had one card up her sleeve. She decided to send the manuscript to Bernard Geis, one of New York's less conventional publishers. Geis, who owned his own firm, had a special talent for turning unusual and edgy books into bestsellers. He had just published Jacqueline Susann's *Valley of the Dolls* (1966), which stayed on the *New York Times* bestseller list for a breathtaking sixty-five weeks before being made into a film starring Patty Duke. Geis had landed another big hit with David Slavitt's *The Exhibitionist* (1967), an erotic potboiler whose edginess had scandalized the literary elites and compelled Slavitt to use a pseudonym. It sold over four million copies. McCall of course knew all this, and so she sent him the manuscript for *Reflections* with a single sentence she knew would get his attention: "I have from Gordon Merrick his fourth novel REFLECTIONS IN THE MIRROR, an explicit homosexual love story, an affirmation rather than an exploitation of the sordid kinds and kookinesses."[4]

Geis took the bait. He quickly sent the manuscript to his two senior editors with instructions to read it and then recommend either publication or rejection. The first editor, Don Preston, was an experienced reader who had worked extensively on the revisions to Susann's *Valley of the Dolls* before it was published. He had started his career with big dreams, imagining himself as "the next Maxwell Perkins" (the iconic editor of Ernest Hemingway and F. Scott Fitzgerald). At Geis's firm he had developed a talent for improving manuscripts by middling writers and making them successful. His initial assessment of Susann, for example, was utterly castigating: "she is a painfully dull, inept, clumsy, undisciplined, rambling and thoroughly amateurish writer whose every sentence, paragraph and scene cries for the hand of a pro." Yet he agreed to overhaul the manuscript, trimming and rewriting it until it became, in his words, a "more readable mediocrity."[5]

Even with his experience of *Valley of the Dolls*, Preston could find no reasons to publish *Reflections in the Mirror*. He didn't think Gordon was a horrible writer (like Susann) and admitted that "there are flashes of something good here and there." He also did not object to the *idea* of an explicitly gay novel. He acknowledged the possibility that an optimistic, sentimental treatment of gay love could be "refreshing." But Preston ultimately concluded that Gordon's story was unbelievable. In his estimation, *Reflections* was simply another heterosexual romance novel, with only the names (and some body parts) changed:

> So much of it is so damned trite. Try reading any one of the love scenes and substituting "Mary" for "Peter." (I know the physical details won't fit, but the point is that that is *all* one has to distinguish the stuff from the most syrupy sort of Ladies' Magazine romantic fiction.)

Throughout his evaluation Preston repeatedly condemns *Reflections* by comparing it to women's magazines, as though he could not imagine a male reader (gay or straight) enjoying a sentimental novel. For him the novel's "sweetness" was its mortal flaw. Its sentimentality made it more like the "cheapie paperbacks" than like Stuart Engstand's *The Sling and the Arrow* or Gore Vidal's *The City and the Pillar*—both gay novels in which the protagonist comes to a tragic end.[6]

Preston's rejection of the novel was not motivated by a deeply rooted homophobia. He appeared fairly comfortable with gay subject matter, especially for an editor in 1968, and he seems to have appreciated the gay liberation movement. Nonetheless, he was simply unable to comprehend the fact that starry-eyed romance between men could truly exist. For him, the same effusive sentimentality that was "trite" in a heterosexual story was "not entirely realistic" in the case of two men. In Preston's gendered view, sex and romance are separate things where men are concerned. Thus while he detected some innovation in the novel's sex scenes, he could not relate them to the novel's optimism: "Aside from the graphic sexual gymnastics, it is pure saccharine." In the end, he deemed romance to be a wasted, unrealistic goal for gay activists: "The new liberation should be used to a better end, it seems to me."[7] (Interestingly, his comments would be echoed by gay critics of the novel after it was published.)

Geis's second editor, Jackie Farber, was less merciful. Like Preston, she thought that the gay relationships in *Reflections in the Mirror* were unbelievable, but she also found them distasteful. Referring to Peter's nonsexual relationship with the older Walter, she is unabashedly frank in her criticism: "No one would go for a guy setting a faggot up and then just giving him 50,000 dollars because he likes to watch him." Farber's two reviews of the manuscript reveal a discomfort toward homosexual acts that she does not take pains to disguise. She openly admits her bias at the beginning of her evaluation: "I'm put off, I'm afraid, by homosexual novels, more than I could ever be put on, so that I expect my negative feelings about this are heavily influenced by a predisposition to dislike." In spite of—or perhaps because of—her avowed distaste for homosexual material, Farber's reviews are fixated on the novel's gay sex scenes. She barely comments on the romantic plot, dismissing it as a "moony relationship," but has more to say about her lack of interest in the size of Charlie's penis: "But the two young men and their bodies—even though one's [penis is] the biggest one ever wouldn't inspire me to read on. It may be, as you say, that the sex is explicit, but it is hardly shocking. I prefer Portnoy's liver myself."[8]

Farber's remark about Portnoy's liver—which she doubtless thought witty—says much about her preconceptions. She was referring to Philip Roth's novel *Portnoy's Complaint*, which was in press at the time and which has a notorious scene where a Jewish boy masturbates with a piece of liver. By comparing the sex scenes in *Reflections* to the liver episode in *Portnoy's Complaint*, Farber reveals her main prejudice about Gordon's novel. For her, the whole point of a gay sex scene is to "shock" and scandalize its reader. Thus for a gay novel to be original, it has to invent new forms of perversion. *Reflections* clearly did not do this, and so Farber did not see how it would stand out among the sea of gay pulp paperbacks in which gay characters almost always ended up as suicides, murder victims, or alone:

> I've read loads of paperbacks at various times no different in any way from this one—as a matter of fact this affirmation Monica McCall speaks so respectfully about makes it even less interesting than its brothers on the Sixth Avenue bookshop shelves.[9]

In other words, for Farber the novel's happy ending was a liability rather than an innovation. The underlying assumption here is that homosexuality is only interesting as a pathology, as an assault on conventional societal mores. The idea that gay sex could actually be "normal" was inconceivable.

In a typical publishing firm, the evaluations by Preston and Farber would have killed the chances of Gordon's novel. However, Bernard Geis was not a typical publishing firm. The damning reviews made *Reflections* even more appealing to Geis, who seems to have regarded the objections by his senior editors as a personal challenge. Within only a few days of reading their reports, Geis agreed to publish the novel, effectively thumbing his nose at his editors. In a letter to Gordon, Geis boasted that his editorial team voted unanimously against publication, but he gave no explanation for his decision other than the fact that he could pull rank: "It just happens, however, that I have one more vote than the rest of the staff put together."[10] As he had done so often before, Geis was happy to play the "bad boy" in his own company. It was this zeal for rebelliousness—which McCall had shrewdly anticipated—as much as (or even more than) any sincere appreciation of the novel's merits that likely accounted for Geis's alacrity in accepting the manuscript and putting it on a fast track for publication.

At this point McCall's skills as a negotiator came into play. She knew that Gordon wanted the novel to be taken seriously and wanted a book contract similar to his previous ones with Morrow and Messner. But she also knew that Geis was taking a significant risk with *Reflections*, so she had to manage the expectations of both. She gently told Gordon that Geis thought the C. B. character could be expanded "to bring some relief to the overwhelming sex content"—this was a very tempered version of the critiques by Geis's editors, which only McCall had seen. She also tried to mitigate the relatively steep terms of Geis's contract (a flat ten percent in royalties regardless of the number of copies sold, and a signing advance of only a thousand dollars) by repeatedly emphasizing Geis's reputation for producing bestsellers like *Valley of the Dolls* and *The Exhibitionist*. She made much of the generous terms for motion picture royalties (thirty percent), using her inside knowledge of other gay-themed works: "The picture rights to a very successful homosexual play here entitled THE BOYS IN THE BAND have been sold, and so it is possible that Hollywood is opening up." (In fact *Boys in the Band* was made into a feature film directed by William Friedkin the following year.) McCall dexterously balanced this optimism with a gentle reminder that *Reflections* had already been rejected by several publishers and that "book sellers are more likely to take this kind of a book from Geis than from, say, the more conventional houses."[11]

At the same time that she was applying gentle pressure to Gordon, McCall was also aggressively bargaining with Geis. She agreed to the flat royalty fee for hardcover editions of the novel, but she managed to squeeze out a number of other concessions from Geis, including higher royalties for film and theatrical rights. Knowing that Gordon was already at work on a sequel to *Reflections*, she cannily negotiated an improved royalty scheme for future novels. She also secured a generous agreement for paperback reprint rights with Avon Books. This would prove to be very lucrative for Gordon, given that sales of paperback copies of the novel would far exceed the hardcover sales. Geis was both humbled and impressed by McCall's command of the negotiations. "At the risk of bringing a blush to your maiden cheek," he wrote after the terms had been settled, "I must say I hope Mr. Merrick appreciates the tough job of agenting you put in on his behalf."[12] Indeed, McCall had pulled off an impressive feat. As she had done many times before, she got both sides to compromise while making each one feel he had gotten the better deal. By the end of January 1969—exactly six months before the Stonewall riots—they both signed a contract to publish *Reflections in the Mirror* within eighteen months.

A book contract was not an absolute guarantee, however. The contract stipulated that publication was contingent on the final version of the novel being accepted by the publisher, and Geis had plenty of ideas for revision. Instead of handing off the manuscript to one of his editors—whom he likely did not trust to work with Gordon—Geis took on the job of editing the novel himself. He dashed off a long list of "problems" for Gordon to fix. The principal issue concerned the character of C. B., who fascinated Geis and who he thought should play a bigger role in the story. In this respect Geis was of the same mind as Preston and Farber, who had both singled out C. B. as the best part of *Reflections*. Geis, however, veered characteristically toward the melodramatic. In his initial letter to McCall, he had proposed making C. B. a demonic character who practiced black magic, "an ominous Evil Genius." Gordon, somewhat horrified at the suggestion, quickly and firmly refused. Geis relented, but he continued to push the idea of making C. B. a more macabre figure who could add suspense to the novel's climax. He raised the possibility of making her a "repressed lesbian" whose internalized homophobia causes her to hate all homosexuals. His most elaborate plan involved a shocking revelation of family secrets and mistaken paternity:

> It could be that C. B.'s evil secret is that Peter is really the adopted son of the General, that he is the offspring of a long-concealed affair between the General and C. B.'s other daughter. (I know this sounds a bit like a Gilbert & Sullivan plot at this point but it's all in the deftness of the telling.)[13]

In the ensuing scenario, Charlie and Peter realize that theirs is an incestuous relationship, and they respond by clinging together even more soundly, in proud defiance of social taboos.

Clearly, in Geis's hands, *Reflections* would have become an operatic potboiler (though he compared it to Gilbert and Sullivan, his proposed ending is actually closer to Wagner's *Die Walküre*). His recommendations show that, like Farber, he thought the main point of a gay romance was to rebel against social mores: "And so, perhaps, at the end, Charlie and Peter defy the devil (C. B.), society, and every convention known to morality, resolving to live according to their definition of love." He was eager to conscript *Reflections* into the sexual liberation movement, comparing the novel to *Hair*, the controversial musical of hippie culture that had just begun its long run on Broadway, and to the growing popularity of unisex fashion.[14] This "revolutionary" reading of the novel put Gordon in a quandary. He had not written the novel as a vehicle for 1960s counterculture—in fact, his aim was much the opposite. He wanted to show that gay relationships *could* be normal, that gays could fit into society without subverting it. His model was not *Hair* but Forster's still-unpublished *Maurice*. If anything, Gordon's novel was more assimilationist than *Maurice* was: while Forster's gay protagonists end up living outside of society, Gordon's gay heroes go on to fight in World War II.

Gordon's solution to the problem of getting his book published *and* keeping his original vision was both ingenious and effective. He agreed to have C. B. reappear at the end of the novel, as Geis had proposed, but instead of making her a practitioner of black magic, he made her financial support the "spell" that had always subdued Charlie and that he ultimately has to relinquish in order to be with Peter. (As before, Gordon was remembering, with mixed emotions, the influence of his own powerful grandmother.) Gordon also followed Geis's suggestion to revise the ending to include the revelation of a scandalous secret. Instead of lesbianism or incest, however, C. B.'s secret is the "truth" of her racial identity:

> Her voice sank again, as if she could barely bring herself to speak. "My mother was a vile and evil woman. My father was a Negro. . . . There's no need to tell you how I learned it," she said in a spent voice. "My mother was very rich. The man I called my father allowed himself to be used by her, but the secret wasn't kept. When I found out, your mother was already born and it was too late. I very nearly opened my veins and let the blood run from them. I would never let any man touch me again. Your grandfather died for failing to respect that resolution."

In revealing her biracial identity, C. B. also confirms her racism, which turns out to be the real reason she tries to prevent Charlie from marrying a woman. She uses her secret to try to convince Charlie to abandon Peter, telling him that her Negro blood is the true source of his "treacherous and insidious passion." Her argument fails utterly. Charlie casts her off for good and rushes back to Peter, affirming their relationship even more than before: "If he was going to be an outcast, he might as well be a thorough one. A bit of black blood was the final touch."[15]

Impressively, Gordon had taken Geis's instructions and used them to improve his novel. By making C. B.'s secret about race, he managed to reinforce the connection between homophobia and racism that he had established earlier in the novel. Admittedly there is some clumsiness here as well—it's ambiguous whether Charlie's sense of "outcast" refers to society's treatment of biracial people or to biracial people themselves. The generous reading of the passage suggests that Charlie is forced to confront his own racist feelings, and his family's influence on them, and that in the end he rejects society's proscriptions on homosexuality and miscegenation. The addition of this episode with C. B. also gave Gordon the opportunity to craft a true "coming out" scene. In the original version Charlie only mentions a telephone call to C. B., who hangs up when she learns about his reunion with Peter.[16] In the revised version, the physical presence of C. B. compels Charlie to explain himself more fully:

> Charlie looked at her levelly. She knew everything, and the heavens hadn't fallen. There was no point in beating around the bush any longer. He thought of Peter's faith in him and found that it wasn't difficult to speak the truth. "I love him, C. B. He explained it to you. How did he say it? 'I love him in every possible way, the way men love women.' I don't know how it happened, but I wouldn't want it to be any different." Unknown to him, a joyful grin began to spread across his face at finally sharing with her some truth about himself.[17]

This is not the first "coming out" scene in American literature, but it is one of the earliest that handles the issue with such frankness and optimism. Gordon may have been remembering things he had said as a young gay man—or perhaps imagining what he *would* have said had he been as brave as Charlie. Near the end of his life Gordon revealed that such a confrontation with his actual grandmother had occurred, when he was seeing Otis Bigelow. In the same breath he also said that he hoped he was "not quite as boring as Charlie," meaning—very ambiguously—that either he had not been as enlightened as Charlie or had not taken so long to figure things out.[18]

In terms of Geis's other main instruction, Gordon was less tractable. Geis, like his editors, had thought that the amount of sex in the novel was excessive: "One marshmallow is good. Two are better. Three or four, however, eaten in rapid succession, can get awfully cloying."[19] In response Gordon made some alterations to the sex scenes, but he retained nearly all of them. Again, he was trusting his own instincts. He had worked meticulously on these scenes, and he was convinced that these episodes were important focal points in the novel, not extraneous "marshmallows." He would have remembered the gentle criticism of *The Strumpet Wind* by Forster, who had found the heterosexual romance in that novel unconvincing, and decided to listen to Forster rather than Geis in this matter. He knew that the novel's success depended on the realism of his gay characters, and sex was indispensable in establishing this credibility.

Despite the fact that Gordon had not fully complied with his instructions, Geis accepted the revised manuscript in the middle of June 1969. Geis either liked the changes that Gordon had made, or he sensed that he could only push Gordon so far. In any case he was grateful for the quick turnaround—Gordon had taken less than two months to complete the bulk of the revisions. Timing was everything in Geis's publishing strategy, and he did not want to delay the book's publication. Though he could not have known it, the Stonewall riots would take place only a couple weeks later, just a few miles from Geis's office in New York. However, he may have sensed—as many others did at the time—a growing momentum for gay liberation and visibility. As always, he was ever on the alert for a possible angle for promoting his books.

One change that Geis *did* insist on was the book's title, which too closely resembled that of another recent book. Gordon thought it over for two days, and he finally decided on *The Lord Won't Mind*—taken from the speech spoken by Sapphire Hall, the black opera singer in the novel. Geis loved the new title, and Gordon himself considered it an improvement, noting that it is "good for a film, too."[20]

At this point the Bernard Geis publicity machine switched into high gear. He began scouting for advance reviews of the novel. Gordon clearly thought of his novel as a serious work, worthy of being endorsed by the leading gay writers of the day, and so he suggested Gore Vidal and Edward Albee. Geis accordingly sent advance copies to Vidal and Albee, as well as Norman Mailer and other illustrious writers, in the hope of getting blurbs to splash on the book's cover.[21] After receiving little response, he took a different approach. He decided to market the novel as a combination of probing psychological study and progressive political treatise. For the book's cover, he selected a stark design in which a silhouette of two male figures appears against a black background—an image that deliberately evoked the genre of psychological "case studies." The cover, designed by an artist named Jay Gendell, contrasted sharply with the paperback edition, whose sensuous, colorful image would eventually come to typify the covers of Gordon's gay novels.

The political angle was promoted even more aggressively. The description on the dust jacket's inside flap, engineered by Geis, places the novel firmly in its cultural moment:

> Seldom does an author dare write a novel or play about homosexuals without ending the story in suicide, disaster, or at least deep despair. Does this mean that all homosexual relationships are inevitably doomed? Or does it mean that, up

to now, our authors have knuckled under to the taboos of the society in which they live?

Gordon Merrick . . . has dared espouse the thesis that not only can a homosexual relationship be a happy one—albeit beset with all of the tribulations and conflicts of any other relationship—but that the author need not tack on an unhappy ending to please the censors. . . . The barbaric attitude of society toward the homosexual is rapidly changing. And that change of attitude can only be accelerated by *The Lord Won't Mind*—the most forthright, explicit and affirmative novel published to date on the subject.[22]

And Geis did not stop here. On the back cover, he plastered a lengthy quotation from Donn Teal's recent manifesto in the *New York Times*—the same article that had prompted Gordon to write a letter to the editor. Geis used the section of Teal's essay that most squarely framed the dearth of affirmative gay literature as a political issue:

Where are Our classics? We have none. One might almost say We have no literature, classic or modern; at least We have no *triumphant* literature, no great story where love conquers all . . . and therefore We have little to turn to for inspiration or for consolation or for that blissful feeling that what We are is Right.

Who are We? We are the American homosexual.

Much like the American Negro of twenty to thirty years ago who saw himself on stage and screen—and read about himself in novels—as Ole Black Joe or Prissy or Shoe Shine Boy, the American homosexual has a complaint: He does not believe his life must end in tragedy and would like to see a change in his image reflected in the entertainment he pays to see and the books he buys to read. Like any minority group, he, too, wants his "Place in the Sun."[23]

To reinforce this marketing strategy, Geis bought advertisements in the *New York Times* and other national publications that trumpeted the novel as "a landmark in the continuing fight against literary censorship."[24] He arranged newspaper and magazine interviews for Gordon to promote the novel, including a radio appearance on the *Dr. Joyce Brothers Show*. Nowhere did the publicity for the novel mention its inclusion of graphic gay sex scenes.

Geis's scheme worked. When *The Lord Won't Mind* hit the bookstore shelves in February 1970, it sold in large numbers almost immediately, and it continued to sell briskly for several months. For whatever reason, a great many people were interested in reading a book that was billed as "the most forthright, explicit and affirmative novel published to date on the subject" of homosexuality.[25] By October 1970, the novel had spent sixteen weeks on the *New York Times* top ten bestseller list, making it the top seller for Bernard Geis that year. It was unquestionably a phenomenon.

NOTES

1. Blake Bailey, *A Tragic Honesty: The Life and Work of Richard Yates* (New York: Picador, 2003), 122–23; John D. Spooner, "What Young Writers Can Learn from a Publishing Pioneer," *Cognoscenti*, July 5, 2013, https://www.wbur.org/cognoscenti/2013/07/05/monica-mccall-john-d-spooner.
2. Alan M. Wald, *Exiles from a Future Time: The Forging of the Mid-Twentieth-Century Literary Left* (Chapel Hill: University of North Carolina Press, 2002), 303; Bailey, *A Tragic Honesty*, 123; Spooner, "What Young Writers Can Learn," *Cognoscenti*.
3. Monica McCall to Gordon Merrick, 16 December 1968, GMP, box 16, folder 1.
4. Monica McCall to Bernard Geis, 14 November 1968, GMP, box 16, folder 1.
5. Jack Stillinger, *Multiple Authorship and the Myth of Solitary Genius* (New York: Oxford University Press, 1991), 145; Barbara Seaman, *Lovely Me: The Life of Jacqueline Susann* (New York: Seven Stories Press, 1996), 286.
6. Don Preston to Bernard Geis, memorandum, 2 December 1968, GMP, box 16, folder 1.
7. Don Preston to Bernard Geis, memoranda, 24 November 1968, 2 December 1968, GMP, box 16, folder 1.
8. Jackie Farber to Bernard Geis, memoranda, 5 December 1968, 22 November 1968, GMP, box 16, folder 1.
9. Jackie Farber to Bernard Geis, memorandum, 5 December 1968.
10. Bernard Geis to Gordon Merrick, 11 February 1969, GMP, box 16, folder 1.
11. Monica McCall to Gordon Merrick, 16 December 1968, GMP, box 16, folder 1.
12. Contract between Bernard Geis Associates and Gordon Merrick for *Reflections in the Mirror*, January 28, 1969; memorandum regarding reprint rights for *Reflections in the Mirror*, January 15, 1969; Bernard Geis to Monica McCall, 6 January 1969, GMP, box 16, folder 1.
13. Bernard Geis to Monica McCall, 6 January 1969; Bernard Geis to Gordon Merrick, 11 February 1969, GMP, box 16, folder 1.
14. Bernard Geis to Gordon Merrick, 11 February 1969.
15. Gordon Merrick, *The Lord Won't Mind* (New York: Bernard Geis, 1970), 272, 274, 278.
16. Gordon Merrick, *Reflections in the Mirror*, manuscript, 335, GMP, box 13, folder 13.
17. Merrick, *The Lord Won't Mind*, 276.
18. Gordon Merrick, interview by Brandon Judell.
19. Bernard Geis to Gordon Merrick, 11 February 1969.
20. Gordon Merrick to Bernard Geis, 26 March 1969, GMP, box 16, folder 1.
21. Bernard Geis to Gordon Merrick, 5 June 1969, GMP, box 16, folder 1.
22. Merrick, *The Lord Won't Mind*, dust jacket.
23. Ronald Forsythe [Donn Teal], "Why Can't 'We' Live Happily Ever After, Too?," *New York Times*, February 23, 1969.

24. Advertisement proof for *The Lord Won't Mind*, undated, GMP, box 21.
25. Merrick, *The Lord Won't Mind*, dust jacket.

Chapter Twelve

The Irene Rockwood Phenomenon

Even if the reading public was ready for an explicitly gay novel like *The Lord Won't Mind*, the literary intelligentsia was considerably less so. Most national newspapers and magazines refused to publish a review of the book, despite the fact that it had been written by an established novelist and published by a leading press. Of the few reviews that *were* published, many were dismissive or highly critical. Some negative reviews were clearly driven by homophobia, but even progressively minded reviewers had few good things to say about the novel. These reviewers, some of them gay themselves, considered the novel irrelevant—or even harmful—to the gay liberation movement. They were not swayed by Geis's marketing of the book as a political manifesto. Thus from the moment it was published, there were two distinct reactions to *The Lord Won't Mind*. One was in the mainstream press and "highbrow" gay periodicals, which ignored or belittled the book. The other was from readers and booksellers around the world, who bought and shared copies of the novel and eagerly devoured its depiction of gay characters.

An unnamed reviewer for the *Brooklyn Record* considered the novel "thoroughly entertaining" and applauded it for "open[ing] the world of the homosexual for all to see"—but this was by far a minority view.[1] Most other reviewers in mainstream newspapers found the novel offensive. Bobby Mather, a married woman with five children who wrote book reviews for the *Detroit Free Press*, summarily dismissed the book as a "trashy novel about Charlie and Peter and their tempestuous homosexual love affair." Rather than being surprised by the novel's sentimentality and idealized characters, she disparaged these qualities as endemic to all gay literature: "As in all homosexual fiction (which tends to be mawkish anyhow), the protagonists are handsome, superbly built, sensitive, intelligent and apt to receive large sums of money from others for no particular reason." The effusive, "mawkish" expressions of love between men seem to have embarrassed her, and she was resolute about the suitability of the novel for other readers like herself: "Maybe the Lord won't [mind], but the reader will."[2]

Janet Quin-Harken, the British book reviewer for the *Pacific Sun*, a San Francisco Bay Area newspaper, was more measured in her criticism. Like Mather she was a married woman with children, but she was also a very cosmopolitan figure, having worked at the BBC in London and the Australian Broadcasting Corporation in Sydney before moving to California with her husband.[3] A fiction writer herself, she had no objection to the *idea* of a gay romance. She had read Donn Teal's article in the *New York Times* about the dearth of positive gay literature, and in her review she wistfully opined that *Lord* "*might* have become a homosexual classic—Peter and Charlie as the first Romeo and Romeo" (my emphasis). But she simply couldn't get past the gay sex scenes. Although she conceded that "graphic depiction" of gay sex might be interesting for a straight reader, the sheer abundance of sex in the novel was a problem for her. She likened *The Lord Won't Mind* to D. H. Lawrence's *Lady Chatterley's Lover*, which had only passingly interested her as a teenage girl: "It reminded me of reading Lady Chatterley at 14. For the first few pages I was keenly interested, yet by the end of the book I could hardly stay awake. One must ask why Merrick is ruining a potentially good book. Even the language suffers, for with the sex scenes come four-letter words by the score, quite out of character."[4] Apparently, for this worldly British journalist, the thought of college-age American men using four-letter words strained the bounds of credibility.

Remarkably, the *National Review*, the conservative bulwark founded by William F. Buckley Jr., agreed to publish a review of *Lord*. Perhaps it was Geis's political marketing that goaded the *Review* to take a stance, or Gordon's previous affiliation with the periodical. Whatever the reason, David Brudnoy, the magazine's book reviewer and a Buckley protégé, took advantage of the opportunity to vent his disgust with the novel. His review was not actually a review, but a synopsis that clearly showed his feelings:

> Grandmother introduces exquisite grandson Charlie to exquisite cousin Peter. Perfect Charlie falls for perfect Peter. Handsome Peter falls for handsome Charlie. Lovely Charlie loves lovely Peter. Precious Peter adores precious Charlie. Magnificent Charlie dotes on magnificent Peter. Virile young Peter moves in with virile young Charlie.

The review goes on and on, outlining the plot of the novel in the same terse, condescending style. Brudnoy saved his only evaluative statements for the end, though still in quippy sentences: "Maybe the Lord won't mind. Discriminating readers will. Gay liberation set back ten years."[5] A quarter century later, Brudnoy would come out as a gay man living with AIDS, noting that he had struggled to conceal his sexuality during his tenure at the *National Review*.[6]

Brudnoy's prediction that *Lord* would "set back" gay rights became a running theme in the reviews. The question was simply how far it would set back gay liberation. Martin Levin, the reviewer for the *New York Times*, put the figure at twenty years in his one-paragraph review:

> Once upon a time, in Rumson, N. J., there were a pair of consenting adult males named Charlie and Peter. But then bad things happened. Charlie got married. To a girl. And Peter got himself kept by a kindly voyeur named Walter Pitney, who sponsored his romance with a lawyer called Tim. Then good things happened. Charlie beat up his wife and left her. Peter left Walter and Tim to be nice to Charlie forever and ever. Unlike "The Staircase" (which developed a pair of interesting characters) this love story focuses on boudoir paraphernalia. It may set homosexuality back at least twenty years.[7]

Even for Levin, who was known for his savage reviews of minor novelists, this was especially snarky.[8] The petulant quips and half-sentences were not his usual style, suggesting he was annoyed at having to review the novel in the first place. (Unlike the more well-known reviewers at the *Times*, Levin did not typically choose the books that he reviewed.) The only specific criticism he could articulate was that the novel was "boudoir paraphernalia"—again, a straight reader offended by the gay sex scenes—and that its characters were less interesting than those in Richard Dyer's *Staircase*.

Levin's allusion to *Staircase* hints at his main problem with *Lord*. Dyer's 1969 novel centers on a middle-aged gay couple, a hairdresser and a pantomime actor, who spend most of their time bickering about their dysfunctional relationship. The work had originally been written as a play that premiered in London in 1966 and was later made into a film starring Rex Harrison and Richard Burton. The play's gay men are campy and stereotypical—"wearisome" and "solipsistic," as Drewey Wayne Gunn puts it—and their relationship is shaped by personal trauma, including prostitution and incest.[9] For Levin, apparently, such trauma makes these gay men more "interesting" than Gordon's characters. In this way he echoed Geis's editors, who instinctively viewed homosexuality as a form of pathology, at least when represented in fiction. They could not see the point of a novel about a successful, stable gay man.

Levin's incredulity was not too surprising. He may have shared Gordon's experience of being an Ivy-educated writer who served in World War II, but he was a heterosexual man with a wife and children. His knowledge of gay men would have largely been shaped by novels and plays that, like Dyer's *Staircase*, represented them as social outcasts and nonconformists. Living in New York City he may very well have seen Crowley's *The Boys in the Band*, which by 1970 had already become a bête noire among gay activists for its putative association of homosexuality and pathology (an interpretation that was reinforced by the 1970 film version).[10]

It is thus ironic that Levin's criticism was also echoed by *gay* reviewers. Like Levin, these critics deplored the novel's sentimentality. The gay activist Peter Ogren wrote a long review of the novel for *Gay*, a weekly New York City magazine, ominously titled "The Lord Won't Mind: The Reader Won't Care." Like the mainstream reviewers, Ogren described the characters of Charlie and Peter with exasperated incredulity: "This novel is about the love affair of two young men, both equally beautiful, handsomely endowed, highly intelligent, and of genteel if somewhat decadent Southern aristocratic stock." However, Ogren did not focus on the sex scenes in the novel and in fact barely mentioned them. Instead he gave a detailed plot synopsis, emphasizing its melodramatic aspects while clearly showing that he had read the novel carefully. His main complaint was about the novel's claim of originality. As far as Ogren was concerned, gay novels with happy endings had been around for years:

> *The Lord Won't Mind* is advertised as a unique gay novel, in that the boys end up happy together. However, this is really no longer unique; witness for example the reunion of the lovers in Baldwin's *Another Country* or more recently the final happy fadeout in *Hours*. Today the publishers of even the sleaziest paperbacks are getting away from the confession-mag complex of punishment for pleasure, and there are many small gay novels, some very well written, with happy endings.

It's unclear which "happy" gay novels Ogren has in mind. Few readers have ever called Baldwin's *Another Country* an optimistic gay novel. Ogren may have been thinking of Richard Amory's *Loon* novels. If so, the fact that *Lord* was published by a hardcover mainstream press and marketed to the general public (unlike Amory's novels) did not impress him. For Ogren it was the utter "happiness" of the ending that made it seem passé: "*The Lord Won't Mind*, weighted against the background of today's literary scene with so many good 'happy' gay novels around, comes off corny, oddly dated, and saccharine."[11]

Ogren's review sheds light on an important strand of gay liberation politics in 1970. On the one hand, gay advocates rightfully fought against the stereotypical and homophobic portrayal of gay men as effete or pathological. On the other hand, many gay activists viewed the movement as a rejection of conservative, heteronormative models of society. This was certainly true of Ogren. At the time he reviewed *Lord*, he was in a relationship with the prominent gay activist Randy Wicker, who later wrote an essay titled "Gay Marriage is a Heterosexual Trap."[12] For gay leaders like Ogren and Wicker, the real problem with *Lord* was that it was too assimilationist. Charlie and Peter's relationship is *too* much like a conventional marriage. As Ogren put it, "the time of this novel is the early forties, and its style and outlook suggest that it was written then, too." Ogren was only partly correct. The novel *was* set in 1939, but it was written nearly thirty years later, by a sixty-two-year-old, Ivy-educated gay man who was living in a long-term relationship with a man and who was *remembering* how he had managed to forge a happy life decades earlier. But this was not the model that many gay activists wanted.

Although Ogren harshly criticized *Lord*, he at least read it carefully and reviewed it at length. Other prominent gay magazines were more cursory, if they reviewed the novel at all. The New York-based *Mattachine Times* declined to review the novel, even though it noted its remarkable sales figures.[13] *Vector*, the leading gay magazine on the West Coast, included only a slender column on *Lord* in its July 1970 issue. Its verdict was short and brutal. The reviewer (whose name was not given) began by acknowledging the novel as a serious literary effort:

> Since this country was conceived nearly two hundred years ago, writers of every inclination have dreamed of creating the "Great American Novel." (Scores of critics still hold up *Moby Dick* as a prime choice.) Thus, discriminating readers who measure the pulse of homophile literature have wondered, in a similar vein, if a *definitive* tale of gay life will someday emerge.

Regular readers of book reviews would likely sense a punch coming at this point. And sure enough: "Let us not postpone the agony any longer. *Lord Won't Mind* is not even in the race." The rest of the review reads as a string of epithets for the novel, calling it a "shallow effort," "a disaster for homosexual feeling on any scale," "a tired sex fantasy," and "a florid piece of Victorian pornography." Unlike Ogren, the *Vector* reviewer gives few specific details about the novel; even so, he still gets basic plot points wrong, suggesting he merely skimmed the novel. He recognizes that *Lord* is an attempt to promote the "gay is good" credo, but he dismisses this as cheap "propaganda." He encourages gay readers instead to turn to Baldwin's *Giovanni's Room* (a novel which ends with the tragic death of its gay protagonist).[14]

The acridity of the *Vector* review may have been motivated by personal reasons as much as aesthetic ones. Although the reviewer is not identified, a likely candidate is Richard Amory, who is listed among the journal's contributors and who officially became its principal book reviewer a few months later.[15] Another possibility is Samuel Steward, also listed as a contributor (under the name Phil Andros), who wrote literary essays for the magazine. Amory, whose *Loon* novels all have happy endings and feature lots of sex and sentimentality, would have had special reason to resent the claim that *Lord* was the "first gay novel with a happy ending." In contrast to *Lord*, Amory's novels were not published in hardcover nor reviewed in the *New York Times*, and they were ineligible for the *Times* bestseller list despite selling thousands of copies. Amory's frustration with the publishing conditions for most gay writers convinced him that gay novels should be published by gay presses, not mainstream ones.[16] This sentiment would explain the condescending tone in the *Vector* review of *Lord*, which seems to resent the novel's aspirations for a mainstream readership. If Amory was personally offended by *Lord*'s success, then it would come as no surprise that *Vector* never again published a review of a Gordon Merrick novel.

Regardless of who wrote the *Vector* review, *The Lord Won't Mind* clearly did not mesh with the magazine's politics. As with *Gay*, the essayists and reviewers at *Vector* tended to reflect the predominant views of gay liberation activists—they were "self-styled reviewer-activists," as the historian Brian Distelberg puts it.[17] The magazine was published by the Society for Individual Rights, a San Francisco-based gay political organization known for advocating for specific legislative action rather than for "abstract principles."[18] In this respect, *Vector* was playing to form by calling *Lord* too "dated" to be considered an advance toward gay equality.

But not all gay periodicals were driven by the same liberationist ideology. *Queens Quarterly* was a New York-based magazine that positioned itself against the gay intelligentsia, billing itself as "the magazine for gay guys who have no hangups." The historian David K. Johnson has noted the magazine's close affiliation with male physique magazines and gay beauty pageants.[19] *Queens Quarterly* was not afraid of expressing views that might be seen as assimilationist: for example, its Summer 1969 issue had featured several articles on gay marriage. Thus it had reason to expect its readers to like *The Lord Won't Mind*. Orlando Paris, the magazine's book reviewer, wrote that the novel was "well written" and that Merrick had "a good ear for dialogue, a good eye for his settings, and the knowledge of his craft." He did not judge it a masterpiece—"Do not expect Great Gay Literature," he warned—since its characters faced problems that were minor compared to those of "the rest of us [gays]." Nonetheless he conceded the artistry of the novel, which he compared to "a serious Joan Crawford movie," and he happily recommended it to his New York-based readers: "Take it with you to [Fire] Island, or borrow a copy for lonely nights."[20]

Reviews were even more favorable in local and regional gay periodicals. In general these were magazines and newsletters published outside the gay meccas of New York City and San Francisco, and they did not have the national and international readership of *Gay, One*, and *The Advocate*.[21] The unnamed reviewer for *David*, a gay beefcake magazine from Jacksonville, Florida, that was affiliated with gay male beauty contests, was unambiguous in his praise for *Lord*.[22] The review is unabashedly sincere and unpretentious, and it calmly acknowledges that the novel's protagonists do not initially appear to be typical gay men:

> The average guy will not be able to identify with the characters in their environment (the John O'Hara wealthy types compete with their own set of politics) and he may have trouble accepting Peter's ability to attract wealthy people who have nothing to do but shower presents on him (even though there aren't many queens who would mind being supported under the conditions offered to Peter).

However, despite such privilege, the review argues that the novel is a fundamentally true representation of gay experience. In the reviewer's mind, Charlie and Peter are "honest" depictions of gay men from a psychological and emotional perspective. The difference in their initial reactions to their sexuality—Charlie's "rationalization that he [is not] 'queer'" and Peter's "wholehearted acceptance of his homosexuality"—is especially authentic. Indeed, the word "honest" is used three times in the review to describe the novel. Ultimately, the reviewer sees *Lord* as an affirmative gay novel that sets a positive example for its gay readers:

> In his novel, Mr. Merrick manages to present the "gay" side of gay life pointing out finally that gay does not necessarily mean sad. Gay life can be, and often is, gay with complete happiness for the people involved. It clearly shows that no life is devoid of hang-ups and that people can be happy by sharing their problems and facing them together.[23]

Although the reviewer does not explicitly say "gay marriage," his description of the possibilities for a same-sex relationship—which he has learned from Gordon's novel—comes very close to it.

The *David* review offers an explanation for the remarkable commercial success of *The Lord Won't Mind*. Explicit sex scenes were not the main reason for the novel's popularity, given the proliferation of gay literary erotica in the 1970s. Rather, the *David* review suggests that it is the novel's "honesty" that makes it so compelling. The same word was used by Hugh Beeson Jr. in his review of the novel for the *Boston Globe*. Beeson was a doctoral student at Harvard who occasionally wrote book reviews for the *Globe*. At the time, he had already published a college grammar textbook and several poems and articles, and he had hosted a Boston radio program on the topic of recent books.[24] His review of *The Lord Won't Mind* may very well be the most positive review of the novel that appeared in *any* gay or mainstream publication at the time. In it, he argued that the critique of the novel as "fantasy" stemmed from a basic disbelief that gay men could live happily together:

The truth of the love of Charlie and Peter, which many will not accept, is that feelings such as theirs do exist. There are, thus, layers of beauty in their saga, and there are levels where thorough honesty makes brightness of graveness, where one palpable hope comes from many hearts.

Beeson accurately intuited that *Lord* was partly a response to works like *The Boys in the Band*, whose characters he described as "caricatures." While he thought that the character of C. B. bordered on caricature, he maintained that Charlie and Peter represented a true portrait of gay men in society. As for the novel's place in gay literature, he was absolutely clear: "This is the novel that James Baldwin would write if he knew how."[25]

The "honest" view of *Lord* expressed by Beeson and others was shared by thousands of gay readers. The evidence of this reception has long been extant, but it has for the most part escaped the notice of literary historians. Some of this material evidence is currently in the Princeton University Library, which owns an archive of letters that were mailed to Gordon's publishers in the 1970s and '80s. The letters—there are hundreds of them—are from readers of Gordon's gay novels who wanted to reach him and share their reactions. In some cases Gordon responded, leading to a conversation over multiple letters. Most of the letters refer to *The Lord Won't Mind*, though many discuss the later novels as well. It is clear that many readers were discovering *The Lord Won't Mind* throughout the 1970s and '80s, well after its initial publication— a testament to the fact that Avon did a good job of keeping the paperback editions in print and in wide distribution. Significantly, the letters are from *everywhere*—not only the gay capitals of New York, San Francisco, and Los Angeles but also Ohio, Houston, Oklahoma, Michigan, Kentucky, Nevada, Florida, upstate New York, and so on, and there are international letters from Canada, Belgium, India, and the Philippines. One letter came from a patient in Atascadero State Hospital, a mental institution in southern California.

Without exception, the writers of these letters see Gordon as a serious novelist. There are no references to *Lord* as pulp or erotica—labels that literary critics attached to the novel and its sequels. One reader, Richard Warnke, a seventeen-year-old boy from Hollywood, California, wrote to tell Gordon that he found the novel both educational and inspirational:

> I am a seventeen year old gay youth. I have known I am gay for five years. Reading your books has shone light on the subject of homosexuality for me. Your written words have inspired me to proceed with my wants and desires without feeling guilty about it. I am proud of myself and my lifestyle and nobody can put it down.

At the same time, Warnke recognized *Lord* as a literary achievement. He praised Gordon's "extremely rare talent" and proclaimed that Charlie and Peter are "fantastic characters." Echoing the reviewer for *David*, Warnke sensed a fundamental truthfulness in the novel's protagonists. As a result, he saw them as a possible model for his own future as a gay man: "I hope to someday find somebody and live just like Charlie and Peter."[26]

The realism of Gordon's characters is a running theme in the letters. Many readers wrote to tell Gordon that they "relate" to his characters, at the same time saying that the novels allowed them to fantasize about different worlds. Several praise Gordon for his ability to create complex, three-dimensional gay characters. Some refer to Charlie and Peter as though they are actual persons who exist outside the novel, even as they praise the novel as literary fiction. This familiarity of Gordon's characters provoked many readers to divulge facts about their own lives—in some cases, writing things they had not revealed to anyone else. One reader, a fifty-four-year-old man in Michigan, wrote to tell Gordon that he had read *The Lord Won't Mind* while caring for his seventeen-year-old autistic son. The novel had given him the courage to come out to his wife after twenty-nine years of marriage.[27] Jack Boles, a reader from San Rafael, California, wrote about his own experience in a same-sex relationship: "Larry and I have a real good relationship and his family accepts me as a good man for their son and brother. We're divinely happy in our affair and are sexually coordinated with each other. I have eyes for no one but him, and he for me. Does that sound phoney?"[28] Many critics would have answered "yes" to this question. Yet for Boles and many other readers, the novels gave them the opportunity to see their own experiences reflected in literature, in most cases for the first time.

The letters in the Princeton archive make clear that *Lord* did not appeal only to one type of gay man. There are letters from younger men and older men, urban readers and rural readers, men who are still in the closet and men who are living openly gay lives. And men were not the only ones drawn to Gordon's novels. There are a surprising number of letters from women, many of whom found Gordon's representation of gay life a revelation. Joyce Webb, a married African-American woman in Del City, Oklahoma, was struck by the verisimilitude of Charlie and Peter, who reminded her of people in her own life. Rather than being repelled by the frank depiction of homosexuality, she had a deeper admiration of gay men after reading the novel: "To me, Homosexual love is the best kind I think, it's more intense and real love." She admitted that she had taken to emulating the characters' language in her daily life, using phrases like "tell me things" and "sublime." Marcia Richardson, a reader from Cincinnati, wrote that she had been so touched by the novels that she had made her husband read the novels also. Her husband subsequently wrote a letter of his own to Gordon.[29]

Maureen Munro, a female reader from Cambridge, Massachusetts, wrote multiple letters to both Gordon and his publisher. Evidently a writer herself, she included in her letters lengthy analyses of Gordon's novels that probed their psychological and social themes. For her, the novels' sentimentality was neither "syrupy" nor trite—the very fact that it occurred in a *male* context made it original and revelatory: "As an amateur writer, I was amazed that a man could write so romantically and with such tenderness and feeling. I always had the misconception that such stories were usually written by women for women, and male writers were far removed from this sort of sentimentality."[30] Ironically, the pejorative remark by Don Preston (Geis's editor) that *Lord* smacked too much of "women's fiction" was validated by Munro, though in a different sense than Preston had intended. As Munro explained, it was not so much that the romance convention itself had changed, but it had been revealed to be much more capacious than most people had realized.

To be sure, some readers had criticisms of Gordon's work. Yet even these letters were written in a context of genuine respect for Gordon's stature as a novelist. One reader from Toronto was bothered by the insularity of Charlie and Peter and their tendency to "close out the world"—though he admitted that "many homosexual couples are forced to do just that." He was also unconvinced by their desire to have children, which seemed to him to be a sublimated form of narcissism. Another reader from Boston made the familiar criticism that most of Gordon's characters are young and beautiful, thus setting up an "impossible standard" for most gay men.[31] Even in these letters, it is clear that the readers have read several of Gordon's novels, often multiple times. Some of them are writers themselves, and their comments to Gordon sound like they are participating in a writers' workshop, offering constructive criticism rather than berating him—and asking for advice about their own writing in return.

Remarkably, almost none of the letters comment on the novel's sex scenes. While these scenes were a frequent lightning rod for harsh editors and reviewers, sympathetic readers did not seem to mind them at all. If anything, the sex scenes made the characters more believable. Mark Alvarez, a reader from Miami, Florida, wrote to commend Gordon's "unique technique" in fleshing out the characters of Charlie and Peter. He confessed to having read *Lord* five times, and he esteemed it above other gay novels that he loved, including those by Christopher Isherwood, Patricia Nell Warren, and Mary Renault—all writers who had crafted positive images of gay men but who only suggested sexual acts in their novels. Alvarez considered *Lord* and its two sequels "marvelous masterpieces," worthy of being grouped with works by J. R. R. Tolkien and Oscar Wilde.[32] The distinction between erotica and "serious" literature that was so prescriptive for mainstream reviewers was simply not meaningful for the thousands of readers who read *Lord* and found it convincing.

One reader, Joe Cosentino, was so influenced by Gordon's novels that he eventually published several gay novels of his own. Cosentino was a young actor when he wrote Gordon in 1981. He had already appeared in the daytime soap opera *Another World* and an ABC Afterschool Special with Holland Taylor. He was struck by the character of Patrice in *The Quirk*, who he thought was a dead ringer for himself. To prove his point he enclosed with his letter a glossy 8" by 10" headshot, with instructions to contact him if a film adaptation of *Quirk* was ever made.[33] After his acting career, Cosentino became a prolific writer of gay mystery novels, his most well known being the Nicky and Noah mystery series.

The attitude of Gordon's appreciative readers was perhaps best expressed by a young woman named Irene Rockwood. Rockwood was eighteen years old and living in Staten Island when she first wrote Gordon. She had read five of Gordon's gay novels and was a devoted fan. Her letter is notable for its effusiveness, but also for its knowledge of other gay writers:

> Mr. Merrick, with your fascinating talent, and enticing style you are my definition of the *perfect* writer. You have written five of the most beautiful books I have ever read. I thank you for that experience. I am impatiently awaiting the arrival of your new book. I check the bookstores every week.
>
> There are two books I have read since I last wrote that remained in my heart. They are *Faggots* by Larry Kramer, and *Lovers: The Story of Two Men* by Michael Denneny. There were both, in my opinion, wonderful books, but of course, they can not compare to yours. You are a true genius. I apologize if I'm getting a bit carried away with the compliments, but I am just writing what I feel.[34]

Rockwood was an aspiring writer herself. She wrote about taking creative writing and playwriting courses in college, noting that her real dream was to write screenplays. Like several other readers, she thought that *Lord* would make a terrific film—and she even had specific ideas about casting choices: Charlie and Peter would be played respectively by Richard Gere and David Marshall Grant, two up-and-coming actors who had recently played gay lovers in the Broadway production of *Bent*. To bolster the case for her inspired idea, Rockwood included with her letter a stunning hand-drawn advertisement by her friend Paul Lanner for an imagined theatrical version of *Lord*.

Gordon almost missed Irene Rockwood's glowing letter. The letter was initially misdirected by the publisher, which would normally forward fan mail directly to the author. (This was the most common way that letters reached Gordon, but not the only one. One writer claimed to have gotten

Gordon's address off a toilet wall in the Sears Tower in Chicago.[35]) In this case, Rockwood's letter was accidentally sent to Bernard Geis, who was no longer Gordon's editor but was still in contact with him. Geis was amused by the letter, so much so that he passed it around his office before sending it on to Gordon. For weeks afterward, "Miss Rockwood" was a running joke in Geis's office, usually accompanied by tongue-in-cheek remarks about Gordon's "genius." When Geis finally sent the letter to Gordon, he again treated it as a laughingstock: "The cost of headwear has gone up greatly in the past few years and if we were to permit you to read the enclosed letter without sedation you would have to throw away all your hats, if any, and buy a completely new set." Yet Gordon, who had been receiving piles of similar letters for years, did not think the letter so funny. In his response to Geis, he dryly noted, "La Rockwood is only a standard-type fan. They all say the same thing."[36]

Geis's cavalier reaction to Irene Rockwood shows how little he and others understood the appeal of Gordon's novels. Readers were not devouring the books because they saw them as political treatises or trashy potboilers. They were drawn to the novels' characters, who seemed "real" to them and with whom they identified. This was a point lost not only on Geis but also on the cadre of gay activist-reviewers who dismissed *The Lord Won't Mind* and excluded it from the category of gay literature. Gordon had gotten bad reviews before, but the critical reaction to *Lord* took him by surprise. He had expected some backlash from straight or mainstream critics, but he was caught off guard by the attacks from gay and liberal publications. In a letter he wrote to the *Village Voice*, he took particular offense at Victor Cotugno's characterization of his writing as "dewy-eyed" and "lavender." He scolded Cotugno for not grasping the bigger picture: "It seems to me that he should welcome books that deal with homosexuality explicitly and approvingly, even ones he doesn't like, if he hopes for a bulk of homosexual literature to develop."[37] This was to be Gordon's persistent attitude toward gay critics who belittled his work. Many years later, in an interview with *Stallion* magazine, he explained that he couldn't understand why the gays had turned against him: "I don't know what the problem was. It seemed to me that dealing with the subject in any way . . . was an act of bravery. I don't know why they didn't welcome my books. More gay culture. What the hell! I mean that's what we want."[38]

In 1970 gay people did not only want explicitly gay books. They needed them. In his magisterial study of the lived experience of gay men in twentieth-century America, John Loughery gives what is probably the most eloquent explanation of why readers responded so zealously to Gordon's novels. He acknowledges their problematic representation of race and their overemphasis on physical beauty, but he argues that these flaws pale in comparison to the affirmation and hope that these novels provided:

> But for the teenager who never imagined that a paperback with descriptions of men in bed together could be on sale at a local drugstore, *The Lord Won't Mind* served a purpose. Twenty-two years after Gore Vidal had been told that he was committing professional suicide with *The City and the Pillar*, New York publishers were talking about a "breakthrough" love story. To the money men following the latest trends, the voices of gay liberation announced something more than radical social change and a new kind of talk-show guest. They announced buyers to be heeded, markets to be tapped. The commercialization of gay life began at the very moment the new activist spirit peaked, with consequences that would be every bit as profound.[39]

As the letters in the Princeton archive show, it was not just gay teenagers but gay men of all ages who found affirmation in Gordon's novels. And while critics wished that a different novel had taken this role, it was Gordon's novels that propelled the "commercialization of gay life" that made later gay novels possible. This is a point that was made, albeit more quietly, by writers like Felice Picano, George Whitmore, and Edmund White.[40]

Despite the critics, readers from all over continued to buy copies of *The Lord Won't Mind* in large numbers for many years after its initial publication in 1970. This readership extended beyond the United States and beyond the English-speaking world, when the novel and its sequels were translated into French, German, Spanish, and Japanese. Moreover, the actual number of readers was likely much higher than the sales figures would suggest. Many letters in the Princeton archive mention getting the novel from a friend or relative who had already read it. For these readers, their edition of *Lord* was a secondhand—or third- or fourth-hand—copy. The relative scarcity of used editions of *Lord*, either in paperback or hardcover, is a sign that most copies were frequently read and reread, often by multiple readers, until they were no longer usable. Gordon was aware of this, and the fact assuaged some of the disappointment he felt after being snubbed by the critics. As he knew, there were many Irene Rockwoods.

NOTES

1. Review of *The Lord Won't Mind*, *Brooklyn Record–Bay Bridge Record*, March 27, 1970.

2. Bobby Mather, "Tempest in a Love Rut," *Detroit Free Press*, May 10, 1970; obituary, Bobby Mather, *Detroit Sunday Journal*, January 17, 1999.

3. Rhys Bowen website, http://rhysbowen.com. Rhys Bowen is Quin-Harken's pen name.

4. Janet Quin-Harkin, "Like Reading Lady Chatterley at Age 14," *Pacific Sun*, May 6, 1970.

5. David Brudnoy, "Books in Brief," *National Review*, June 16, 1971.

6. Thomas S. Hibbs, "David Brudnoy Signs Off," *National Review*, December 10, 2004; Andrew Sullivan, "Buckley and the Gays," *Atlantic*, February 28, 2008.

7. Martin Levin, "Reader Report," *New York Times*, April 26, 1970.

8. Margalit Fox, "Martin Levin, Prolific Book Reviewer, Dies at 89," *New York Times*, May 30, 2008.

9. Drewey Wayne Gunn, *Gay Novels of Britain, Ireland and the Commonwealth, 1881–1981: A Reader's Guide* (Jefferson, NC: McFarland, 2014), 151–52.

10. Matt Bell, ed., *The Boys in The Band: Flashpoints of Cinema, History, and Queer Politics* (Detroit: Wayne State University Press, 2016), 5. This reading of the film is productively complicated in this excellent collection of essays.

11. Peter Ogren, "The Lord Won't Mind: The Reader Won't Care," *Gay*, April 20, 1970. In this respect, Ogren's review of *Lord* is similar to the negative comments made about Forster's *Maurice* after it was published in 1971. See Robert K. Martin and George Piggford, eds., *Queer Forster* (Chicago: University of Chicago Press, 1997), 19–20.

12. Michael G. Long, ed., *Gay Is Good: The Life and Letters of Gay Rights Pioneer Franklin Kameny* (Syracuse: Syracuse University Press, 2014), 165. Interestingly, Wicker started his activist career sounding more like an assimilationist, arguing on a New York radio program that gay people had "a very strong moral fiber and a very definite set of rules." See Eric Cervini, *The Deviant's War: The Homosexual vs. the United States of America* (New York: Farrar, Straus and Giroux, 2020), 94–99, 171–74.

13. See the mentions of *Lord* in the "Around the Arts" sections in the August and October 1970 issues of the *Mattachine Times*.

14. "Book Review," *Vector*, July 1970.

15. The likelihood that Amory is the review writer is bolstered by the fact that very similar language appears in an interview of Amory published in *Vector* the previous month. See "Richard Amory Interview," *Vector*, June 1970.

16. See Michael Bronski's discussion of Amory's publication frustrations in Richard Amory, *Song of the Loon*, 19–20. See also Justin Spring, *Secret Historian: The Life and Times of Samuel Steward, Professor, Tattoo Artist, and Sexual Renegade* (New York: Farrar, Straus and Giroux, 2010), 351–55.

17. Brian J. Distelberg, "Mainstream Fiction, Gay Reviewers, and Gay Male Cultural Politics in the 1970s," *GLQ* 16, no. 3 (2010): 390.

18. Cervini, *The Deviant's War*, 224–25.

19. David K. Johnson, *Buying Gay: How Physique Entrepreneurs Sparked a Movement* (New York: Columbia University Press, 2019), 229–31.

20. Orlando Paris, review of *The Lord Won't Mind*, *Queens Quarterly*, Summer 1970.

21. On the importance of these less "respectable" publications for the study of gay history, see Marc Stein, "Canonizing Homophile Sexual Respectability: Archives, History, and Memory," *Radical History Review*, no. 120 (Fall 2014): 53–73.

22. Johnson, *Buying Gay*, 229–32.

23. Review of *The Lord Won't Mind, David*, July 1971.

24. "Former City Boy Writes Grammar," *Pantagraph* (Bloomington, Indiana), April 3, 1966.

25. Hugh Beeson Jr., "Love Story with a Twist," *Boston Globe*, August 30, 1970.

26. Richard Warnke to Gordon Merrick, 22 October 1979, GMP, box 19, folder 6.

27. Peter Reale to Gordon Merrick, 7 September 1978, GMP, box 19, folder 6.

28. Jack L. Boles to Gordon Merrick, 30 August 1977, GMP, box 19, folder 6.

29. Joyce Webb to Gordon Merrick, 23 and 25 April 1978; Marcia J. Richardson to Gordon Merrick, 26 August 1979, 22 September 1979; Michael J. Richardson to Gordon Merrick, 24 September 1979, GMP, box 19, folder 6.

30. Maureen Munro to Gordon Merrick, 16 August 1978; Maureen Munro to President of Avon Books, 17 July 1978, GMP, box 19, folder 6.

31. T. P. Snow to Gordon Merrick, 19 February 1978, GMP, box 19, folder 6; Ken Westhassel to Gordon Merrick, 7 July 1981, GMP, box 19, folder 7.

32. Mark Alvarez to Gordon Merrick, 16 August 1978, GMP, box 19, folder 6.

33. Joe Cosentino, email to the author.

34. Irene Rockwood to Gordon Merrick, 4 March 1981, GMP, box 17, folder 7. See also Joseph M. Ortiz, "'The World Won't Mind': The Accidental Success of Gordon Merrick." *Princeton University Library Chronicle* 68, no. 3 (Spring 2007): 611–26.

35. Frank Phillips to Gordon Merrick, 9 June 1979, GMP, box 19, folder 6.

36. Bernard Geis to Gordon Merrick, 12 March 1981; Gordon Merrick to Bernard Geis, 25 March 1981, GMP, box 17, folder 7.

37. Gordon Merrick, Letter to the Editor, *Village Voice*, July 11, 1974.

38. Brandon Judell, "A Conversation with Gordon Merrick," *Stallion*, July 1987.

39. John Loughery, *The Other Side of Silence: Men's Lives and Gay Identities: A Twentieth-Century History* (New York: Henry Holt, 1998), 338.

40. George Whitmore, "The Gay Novel Now," *Gaysweek*, October 9, 1978; Edmund White, interview by the author; Daniel M. Jaffe, "Talking Across the Table: Felice Picano: An Interview," Bibliobuffet.com, July 2007. Although the website is no longer available, details of the article's online publication were confirmed by Daniel Jaffe, email to the author.

Chapter Thirteen

Going Greek, or Making a Gay Mythology

Gordon Merrick the novelist was back. After a twelve-year hiatus, he had reemerged on the literary scene in a big way. *The Lord Won't Mind* had been on the *New York Times* bestseller list for sixteen weeks, and the Avon paperback edition of the novel was selling in even greater numbers. Gordon had taken a chance, and it had proved more profitable than he could have expected. He had not only resuscitated his career; he had reinvented it. He was no longer the postwar protest novelist who looked at America from a distance. He was a wildly successful *gay* novelist. Even if most critics had panned *Lord*, there was no question that it marked a watershed moment in gay literature.

Gordon did not, however, rest on his laurels. Even before *Lord* was published, he was already working on a sequel from his home in Hydra, and he even had an additional sequel in mind. The idea of a gay romance trilogy was not unprecedented. When Richard Amory published *Song of the Loon*, he had advertised it as the first of a trilogy of gay pastoral novels (*Song of Aaron* and *Listen, the Loon Sings* followed shortly after). Richard Fullmer, writing as Dirk Vanden, also produced his popular *All* trilogy starting in 1969. If Gordon knew about these, he might have been confident about the marketability of sequels. And he may simply have wanted to write more about himself. Much had happened in his life after 1940, the year in which *Lord* takes place, and so there was an abundance of material available to him—especially now that he was willing to draw more directly from his personal experiences.

The sequel, *One for the Gods*, takes place in 1950, ten years after *Lord*. Charlie and Peter are still together, having endured a brief separation when Peter was in the army during World War II. The two live in a farmhouse in Connecticut, where Charlie is a moderately successful painter and Peter is an extraordinarily successful financier. The novel begins with them vacationing on the French Riviera. As in *Lord*, the main focus is their relationship, which after ten years has a different set of challenges.

After a brief prologue, the first chapter begins with a question: "Is it true you two go in for fidelity and all that?"[1] The speaker is a young Frenchman named Guy, who is flirting heavily with Charlie, and his question stokes a brewing conflict between Charlie and Peter. Except for their separation during the war, they have been completely monogamous, in contrast to most gay couples they know. Since coming to Saint-Tropez, however, Charlie has become suspicious of Jean-Claude, another young Frenchman who actually is having an affair with Peter. Peter's love for Charlie is as strong as ever, but he finds Jean-Claude irresistibly exciting. In particular, he discovers with Jean-Claude that he enjoys being the "top" during sex (he is always the "bottom" with Charlie).

Peter decides to end the affair, but not before it is discovered by Charlie, who erupts in seething rage. He is plagued by the usual feelings of jealousy and betrayal, but the affair also exposes a deep fissure in his and Peter's attitudes about their sexuality. Although Peter had long ago accepted his homosexuality, Charlie still refuses to see himself as definitively "queer": "They weren't queers like these others. They were two people who were in love with each other and had made a decent life for themselves."[2] He has made big strides toward self-acceptance since his early days with Peter (when he insisted on hiding their relationship from his family), but he still struggles with internalized homophobia. For one thing, his sensitivity to social stigmas against homosexuality compels him to avoid gay communities altogether: "Together, they had never frequented a homosexual world. They had found their friends among their neighbors, professional people, married couples with children, and among the rich, whom Peter cultivated as clients."[3] Gordon, who for much of his life was uncomfortable in gay spaces, was here effectively describing himself.

Peter's affair also exposes another of Charlie's internalized defenses against homophobia: his idealization of their relationship. His need for perfection is a running theme in the novel, and so when Peter tries to reason that his affair is a "human" mistake, Charlie explodes in rage:

> Who said anything about being human. We're a couple of faggots. We have to be goddamn supermen to get by. I thought maybe we were, but no. You lie, you cheat . . . you lie to me over and over again, all for the sake of a big, dull body. Some superman. . . . Now we're like everybody else. *And* queers, to boot.[4]

For Charlie, gay men are either "supermen" or "faggots." They must be better than everyone else to be accepted. His perfectionism exemplifies what the writer Andrew Tobias describes as a common coping strategy among gay men in his autobiographical memoir *The Best Little Boy in the World*.[5] Like the young Tobias, Charlie is the quintessential gay overachiever who takes every opportunity to prove his strength and masculinity. In one scene, when he heroically guides a sailboat through a storm and saves the lives of its passengers, his first reaction is to frame the event as a refutation of gay stereotypes: "What can you expect of queers? He hoped he had shown them what they could expect: a sense of duty, some courage, and tenacity . . . he had nothing to be ashamed of."[6]

Charlie and Peter are clearly at a crisis point in their "marriage." In an attempt to work through it, they decide to leave the French crowd and travel with an American couple, Jack and Martha Kingsley, who conveniently invite them to travel on their boat for two months on the Mediterranean. The ensuing cruise, which occupies most of the novel, is transformative. It gives Charlie and Peter an opportunity to reestablish the bonds of their relationship, and it spurs Charlie to confront his inner demons.

The boat trip also becomes the impetus for two other significant events in their lives. During a port stop near Patras, Greece, Peter is accosted by three Greek men who rob him and nearly rape him (in an early version of the novel, Peter is actually raped by the men). He escapes, but the incident triggers a traumatic memory from the war when he was caught naked in bed with his captain, a gay Princeton alumnus who had sex with Charlie in college. After being caught, Peter was forced to undergo a psychiatric evaluation, and after a humiliating court-martial he was dishonorably discharged from the army. The experience had traumatized Peter, who had never before been the target of antigay prejudice. He had mostly suppressed the memory until the incident in Greece, which unleashes his fear and anger over society's homophobia.

The second event concerns Martha, who develops a strong friendship with Charlie and Peter during the cruise. She is attracted to both men, particularly Charlie, even though she knows they are a couple. Charlie is likewise drawn to her, and eventually the two have sex. After learning that Martha's husband is sterile, Charlie gets inspired with the idea of having a child with her—and of Peter doing the same. Martha is initially shocked by the proposal, but she eventually agrees, happy for an excuse to leave her marriage and secretly hoping to keep Charlie for herself. Peter, who has never had sex with a woman, is harder to convince, but the prospect of raising a family with Charlie finally persuades him. Unsurprisingly the situation becomes an emotional minefield. At one point the scheme almost ends Charlie and Peter's relationship, but they manage to fight their way (including, at one point, an actual fistfight) to a common understanding. The novel ends cinematically, with the two making love under the stars in a house in Hydra—just like the one where Gordon and Hulse were living.

Gordon had again given his two golden boys a happy ending. This time the conflict was not over "coming out" but over the challenges inherent in a long-term relationship between two men—in other words, the challenge of a same-sex marriage. The word "marriage" appears frequently in the novel, most often spoken by Peter, who thinks of their relationship as "a truer marriage than that of most people he knew." He craves public acknowledgment of the fact, so much so that the simple act of holding hands in public makes him euphoric: "[Charlie] was who he belonged to, always had and always would; he would love to have it publicly recognized as a marriage, which was what it was." Charlie also thinks of their union as a marriage, but the fact that their relationship is not fully recognized by the heterosexual world in which they live is a constant source of resentment: "No matter how much they know about us," he tells Peter, "they can't understand it's like being married." For Charlie, the lack of a social structure threatens to lead to a future of isolation and piteousness:

> Doesn't the future scare you sometime? We've known enough old queens. In another few years, we might not find it so easy to turn down pretty boys like your Dimitri. In another few years after that, they won't be offering themselves any more. That's when the horror begins.... I'm trying to find something that'll give more stability—no, a broader base for our lives so that we'll be better prepared to cope when time catches up with us.[7]

This specter of the aging gay couple appears often in Gordon's gay novels, suggesting it was something he often thought about. The fear seems to be that an older gay couple has no *meaning*, no established set of routines and signs by which they are intelligible to the rest of the world.

The complex set of feelings that Gordon ascribed to Charlie and Peter is realistic. In a profound way, Gordon was anticipating the legal battle for same-sex marriage in the United States, which proved that the *social* recognition of marriage is an indispensable part of the institution, one that profoundly affects the emotional and psychological well-being of the married couple. This was a timely topic in 2013, when *United States v. Windsor* affirmed the right for same-sex couples to marry nationwide—and it was a timely topic in 1971 when *One for the Gods* was published. The previous year, a gay couple in Minnesota had sued for the right to a marriage license, and a few months later the *San Francisco Chronicle* wrote about a "gay marriage boom" in the United States.[8] The issue was a point of debate among gay rights activists themselves, most of whom saw marriage as essentially assimilationist and conservative.[9] Indeed, the timeliness of the issue was clearly understood by the marketing team at Avon, the publisher of the paperback edition of *One for the Gods*; a press release for the novel explicitly advertised it in relation to "homosexual marriage."[10] Likewise, in an interview that Gordon gave while doing publicity for the novel, he was asked about the push for marriage equality. He was strangely dispassionate on the topic, given how much he had made the novel read like a manifesto for same-sex marriage. He admitted that marriage is "a natural human instinct" but claimed not to need such ritualization himself.[11] Perhaps he was trying to avoid putting himself in the crosshairs of the debate, or perhaps he was trying to convince himself (as Charlie does at times) that he did not need society's validation.

In addition to the issue of gay marriage, *One for the Gods* tapped into another, very different, current in American gay culture—one that looked back in time rather than forward. Gordon heavily imbued the novel with Hellenism, the idealization of classical Greek culture that had long been used by gay men to justify their sexuality. For example, in Victorian England the study of classical Greek texts was used by gay men at Oxford as a "homosexual code" through which to communicate and defend same-sex desire. (In Forster's *Maurice*, Clive and Maurice initially discover their mutual attraction by discussing Plato's *Phaedrus* and *Symposium*.) A similar practice was carried on by German classicists earlier in the nineteenth century.[12] In 1950s America, a more explicit linking of Hellenism and homosexuality appeared in the pages of male physique magazines. When Randolph Benson and John Bullock, a gay couple who had met as undergraduates at the University of Virginia, launched the first issue of their physique magazine *Grecian Guild Pictorial* in 1955, they strategically used the term "Grecian" as a euphemism for gay men: "Since you who read this are manifestly interested in the male body as an object of admiration and respect in its highest form, perhaps you already understand why we are the GRECIAN Guild."[13] The magazine likewise used Hellenistic language and imagery to create the sense of a gay community that stretched across the centuries. Other physique magazines targeted at gay men also used Hellenistic rhetoric, and classical settings became a "safe" vehicle for gay themes in midcentury novels, such as Mary Renault's *The Last of the Wine* (1956) and *Fire from Heaven* (1969).[14] By the 1970s classical references were ubiquitous in gay publications, appearing in everything from gay political manifestos to advertisements for gay book clubs and bathhouses.

One for the Gods wore its Hellenism on its sleeve—literally—when it first appeared. In addition to the classicizing title, the cover for the hardback edition features the head of a classical male statue, an image almost identical to the cover of the first issue of *Grecian Guild Pictorial*.[15] The novel itself contains dozens of classical allusions, which gave Gordon the opportunity to show off the deep Latin education he had received at Princeton and the Episcopal Academy. For example, in a scene where Charlie is having sex with Jean-Claude, the younger man yells out in ecstasy, "You are a bull raping me," a line which makes Charlie think of Zeus and Europa. In other scenes the classical allusions add texture to the novel's descriptions of Mediterranean locales. Most importantly, the novel's Hellenism functions as a subtext for the nobility of gay relationships—much like it does in homophile magazines in the 1960s and '70s. A poignant example of this occurs near the end of the novel, when Charlie and Peter discover a set of ancient inscriptions while visiting the Greek island of Santorini:

> The island had been a cult center in antiquity, celebrated for the beauty of its naked dancing boys; dedications to them from their male suitors remained, carved in stone. When they reached the town at the top of the cliff, Peter tried to make him laugh with joking references to "their" shrine and naked dancing boys in general but he failed.[16]

This graffiti, made during the ancient *gymnopediés* festivals, can still be seen in Santorini. In the novel, the inscriptions do not however comfort Charlie, since they make him feel further cut off from the modern world.

Unfortunately, Gordon also tapped into the darker side of gay Hellenism, which could at times fuel a "homosexual chauvinism," the valorization of gay masculinity through the degradation of campy or effeminate gay men—what the historian Craig Loftin calls "anti-swish prejudice."[17] Charlie, who shuns gay bars and has a knee-jerk aversion to effeminate gay men, is clearly guilty of "anti-swish prejudice." His reunion with Peter at the end of the novel happens not because he finally accepts Peter's "feminine streak" but because he interprets their fistfight as a sign of Peter's true masculinity: "Peter landed a strong blow to the side of Charlie's jaw. . . . This is a *man*, Charlie thought with wonder as his breath was cut off; I'm in love with a man." There is an inherent sexism here, and it accords with the novel's larger representation of women. When Peter has sex with a woman for the first time, he experiences it as "a ritual of power that perhaps could only be performed only by a man and a woman."[18] In other words, the novel seems to say, heterosexual sex is naturally between a dominant man and a submissive woman, while homosexual sex, by contrast, at least holds the possibility of equality.

Many readers were delighted by the sequel to *Lord*, but some were puzzled by it. Readers who had fallen in love with Charlie and Peter were dubious about the character of Martha. They were confused as to why both men, especially the assuredly gay Peter, have sex with her. The new novel seemed like a defense of bisexuality, or even pansexuality; at one point Charlie even refers to himself as "probably bisexual."[19] This reading was inadvertently reinforced when Geis placed a full-page ad for the novel in the *New York Times* that featured two men and a woman in a sexually suggestive pose. He later pulled the ad when he got reports that it was hampering sales of the novel.[20]

Critics were also puzzled, though for different reasons. Dotson Rader, reviewing the book in the *New York Times*, called it an "intriguing" and "enlightening" novel, but also "so awful that by sheer artlessness and banality it is a source of perverse fascination." He was not offended by the novel's sexual explicitness or sexual fluidity—he hardly could have been, being a straight man who had once worked as a homosexual hustler and who had said that "all boys should spend a year or two hustling.[21] He was bothered, rather, by the novel's unabashed sentimentality. And while he noted the novel's Hellenism, which he identified as "homosexual romanticism and myth," he saw it as a type of escapism. In sum, he couldn't fathom the possibility that two gay men could stay in a long-term relationship: "two stunningly handsome homosexuals who maintain an incredibly intense and beautiful love affair for decades . . . that triumph alone truly makes his novel a fiction."[22] Rader was not a homophobe; in the same article he argues passionately for an end to gay discrimination. But he did not know many gay people. He certainly did not know Gordon, who by that time had been in a gay relationship for fifteen years. (As it turned out, Rader met Gordon in person five years later, at the famous masked ball on Hydra where Gordon appeared as a Carpathian prince. Rader was dressed, appropriately, as an executioner.[23])

Gordon did not spend much time worrying about reviews. Before *One for the Gods* had hit the bookstore shelves, he was already finishing the next novel: *Forth into Light*, the final and longest installment in the "Charlie and Peter" saga. Part of the reason he was able to write it so quickly was that he incorporated into it nearly all of *A Day with Leighton*, the Hydra novel he had been unable to publish a few years earlier. In adapting the *Leighton* material, he changed the characters of Bob and Paul (who were already fictionalized versions of Gordon and Hulse) into Charlie and Peter. He expanded the storyline about Leighton's own gay son Peter (whose name was changed to Jeff) and developed a major storyline for Charlie and Peter. And as he had done twice before, he made sure to give his now-iconic gay couple a happy ending.

Forth into Light takes place in Hydra in 1960, ten years after *One for the Gods*. By this time Charlie and Peter are established residents of the island, living openly as a "married" couple. The island's residents accept and refer to them as "the Mills-Martins." They also now have two children, both from Martha: Charlotte, Charlie's nine-year-old biological daughter, and Petey, Peter's four-year-old biological son. Martha lives in the same house, caring for the children and maintaining a (mostly) platonic friendship with the two men. Half of the novel focuses on Charlie and Peter as they adjust to this phase of their lives. The other half focuses on George Leighton, an American novelist whose dysfunctional family is a stark contrast to the Mills-Martins. His wife Sarah is having an affair with Pavlo, a local muscle body, while his son Jeff is coming to terms with his homosexuality and having an affair with

Dimitri, the island's drug dealer. The novel's two plot strands intersect mostly through Jeff, who sees Charlie and Peter as gay role models and turns to them for guidance. Gordon kept virtually all of the "Forsterian" plot of *Leighton*: Leighton's accusation of theft against Costa, a local Greek man.

As with the first two Charlie and Peter novels, Gordon included much autobiographical material in *Forth into Light*. The fact that Charlie and Peter are approaching their forties gave Gordon the opportunity to reflect on the complexity of sexual desire in a long-term gay relationship in a very personal way. At one point, he seems to have thought he was getting *too* personal. In an early draft of *Light*, he wrote a remarkably intimate scene between Peter and Jeff that he later backtracked, presumably because it showed the shifting sexual desires of Peter as an older man. In the early version, the seventeen-year-old Jeff comes out as gay to the thirty-nine-year-old Peter and confesses his infatuation with him. What follows is a tender scene that captures Jeff's nervous excitement and Peter's thrill at the young man's beauty:

> Jeff's voice was deep and pleasing. A lot of dark hair fell over his forehead. Heavy brows rose into it. He had a strong straight nose and a delicately sculpted mouth. His face would probably be slightly craggy when finally formed but there was still something softly androgynous about it that Peter found highly provocative.

When Jeff asks Peter to teach him how to have sex with a man, Peter hesitates but eventually complies. As Peter tries to reassure Jeff about the normalcy of his sexuality, he is caught off guard by the depth of his own response to the lovestruck youth:

> It was an undeniable thrill to have the lovely young mouth pressed so intimately to him. . . . Jeff rose and Peter took his hands and placed them on the erect sexes so that they were side by side. The contact of hand and rigid flesh sent a shock of desire down to the soles of Peter's feet.

As the scene progresses, the narrative delicately oscillates between Peter's determination to play the role of caring mentor and his newly discovered vulnerability. Jeff's youthful beauty causes the normally self-assured Peter to become self-conscious of his own looks, which have changed with age: "Peter ran the tips of his fingers over the soft down of his chest and lowered them to the flat abdomen. He had kept himself flat but he no longer had the thrilling convexity of this youth."[24] Gordon had always labored over sex scenes, but the handwritten changes in this episode are unusually dense. The episode, in which an older, experienced man has sex with a younger, inexperienced man—could easily have come off as exploitative, but Gordon's fine-tuning makes it so that it insightfully reveals the vulnerabilities and insecurities of both men.

The episode never made it into print. For whatever reason, Gordon cut these passages, and he changed the episode so that Peter feels little attraction to Jeff and brusquely refuses to have sex with him. Instead, Peter gives Jeff a long, clinical-sounding lecture on gay relationships. This revised Peter is a conspicuously chaste man who is impervious to sexual temptation:

> Peter was moved by him, but not remotely tempted. It had been years since he had even thought of making love to a boy, not necessarily out of loyalty to Charlie or because his basic sexual drive was any less unequivocally homosexual but because he was simply no longer interested. . . . As Charlie had doubtless hoped, they had somehow eliminated the temptation of boys.[25]

Given the autobiographical nature of the novel, Gordon may have not wanted to write what seemed like an admission of his or Hulse's infidelity. Or he may have not wanted to complicate his heroes. He knew that many readers of *The Lord Won't Mind* identified with Charlie and Peter, and he didn't want to disappoint them by suggesting their love had waned. He also knew that his novels were used by some reviewers (like Rader) as "evidence" of the gay lifestyle, and may not have wanted to reinforce the view of gay men as promiscuous. In the final published version, Peter turns down Jeff, saying, "A lot of people think queers will go for any guy they can get their hands on."[26] Gordon was preserving Peter's noble reputation, but he was likely also thinking of his own.

In his revisions Gordon also added a new episode that further developed the issue of monogamy—and that commented on his own literary reputation. Near the end of the novel, Charlie has a tender moment with Jeff that nearly leads to sex. As the one who has always argued for monogamy, he feels guilty about his attraction to Jeff. Finally, after a sleepless night, he is struck with artistic inspiration:

> [He] want[ed] to let loose and fling paint about, get his hands in it and throw away the rules. He finished his coffee hastily and got out a virgin canvas and went to work, the final result he wanted to achieve for once eluding him. When he stepped back to survey his progress, he laughed out loud at what he was doing. Let his public make what they would of it. He felt reckless and inspired. Perhaps he was entering a new Period. This was the area in which to consolidate his new sense of liberation, not with treacherous young lovers. He couldn't wait to show Peter.[27]

Gordon rarely wrote such intensely metafictional passages (though he came close in *The Vallency Tradition*). Here, Charlie's "reckless" paintings are a clear stand-in for Gordon's new gay novels, in which he "threw away the rules" and wrote with a "new sense of liberation." The episode expresses Gordon's own satisfaction at being able, as a man in his fifties, to reinvent his literary career. At the same time, it connects Gordon's professional breakthrough to his relationship with Hulse. It is possible that Gordon and Hulse had in fact been dealing with some kind of marital midlife crisis. If so, Gordon wrote the scene in *Forth into Light* as a way of acknowledging that they had survived it and that their relationship had been a pivotal influence on his writing. Gordon said as much on the book's dedication page, which he addressed solely to Hulse, "who invented this book."

Gordon was again thinking of his literary reputation when he wrote the novel's ending, which is also self-reflexive, though in a more subtle way than the scene of Charlie's painting. At the end of *Forth into Light*, Jeff commits suicide by jumping off a cliff—the tragic outcome of his destructive affair with a famous American writer named Michael Cochran, a cruel older man who has many ex-wives but enjoys sex with young men. When the islanders discover his body, they explain his death as the inevitable result of his "unnatural" sexual desires. The novel then ends with a proleptic final sentence that notes the interpretation of Jeff's suicide as a lesson on the evils of homosexuality: "He entered into island legend, an example to sinners, as a lovelorn boy who had been driven to destroy himself by the enormity of his unnatural crimes."[28] (An early working title for the novel had actually been *An Example to Sinners*.[29]) This is an utterly bleak ending, typical of Gordon's earlier protest novels but unexpected for the final note in the Charlie and Peter trilogy. It was, however, more self-conscious and intertextual than the protest novels. The episode of Jeff's suicide is actually a carefully orchestrated imitation of earlier gay novels—in particular, Fritz Peters' *Finistère*, a popular gay novel published in 1951 whose protagonist, a gay American teenager, commits suicide in almost exactly the same way. By writing such an ending, Gordon was giving a sardonic nod to the literary convention of tragic gay endings while commenting indirectly on the relationship of his own, far more affirmative, gay novels to this tradition.

In fact, *Forth into Light* has *two* endings. Gordon's brilliant masterstroke was to juxtapose the *Finistère* ending with another scene, placed two paragraphs earlier, in which Charlie and Peter are greeted by their two children:

> Little Pete came hurtling down the stairs, a brief golden streak in space (God, how beautiful, Peter thought. And then with quick alarm: take it easy, darling), hurtling down the stairs (Oh lord, Charlie thought, his chest stretching with uncontainable love for this splinter of Peter's magic, reproduced in gold), hurtling down the stairs to greet them.[30]

Gordon's literature professors at Princeton would have been impressed by this expert handling of chiasmic form. The image of Jeff's body falling into the sea is paralleled by the image of little Petey "hurtling down the stairs" into the arms of his two gay dads. Gordon also manages to reprise the end of *The Lord Won't Mind*, which ends with Charlie and Peter gazing at each other, by having Charlie and Peter look at each other through the mirroring figures of their children. Through this artful structuring, Gordon emphasized the way that his gay novels had transformed the conventional tragic gay novel into a narrative of gay domesticity.

Not surprisingly, Gordon considered *Forth into Light* the best of the Charlie and Peter novels. He had drawn on Greek mythology in *One for the Gods*, but he now saw himself creating a new mythology—a canon of gay literature in which Charlie and Peter stood alongside Forster's Maurice as a new heroic type of gay character. He had originally named the novel *Who'll Go Down in History?*, a title that notionally refers to Jeff's mythologized suicide, but that from another angle sounds like a taunt at Gordon's critics. Gordon was not shy about writing angry rebuttals to newspapers that criticized his writers, but this time he thought it would be more effective to have his characters speak for him. In one scene, Charlie bellows out a speech that could just as easily be Gordon yelling at his critics: "Two aging men clinging to each other? What's absurd about that? It's heroic. It's as moving as the survival of anything beautiful. Don't ever laugh again at something that's too big and deep for you to know anything about."[31]

Some people were happy to include Gordon in the new canon of gay literature. Gay booksellers routinely placed Gordon Merrick novels alongside works by Vidal and Isherwood in their catalogues and advertisements. In 1974, an advertisement for the Oscar Wilde Bookshop in New York City put *Forth into Light* near the top of its list of new and notable books, next to novels by Patricia Nell Warren and Richard Amory.[32] Likewise, a 1975 newsletter published by Lambda Rising, the iconic gay bookstore in Washington, DC, gave Merrick a prominent space alongside Burroughs, Genet, Renault, and Wilde—more prominent than the space it gave to Vidal, Isherwood, Rechy, Warren, Gide, or Maugham.[33]

As usual, the gay intelligentsia saw things differently. While most gay literary critics derided or dismissed *Lord* and its sequels, they could not ignore the unprecedented commercial success of Gordon's novels. The *Mattachine Times* regularly noted the appearances of Gordon Merrick novels on the *New York Times* bestseller list, while refusing to review them. In a 1973 *Vector* article on the status of gay literature, the gay playwright Dean Goodman (writing under the pseudonym of Douglas Dean) also noted the bestselling status of the Charlie and Peter novels, though he felt they represented gay men as "highly neurotic types in extreme, melodramatic situations."[34] More influential was the reaction by the activist Larry Townsend, who would go on to write a number of gay novels himself. At a meeting of the Society for Individual Rights in 1970, Townsend participated in a panel with Richard Amory, Dirk Vanden (Richard Fullmer), and Phil Andros (Samuel Steward). The topic of the panel was the future of gay literature, and afterward Townsend published an article in *The Advocate* summarizing the main points that had been raised by the panel. He singled out Gordon's work as having broken the glass ceiling for gay writers:

> Our problem now, and the problem we discussed in San Francisco, is: *Where do we go from here?* At the moment, the future seems a bit nebulous, although the hard-cover publication of Gordon Merrick's *The Lord Won't Mind* would seem to offer a potential alternative. This book is now a best-seller, with sales approaching the 30,000 mark. It is distributed through the regular (non-porno) channels, although it is frankly homosexual and every bit as explicit as anything any of us have written. Just as *Loon* changed the market four years ago, this new book may open the doors which have continued to be closed. Let's hope it does.[35]

It was clear to Townsend that Gordon was a new kind of gay writer, but exactly what kind of writer was he?

This question was never fully answered, and part of the reason had to do with Gordon himself. Ironically, as much as he wrote about himself in his novels, he was not comfortable talking about himself in public. This made him a poor vehicle for public relations, a fact which became evident during a New York publicity tour in the spring of 1971 that Bernard Geis had arranged to promote *One for the Gods*. Gordon agreed to do the tour because he wanted a free trip to New York to see friends and theater shows. Geis's publicity assistant Sheri Safran put together a full itinerary of events, including interviews with newspapers and magazines (*Village Voice*, *Gay*, *The Advocate*) and an hourlong taping session with Dr. Joyce Brothers for her daily radio show. Safran advertised Gordon as a "forerunner of the current homosexual movement," telling the magazine editors and program directors that Gordon would be an expert speaker on the current debates over homosexuality.[36]

The tour was a flop. Safran was not able to secure all the interviews she had promised, and, with one exception, the ones that did happen were not published. At the time, magazines like *Gay* and *The Advocate* were not interested in novelists like Gordon; they wanted stories that spoke to specific social or political issues in the gay community. Gordon did get a spot on *The Dr. Joyce Brothers Show*, but he was not prepared for the incisive, clinical questions that Brothers fired at him. At one point during the show, Brothers asked Gordon "whether many homosexuals hope to be cured." Gordon responded as tactfully as he could, but he was not an authority on the psychological health of gay men.[37] He might have made a stronger impression if he had talked about his experiences as a young gay man in the 1930s and '40s, or about his long-term relationship with Hulse, but his habitual privacy kept him to generalities. Admittedly, when Geis had originally proposed the tour, Gordon refused to promote the book as an openly gay man. "The only thing I won't permit is any invasion of privacy," he had protested. Geis had gently pointed out that his readers would likely assume he was gay either way, but Gordon was adamant. "The book doesn't prove anything about me," he argued, "any more than 'Crime and Punishment' proves that Dostoevsky murdered old ladies. That's my line and I'm sticking to it right up to the Supreme Court."[38] Geis was right, even if Gordon kept to his line. In an interview he gave to *Michael's Thing*, a New York weekly gay guide, he admitted only to "know[ing] many happy homosexuals." Nonetheless it's impossible to read the article and not get the impression that Gordon is gay.[39]

Public relations were not the only way for Gordon to boost his literary stature. After the success of *The Lord Won't Mind*, the possibility of film and theatrical adaptations arose. Stephen Warner, a young enterprising man from Hollywood working for Paramount Pictures, approached Gordon with a plan for turning the novel into a film. He offered five thousand dollars for the motion picture rights, having already found a screenplay writer and two studios interested in producing the film.[40] Warner had good reason to think that a film version of *Lord* was possible. Gore Vidal's *City and the Pillar* was reportedly being made into a film, and *Midnight Cowboy*, a film that included homosexual characters, had recently won multiple Academy Awards. Warner planned to follow the same plan that the producer Stanley Jaffe had used to make *Cowboy*.[41]

Warner's offer languished for months, in part because McCall, Gordon's agent, insisted on squabbling over money. McCall thought she could command a high price in light of the novel's bestselling status, so she persuaded Gordon to stall Warner while she pitched the novel to other producers. This strategy turned out to be a mistake. McCall was unable to get any more offers, and when Warner increased his offer to ten thousand dollars, she continued to haggle over contract terms.[42] By the time a contract was finally signed, over a year had passed since *Lord* was on the bestseller lists, and interest from the film studios had cooled.[43] The film prospects only worsened when *One for the Gods* failed to make the bestseller list. In retrospect, both Warner and McCall underestimated the difficulty of making a gay-themed film. Only a few years later, the actor Paul Newman optioned the film rights for Patricia Nell Warren's popular gay novel *The Front Runner*. Although Newman had every intention of making a film, the studios were too queasy—even with a headliner like Newman—and the film was never made.[44] McCall thought she was acting in Gordon's best interest by negotiating aggressively, but in this case timing was more important than contract terms. Even if a film did not make Gordon a lot of money, it could have opened up a new market for his novels and broadened his reputation.

As disappointing as this failed venture was, the biggest blow came with the implosion of Bernard Geis. Signs that Geis's firm was in trouble started appearing in 1971 during production of *One for the Gods*. Geis gave much less attention to this novel than he had for *Lord*, and the production process was riddled with problems, including errors in the printed text and a weak advertising campaign. At one point, Avon Books, the paperback publisher of the novel, accused Geis of misusing money that had been specifically earmarked for advertising and promotion. As was customary for a paperback press, Avon had contributed money—in this case, fifteen thousand dollars—to promote the hardcover release of the novel, and so they were alarmed when it appeared that only a fraction of the amount was actually being spent on advertisements. The situation grew worse when Geis began to neglect royalty payments. For Gordon, who relied on this income, this would not do. He quickly enlisted McCall and her legal team to demand all royalties due to him.[45] Finally, in November 1971, the axe fell. Citing a recession in the fiction market, Geis filed a motion for reorganization in federal district court—a clear first step in bankruptcy filing.[46] At this point all royalty payments due to authors were temporarily halted, and the firm's publishing projects were effectively in limbo.

The Geis bankruptcy created several problems for Gordon. In addition to the loss of royalties, any planned promotional work for *One for the Gods* was now impossible—a big missed opportunity, not least because Gordon was in the middle of negotiations for the film rights to *Lord*. But the biggest problem was the fact that Gordon was now without a publisher. He was nearly done with the manuscript for *Forth into Light*, but there was no clear means of getting the novel into print. Luckily, McCall had anticipated problems with Geis, and so when negotiating the contract for *Gods*, she had insisted on stripping out the clause regarding sequel rights.[47] This meant that she could sell the manuscript directly to any publisher without going through the byzantine process of extricating it from an earlier agreement with Geis. Given the fact that *Lord* had been a national bestseller, as well as the perception that gay-themed novels were less controversial in 1972 than they had been in 1968, McCall surely thought that placing Gordon's novel would simply be a matter of due diligence.

The task was more difficult than McCall had expected. All of the publishing houses she approached—William Morrow, Putnam's, David McKay, Delacorte-Dell, Arbor House—rejected the novel, despite *Lord*'s unprecedented success. Harvey Ginsberg, the veteran editor who had made an unsuccessful bid for Forster's *Maurice* the previous year (and who would later encourage Armistead Maupin to publish *Tales of the City* as a book) tried to put together a package at Putnam's. He had regretted turning down the manuscript for *Lord* after it became a bestseller, and he didn't want to miss an opportunity this time.[48] Somehow, the deal fell through amid mysterious circumstances.[49] McCall blamed the multiple rejections on Geis, who she claimed had done a disastrous job on the reprint campaign for *Lord*, thereby depriving the book of valuable hardcover sales.[50] Whatever the reason, the mainstream firms balked. For a worrying moment, it seemed as though *Forth into Light* might never be published.

Fortunately, Avon came to the rescue. Peter Mayer, Avon's editor in chief, had overseen the robust paperback sales of *The Lord Won't Mind*, and he knew there was a large readership for Gordon's gay novels. He was not concerned about the negative critical reception of *Lord* and *One for the Gods*, since he could reach readers directly through Avon's distribution channels, which didn't rely on mainstream reviews for book sales. He offered to publish *Forth into Light* as a paperback original, with an advance of ten thousand dollars—the same amount Gordon had wanted from the hardcover presses.[51] Gordon accepted Mayer's offer. Although his six previous novels had all been published in hardcover, he was anxious to see *Forth into Light* in print—and he was anxious to get his paycheck. "I'm more interested in money than in whatever prestige accrues from hardcover publication," he told McCall, "I think it's absurd to expect people to pay seven dollars for a novel anyway."[52]

Avon wasted no time getting *Forth into Light* into bookstores. As soon as Gordon signed the contract, Mayer assigned his novels to Robert ("Bob") Wyatt, a handsome thirty-two-year-old rising editor in the firm. Wyatt was a wunderkind in the publishing history. A workaholic and voracious reader, he was known for his sexy beard and for having a small apartment in the Upper West Side that was crammed with books from top to bottom. He had attended the University of Tulsa and worked for a Tulsa newspaper before coming to New York, and outside the office he was most comfortable in Levis and boots. A gay man himself, he knew the gay literary scene in New York well. He was a regular at Fire Island, where he socialized with Felice Picano, Lawrence Kramer, and other New York writers. He also had an impeccable instinct for appealing to gay readers. He knew that the gay reading market was significantly variegated, and he knew that different readers required different marketing approaches.[53]

Wyatt had a few ideas about what to do with Gordon's books. First, he jettisoned the approach taken by Geis, who had promoted *Lord* and *Gods* as political and sociological manifestos.[54] Instead he capitalized on the popularity of the novels' characters. He promoted *Forth into Light* as the dramatic conclusion to the story of Charlie and Peter; for some marketing cycles he even sold all three novels as a boxed set, "The Charlie and Peter Trilogy." Second, he bypassed the critics, both straight and gay, instead reaching readers through straightforward advertising. He put glossy ads in *The Advocate* and *Christopher Street*, as well as in "gay-adjacent" periodicals like the *Village Voice* and *After Dark*.[55]

Third, Wyatt ensured that the books were visually appealing. When the Avon paperback edition of *The Lord Won't Mind* came out, it featured a lush, colorful image of Charlie and Peter holding hands and gazing into each other's eyes against the backdrop of Princeton's campus. The paperback cover of *One for the Gods* also had Charlie and Peter holding hands and looking at each other, though now in skimpy revealing bathing suits. The creator of these daring images was Victor Gadino, a young New York-based artist who had just graduated from the Pratt Institute, where he had sometimes unnerved his professors with his graphic homoerotic paintings.[56] Gadino had taken his portfolio to Hearst Publishing in the hopes of getting work, and he caught the attention of the art director of Avon Books (a division of Hearst). She liked Gadino's work, and she also suspected he was gay, so she decided to assign him the covers for Gordon's books. She gave Gadino a copy of *Lord* to read, and he was "shocked" at the explicitness of the gay sex scenes. He had created illustrations for historical romance covers, so he had an idea of what to do with Gordon's novels. One challenge, however, was finding models. Gadino's normal method was to hire a photographer to create an image using real-life models and then create an oil painting based on the photograph. Even though most male models in New York were gay, many of them were wary of being identified as gay and losing potential jobs. Gadino knew some models who were less concerned, and these became the templates for the Avon Merrick books.[57]

The Gadino covers were more effective than Avon could have hoped. Over the next several years his paintings became synonymous with Gordon's novels, so much so that readers and reviewers would regularly talk about the covers as indistinguishable from the novels themselves. Gadino even received his own fan mail. In one instance he got a letter from an archbishop in New Jersey, on church letterhead, warmly telling Gadino how much he had been moved by the books' covers.[58] Wyatt decided that Gadino would continue to make the cover art for all of Gordon's novels. While this was a clever branding strategy, it was also historically significant. As the historian Ian Young has shown, the Avon covers for Gordon's books were revolutionary in the context of gay literature. Earlier gay-themed paperback novels always had their men looking away from each other, often with shamed or despondent expressions. By contrast, the men in Gadino's paintings are confident,

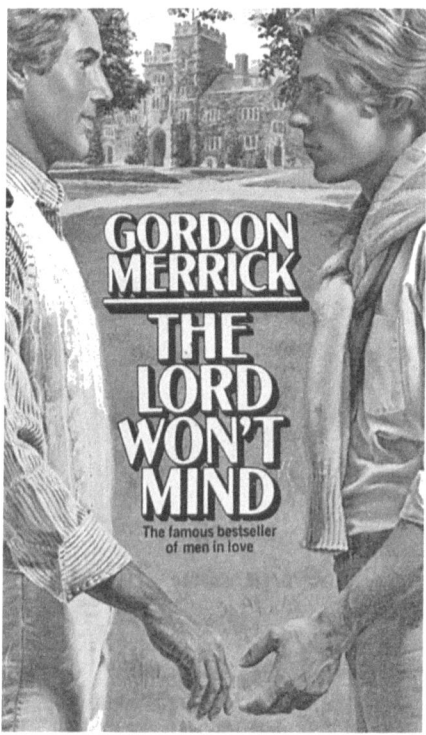

Figure 13.1 Original Avon paperback cover for *The Lord Won't Mind* (1970).
Source: Estate of Gordon Merrick.

self-aware, and seductive.[59] Gadino would continue as a prolific portraitist and book cover illustrator for the next several decades.

Through its aggressive marketing and branding strategy, Avon was also transforming Gordon's literary reputation. He was no more the subversive postwar novelist who had written critiques of American capitalism in Fitzgeraldesque prose. He was becoming known instead as a writer of "escapist" fiction, a purveyor of unrealistic gay fantasies. One reason for this was the sheer snobbery of hardcover publishing. Paperback originals were not regularly reviewed by the mainstream newspapers, and subsequently none of Gordon's novels after *One for the Gods* was reviewed by the *New York Times*. Likewise, Gadino's sexy images, which made the novels visually unforgettable, also contributed to the growing perception of Gordon as a "pulpy" romance writer. Years later, historians of gay literature would cite the paperback editions as evidence of their "pulp" status, some of them unaware that his first gay novels had in fact been published in hardcover.[60] Gordon had imagined himself creating a gay mythology through the Charlie and Peter saga, but Avon was also mythologizing "Gordon Merrick" as a certain kind of gay writer.

Gordon would later regret his quick dismissal of hardcover "prestige." To be sure, Avon had lived up to its promise to sell his work. They put his novels in the hands of thousands of readers, for many years and in many places, and they cemented his household name status in the gay community. At the same time they constructed an image of him that he did not recognize.[61] He had always thought of himself as a "serious" novelist first, worthy of being reviewed by the *New York Times*. He may have bristled whenever he got a bad review in the national press, but he was now realizing that, in this arena, negative publicity was still better than no publicity.

NOTES

1. Gordon Merrick, *One for the Gods* (New York: Bernard Geis, 1971), 5.
2. Merrick, *One for the Gods*, 28.
3. Merrick, *One for the Gods*, 7.
4. Merrick, *One for the Gods*, 84, 88.
5. Tobias published the memoir under a pseudonym, John Reid, in 1973. In 1986 he used his own name for a new edition of the book and wrote a sequel, *The Best Little Boy in the World Grows Up*.
6. Merrick, *One for the Gods*, 126.
7. Merrick, *One for the Gods*, 20, 132, 293, 271.
8. Michael McConnell and Jack Baker, *The Wedding Heard 'Round the World: America's First Gay Marriage* (Minneapolis: University of Minnesota Press, 2016); Rob Cole, "Gay Marriage 'Boom': Suddenly, It's News," *The Advocate*, August 6–18, 1970.
9. Elise Chenier, "Gay Marriage, 1970s Style," *Gay & Lesbian Review*, March–April 2013; Craig M. Loftin, *Masked Voices: Gay Men and Lesbians in Cold War America* (Albany: State University of New York Press, 2012), 157–59, 168–77.
10. Avon Books press release, December 2, 1972, GMP, box 22, folder 8.
11. "An Exclusive Interview with Gordon Merrick," *Michael's Thing* 1, no. 30 (1971): 13.
12. Linda C. Dowling, *Hellenism and Homosexuality in Victorian Oxford* (Ithaca: Cornell University Press, 1994), xiii; Sebastian Matzner, "From Uranians to Homosexuals: Philhellenism, Greek Homoeroticism and Gay Emancipation in Germany 1835–1915," *Classical Receptions Journal* 2, no. 1 (2010): 60–91; Amy Richlin, "Eros Underground: Greece and Rome in Gay Print Culture, 1953–65," *Journal of Homosexuality* 49, nos. 3–4 (2005): 421–61.
13. Quoted in David K. Johnson, *Buying Gay: How Physique Entrepreneurs Sparked a Movement* (New York: Columbia University Press, 2019), 90. Johnson gives an authoritative account of *Grecian Guild Pictorial* and its founders, and his

chapter on the physique magazines perceptively explains the genre's Hellenistic rhetoric.

14. Bernard F. Dick, *The Hellenism of Mary Renault* (Carbondale: Southern Illinois University Press, 1972); Caroline Zilboorg, *The Masks of Mary Renault: A Literary Biography* (Columbia: University of Missouri Press, 2001).

15. The design was created by Roy E. La Grone, an artist who served in the Air Force during World War II before studying art at the Pratt Institute. He is best known for his paintings of the Tuskegee Airmen, with whom he served. See Joseph Caver, Jerome Ennels, and Daniel Haulmen, *The Tuskegee Airmen, An Illustrated History: 1939–1949* (Montgomery, AL: NewSouth Books, 2011), 149.

16. Merrick, *One for the Gods*, 68, 281–82.

17. Quoted in Johnson, *Buying Gay*, 89, 94–98. See also Robert Aldrich, *The Seduction of the Mediterranean: Writing, Art and Homosexual Fantasy* (London: Routledge, 1993), 82; Craig Loftin, "Unacceptable Mannerisms: Gender Anxieties, Homosexual Activism, and Swish in the United States, 1945–1965," *Journal of Social History* 40 (2007): 557–96. Critics of gay Hellenism have also pointed out its tendency toward racial exclusion. See Scott Bravmann, *Queer Fictions of the Past: History, Culture, and Difference* (Cambridge: Cambridge University Press, 1997), 67.

18. Merrick, *One for the Gods*, 309, 266.

19. Merrick, *One for the Gods*, 252.

20. Monica McCall to Gordon Merrick, 11 October 1971, GMP, box 16, folder 3.

21. Jim Watters, "Ruth Ford & Dotson Rader: A December Mistress-Muse to May," *People*, March 24, 1975.

22. Dotson Rader, "The Gay Militants," *New York Times*, October 3, 1971.

23. "Ode to a Grecian Isle," *New York Daily News*, September 12, 1976, p. 39.

24. Gordon Merrick, *Who'll Go Down in History?*, draft, Merrick Papers, box 14, folders 1–2.

25. Gordon Merrick, *Forth into Light* (New York: Avon Books, 1974), 85–86.

26. Merrick, *Forth into Light*, 90.

27. Merrick, *Forth into Light*, 336.

28. Merrick, *Forth into Light*, 348.

29. Robert Wyatt to Gordon Merrick, 7 January 1974, GMP, box 16, folder 6.

30. Merrick, *Forth into Light*, 347.

31. Merrick, *Forth into Light*, 253.

32. Advertisement, Oscar Wilde Memorial Bookshop, Summer 1974, George Fisher Papers, box 38, folder 17.

33. Newsletter, Lambda Rising, Washington, DC, 1975, George Fisher Papers, box 38, folder 10.

34. Douglas Dean, "Fuck Books or Gay Literature?" *Vector*, May 1973.

35. Larry Townsend, "Who Gauges Market Correctly, Publishers or Writers?" *The Advocate*, August 19–September 1, 1970.

36. Sheri Safran to Bernard Geis, memorandum, 19 May 1971; Sheri Safran to Gordon Merrick, 25 May 1971, GMP, box 16, folder 3.

37. Bernard Geis to Gordon Merrick, 18 and 31 August 1971, GMP, box 16, folder 3.

38. Gordon Merrick to Bernard Geis, 26 March 1969, GMP, box 16, folder 1.

39. "An Exclusive Interview with Gordon Merrick."

40. Stephen R. Warner to Monica McCall, 16 July 1970; Stephen R. Warner to Gordon Merrick, 28 October 1970, GMP, box 16, folder 2.

41. "Around the Arts," *Mattachine Times*, August 1970, p. 16; Monica McCall to Gordon Merrick, 18 November 1970, GMP, box 16, folder 2.

42. George Willner to Stephen R. Warner, 21 July 1970; Monica McCall to Gordon Merrick, 22 September 1970; George C. Shelton Jr., representing Stephen R. Warner, to Bernard Geis, 24 November 1970; Monica McCall to Gordon Merrick, 30 November 1970; Monica McCall to Gordon Merrick, 21 January 1971, 9 March 1971, 10 March 1971, 2 April 1971, 13 April 1971, 5 May 1971, GMP, box 16, folders 2–3.

43. Monica McCall to Lawrence Livingston, 19 October 1972; Monica McCall to Gordon Merrick, 14 January 1974, GMP, box 16, folder 6.

44. "New York Times Best-Selling Book 'The Front Runner' Film Rights Up for Grabs," *Business Wire*, June 28, 2013, http://www.businesswire.com.

45. Bernard Geis to Gordon Merrick, 18 and 31 August 1971; Monica McCall to Gordon Merrick, 22 October 1971, 2 November 1971; Peter Mayer to Bernard Geis, 11 November 1971; Monica McCall to Bernard Geis, 9 March 1971; Monica McCall to Gordon Merrick, 10 March 1971, 2 April 1971, 6 April 1971, 22 April 1971, 12 May 1971, 24 August 1971; agreement between Bernard Geis Associates and Gordon Merrick, 21 June 1971; Monica McCall to Bella Linden, 27 August 1971, GMP, box 16, folder 3.

46. Henry Raymont, "Bankruptcy Step Is Taken by Geis," *New York Times*, November 13, 1971; "Geis Reorganizes Prior to Merger," *Publishers Weekly*, November 22, 1971; Monica McCall to Gordon Merrick, 16 November 1971, GMP, box 16, folder 3.

47. Joseph Calderon to Monica McCall, 6 January 1972, GMP, box 16, folder 4.

48. Monica McCall to Gordon Merrick, 3 September 1975, GMP, box 17, folder 1.

49. "'What Am I Bid for Lyndon Johnson?': Or How the Literary Auction Works," *New York Magazine*, August 30, 1971; Patrick Gale, *Armistead Maupin* (New York: Open Road Media, 2016), n.p.; Monica McCall to Gordon Merrick, 16 May 1972, GMP, box 16, folder 4.

50. Monica McCall to Gordon Merrick, 23 March 1972, 5 April 1972, GMP, box 16, folder 4.

51. Monica McCall to Gordon Merrick, 13 March 1972, 16 May 1972, 30 May 1972, 6 July 1972, 20 July 1972; Contract between Avon Books and Gordon Merrick, 11 September 1972, GMP, box 16, folder 4.

52. Gordon Merrick to Monica McCall, 18 December 1971, GMP, box 16, folder 3.

53. Richard Hall, "Is the Future of Gay Publishing a Fiction?" *The Advocate*, May 31, 1979.

54. Robert Wyatt to Monica McCall, 20 August 1973, GMP, box 16, folder 5.

55. Robert Wyatt to Gordon Merrick, 2 July 1974, GMP, box 16, folder 6.

56. Christopher Harrity, "Artist Spotlight: Victor Gadino," *The Advocate*, September 17, 2011.

57. Victor Gadino, email to the author.

58. Ibid.

59. Ian Young, *Out in Paperback: A Visual History of Gay Pulps* (Albion, NY: MLR Press, 2012), 66–67; "The Paperback Explosion: How Gay Paperbacks Changed America," in *The Golden Age of Gay Fiction*, ed. Drewey Wayne Gunn, 3–12 (Albion, NY: MLR Press, 2009), 10–11.

60. Other early gay novelists met a similar fate. See for example Susan Stryker's discussion of the paperback edition of Geoff Brown's *I Want What I Want*, which had been published in hardcover the previous year. Susan Stryker, *Queer Pulp: Perverted Passions from the Golden Age of the Paperback* (San Francisco: Chronicle Books, 2001), 88–89.

61. Harrity, "Victor Gadino"; Brandon Judell, "Conversation with Gordon Merrick," *Stallion*, July 1987.

Chapter Fourteen
A Return to the Stage

Publishing three novels in four years was the most productive Gordon had ever been, and the strong sales of his books promised prosperity for the foreseeable future. The Geis situation was an intermittent headache, but the Avon paperback sales gave Gordon a fairly regular stream of income, which was more than he needed in inexpensive Hydra. He had already received a small inheritance when his grandfather Melvin Billups died in 1969, a few months before *The Lord Won't Mind* appeared.[1] With his finances looking up and his health improving, Gordon was now able to do more of what he loved, like travel. He still kept to his daily writing regimen—he was almost always working on the next novel—but he filled the rest of his time with an active social life in Hydra and with increasingly frequent trips to France, England, and Asia.

Trips to England inevitably meant more theater. By now Gordon had given up the Paris apartment, and he and Hulse were spending more of the winter months in London. He had rediscovered his love of the theater, and, while he did not have the slightest intention of acting again, he ingratiated himself more and more into the city's theater scene. He shrewdly invested money in a London production of *Gypsy* that was originally supposed to star Elaine Stritch until she was replaced by Angela Lansbury right before rehearsals began.[2] The show was a smash. Gordon enjoyed the financial return on his investment, but he was more excited by the fact that he had contributed to a show that was by all accounts a spectacular triumph.

An opportunity for a different kind of theatrical venture arose when Gordon was contacted in 1974 by a young, handsome actor named Richard Drew, who wanted to produce a stage version of *The Lord Won't Mind* in New York. Drew and his romantic partner, Keith Carsey, were members of the Splinters Company, an off-off Broadway operation that staged plays in Greenwich Village. Drew proposed adapting the novel himself and starring in the play, and he made a modest offer for dramatization rights.[3] McCall was lukewarm about an off-off Broadway production, with its meager financial rewards, but

Gordon insisted that she pursue the deal. On the face of it, Drew had a viable plan, given that the Splinters Company had just staged Neal Weaver's *The Cure*, a play with explicit homosexual content.[4] And if any place was likely to welcome a theatrical *Lord*, it would surely be Greenwich Village, which had been a hot spot for sales of the novel when it first appeared. Drew drafted a script, which Gordon thought was "pretty good," and had meetings with prospective backers. Ultimately, however, the play never materialized. Either Drew was unable to find financial backing or got distracted by other projects. Gordon, who had been hoping to see his work on the stage, sent Drew's script to Richard Barr, his old friend from Princeton who had produced *The Boys in the Band* a few years earlier. Barr said he liked the script, but he politely declined.[5]

At least Barr was polite. Around the same time, Gordon met the playwright Edward Albee, whose plays Barr had produced in the 1960s. Both Gordon and Albee were at a party in London, most likely one of the many theatrical gatherings that Gordon had gotten in the habit of attending, and Albee had already had a few drinks when the two got into a conversation. Apparently Albee had read enough of *The Lord Won't Mind* to know that he was not a fan. At one point the famous playwright lost his temper and screamed at Gordon, "Merrick, how dare you write all that crap! You have an 8-inch cock and I have an 8-inch cock but we don't have to write about it, do we?" Afterward Gordon professed to have been confused by Albee's reaction to his novels. "I didn't know what it was about," he said. "It was as if I were giving away trade secrets." Noël Coward was of the same mind as Albee. "My dear boy, that isn't done," he supposedly told Gordon. "We don't talk about *it*."[6]

A friendlier person in the London theater scene was Patrick Newley, an Irish journalist who, like Gordon, had enjoyed a short theatrical career before turning to writing. Gordon and Hulse sometimes stayed at Newley's flat during their trips to London. Another good friend was Emlyn Williams, the distinguished Welsh playwright who had made a big splash in the 1930s with a number of hit plays in the West End. It is unclear when Gordon and Williams first met, but by the 1970s they were good friends and would regularly go to the theater together. Williams had been married to the actress Molly Shan for thirty-five years, but it was widely known in the theater world that he was bisexual and that he had had several relationships with men over the years. It is possible that it was Williams who had taken Gordon to see the London production of *Boys in the Band* back in 1969, since he had seen it around the same time. It is also possible—though the evidence is only circumstantial—that Williams was one of the people who gave Gordon the idea to write *The Lord Won't Mind*. In 1968 Williams had started work on an autobiography (his third) that was remarkably candid about his sexuality.[7]

Besides his connections through friends, Gordon was able to inject himself into the London theater scene by brushing up on his old journalist skills. He got the idea to interview Ian McKellen, who was by then one of the biggest stars in the Royal Shakespeare Company. Gordon had long admired McKellen, and he had a friend in the RSC's press office who was persuaded to arrange a meeting between them. When Gordon met McKellen in the summer of 1976, he was starring simultaneously in *The Winter's Tale*, *Romeo and Juliet*, and *Macbeth*, all in Stratford. The *Macbeth* production, directed by Trevor Nunn and starring a young Judi Dench as Lady Macbeth, had caused a huge sensation among theater critics. McKellen in particular was singled out for his performance, which the *New York Times* hailed as cementing his status as "physically and intellectually the best equipped British actor of his generation."[8] The show's subsequent popularity meant that Gordon couldn't get a seat even with his theater connections. He had told McKellen that he wanted to write a magazine profile of him, but he wanted to see the *Macbeth* production first. So he proposed returning to England in the spring to see McKellen in the play and then interview him at length. To Gordon's delight, McKellen agreed.

The piece that resulted was more a long essay than a magazine article. When Gordon came back in May 1977 to see the RSC *Macbeth*, he spent three days at McKellen's side. He watched him in rehearsals for a production of Ben Jonson's *The Alchemist*, tagged along to a costume fitting session, and took him for drinks and a late supper at a nearby pub after the performance. McKellen was at first guarded around Gordon, but he eventually warmed up to him, even inviting him to a *Macbeth* cast party after the show. (At the party Gordon charmed Judi Dench, whom he found "adorable" and "bubbly.") As a result, most of Gordon's article is about McKellen's personality and behavior, with relatively little on the performances themselves. The descriptions of McKellen are quintessential Gordon Merrick prose, as if Gordon were describing a character in one of his novels:

> His manner is direct but slightly guarded. One thinks immediately of a schoolmaster or an editor of a serious publishing house although I've seen his physical type working on construction gangs in London. He reflects an undefinable aura of the underprivileged English working masses—something in the lackluster skin tone, in the formation of the teeth and limbs—although his background is solidly middle class. His hands, which he uses with such effect on stage that much comment has been focused on their expressiveness, are big coarse workman's hands. He is average tall, a bit less than six feet, with a serviceable but not strikingly graceful body whose most salient feature is an unusually well-rounded bottom. No matter how well-kept his secret is, the record shows that he has to be in his late thirties but he looks younger, about thirty, at moments even less. His hair, short enough to show his ears, is brown with hints of auburn and sits

on his head like an unruly mop, which may contribute to his occasional, fleeting resemblance to Harpo Marx.[9]

Gordon's portrait of McKellen is undeniably sensual, lingering almost a tad too long on his "big coarse workman's hands" and "unusually well-rounded bottom." Later in the article, when Gordon has the opportunity to watch McKellen undress during a costume fitting, he recalls a performance of *King Lear* two years earlier, when McKellen (as Poor Tom) appeared on stage completely naked. He again lingers on the shape of McKellen's body in sensuous detail: "His shoulders are slight, his torso slim, almost skinny, with substantial buttocks and thighs and calves, ideal for wearing tights." In many ways Gordon was trying to humanize the godlike McKellen—drawing comparisons to construction workers and Harpo Marx—and thus make him more interesting for a general nontheatrical audience. But he also makes him into a pinup boy for gay readers.

In keeping with his newly liberated reputation as a gay novelist, Gordon did not avoid the subject of McKellen's sexuality. At one point in the article he basically admits that McKellen's homosexuality is common knowledge among his theatrical circle of friends:

> The theatre being what it is, Ian is much gossiped about and many of my theatre friends in London take it for granted, as a matter of no great consequence, that he is a homosexual, backed up by the fact that he has never married, that he has had no known important heterosexual relationships and that a few years ago he lived with a friend in a neighborhood in Kensington where several prominent young actors had set up housekeeping with their male mates and where it had all been quite open and above board. I've never met anybody who claims to have been to bed with him. Does it matter? Laurence Olivier is reported to have turned down a friend of mine for the National Theatre on the grounds that "he's that queer who pretends he isn't."

Gordon is being disingenuous here. Like his "gossipy" theater friends, he knew very well that McKellen had been in an eight-year relationship with Brian "Brodie" Taylor, a history teacher from Manchester.[10] Likewise, McKellen would have known that Gordon had published three explicitly gay novels and likely knew about his relationship with Hulse. In this light, Gordon's coyness about McKellen's sexuality reads as a performance for his *straight* readers: "If I had asked [McKellen] the straightforward question—are you or aren't you [gay]?—I felt reasonably sure that he would have neither confirmed nor denied it but simply refused to answer it as being none of my bloody business." In effect Gordon was playing it both ways. He leaves out enough information so as not to publicly "out" McKellen (it would be another eleven years until McKellen did so himself), but he drops enough hints for his gay readers to grasp what is going on here: two gay men of the theater gadding about London. For his readers who were clued into the London theater scene, Gordon removed any doubt by quoting his friend Emlyn Williams, who, after learning that Gordon had seen the *King Lear* production, asked whether "Ian was well hung." Gordon's answer: he had been too spellbound by the performance to notice.

For reasons that are not clear, the essay was never published. It is entertaining and skillfully written, and it shows that Gordon had not lost his touch as a journalist. The article would have fit well in a magazine like the *New Yorker*, and it would have been perfect for *Christopher Street*, the national gay magazine that tried to emulate the *New Yorker*. McCall tried to find a home for the article, but she was not confident about its prospects since, as she put it, McKellen was simply "not known" to Americans. She sent the article to *Esquire* and *Playboy*, which rejected it, and instead of contacting more highbrow magazines, she pawned it off on Murray Pollinger, her literary agent friend in London who was also representing Roald Dahl.[11] This was a dead-end as well, and the essay was eventually consigned to Gordon's pile of unpublished works. McKellen himself found it amusing. When Gordon sent him a copy to get his approval, McKellen replied with a short, friendly letter: "Of course the Ian McKellen you write about is not someone *I* recognize but so what? Publish anything you can."[12]

The McKellen piece was Gordon's love letter to the theater. While he was disappointed about the failure to get it published, he could at least console himself with the fact that he had just published another, longer tribute to the theater: *An Idol for Others*, his fourth gay novel, and his eighth overall. Stretching to over four hundred pages, this was the longest work he had ever written. Unlike *The Lord Won't Mind*, Gordon did not include a fictionalized version of himself in *Idol,* but he based it on someone he had known very well, and he set it in places and times he knew very well. With the novel he was returning to his formative years in New York before the war, and in it he also revisited his brief time in California. Moreover, unlike nearly all of his other gay novels, *Idol* does not have a happy ending.

The novel focuses on Walter Makin, a wildly successful theater producer in New York in 1970. He is married to Clara, a wealthy socialite, and has two teenage sons. On the cusp of his fiftieth birthday, he is about to receive a lifetime achievement award when he meets Tom Jennings, a young, talented writer who is in New York for a few days. The two men instantly fall for each other. Walter wants to pursue a relationship, but Tom is preparing to go back home to California. At this point the novel flashes back thirty years, when Walter is a high school student at a prep school in New Jersey. He recalls his infatuation with Harry, the school's top athlete, who one day seduces the inexperienced Walter in the school's shower room. They fall into a regular pattern of sex, and Walter is surprised that the hypermasculine Harry is an intensely passionate bottom in bed. After graduation, Walter has sex with women for the first time and convinces himself that sex with Harry was just a phase.

The novel continues to retrace Walter's early years as a student at Rutgers, which for a brief while seems to reprise Gordon's own experiences. Walter is the star of his college theater group, and he goes to New York to see Broadway productions. (Walter's thoughts about Gielgud's Hamlet are almost a quotation of Gordon's review of the production in the *Daily Princetonian*.) Walter is recruited to work at a summer theater company on Long Island, where he shows a talent for directing and quickly moves up the company's ranks. Meanwhile, he gets sexually involved with Philip, a sensitive theater technician (with echoes of Otis Bigelow), and Clara, an actress from a wealthy Cleveland family. At this point the resemblance to Gordon's life quickly dissipates. Walter dumps Philip for Clara, causing the brokenhearted Philip to commit suicide. The incident shocks Walter and convinces him of the hopelessness of homosexuality. "This thing of being queer is horrible," he says, and clings to Clara ever more firmly.[13] Afterward he drops out of Rutgers to take a theater job in New York, and he moves into a small apartment with Clara. His big break comes when Johnny Bainbridge, a classmate from Rutgers, brings him a play written by a French communist writer. Walter deems the play a masterpiece and quickly sets about procuring funds for a production—including having sex with Fay Kennicutt, the wife of a wealthy businessman who agrees to sponsor the play.

The first half of the novel builds toward the play's debut, and it is here that Gordon lovingly details the long and exhilarating process of mounting a Broadway production. He describes the work of finding a theater and assembling a cast and crew, the excitement of the first read-through, and the painstaking rehearsals leading up to the first performance. When the play gets a lukewarm audience response in previews, Walter determines that the actors, particularly the lead actor Greg, are playing it too safe. So he personally coaches Greg, putting him through a demanding series of acting exercises. The ritual is so physically and emotionally exhausting that it causes Greg to break down during a performance, which Walter sees as an epiphanic breakthrough. He takes Greg home and has sex with him, more as an attempt to steady Greg than because of a personal sexual interest. The approach works, and Greg delivers a knockout performance the next night. The play is a spectacular hit and launches Walter into the upper echelon of Broadway theater directors. He marries Clara and enjoys a prominent theatrical career, interrupted only briefly by his army service during the war.

The second half of the novel traces the second twenty-five years of Walter's life: his success as a theater producer, his increasingly stifling marriage, and his recurring attraction to men. Walter's struggle with his sexuality plays out against the backdrop of McCarthyism and the Lavender Scare, the homophobic "panic" that fueled the persecution of gay men and lesbians.[14] In this environment Walter is always on guard against appearing too "lily" in public or getting himself into situations where he could be blackmailed. In one scene he meets a model, Mark Travere, who was dishonorably discharged from the army after being caught in bed with another soldier. The incident led to a prison term and a permanent stain on his record, making it impossible for him to find a steady job. "We weren't doing anybody any harm," the young man says wistfully about himself and the other soldier. "If it hadn't been for [the dishonorable discharge], I probably would've gone to college on the GI Bill." At another point Walter is ordered by a film studio head to create a list of homosexuals to be fired from the studio, a purge directly mandated by the House Un-American Activities Committee. He refuses to make a list, and instead he makes a point of hiring people who had lost their jobs because of the witch hunts.

Idol offers a tantalizing view of New York's midcentury gay subculture, a milieu that Gordon had avoided in all his previous novels. For example, when Walter is picked up by a young man in a hotel bar, Gordon uses the opportunity to show how gay men discreetly identified each other in the city's public spaces. Later, when Walter visits a gay bar for the first time, an unnamed spot in the East Fifties, he is surprised by the ordinariness of the bar's patrons:

> They entered a nondescript bar that was crowded, noisy, and populated exclusively by males. As soon as he could bring himself to look around, he was struck by the low esthetic level of the assemblage. He had always thought of homosexuals as pretty youths, limp-wristed, shrill, perhaps even painted but more attractive in a strictly physical sense than the general run. A second glance revealed a scattering of presentable young men, but there was a generous share of paunches and bald heads and ill-formed features.

Gordon also represented the fact that the preferred term for gay people was remarkably fluid during the period. For example, as a young man in the 1930s, Walter refers to gay men as "queer," but his more experienced friend Harry prefers the newfangled term "gay."[15] Gordon uses the large time span of the novel—three and a half decades—to register methodically the changing popularity of specific terms, including the shifting connotations and effects of the word "faggot."

Gordon's original title for the novel was *Mister Makin*, which he changed to *The Award*. He finally settled on *An Idol for Others*, which he took from a passage that describes the main contradiction of Walter's life: he is "idolized" by people who do not truly know him. The novel's main conflict hinges on Walter's struggle to accept his homosexuality and have an openly loving relationship with another man. He was on the verge of doing so when he met Mark, the expelled army serviceman. At that time Walter was twenty-nine and married, but the intensity of his feelings for Mark prompted him to imagine himself in a gay relationship. In the end, however, Walter's fear of being publicly branded as a homosexual was too great. The next real opportunity comes twenty years later when Walter meets Tom. By now Walter is jaded with his marriage and career. In a bold move, he leaves Clara and moves in with Tom in his home in San Francisco.

Walter's relationship with Tom is exhilarating but not without problems. There is a significant age gap between them, and Walter struggles to fit in with Tom's gay community in San Francisco. (Gordon was remembering his own experience living in San Francisco with Hulse.) He is discomfited by the city's drag shows, campy gay bars, and men who greet each other with kisses. Moreover, Tom refuses to emulate a conventional heterosexual marriage, with prescribed roles and strict monogamy. During one fight, which erupts after a sexual threesome with a younger man, Tom defends his beliefs in a speech that reads like a 1970s queer manifesto:

> People talk about gays as if we're just like everybody else except that we happen to like our own sex. We're supposed to want what everybody else wants—acceptance in the community, marriage after our fashion and all the rest of it. People talk about our minority rights, as if we were blacks with a legitimate grievance. That's not it at all. We're unique. I'll never be your wife, no matter how much you fuck me. We're two men. We're rebels. . . . I don't want a model homosexual marriage so that everybody can say we're really nice—considering. I'll break any law if it means getting closer to you.[16]

Walter learns to accept Tom's perspective, and in the process he recognizes that his conformity to societal norms has been a defense against his internalized homophobia. The two appear to be forming a stable relationship, but things take a tragic turn when Walter is diagnosed with skin cancer. The novel ends with Walter dying in his bed after being given an overdose of painkillers by Clara. A devastated Tom kills himself the next day by taking barbiturates.

In a sense, *An Idol for Others* is an *anti*-autobiographical novel. It suggests what might have happened if Gordon hadn't become disillusioned with the theater as a young man—if he *had* become a huge Broadway star, *had* married a socialite, *hadn't* gone to Princeton, *hadn't* been born into an influential family. But it is also not autobiographical insofar as it is partly based on the life of Lemuel Ayers, Gordon's longtime friend from Princeton who became a successful theatrical designer and producer. Although Ayers had confessed to Gordon his attraction to men, he had avoided gay relationships out of the "fear of persecution" and had urged Gordon to do the same. "Don't let it happen to you," he warned Gordon, while advising him to marry a woman. Gordon momentarily considered taking Ayers' advice, but decided in the end it would be impossible for him. Ayers, on the other hand, did marry and have children and by all appearances had a stable and successful life before dying of cancer at the early age of forty. Gordon later admitted that the character of Walter was based on Ayers, but that the romance plot with Tom was an imagined alternate scenario—what might have occurred if Ayers had met someone who could have given him the courage to live openly as a gay man before his untimely death.[17] By imagining this alternate reality, Gordon was able to explore the difficulty of living as a gay man in midcentury America—a challenge he had largely avoided through his economic status and his decision to live abroad.

Gordon's approach in *Idol* shows that, despite all his protestations to the contrary, he had listened carefully to his critics. In many ways the novel reads as a response to the harsh reviews of *Lord* and its sequels. Most of the main characters are not rich, Ivy League brats. They work at low-paying jobs and scrape by for years before achieving financial success. The gay men in the novel are attractive but not in a conventional way—the main romance occurs when Walter is fifty years old, far from a young Greek god. Likewise, Walter and Tom do not retreat into a solipsistic world of their own. They integrate themselves into the city's gay community, going to gay parties and bars and cultivating networks of gay friends. In addition, Gordon restrained himself in the sex scenes, which had been a perennial lightning rod for critics. While there are certainly Gordon-Merrick-trademark sex scenes, many sexual episodes are glossed over in a couple sentences. And the sex scenes that are detailed at length are not as *perfect*. When Tom bottoms for the first time, the experience is an uncomfortable one despite his wish to please Walter. "So you didn't like it," Walter states frankly and then reassures him; "It doesn't matter." The realism of the scene accords with the other details of gay coupling that Gordon includes—like the mundane business of combining finances.

Most immediately obvious, the novel's tragic ending is an about-face from the "saccharine" endings that Gordon's critics had lambasted in the Charlie and Peter novels. Even here, though, Gordon did not revert to the stereotypical gay novels of the '50s and '60s. Walter's tragic ending does not happen because same-sex love is doomed or because gay men are helpless or neurotic. The tragedy stems from an incurable disease, made worse when Walter's gay partner is not allowed to see him in the hospital. Gordon did not know, in 1976, how common such a scenario would become.

Gordon had also heard the complaint that his novels were not politically relevant. This was surely annoying for a writer whose first novel had been political enough to make him a "passive fascist" in the *New York Times*. Yet he made an effort in *Idol* at least to address issues that had been important in midcentury America, like McCarthyism and racial segregation. For example, when Walter learns that one of his financial backers is anti-Semitic, he lashes back with plans for a progressive theater: "What I'm getting at is a theater for all the people. . . . Jews. Negroes. For instance, most theaters make a policy of keeping Negroes out of the orchestra. I won't have that. I'm looking for plays by Negroes. We're not going to make concessions to anybody's prejudices."[18] The speech feels contrived, but it shows Gordon trying to tap into his memories of the New York theater scene and connect them to present-day concerns. At the same time he was writing *Idol*, he tried to get up to date on American politics. He had McCall send him a copy of *The Final Days*, the book by Bob Woodward and Carl Bernstein about the Nixon Watergate scandal. He also wrote an open letter attacking Anita Bryant, the beauty-pageant-winner-turned-anti-gay-crusader who referred to gays as child molesters and worked to repeal an antidiscrimination law in Dade County, Florida. Gordon had asked McCall to find a national magazine or newspaper to publish his letter, but she demurred, claiming it was not the right "moment."[19]

As he had done in *Forth into Light*, Gordon also included metafictional self-commentary in *Idol*. In one section Walter tries to produce a controversial gay-themed play in San Francisco, a nod to his own unsuccessful effort to get a staged version of *The Lord Won't Mind* in New York. More cheekily, in one scene Gordon has a character—Jerry, a young, campy, self-assured gay man—imagine himself as a character in a Gordon Merrick novel: "It's one of those things that should happen but doesn't. It's in that new novel—it's a big bestseller—called 'The Lord Won't Mind.' It's about two beautiful boys who find undying love. Utter fantasy, but I loved it."[20] His remark leads to a discussion about the problems created by gay men who try to live up to an idealized model of beauty. "I hope you don't develop blond god problems," Jerry warns his friends. Such a Hitchcock-like cameo was unprecedented for Gordon, but it allowed him to show that he understood very well the problem of reading his gay novels too prescriptively.

Gordon was determined to regain his status as a "serious" novelist. He enjoyed the piles of fan letters—and the big royalty checks—but he was not immune to the desire for critical respectability. He made a big push to get *Idol* published by a hardcover press, even though Avon again made him a lucrative offer to publish the novel as a paperback original. He had McCall send the manuscript to several publishers, including William Morrow and Putnam's, who considered the novel but ultimately rejected it. McCall agreed that *Idol* was the best novel that Gordon had written, but she was reluctant to turn down Avon's generous offer. She was also not as effective an agent as before. She was increasingly plagued by health problems, which may have caused her to make uncharacteristic missteps. A particularly embarrassing blunder occurred when she sent *Idol* to Jackie Farber at William Morrow, thinking that Farber was a longtime admirer of Gordon's work. (Farber had actually been the editor at Bernard Geis who lobbied vociferously against *The Lord Won't Mind*.) Naturally, Gordon erupted when he learned about the mistake, which effectively killed the novel's chances at William Morrow.[21]

Gordon had good reasons for being wary about staying with Avon. At the same time that McCall was testing the waters with the hardcover presses, the *Village Voice* published an article about gay fiction that included a few incendiary paragraphs about Avon's "true" feelings about Gordon's work. John Lombardi, the article's author, claimed to have run into Bob Wyatt at the train station and gotten him to speak candidly about the Charlie and Peter novels. "If we publish Merrick again, it'll be over my dead body," the article quoted Wyatt as saying. "He's a horse's ass, living over there in Greece."[22] Within minutes of seeing the article, McCall was on the phone with Peter Mayer, who swiftly tried to diffuse the situation. He assured McCall that Avon was firmly committed to Gordon, and he had Bob Wyatt write a long letter detailing how horrified he was at the *Village Voice* article and maintaining that Lombardi "had simply invented his own dialogue." McCall persuaded Gordon that Wyatt was probably correct, given Lombardi's reputation as an unscrupulous tabloid writer, and after a while their normal working relations resumed.[23] But Gordon always wondered in the back of his mind what Wyatt might have actually said to Lombardi at the train station.

Ultimately Gordon was compelled to stay with Avon. Bob Wyatt, who had engineered the production of *Forth Into Light*, was again tapped to see *Idol* through to publication.[24] Despite the fact that the new novel was markedly different from the Charlie and Peter trilogy, he used the same marketing strategy, including another steamy cover by Victor Gadino. Gordon had initially liked Gadino's illustrations, but he was troubled by this one, which he thought misrepresented the novel. He also disliked the blurb on the back cover, which said nothing about the novel's theatrical setting or about Walter's struggle as a closeted gay man.[25] Instead it highlighted and exaggerated a minor plot point about an incestuous meeting between Walter and his illegitimate son Jerry.

The Gadino cover was widely used to advertise the book, and so readers naturally expected *Idol* to be a sex-fueled melodrama. The provocative marketing was enough to scandalize Gordon's brother Samuel, who wrote Gordon as soon as *Idol* was published, telling him, "You go too far!"[26] One newspaper, the *Miami News*, went so far as to ban advertisements for *Idol* because of the sexual suggestiveness of the image.[27] Richard Hall, the book critic for *The Advocate*, wrote a preview of the novel in his monthly column that reinforced these expectations. He had chatted with Wyatt, who told him the forthcoming book was "complex" and different from the Charlie and

Peter novels, but Hall ignored Wyatt's comments and based his preview on the novel's cover, which he had seen in advance: "Merely being seen with this novel in your hand may be equivalent to coming out; then again, it may trigger a boom in plain brown wrappers." A few months later Hall again predicted that *Idol* would be no different from the Charlie and Peter novels.[28]

Not surprisingly, *An Idol for Others* was largely ignored by critics, both straight and gay. None of the leading gay magazines reviewed the novel, even though they happily printed the large, revenue-generating advertisements for it. Gordon heard reports from Avon that some gay organizations were protesting the novel, which accused it of being "anti-homosexual" because its hero was a "self-hating" gay man.[29] As usual, it was the booksellers and distributors who understood Gordon's work better. They gave *Idol* a prominent place in their advertisements for gay titles, putting it next to books like Wallace Hamilton's *Coming Out* and David Kopay's *The David Kopay Story*. Like *Idol*, both of these works were about older, married, successful men who struggled with their sexuality before coming out as gay men. *Publishers Weekly*, in a feature article that interviewed fifteen booksellers about their handling of gay books, listed *Idol* alongside Avon's other gay title that year, the paperback edition of Isherwood's *Christopher and His Kind*.[30] At the same time that *Idol* was published, the nonfiction writer Richard R. Lingeman had written an article in the *New York Times* in which he divided contemporary gay books into two categories—the "clean-cut," "coming out" strand, typified by *The David Kopay Story*, and the "pornographic," "homosexual as sexual outlaw" strand, typified by John Rechy's *Sexual Outlaw*.[31] Booksellers routinely put Gordon's book in the first category.

Beyond the booksellers, there was at least one journal that looked past the novel's cover and read it seriously. The *West Coast Review of Books* was a bimonthly literary magazine from Los Angeles that set itself apart by giving serious attention to paperback originals. In 1977 it started giving more attention to books on "controversial" themes (a move that irritated some of its readers) and inaugurated its annual Porgie Awards, for "the most outstanding original paperbacks of the year." The following year it awarded the top prize to *An Idol for Others*. In explaining the reason for this choice, the magazine noted the lack of respect given to paperback originals as well as the difficulty of publishing gay-themed novels. It heaped lavish praise on *Idol* for its treatment of gay characters, which it deemed both enlightening and moving:

> Merrick's story of the love between producer-director Walter Makin and novelist Tom Jennings rings true from their first meeting and through to their last; indeed, we understand, through Merrick's writings, what it is, this homosexual love, and how different it is, from heterosexual love.... While there is, of necessity, graphic description, the author never succumbs to the gross exaggerations

of display one might find in cheapo novels handled by irresponsible hacks. [Merrick] is a super writer turning out an exceptional novel that has all of the colors necessary to entertain and illuminate. When Walter and Tom fall in love, it is real love, and when they battle, in an absolutely brilliant scene, it is one of the great scenes from a novel. . . . Homosexuality is with our society today, as indeed it has always been, but it's now in the open. You can read tons of non-fiction material to try get an understanding of what it means to people, but Merrick tells it to us in a dynamic, never to be forgotten manner. It is a beautiful story, well told, with a finish that is devastating.

Such language could have come from one of Gordon's middle America fan letters, but this was a magazine in Hollywood, only a few miles from the editorial offices of *The Advocate*. The journal's editor and publisher, D. David Dreis, a New Yorker who had moved to Los Angeles in the 1960s, was hardly ignorant of other gay writers. The same issue of *West Coast Review* featured a review of Gore Vidal's *Kalki*. Yet he and his editorial team saw Gordon's work very differently than the gay intelligentsia did. Dreis's team recognized the stylistic quality of the writing, which admittedly was better than most paperback originals, and more importantly they read the novel as an authentic representation of gay experience. The review quoted nearly all of Tom's manifesto against gay assimilationism, as evidence of the novel's relevance to the gay liberation movement. And it was absolutely clear about its opinion of Gordon's status as a serious writer: "Merrick is, without qualification, one of the best authors being published today hardcover or paperback."[32]

The mixed reception of *An Idol for Others* shows just how large a divide there was between highbrow gay culture and the national gay consumer market. Ironically, it was one of these highbrow magazines, the New York-based *Christopher Street*, that shed light on this divide, in an article it published a few months before *Idol* appeared. In the article, Tim Dlugos, a gay Manhattanite poet, interviewed Terry McClymonds, the Avon sales representative overseeing the Southern states market, about the challenges of selling gay literature. In the article the urbanite Dlugos is surprised to hear about Avon's effective strategy for getting gay books—*especially* Gordon Merrick books—into bookstores in the rural South:

> "Down there," says McClymonds, "most of your readership is *very* mass-oriented." Predictably, Avon's biggest "gay" titles are those written by "Gordon Merrick," whose continuing adventure of two hunky men began with *The Lord Won't Mind*. "You hate to call a book like *The Lord Won't Mind* a classic," says McClymonds, "but it's been around long enough to be a significant part of the masscult scene. The Merrick books are like Rosemary Rogers romances—they're standards, and they get recognized."

In other words, Avon was *not* targeting gay readers in Manhattan or San Francisco, who could find any book they wanted. It was aiming for the gay readers in places that were, as Dlugos put it, "not exactly hotbeds of sympathy for alternative lifestyles."[33] This was directly the work of Wyatt, who had devised a strategy for getting around the problem of timid salespeople in less gay-friendly areas of the country.[34] There is a trenchant irony in the fact that Wyatt's strategy, which all but ensured the critical dismissal of *An Idol for Others*, was precisely the means by which Gordon's novels reached a wide, geographically diverse readership.

The partial success of *An Idol for Others* is evidence of the kind of writing that Gordon was capable of when he responded constructively to criticism rather than getting angry at it. It is no coincidence that this was happening at the same time that he started mentoring other writers. Hulse had just started work on a novel of his own, based on his childhood in Arkansas, and Hulse's brother Larry was also working on his first book, also inspired by his childhood memories in the South. Gordon read and gave feedback on both their manuscripts, even getting his agent to take on Larry Hulse as a client.[35] Gordon was evidently thinking of Larry's book when he finished writing *Idol*, since he dedicated the book to him, with a cheering prediction of the future of Larry's book. Gordon had just gone through a growing period of his own, in which he had tried hard to connect his writing to contemporary political and social issues in America. This had not been easy for him[36]—he admitted later that the novel had been extremely difficult for him to write—but his pains had yielded dividends. Had he continued on this path, paying attention to what was going on in America and listening to American writers and critics, he might have found himself among an emerging group of gay writers who would eventually come to define "post-Stonewall" gay literature.

However, the impulse did not last. Although the lure of the stage had drawn Gordon's attention back to America and England for a few years, by the late 1970s he was being pulled in a very different direction, both geographically and culturally. For better or worse, this new trajectory would lead him back to the kind of worldly, cosmopolitan settings with which he had been most comfortable.

NOTES

1. Notice of Last Will and Testament of Melvin P. Billlups, August 28, 1969, GMP, box 16, folder 1.
2. Monica McCall to Gordon Merrick, 11 June 1973, GMP, box 16, folder 5.

3. Letter of agreement from Richard Drew and Keith Carsey for dramatic rights to *The Lord Won't Mind*, 30 April 1974, GMP, box 16, folder 6; Obituary, Keith DeVon Carsey, *Salt Lake Tribune*, November 5, 2013.

4. "Off Off Broadway Shows," *New York Times*, June 15, 1973.

5. Gordon Merrick to Monica McCall, 20 November 1974; Monica McCall to Gordon Merrick, 20 November 1974, GMP, box 16, folder 6; Monica McCall to Gordon Merrick, 27 May 1975, 25 March 1976, 1 and 15 April 1976, 3 May 1976, 11 and 19 January 1976, GMP, box 17, folders 1–3.

6. Keith Howes, "Once A Spy . . . ," *Gay News*, August 10, 1978; Brandon Judell, "Orgasm and Organdy: Gordon Merrick, the Champion of Gay Romance," *The Advocate*, October 14, 1986.

7. John Russell Stephens, *Emlyn Williams: The Making of A Dramatist* (Wales: Seren, 2000), 12–13.

8. Robert Cushman, "A Stunning *Macbeth* from the RSC," *New York Times*, February 5, 1978; Michael Mullin, "Stage and Screen: The Trevor Nunn *Macbeth*," *Shakespeare Quarterly* 38, no. 3 (1987): 350–59.

9. "Reflections on British Actor Ian McKellen," unpublished manuscript, c. 1977, GMP, box 15, folder 14. All details about Merrick's meeting with McKellen, including quotations of their conversations, are taken from this manuscript unless otherwise noted.

10. Garry O'Connor, *Ian McKellen: A Biography* (New York: St. Martin's Press, 2019), 80.

11. Monica McCall to Gordon Merrick, 15 and 30 September 1977, 12 October 1977, GMP, box 17, folder 3.

12. Ian McKellen to Gordon Merrick, 5 October 1977, GMP, box 19, folder 5.

13. Gordon Merrick, *An Idol for Others* (New York: Avon Books, 1977), 94.

14. See David K. Johnson, *The Lavender Scare: The Cold War Persecution of Gays and Lesbians in the Federal Government* (Chicago: University of Chicago Press, 2004).

15. Merrick, *An Idol for Others*, 242, 41.

16. Merrick, *An Idol for Others*, 390.

17. Howes, "Once A Spy"; Michel Mabille, "Ceylon to Tricqueville: The Restless Life of an American Author," *L'Éveil de Pont-Audemer*, August 27, 1981; Gordon Merrick, interview by Brandon Judell. Gordon did not give Ayers' name in the Howes and Mabille interviews, though he gave enough details to identify Ayers. He did name Ayers in the Judell interview, though Judell did not include the name in the published version.

18. Merrick, *An Idol for Others*, 192.

19. Monica McCall to Gordon Merrick, 15 April 1975, 22 August 1976, GMP, box 17, folders 2–3.

20. Merrick, *An Idol for Others*, 379–80.

21. Monica McCall to Gordon Merrick, 16 July 1975, 3 and 19 September 1975, GMP, box 17, folder 1; Mitch Douglas to Gordon Merrick, 14 April 1978, GMP, box 17, folder 4.

22. John Lombardi, "Selling Gay to the Masses," *Village Voice*, June 30, 1975.

23. Monica McCall to Gordon Merrick, July 16, 1975, GMP, box 17, folder 1.

24. Contract between Gordon Merrick and Avon Books, October 31, 1975; Jo Stewart to Gordon Merrick, 12 December 1975, GMP, box 17, folder 1; Monica McCall to Gordon Merrick, 4 January 1976, 15 April 1976, GMP, box 17, folder 2.

25. Christopher Harrity, "Artist Spotlight: Victor Gadino," *The Advocate*, September 17, 2011.

26. Bjorn Rye, "Idylls for Others," *The Advocate*, April 5, 1979.

27. Richard Hall, "The Problem's Distribution," *The Advocate*, August 10, 1977.

28. Richard Hall, "Reviews & Previews," *The Advocate*, March 9 and June 15, 1977.

29. Rye, "Idylls for Others"; Howes, "Once A Spy."

30. Daisy Maryles and Robert Dahlin, "Books on Homosexuality: A Current Checklist," *Publishers Weekly*, August 8, 1977.

31. Richard R. Lingeman, "Homosexual Titles," *New York Times*, July 17, 1977.

32. "The Second Annual Porgie Awards," *West Coast Review of Books*, July 1978.

33. Tim Dlugos, "Rough Trade: Notes on the Book World," *Christopher Street*, March 1977.

34. Hall, "Problem's Distribution." See also Richard Hall, "Books," *The Advocate*, October 5, 1977. Hall wrote a longer piece on the difficulty faced by gay writers in the *Village Voice*, though without mentioning Merrick: Richard Hall, "The Unnatural History of Homosexual Literature," *Village Voice*, August 22, 1977.

35. Monica McCall to Gordon Merrick, 1 January 1976, GMP, box 17, folder 2.

36. Mabille, "Ceylon to Tricqueville."

Chapter Fifteen

Adventures in the East

By the mid-1970s Gordon was getting restless. He had lived in Hydra for over fifteen years, and the island had started to lose its charm. It was not as popular among celebrities as it had been a decade earlier, when Jackie Kennedy had sailed in on her yacht, yet the steady influx of tourists made it feel more congested. The cost of living for American expatriates was also not as cheap as it had been before. The discovery of the island by Americans and Europeans had brought in a horde of emigrés and part-time residents who added little to their social circle but who drove up the price of real estate. The situation got bad enough that Gordon led a group of residents to petition the Greek president of Tourism to restrict the amount of sea traffic, which was causing air pollution.[1] When an interviewer asked him if he thought Hydra was beautiful, Gordon answered bluntly: "It was *once*. Now the crowds are so big, you know, and everyone is trying to outdo one another with a larger pool and more fabulous parties. It's not the place at all it once was. I think I've had it."[2] In addition, Gordon's back problems were getting worse again, making the daily trek home up a steep rocky footpath more arduous with each passing year.[3]

An opportunity for change came when Gordon and Charlie got the idea to visit Sri Lanka (previously Ceylon). The tropical island, near the southern tip of India, had gained its independence in 1948 after four centuries of Dutch and British imperial rule, opening the door for a new wave of American and European expatriates. The writer Paul Bowles had been living there since the 1950s, and the science fiction writer Arthur C. Clarke was there by 1956. Clarke, who was a year younger than Gordon, was a discreet gay man who neither confirmed nor hid his homosexuality. Many of Clarke's friends later speculated that one of his reasons for moving to Sri Lanka was the country's relatively tolerant attitude toward gay people. The other reason was the extremely low cost of living. Westerners could buy a sprawling villa with lush surroundings for a fraction of the cost of a modest building back home. Servants were even cheaper. People who could not afford a maid or cook in America or Europe could easily maintain a full house staff in Sri Lanka. In

1976 Clarke and other expatriates were successful in getting Sri Lanka to pass the "Clarke Act," which exempted certain expatriate residents from local income tax. This made the island even more affordable for incomers, and soon Colombo became home to a small but active circle of expatriate writers and artists.[4]

Having long wanted to tour the East, Gordon and Hulse took a long, three-month trip at the beginning of 1975. They visited India, Nepal, Thailand, Malaysia, Singapore, Indonesia, and finally Sri Lanka, where they stayed for two weeks before making the trip back to Athens. The island must have made a good impression, since they went back in January 1976, this time staying at the New Oriental Hotel in Galle, a city on the southwestern coast whose center is a massive stone fort built by the Dutch in the seventeenth-century.[5] The hotel itself was very much in Gordon's style—Victorian-period furnishings, twenty-foot-high ceilings, dramatic verandas, obsequious hotel staff. Apparently, the visit went very well. Before the year was over they had bought a house—a charming bungalow which they christened "Cap Coco"—in the Galle suburb of Unawatuna, a lush coastal town known for its purple-faced langurs (leaf monkeys).[6] Unlike their home in Hydra, which had been a big renovation project, Cap Coco was brand new. It was custom built for Gordon and Hulse in twelve days by an army of 150 construction workers.[7] For the next twelve years, they would spend most of their time in Galle, occasionally taking trips to England or America and later spending a few months each year in Normandy. Hulse's brother Larry visited them in Sri Lanka frequently, and eventually they set him up in a nearby point house, a building that was later destroyed by the 2004 tsunami that devastated the island's coast.

Gordon and Hulse took little time acclimating to their new home. They enjoyed the sunny, temperate climate, and they found the local community to be warm and hospitable. Their introduction to Galle took place against a backdrop of increasing political volatility. Since gaining independence, political power in Sri Lanka had shifted regularly between the Sri Lanka Freedom Party, which was committed to the nationalization of Buddhism and Sinhala culture, and the United National Party, which advocated for a more "popular, multicultural and modernist" state. In 1977, only a few months after Gordon had moved to Sri Lanka, the United National Party had won control of the government. At the same time Tamil separatist groups were pushing more aggressively for independent sovereignty, and the increasing threat of ethnic riots and violence was a constant force in Sri Lankan politics.[8]

Despite the political situation, Gordon and Hulse, like most other expatriate residents, were relatively inoculated in their home in Galle. They bought a couple of bikes which they used to go to the local food markets. Gordon's culinary talents were tested by the change of amenities and available ingredients, but he adapted quickly. "You can find chickens everywhere," he told a *Gay News* reporter. "It's easy to do anything to a chicken." Cheese was nearly impossible to find, which was a challenge for someone who had learned how to cook in France, but he found other ingredients to play with. One of his specialties was crab, which was easy to get, cooked with onions, tomatoes, and pesto sauce. He also discovered a love for pork crackling, which he had never been allowed to eat as a child.

As they had in Greece, Gordon and Hulse welcomed many guests to Galle. Gordon was an impeccable—and imperious—host. Guests staying at their home would get a breakfast tray with café au lait, fresh fruit juice, and a long list of rules: "Please don't offer to help in the kitchen. Keep your room tidy. Don't feed stray cats at restaurants. Don't stack plates at table. Don't come into the kitchen. Don't ask for special menus—take what we can find and want to cook."[9] Guests who did not follow basic rules of decorum ran the risk of provoking Gordon's temper. On one occasion, when they were selling the Cap Coco home in order to move closer to town, they invited the buyer over for a dinner party. Gordon spared no effort and produced an elaborate dinner, including soufflés with cheese, a luxury in Sri Lanka. Unfortunately the buyer never tasted Gordon's soufflé, since she arrived to the dinner party three hours late. Gordon was livid. He remained quiet throughout the entire dinner, steaming. Finally, when the buyer mentioned something about the house, he erupted. "There is no way in hell you will ever get this fucking house," he raged, and announced he would be returning her down payment. Charley later smoothed things between them, and the sale went through. Usually the less easily rankled one, Charley had not minded their guest's lateness as much, especially since it meant he got two soufflés.[10]

At the same time that Gordon was settling in Sri Lanka, he was at work on his fifth, and perhaps strangest, gay novel. He initially called it *The Fluke*, though his publisher convinced him to change it to *The Quirk*.[11] The original idea for the novel came from an earlier novella that Gordon had drafted, probably in the 1960s, but never published. In the novella the main character, Charlie, is an idealistic American painter who moves to postwar France to work on his art. While there, he falls in love with Nicky, a young French woman. Charlie is on the verge of having a big exhibition of his work in America when his financial backers pull out. Nicky tries to help by arranging an exhibit in Paris with help from Gerárd, a wealthy but shady acquaintance from her past. When Gerárd demands sex from Nicky in return, she complies and is plagued with interminable guilt. Her shame ultimately drives her to commit suicide, and the novella ends with Charlie discovering her dead body.[12]

In transforming the novella into *The Quirk*, Gordon made several changes. He changed Charlie's name to Rod MacIntyre and, more significantly, made him bisexual. As in the novella, Rod is an aspiring American painter who falls for a French woman named Nicole. However, the main plot of *Quirk* focuses on Rod's gradual discovery of his bisexuality. For this storyline Gordon added two new gay characters: Patrice, a young, impish French boy, and "the prince," a devastatingly handsome European aristocrat who is the toast of the Parisian gay scene. Patrice is by far the most original and complex character in the novel. He is immediately infatuated with Rod and determines to help advance his career. For his part, Rod is impressed by Patrice's knowledge of art and disarmed by his selfless devotion. Although Patrice does not deliberately try to seduce Rod, their growing friendship and mutual affection prompts Rod to experiment sexually with Patrice on multiple occasions. At first, Rod decides that sex with Patrice is only a "quirk." He is not queer, he tells himself, but simply letting go of inhibitions and giving pleasure to a friend. This theory falls apart when he meets the prince, who captivates him. By the end of the novel Rod realizes that his attraction to both men stems from his essential bisexuality.[13]

Gordon set this drama of self-discovery against a backdrop of intrigue and adventure. He kept the character of Gerárd but transformed him into Patrice's former pimp, an older gay man who controls a group of young male prostitutes. He created a new character, Francois, an experienced drug trafficker who manages to recruit Rod for a drug deal in Marseille. The scheme leads to a dramatic car chase, which ends only when Patrice tragically sacrifices himself in order to save Rod. At one point, Rod inadvertently gets mixed up in a demonstration for Algerian independence and is arrested with the other protestors. The incident leads to Rod's detainment by the American CIA, which tries to recruit him for a French espionage mission. Later, Rod is committed to a mental hospital when his grief over Patrice's death spirals into a violent dissociative disorder. The novel ends on an ominous note, with the CIA planning to blackmail Rod to ensure his cooperation with their espionage efforts.

Although *The Quirk* was published only a year after *An Idol for Others*, it could hardly be a more different gay novel. This time Gordon had chosen a European setting instead of an American one, and had chosen intrigue over cultural critique. In many ways he was reverting to the formula of his postwar novels: an American expatriate whose idealism is shaken by living in a foreign country. At the same time, the protagonist of *The Quirk* is not a conventional gay character. Unlike Charlie in *The Lord Won't Mind* or Walter in *Idol*, Rod is not a married gay man who overcomes internalized homophobia and accepts his sexuality. In modern terms, Rod's sexuality is more "fluid." Gordon had bypassed the typical coming-of-age and romance plots, producing something that was more cosmopolitan and experimental. He hoped this originality would compel the critics, both gay and straight, to take him more seriously.

Unfortunately, *The Quirk* was the wrong novel for 1978. Although Gordon could not have foreseen it, his novel came out amid an unprecedented explosion of significant gay writing. Several groundbreaking gay novels from major publishers were released at nearly the same time: Andrew Holleran's *Dancer from the Dance*, Paul Monette's *Taking Care of Mrs. Carroll*, Armistead Maupin's *Tales of the City*, Edmund White's *Nocturnes for the King of Naples*, Gore Vidal's *Kalki*, Lawrence Kramer's *Faggots*. The appearance of so many books, by authors who were heralded (or soon would be) as major gay authors, was immediately registered by gay reviewers and journalists as a watershed moment. Yet Gordon hardly figured in these discussions. The gay novelist and critic George Whitmore, who wrote about this "flood" of gay novels in a September 1978 issue of *Body Politic*, a national gay magazine, was one of the few to discuss *The Quirk*—though he was very clear where he thought it ranked among the others:

> Let's start with Gordon Merrick, whom we would ignore at our own peril, since he sells a lot of books, if nothing else. His latest offering is *The Quirk*, a paranoid fantasy set in Paris in the early 1960s. Just as Merrick no longer bothers to publish in hardcover, he no longer pretends that gay love or gay identity—as in the Peter and Charlie books, *The Lord Won't Mind*, etc.—are his themes, and his predominant fantasy is in full flower in *The Quirk*—that of a big, butch man with a big cock who is, moreover, able to stick it up everyone, but everyone, in the course of a book. . . . For we are here dealing not with any healthy sexual kind of masochism, but with the very worst variety, in which an author and readers must conspire together to strip a character down to the absolute basics and flay the soul out of him. In hard core pornography this would be obligatory. In a mass market paperback it's reprehensible. It seems to be Merrick's solution to dealing with gay material.[14]

In an earlier *Washington Post* article about gay literature, Whitmore had discussed Merrick's novels approvingly, calling them a "good read." He had even singled out *An Idol for Others*, which, despite its tragic ending, featured a "liberated" gay character.[15] Apparently, however, *The Quirk* changed his mind about Gordon's writing. Whitmore had clearly read the novel, and his representation of it is mostly accurate, but the *Body Politic* article gives it the worst spin possible. Whitmore sees the bisexual Rod as a betrayal of Gordon's erstwhile commitment to "gay love or gay identity." In effect, he reviews *The Quirk* only to marginalize it, to exclude it from "gay literature." Even though Whitmore saves his harshest words for Kramer's *Faggots* ("sleazy," "excremental prose," "homophobic"), he does not dispute Kramer's status as a gay novelist. As if this were not damning enough, Whitmore takes Gordon to task for not "bother[ing] to publish in hardcover." No doubt this remark would have infuriated Gordon, who had tried so hard to publish his last three novels in hardcover.

In an article that appeared the following month in *Gaysweek*, Whitmore again meditated on the "new" gay literature by focusing on the same set of novels that he had discussed in the *Body Politic* piece. He was kinder to Gordon here, admitting that the Charlie and Peter novels, along with Patricia Nell Warren's *The Front Runner*, had in fact "paved the way" for the current "revolution" in gay writing. However, his point was still the same. Gordon's books were not truly *gay* novels. For Whitmore, a gay novel was not simply defined by a focus on gay characters or gay plots; rather, as he put it, "it's a matter of style . . . effeminate, arch, bitchy, artificial." By this logic even Vidal's *City and the Pillar* could not be considered a gay novel in the modern sense: "What is now being written by gay fiction writers shows that Vidal's book is as remote from mainstream gay literature as Wonder Bread is from kosher rye."[16]

It is important to note that, although Whitmore does not emphasize it in his article, he is himself a gay writer. A year and a half later he would form a group with six other gay writers that got together to share their work and discuss the future of gay literature. The other members of the Violet Quill, as they called themselves, were Christopher Cox, Robert Ferro, Michael Grumley, Andrew Holleran, Felice Picano, and Edmund White. As David Bergman points out, Whitmore's exclusion of Vidal and other writers from the category of gay literature is as much prescriptive as it is descriptive; it is a carefully worded statement about what he and his fellow like-minded writers should be doing.[17] This prima facie conflict of interest was typical of much of the negative critical reception of Gordon's works. For example, when Edmund White, another member of the Violet Quill, wrote a short history of gay literature for the *New York Times*, he conveniently pretended that there had been no notable gay novels produced between 1969 and 1978.[18] Daniel Curzon, one of Gordon's most choleric critics, was himself a working writer whose books competed directly with Gordon's novels. When his 1971 novel *Something You Do in the Dark* failed to catch fire with gay readers, he reacted by writing a vitriolic article for *The Advocate* that branded Gordon's novels as "gay trash": "The Lord won't mind because not only does He tolerate trash. He absolutely prefers it!"[19] (In the magazine's next issue the novelist Vincent Lardo wrote a vigorous rebuttal: "Being Erotic Doesn't Make It Trash."[20]) Gordon seems to have been a bête noire for Curzon, who later wrote a full-blown parody of *The Lord Won't Mind*, which he titled "The Lord May Barf, by Gordon Meretricious."

Yet even if he wasn't completely objective, Whitmore understood far better than Gordon the direction in which American gay literature was going. A comparison with *Dancer from the Dance* shows just how far *The Quirk* was from the main current of American gay writing in 1978. Holleran's novel centers on Malone, an attractive young gay man who discovers New York's gay scene in the early 1970s. It takes place in actual gay venues in New York, from the Tenth Floor disco club (renamed the Twelfth Floor) to the Everard Baths to Fire Island, quotes disco songs that were popular in gay clubs at the time, and details the clothing that gay men wore to these clubs. It offers up a diverse montage of gay figures, from straitlaced investment bankers to flamboyantly effeminate queens. In terms of the writing, *Dancer* is a lyrical masterpiece. But more importantly in terms of its trendiness, *Dancer* is a *contemporary* novel. It features the types of places and persons that its earliest readers knew—or could know if they wanted to. This contemporaneity was of singular importance for book critics in the leading gay magazines. In an important essay on these reviewers, the historian Brian J. Distelberg notes their rejection of novels that were deemed "out of step with contemporary gay life."[21] A novel like *An Idol for Others* had a fighting chance in this climate, but *The Quirk* was dead on arrival. American gay critics had no interest in the Paris art scene, Algerian politics, international espionage, or any of the other exotic elements that Gordon had stuffed into his novel, even if they were based on actual figures and events.

Admittedly, Gordon had not gotten much help from his editorial team in grasping the gay literary zeitgeist. McCall had praised *Idol*, but she had little to say about *Quirk*. When Gordon asked her about *Quirk*'s hardcover prospects, she demurred on the grounds that the novel had too much sex for a hardcover press. Gordon revised the manuscript accordingly and offered to revise it further, but McCall showed little interest in giving up the lucrative paperback deals.[22] Bob Wyatt was an even worse advocate. He knew what kind of fiction the gay reviewers wanted, but he wasn't interested in appealing to them. When the idea arose to publish an excerpt of *Idol* in a gay magazine, he quickly dismissed the possibility of going to *The Advocate* or *Christopher Street*—magazines that had published excerpts by White, Isherwood, and Holleran. Instead he went to *Blueboy*, a glossy gay magazine that was known for its erotic fiction and "softcore" nude photos.[23] Worse still, he encouraged rather than curbed Gordon's outmoded literary impulses. After reading the manuscript for *Quirk* (*The Fluke*), he had nothing but praise for Gordon:

> It may well be your best book. There is a concise quality and a control that I admire. The fact that you are dealing with comparatively few people over a short space of time is attractive and gives the book a theatrical quality which the broader canvasses of the trilogy and IDOL could not afford. I particularly like the setting. I've never been to Europe proper (Paris, Rome, Madrid) but I get a sense of the milieu in THE FLUKE. It would clearly make a wonderful movie,

wouldn't it? You are clearly more relaxed and comfortable in THE FLUKE than in IDOL. That's a joy![24]

Wyatt was not entirely off base here. With its car chases, street riots, drug deals, and French stereotypes, *The Quirk* was certainly more "cinematic" than the earlier novels. But for a writer who was trying to get back into hardcover and regain some modicum of critical respectability, such advice could not have been more misguided. To say that *Quirk* was a better novel than *An Idol for Others*—much less to say that *Quirk* was Gordon's best novel—was to express a minority viewpoint, to put it mildly.[25] It was, however, the viewpoint of an expert marketer. Wyatt knew better than anyone how to sell Gordon's books in the paperback market, and so his advice to Gordon typically addressed the aspects of his novels that he knew he could sell. As usual he went to Victor Gadino for the cover image, and he was especially proud of the *Quirk* cover, which, instead of featuring a shirtless bronzed chest, had a shapely leg splayed across the front. "That probably makes me some kind of 'leg man,'" Wyatt joked to Gordon.[26]

Gordon began to realize he had been placed in a box. Despite the fact that he had written nine novels that collectively showed a decent range, publishers and reviewers almost always approached his works with rigid preconceptions (when they deigned to read them at all). He was now seen more as a brand than a serious writer. The fact of this became painfully clear when he learned that his own agent and publisher were no longer reading his manuscripts in their entirety. In a letter to McCall, he vented his growing exasperation: "It's rather odd negotiating for a novel about which nobody has expressed an opinion. Or do I produce a standard commodity like Campbell's Soup which makes an opinion irrelevant? A Merrick is a Merrick?"[27]

At the same time, Gordon also started to understand why the gay literati ignored him or savaged him. In an interview he gave to a British gay newspaper shortly after *The Quirk* was published, he admitted the fact that he simply couldn't relate to the experiences of younger gay men in New York and San Francisco:

> I've been attacked for not dealing with ordinary gay life. But I don't know much about it. I've never frequented gay bars. I'm from a generation which hid from it. I've never hidden but I've never got myself into situations where it would be dangerous. Living in Europe as a writer and knowing the people I know, who couldn't care less, has meant that I haven't been subjected to any of the pressures that the gay liberation movement is all about.[28]

He may have overstated the tolerance of Europeans (particularly in light of the backlash against gay activists in Britain at the time[29]), but he was correct about his alienation from American urban gay culture. Even when he did make the rare trip to New York, he didn't visit gay bars or bookstores. He didn't mingle with rising gay writers and artists as he had as a young man in New York in the 1940s. He couldn't do what writers like Holleran and White were doing, because he simply wasn't part of their culture.

Gordon admitted, somewhat defensively, his alienation from American gay culture a few months later, in an interview he gave to *The Advocate*:

> Obviously, one has to set things in the certain milieu one knows. What I've known is people who've had a fairly easy life. I think that's perfectly legitimate. The books are about simply being true to one's self. I'm trying to deal with homosexuals not as problems, but just as people. In all the books there's always been someone struggling to face the truth of their own sexuality.[30]

This is quintessential Gordon. He had always based his novels on his own experiences, and here he was candidly admitting that he didn't know any other way to write. At the same time, he was explaining—far better than his critics—why his novels were so poorly received by gay reviewers. His characters were, much like himself, privileged men who had been able to deal with their homosexuality largely outside of the oppressive confines of American society. Their "struggles to face the truth of their own sexuality" were psychological or philosophical problems rather than political or social problems. By admitting this, he identified the precise reason for the critical backlash. In 1978, gay reviewers were debating *what* kinds of gay writing would best advance the status of gay people in American society; there was no question that gay writing *should* do this.[31] Thus by making homosexuality a matter of *character* rather than a matter of *culture* in his novels (with the exception of *An Idol for Others*), Gordon had made himself irrelevant to the gay movement and its spokespersons.

He was facing a question of direction. Should he try again to connect his writing to current gay issues, as he had done in *Idol*? Or should he continue on the same path as *The Quirk* and write about the places and people he knew best? He decided, to the detriment of his critical fortunes, to follow his old instincts. His sixth gay novel, *Now Let's Talk about Music*, begins with a description of Sri Lanka, where he and Hulse were currently living:

> Just off the southern tip of the distant land called Ceylon, more recently Sri Lanka, within plain sight of the old Dutch port of Galle, a luxury yacht skewered on a coral reef has been slowly disintegrating since 1975. Every year, pounded by the heavy surf of the Indian Ocean, buffeted by the gales of the Southwest monsoon, it settles deeper into the sea. It has long since broken in two, evident from the wide inverted V of its profile, both bow and stern pointing into the deep. Within the first year, it was stripped of everything of use or value by the

efficient fishermen based in Galle, several of whom sacrificed their lives to their arduous quest.³²

As a setting for a novel, this was as exotic as anything Gordon had written before. He was clearly thumbing his nose at the reviewers who complained that his novels did not focus on American culture, and he made no effort to "democratize" his writing. He showed off his boating knowledge by including glamorous boating episodes—on boats with names like *Hephaiston*, thus showing off his classics knowledge as well. He made the novel's main characters not only beautiful and rich but incalculably beautiful and rich. In the first thirty pages the protagonist goes on an extravagant shopping spree, buying a bespoke suit made entirely of white silk and accessorizing it with an opulent gold necklace. Much of the novel takes place on a yacht in the middle of the Indian Ocean—as far removed from American gay culture as one could imagine. Gordon dedicated the novel, appropriately, to Nesta Brohier, the owner of the New Oriental Hotel and the "grand dame of Galle," who had made Gordon and Hulse—"her boys," as she called them—feel at home on the island.

The novel focuses on Gerry Kennicutt, an attractive gay man who was a minor character in *An Idol for Others*. In *Music*, Gordon gives Gerry's backstory from the age of fifteen, when he meets other gay men for the first time and has a long string of turbulent affairs. Gerry is initiated into New York's gay party scene, which is typified by booze-fueled orgies and dandyish, effeminate men. For several years he roams from New York to Paris to San Francisco, finally ending up in Vietnam, where he meets Jack, a U.S. Air Force colonel stationed in Vietnam at the end of the Vietnam War. When Jack is killed during a military mission, Gerry, now thirty-five, escapes to Bangkok. There he meets and begins a passionate affair with Ernst von Hallers, an obscenely rich baron who spends his time traveling around the world in his yacht. Gordon had based the character on Arndt von Bohlen, an heir of the German Krupp dynasty who had married an Austrian princess and who was notorious for his jet-setting lifestyle and for his rumored homosexuality.³³ The Italian director Luchino Visconti had portrayed Bohlen in his 1969 film *Die Verdammten* (*The Damned*), with Helmut Berger playing the Bohlen role. Gordon had actually met Bohlen the previous year during a trip to Bangkok. When Gordon told him about his plans to write a novel about him, the publicity-hungry Bohlen eagerly assented, promising that he "wouldn't sue."³⁴

For the most part, *Now Let's Talk about Music* is a decadent romp. There are some poignant flashback sequences involving Gerry's experiences as a gay teenager, but most of the novel reads like an exotic Orientalist fantasy. Gerry's melodramatic affair with Ernst plays out against a backdrop of South

Asian locales, punctuated by a series of opiate-infused orgies, extravagant champagne parties, and garish displays of luxury fashion. As a romantic character, Ernst (Bohlen) is a strikingly unsympathetic figure. Gordon's presentation of him is closer to Helmut Berger's hysterical grotesque in Visconti's film. Gordon had often been accused of writing potboilers, and in this case the charge would have been merited.

Yet Gordon was also enjoying himself. He peppered the novel with veiled cameos of celebrities and artists whom he had personally known, and he painted an enchanting picture of the places he had been recently visiting in South Asia. He had fun by recalling and flaunting the literary figures who had inspired him to become a writer in the first place; in one scene, Gerry stays in a hotel in Bangkok whose best suites are named Maugham, Conrad, and Coward. The novel is staunchly unapologetic about its Old World cosmopolitan vantage point, and Gordon was just as unapologetic in an interview he gave to London's *Gay Times* in which he discussed the novel: "I'm still the only one who writes my kind of books. I just carry on using my own material—it's mine and has a special expatriate viewpoint, well-heeled, unrooted people who come to Europe and find a very tolerant society."[35] This rarefied perspective is encapsulated in the novel's title, which would have only been intelligible to a select few. Asked by an interviewer to explain it, Gordon replied:

> There was a wonderful old lesbian in Paris, one of the Singer sewing machine daughters, who was married to a Frenchman—she became the Princesse de Polignac—and she *lived* for music. She gave salons at which nearly all the guests were what we'd now call gay. Well, one of her famous stock lines when someone new was brought in and introduced to her was, "I *assume* you're a homosexual—now let's talk about music."[36]

Gordon worked this anecdote into the novel and managed to make it sound even more snobby. The line appears in a scene where an older gay actor (modeled on Clifton Webb, Gordon's old friend) is telling a story about being taken to Winnaretta Singer's salon by Jean Cocteau.

With *Music*, Gordon was digging in his heels and reclaiming the genteel pose he had struck in his (mostly unpublished) novels in the 1950s and '60s. In this respect he put himself on a trajectory that was the stark opposite of Christopher Isherwood, his old acquaintance. When the two had met in the 1940s, they had shared the same literary mentors: Forster, Wescott, Maugham. Both had been shaped by World War II and had written semi-autobiographical, postwar novels, and both had been alternately praised and derided as "middlebrow" novelists who brought sentimentality to their writing.[37] However, at the same time that Gordon was becoming more alienated from American gay culture, Isherwood was becoming more immersed in the scene. Unlike Gordon, Isherwood was unflagging in his efforts to understand American gay men, which paid off in the reception of his writing. As an outsider who immersed himself in American gay culture, he was able to provide a uniquely perceptive viewpoint for gay readers. Accordingly, the American gay intelligentsia embraced Isherwood in a way they never could have done with Gordon. Thus while Gordon had liked and admired Isherwood, comparisons with him inevitably made him uncomfortable since it reminded him of his snubbing by critics. At the same time that a magazine like *Christopher Street* was refusing to review his novels, it was featuring an excerpt from Isherwood's forthcoming *Christopher and his Kind*.

Gordon's frustration with the gay critics had been a regular fact of life, but a tipping point came in 1979 when he did an interview for *The Advocate*. Gordon had been in New York visiting friends, and he agreed to meet with Bjorn Rye, one of the magazine's writers, at the friend's apartment where Gordon was staying. Rye was a struggling novelist with an undergraduate degree from Columbia who did freelance work for *The Advocate* and other magazines. He eventually abandoned writing to pursue his dream as a painter. Rye had pitched the interview to Gordon as an opportunity to explain himself to his critics and generate publicity for *Music*. He asked to record the interview, ostensibly to ensure that Gordon's comments were accurately represented in the published article. Gordon was very genial during the interview, and he took special care to explain why he felt out of step with the gay rights movement in America:

> God knows, I've been awfully misquoted about this whole gay-lib thing—the *last* thing in the world I'd be against. It's the side issues, the side effect of forcing all of us . . . I've been terribly misquoted, and I've come out sounding anti-gay lib and all that sort of thing, which I'm *not*. I simply feel that the legitimate activities like fighting for rights are absolutely necessary. But I don't believe that everybody *need* do it any more than anybody *has* to be the governor of California. I mean, people are given to that sort of political activity or they do something else—like write a book. The only thing about it that I still am not sold on is the tendency that it inevitably has of solidifying a sort of ghetto feeling.[38]

Careful as this was, Gordon was saying the wrong thing to the wrong person. The entire raison d'être for a magazine like *The Advocate* was the idea that there *is* a distinct gay community, with unique concerns and a unique culture. Gordon's stance was not unreasonable: there were many gay men and lesbians in 1979 who were wary of a "ghetto-izing" effect of gay politics (indeed, fifteen years later, the cultural critic Bruce Bawer made this concern the basis of his landmark book *A Place at the Table*).[39] But Rye did what he could to marginalize Gordon's explanation and make it seem like a tiresome rant: he (or his editor) edited the article so that it cuts off Gordon in midsentence and leaves out the main reason for his view. There is a bitter irony in the fact that Rye effectively misquotes Gordon in a paragraph where Gordon is complaining about being misquoted by gay journalists.

Rye's unscrupulous editing was actually one of the least offensive aspects of the article, which is essentially a hatchet job. The article was titled "Idylls for Others," a play on *An Idol for Others*—one that makes Gordon's politically relevant novel seem like a trivial affair. And lest the reader miss the insinuation, Rye begins the article by framing Gordon as a sensationalist hack:

> GORDON MERRICK writes the kind of novel in which men screw (one another) with shrill little cries of "Oh, my darling, it's ecstasy." His books are vital, vulgar, short on meaning and long on plot. The most recent, *An Idol for Others*, has aroused the wrath of gay groups for its portrait of a hero horrified by the whole idea of homosexuality.

The misrepresentation of *Idol* here is glaring. Walter Makin struggles with his *own* homosexuality, not "the whole idea of homosexuality." Had Rye actually read the novel, he would have learned that by the end, Walter overcomes his internalized homophobia—a process that was all too real for many gay men, even in 1979.

Rye did not refrain from tabloid-style fodder. At one point he digresses from the interview to ruminate on Gordon's trembling hand, which he speculates may be related to some illness. He takes every opportunity to remind his reader that Gordon is an *older* gay man:

> Gordon Merrick himself looks like the hero from one of his own books—handsome, lean and sixtyish. He has close-cropped gray hair, a chiseled nose, blue eyes. He wears an old blue turtleneck (to match the eyes?) and well-tailored gray slacks. His manner is old-line polite. His voice is soft—hardly more than an elegant, exhausted whisper—and the accent is transatlantic. He reminds me of the older gay men—all wealthy, all very refined—whom I met when I first came out. Seems like old times.

Perhaps only another gay man can fully appreciate the shade that Rye is throwing here, but any reader can notice that the word "old" is used four times in a single paragraph. Rye may have learned in a college journalism class somewhere the importance of giving an article, even an interview, an editorial "slant." In this case, his slant was clear: Gordon Merrick is a *relic*, a curious and somewhat interesting museum piece for the younger, more enlightened gays.

Gordon was outraged. His agent had been afraid to send him a copy of the article, and when he finally read it he decided he was done with the American gay press. When his agent proposed publishing his next novel with St. Martin's Press, a new firm that was specializing in gay books, Gordon flatly refused. "I want to be published as general fiction or give up and stick with Avon," he told her.[40] He had tried to explain himself to the gay critics, but it had failed. So he was going to be a respectable mainstream author, as he had been at the start of his career, or he was going to continue making lots of money from the glossy paperbacks. If that made him a "fagtrash" writer (as Isherwood called them), then so be it.

NOTES

1. Gordon Merrick et al. to Professor Daskalikis, 5 August 1977, GMP, box 19, folder 2.
2. Bjorn Rye, "Idylls for Others," *The Advocate*, April 5, 1979.
3. Monica McCall to Gordon Merrick, 14 January 1974, GMP, box 16, folder 6.
4. Neil McAleer, *Arthur C. Clarke: The Authorized Biography* (Chicago: Contemporary Books, 1992), 254.
5. Monica McCall to Gordon Merrick, 4 January 1976, Merrick Papers, box 17, folder 3.
6. Monica McCall to Gordon Merrick, 19 January 1977, GMP, box 17, folder 4.
7. "About Olanda Villas," Olanda Villas website, http://olandavillas.com/about-us.html.
8. Nira Wickramasinghe, *Sri Lanka in the Modern Age: A History* (Oxford: Oxford University Press, 2014), esp. 163–68.
9. "Bill's Cuisine: Writer's Fare," *Gay News*, January 10, 1980.
10. Charles Hulse, interview by the author.
11. Monica McCall to Gordon Merrick, 4 January 1976, GMP, box 17, folder 3.
12. Gordon Merrick, unidentified novel fragment, GMP, box 15, folders 1–2. About half of the draft is missing, but the extant sections give a fairly clear picture of the novella's plot. A short story written by Gordon, also never published, also features similar characters and events, suggesting that he had been thinking about the idea for a while. Gordon Merrick, "An American in Paris," GMP, box 15, folder 6.
13. Gordon Merrick, *The Quirk* (New York: Avon Books, 1978), 275.
14. George Whitmore, "Beer, Baloney, and Champagne," *Body Politic*, Review Supplement, September 1978.
15. George Whitmore, "Out of the Closet and onto the Shelves," *Washington Post*, January 8, 1978.
16. George Whitmore, "The Gay Novel Now," *Gaysweek*, October 9, 1978.
17. David Bergman, *The Violet Hour: The Violet Quill and the Making of Gay Culture* (New York: Columbia University Press, 2004), 44–45.

18. Edmund White, "Out of the Closet, onto the Bookshelf," *New York Times*, June 16, 1991.

19. Daniel Curzon, "Gay Trash Driving Out the Good," *The Advocate*, April 13, 1974.

20. Julian Mark [Vincent Lardo], "Being Erotic Doesn't Make It Trash," *The Advocate*, April 24, 1974.

21. Brian J. Distelberg, "Mainstream Fiction, Gay Reviewers, and Gay Male Cultural Politics in the 1970s," *GLQ* 16, no. 3 (2010): 389–427 (406).

22. Gordon Merrick to Monica McCall, 15 June 1977, GMP, box 17, folder 3.

23. Robert Wyatt to Gordon Merrick, 6 March 1977, GMP, box 17, folder 3. On the reputation of *Blueboy* magazine in the 1970s, see Leigh W. Rutledge, *The Gay Decades: From Stonewall to the Present: The People and Events that Shaped Gay Lives* (New York: Plume, 1992), 75.

24. Robert Wyatt to Gordon Merrick, 27 September 1977, GMP, box 17, folder 3.

25. Frank J. Howell, the reviewer for the *Bay Area Reporter*, said much the same thing in his review of *The Quirk*. While he thought that Gordon's writing had "matured" since *The Lord Won't Mind*, he was confused by the proliferation of action sequences in the second half of the novel: "One has the feeling another author took over the typewriter and the publisher told him to jazz up the plot for a smashing finale." Frank J. Howell, review of *The Quirk*, *Bay Area Reporter*, November 9, 1978.

26. Robert Wyatt to Gordon Merrick, 2 February 1982, GMP, box 17, folder 8.

27. Gordon Merrick to Monica McCall, 30 June 1977, GMP, box 17, folder 3.

28. Keith Howes, "Once A Spy . . . ," *Gay News*, August 24, 1978.

29. Gregory Woods, "No Source of Pride," *Times Literary Supplement*, May 5, 2017.

30. Rye, "Idylls for Others."

31. Distelberg, "Mainstream Fiction, Gay Reviewers," 394.

32. Gordon Merrick, *Now Let's Talk about Music* (New York: Avon Books, 1981), 1.

33. "Arndt Von Bohlen, Last Surviving Heir of Krupp Fortune," *New York Times*, May 13, 1986.

34. "'Quirk' Author on the Move," *Gay News*, November 15, 1979.

35. "'Quirk' Author on the Move."

36. Rye, "Idylls for Others."

37. See Jaime Harker, *Middlebrow Queer: Christopher Isherwood in America* (Minneapolis: University of Minnesota Press, 2013), 1–24.

38. Rye, "Idylls for Others." The ellipsis is Rye's, not mine.

39. Bruce Bawer, *A Place at the Table: The Gay Individual in American Society* (New York: Poseidon, 1993).

40. Gordon Merrick to Jeanne Sakol, 11 July 1979, GMP, box 17, folder 5.

Chapter Sixteen

Rewriting the Past

In 1980 Gordon was missing France. Having given up the Paris apartment years earlier, he started looking for places to live in the northern part of the country, close enough to Paris and London to be able to get to them easily. He visited Tocqueville, a lush wooded area in Normandy a hundred miles from Paris and only thirty miles from the port of Le Havre. For Gordon, it was "love at first sight." He and Hulse bought a large, three-storied country house in Pont-Audemer, a picturesque medieval town known for its historic buildings and Venetian-like canals. This meant selling the house in Hydra, which Gordon was happy to do, having grown weary of the island. Hulse, who preferred Greece to France, was less eager, but as usual he went along with Gordon. When Gordon asked him if he wanted to sell the Hydra house, he replied with the same line he used when they left California: "No, but I will."[1]

Gordon was welcomed back to France with open arms. Ironically, just as the American gay critics were consigning Gordon to the closet of literary history, his star was rising in France and Britain. The success of his gay novels in Britain had been stalled for many years, first by the collapse of Bernard Geis and then by McCall's inability to find a British distributor.[2] Bob Wyatt had tried to include British distribution rights in the contract for *Forth into Light* and *An Idol for Others*, but McCall objected on the grounds that her agency would not get a commission on British sales.[3] Such squabbles kept Gordon's novels out of the hands of British readers until a new distribution channel opened up. *Gay News* was a biweekly gay newspaper in London that featured a mail order service through which readers could get gay books outside of the normal bookstore venues. In 1978 the newspaper began advertising Gordon Merrick titles for £1.40 each. They were grouped with other gay books—Warren's *The Front Runner*, Waugh's *Brideshead Revisited*, Joe Orton's plays, *Spartacus* gay travel guides—but the eye-grabbing nature of the Merrick covers meant that they were shown more prominently in the ads.[4]

Once they discovered Gordon's novels, British readers devoured them as avidly as the Americans had done. The books regularly appeared in gay bestseller lists, and gay journalists in England and Scotland started using Gordon's name as shorthand for popular gay romance—sometimes just for beautiful men or explicit sex. Phrases like "he resembled a Gordon Merrick hero" were common.[5] There were public readings of Gordon's novels in Scotland. A soiree at Edinburgh's annual arts festival (later known as the Fringe festival) featured a reading from *One for the Gods* alongside other gay and lesbian authors.[6] A 1979 *Gay News* piece on Mediterranean travel recommended Hydra as a gay destination, breathlessly noting that the island was "one of the homes of the bestselling gay novelist Gordon Merrick."[7] The Lavender Menace Bookshop, the first gay bookstore in Scotland, celebrated its second anniversary with a party headlined by the activist Paul Trainer, who "did his now-famous rendition of the most poignant movements from that great literary classic, *The Lord Won't Mind* by Gordon Merrick."[8]

The prominence of Gordon's novels in Britain was made especially clear in 1984 when the Gay's The Word, a popular gay bookstore in London, was raided by customs agents seeking to curtail the circulation of "indecent or obscene" books. (A year earlier, Gordon's books had been the target of a book banning campaign at a public library in Michigan, but the campaign had proved a moot point when the library revealed that the books had already been stolen.[9]) Articles about the British raid in gay newspapers noted that Gordon's novels had been a primary target. Together with titles like Warren's *Front Runner* and Genet's *Querelle*, Gordon's novels were seized from the bookstore shelves and marked for disposal. Around the same time, customs officials also confiscated a shipment of books mailed to Edinburgh's Lavender Menace bookstore, again singling out Gordon's novels as justification for the seizure.[10] Gay's The Word responded quickly and forcefully to the seizures, initiating a court battle and establishing a legal defense fund. The National Council for Civil Liberties agreed to represent the bookstore, and as part of its publicity efforts it staged an exhibition of Gordon's novels and other seized books at its London offices. Several MPs were personally invited to attend the exhibition and view the books.[11]

It was not only readers and bookshops that embraced Gordon in Britain. Unlike their American counterparts, the British gay literati found his novels fascinating. The *Gay Times* journalist Hugh Miller recounted a dinner party with other gay intellectuals, in which the conversation moved "from Hazell Dean versus Laura Pallas [to] the literary insights of Gordon Merrick to Poland [and] AIDS." In Britain, the gay press was not merely following its readers and advertisers in giving Gordon a warm reception—it also led the way by introducing its readers to his work. In 1978 the journalist Keith Howes wrote a feature article about Gordon in *Gay News*, the leading gay newspaper in England. This was no mean honor. Howes had interviewed many of the most important gay figures for *Gay News* in the 1970s, including

Tennessee Williams, Derek Jarman, Stephen Sondheim, Dame Edna Everage, Derek Jacobi, David Hockney, Bette Midler, Eartha Kitt, and Liberace.[12] To be interviewed by him was to be identified as a significant figure in gay culture. A year later he also interviewed Andrew Holleran and Lawrence Kramer while in New York, though he did not give them a feature, instead squeezing them into an article about the bleakness of literary representations of New York gay life.[13]

Howes' interview could not have been more different than the tabloid piece Bjorn Rye had written for *The Advocate*. Howes did not portray Gordon as an aging queen or a hackneyed writer. Instead, he titled the piece "Once A Spy . . . " and devoted the first few paragraphs to Gordon's OSS adventures in World War II. While Gordon had long ago fictionalized these stories in *The Strumpet Wind*, Howes managed to get more specific information out of Gordon about his wartime activities than any journalist had done before. He also engaged Gordon in a long discussion about his theatrical career, in the process revealing that the protagonist of *An Idol for Others* was based on a close personal friend (Lemuel Ayers, though at this point Gordon did not give his name). In essence, Howes' interview showed that Gordon's novels, even when they seemed most sensational, were firmly grounded in his life experiences.

Howes was able to get a revealing interview from Gordon in part because, unlike Rye and many of the other American journalists, he had actually read the novels. He was not blinded by the novels' advertising but instead approached them as an open-minded, sympathetic reader. For example, in his article he accurately summarizes the plot of *Idol* and then gives it a fair assessment: "[The plot] sounds awful but the careful characterization and erotic detail gets the plot over the shallows of cliché." He also let Hulse be part of the interview, asking for his view of *The Quirk* and prompting him to recount his first meeting with Gordon in France. Most importantly, Howes gave Gordon a chance to explain fully his reasons for feeling alienated from the American gay liberation movement. As before, Gordon expressed his fears of ghettoization, but Howes gave him more space to contextualize them:

> I think the world of the future will probably see all distinctions fading away. At the moment there's a terrible pressure towards conformity and I think it's a pity that the gay movement is trying to create one gay lifestyle. By trying to isolate themselves they're undoing all the work I thought we'd been doing on integration.

Howes not only acknowledged the validity of this point of view; he pointed out the irony of the fact that the American gay "literati" and "politicos," who staked their advocacy on a politics of visibility, never credited Gordon for living openly as a gay man and writing gay characters two decades before Stonewall. He noted this irony again in his later interview with Holleran. When Holleran made a condescending remark about Gordon's novels, Howes drily noted that, unlike Gordon, Holleran had not done media appearances or put biographical information on his novel's dust jacket. He also noted that Holleran had published *Dancer from the Dance* under a pseudonym in order to shield himself from a homophobic press (Holleran's real name is Eric Gerber).[14]

As he had felt while spending time with Ian McKellen, Gordon thought that the Brits understood and appreciated him better than his own countrymen did. Such warm reception caused Gordon to toy briefly with the idea of moving to England. The political situation in Sri Lanka had become more volatile with the presidency of Jayewardene, who was aggressively consolidating power in his government. Concerns about an escalation of political tensions, along with a nasty bout of diabetic foot disease, gave Gordon and Hulse an excuse to shop around for flats in Chelsea during a visit in 1979.[15]

In the end they did not leave Sri Lanka. For all his Anglophilia, he felt more at home in France, and so he decided the best thing would be to split his time between Galle and Normandy. Gordon had not forgotten that it was the French media who had made him a minor celebrity in the 1950s, at the same time that the American critics were cooling on his novels. Nearly thirty years later, he returned to France to find that French readers had already discovered his gay novels, even though they had not yet been translated into French. A few months after buying the house in Normandy, Gordon was profiled by Michel Mabille in *L'Éveil de Pont-Audemer*, a French weekly newsmagazine that covered French and European culture. As far as the magazine was concerned, Gordon was an international celebrity. The magazine's front page is filled by a larger-than-life photograph of Gordon, looking debonair in an unbuttoned shirt and heavy gold chain, and the big splashy headline makes it sound as though America is too small for Gordon's worldly vision: "De Ceylan a Tricqueville: La vie mouvementée d'un écrivain américain" ("Ceylon to Tricqueville: The Restless Life of an American Author"). The article itself occupies three full newspaper-size pages, tracing Gordon's life story and his dual career as postwar novelist and gay romance writer. A large insert provides a chronological list of all of his novels, both straight and gay, each with a short synopsis. Several attractive photographs are included, many of which show Gordon at his home in Sri Lanka, where framed dust jackets from his hardcover novels are artfully arranged on the walls. One picture stands out among all the rest: a shirtless, beaming Hulse standing outside their house in Normandy, while Gordon gazes at him adoringly.[16]

The Gordon Merrick described in the French magazine bears little resemblance to the image constructed by the American gay press. Mabille paints him as a gay pioneer who is brave enough to tackle the "taboo" subject of homosexuality (*un sujet tabou*) and committed to "destigmatizing" (*dédramatisé*) the subject for heterosexual readers. Mabille clearly put Gordon at ease during the interview, since he admitted things he had never said to an English-speaking journalist. He spoke frankly about his disappointment with the changes in French society since the war and his even greater disappointment with America:

> I love France. The French were much more individual before, now they are losing their individuality to materialism. It's progress, of course, but it's not like it was before. I almost got French citizenship, but it was during McCarthyism, the witch hunt. The US was against it, I had some trouble and then I gave up. But I have to say that I hate America and Americans. It's kind of the family tradition on my father's side . . . I followed the trend.[17]

At first this sounds like a crotchety old man who is nostalgically pining for the "good old days." But Gordon had said much the same thing when he was living in France in the 1950s. Thirty-five years later, he found that his feelings about France and America were fundamentally the same. He was more at home in France, whose people he understood—and who seemed to understand him.

The French appreciation for Gordon's work was confirmed a few years later when he received a letter in August 1986 from Jean-Michel Senecal, a forty-two-year-old actor and writer who had just started up a small publishing venture. He had had a checkered but interesting film career, including a role as Magnus Hirschfeld's assistant in *Race D'Ep*, an experimental film about the long history of gay liberation.[18] Senecal had long been an admirer of the Charlie and Peter trilogy, and he wanted to publish a French translation of the novels. He had learned that Gordon was spending time in Normandy and Paris, and he offered to meet Gordon in either place.[19] They settled on meeting in a café near the Saint-Lazare train station in Paris. Senecal took one of his editors, Christian Hym, a young man who had discovered *The Lord Won't Mind* as an exchange student at Manchester College in Indiana in 1982. Hym was enchanted with Gordon, who looked to him like a character from one of his novels. A deal was quickly agreed on, and by early 1987 a French version of *The Lord Won't Mind* was released. Hym had initially suggested using the title *Un Amour Sans Blasphème* ("A Love without Sin"), since the French equivalent of *The Lord Won't Mind* sounded awkward.[20] In the end the novel was published as *Beaux à se damner* ("Beauties to Die For"). Senecal hosted a book-signing party in Paris to publicize the book, and Gordon arrived looking dapper in a plaid sportcoat and silk scarf.

Figure 16.1 Gordon Merrick at a book-signing for the French translation of *The Lord Won't Mind*, Paris 1987.
Source: Estate of Gordon Merrick.

For a small publishing firm, *Beaux à se damner* was a huge success. The novel got a lot of high-profile press coverage, including an article in *Le Monde* by Claude Sarraute, the famous actress and journalist. In her article, "Rose et bleu" ("Pink and Blue"), Sarraute cited the French translation of *Lord* as evidence that romance was undergoing a profound change in American culture. What is striking about Sarraute's article is that she repeats many of the observations that American critics had made about Gordon's novels but then draws from them a very different conclusion:

> The pink-tinged pages of your wife's romance novels are now turning shades of blue. . . . The books are here, they've arrived, you can find them now in stations and airports. They are signed Gordon Merrick, the king of best-sellers across the pond. . . . They consist entirely of love stories between multimillionaire gays who go out on yachts and private jets from Hong Kong to Acapulco on the flying carpet of a sentimental, champagne-drenched dream. . . . They're handsome, they're rich, and they love each other. Strange, isn't it, this inversion of traditional gender roles?[21]

It doesn't matter that none of this actually happens in *Lord*. Sarraute's point is that Gordon's novels are transforming gender roles in a profound way. There is a distinct echo here of the fan letter from Maureen Munro, who explained that the originality of Gordon's novels was their translation of the conventions of heterosexual romance to a gay context.

Sarraute's characterization of Gordon's novels echoed an earlier article by Didier Lestrade in *Gai Pied Hebdo*, the leading French gay magazine. Lestrade was a gay activist who had founded the first French chapter of ACT UP, and he was well acquainted with Gordon's other gay novels besides *Lord*, even though they had not yet been translated into French. He compared Gordon favorably to writers like Holleran and Boyd McDonald, and, like Sarraute, he saw the novels as both the cause and effect of a big cultural change. Unlike Sarraute, he identified this development as specifically American. For him, Gordon was the perfect example of "the American inclination to recreate the entire world in the image of homosexuality." For Lestrade, Gordon's novels were not out of step with the gay liberation movement in America—they were the embodiment of it. As he put it, they "are no more out-of-place [in America] than gay laundromats, gay vacation centers, gay radio stations, etc."[22]

Not surprisingly, Gordon's return to France in 1980 reminded him of *The Demon of Noon*, his postwar novel that had been inspired by his time in Provence. As he was thinking of ideas for his next novel, he devised an ingenious plan. He would revive *Demon of Noon* and rewrite it *as a gay novel*. He had done something similar with *A Day with Leighton*, which he had revised and expanded as *Forth into Light*. The difference was that *Leighton* was never published. *Demon* had not only been published but it had been widely reviewed and translated into French. Thus, revising it would be a more conspicuous affair. In a sense, Gordon was proposing to rewrite *Demon* as a gay novel that had been "in the closet" in the 1950s.

Gordon had actually been trying to revive his "straight" novels for some time. Years earlier he had tried to persuade Avon to reprint his postwar novels, without success.[23] His interest in reprints had also been spurred by the possibility of film adaptations. Del Tenney, a film producer who had a reputation for making low-budget horror films (*The Curse of the Living Corpse*, *The Horror of Party Beach*), made an offer for motion picture rights to *Demon of Noon*. Working with Edgar Rosenberg (the husband of comedian Joan Rivers), Tenney had also made a number of politically oriented, international films, and he saw *Demon* as fitting into this category.[24] Although the project never came to fruition, Gordon was convinced of a potential new audience for the decades-old novels. As late as 1979 he was still trying to get his first novel *The Strumpet Wind* reprinted—this time as a "homosexual" novel. He wrote an introduction for a new edition in which he grouped *Strumpet* with two other "homosexual" postwar novels: Burne's *The Gallery* and Wescott's *An Apartment in Athens*. All three, he claimed, had been criticized for their "subversive" representation of war, a perspective he directly attributed to the writers' gay sensibility. He went further, making *Strumpet* into a manifesto for gays in the military:

> This is not to perpetuate the myth that homosexuals are unfit for the manly arts of war. There were plenty of gun-slinging heroes who lusted for their buddies, despite the misbegotten efforts of the authorities to reject them. My own service, the OSS, contrived a rather ludicrous apparatus to screen them out, doubtless successful if any screaming queens had come up for consideration, but helpless when a "normal" homosexual chose to slip through the psychiatric traps laid for him. We suffered from thugs and dotty visionaries, against whom no screens had been erected, not from homosexuals.

This is fairly revisionist, given that the novel's only gay character is a villain. Gordon acknowledged this fact and apologized for it, explaining that he had merely "succumbed to the prevailing sentiments of the time."[25] He suggested that the novel's *true* gay character was Roger Chandler, who, despite his sexual relationships with women, was in actuality a fictionalized version of himself. Again, Gordon was representing his older work as "closeted" gay material.

Gordon was not the only gay writer trying to resuscitate his pre-Stonewall work. Around the same time, Charles Henri Ford had authorized a new edition of *The Young and Evil*, which he had co-authored with Parker Tyler in

1933 and which was sometimes billed as the "first true homosexual novel."[26] (Gordon had known Ford while living in Hydra and may have gotten the idea from him, if not the other way around.) Early novels by Burns, Vidal, and Isherwood were all being reissued—as *The Advocate*'s Richard Hall wrote at the time, such new editions of "neglected pre-lib masterworks" were suddenly all the rage.[27] Even so, Gordon's exhumation of *Demon of Noon* was more substantial than any of these. His "revision" expanded the original novel by more than two hundred pages, doubling its size. His method for making this weightier version was to take apart his old copy of *Demon* and write his changes directly on the printed pages. In sections where he added a longer new section, he interleaved manuscript pages, often several at a time.

The resulting work, retitled as *Perfect Freedom*, was a sweeping epic saga. Gordon successfully managed to combine the Fitzgeraldesque austerity of the earlier novel with the sumptuous romance (and sexual explicitness) of his gay novels. He retained the main plot of *Demon*, concerning Stuart Cosling's expatriate life in France, mostly unchanged except for more graphic details in the sex scenes. The main revision was his elaboration of Robbie's story, which takes up most of the last two-thirds of *Perfect Freedom*. In *Demon*, Robbie is clearly a gay character but only a supporting one; his sexuality is important mainly as a test for Stuart. By contrast, in *Perfect Freedom*, Robbie

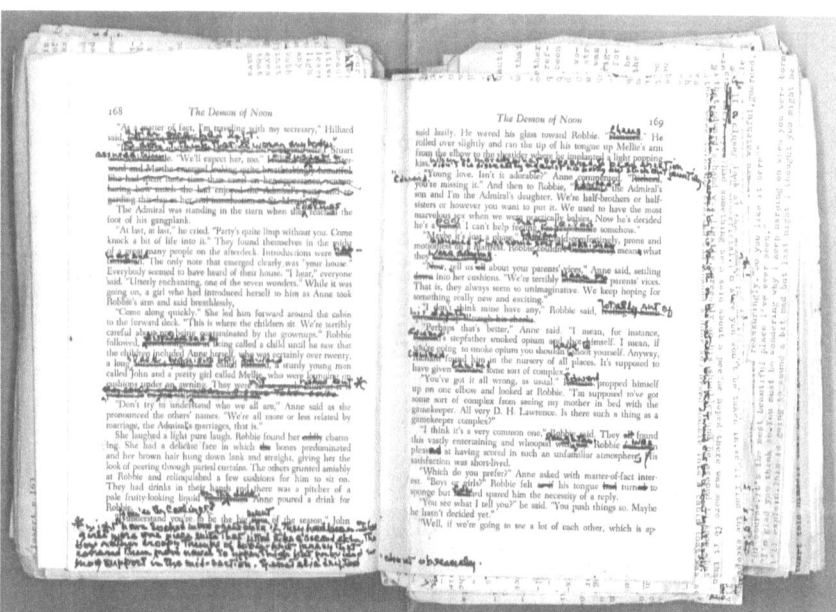

Figure 16.2 Pages of *The Demon of Noon* (1955) being revised for *Perfect Freedom* (1982). Longer additions were interleaved in the book as inserts.
Source: Estate of Gordon Merrick.

steals the spotlight midway through the novel and proceeds on his own journey of self-discovery.

Much of the novel takes the form of a picaresque, with Robbie traveling around the Mediterranean coast and meeting a diverse group of sexual partners along the way. His first real sexual experience takes place with Rico, an Italian deckhand on his father's yacht who seduces Robbie in the absence of any available women. For Robbie, the episode confirms the truth of his sexual preferences, and during the next several months his sexual education is aided by a young Greek boatman, an Italian tour guide, an American naval officer, an Ionian motorcyclist, and a Teutonic German playboy who later seduces Robbie's mother. The episodes are typical Gordon Merrick fare, with graphic bodily descriptions and a variety of sexual positions, but they also provide a glimpse into an earlier gay male cruising culture. Through his gallivanting, Robbie learns a "code" of eye contact and body gestures by which he is able to have sex with other men, even those who do not speak English or French.

Robbie is a fast sexual learner, but he struggles to make sense of his experiences. Having grown up in relative isolation, his only notions of gay men are as "doomed" and "freaks."[28] It is only when Carl, the German playboy, assures him that homosexuality is perfectly "natural" and that he will one day have a "happy life" that Robbie begins to accept his homosexuality.[29] Almost simultaneously he falls in love with Toni, a beautiful nightclub dancer who is staying with the Coslings. As in *Demon*, Toni is straight, but his affection for Robbie makes sex between them possible. While the early version of Toni is slightly annoyed by Robbie's sexuality, the revised Toni is more fluid. His feelings for Robbie are more romantic, if not quite libidinous. He willingly enmeshes himself in a sexual relationship with Robbie, telling himself it will help "wean" Robbie from same-sex desires. The affair is tempestuous and ultimately impossible, but Gordon frames it as an important stage in Robbie's sexual and psychological maturation. The increased importance of their relationship in the revised novel was highlighted on the novel's cover, in another exquisite Victor Gadino illustration.

Compared to Gordon's other novels, *Perfect Freedom* is not very autobiographical. Much of it, especially the new material, reads like a European travel fantasy, with cameos by Greta Garbo, Marlene Dietrich, and Pablo Picasso. Yet Gordon still took the opportunity to express his own personal thoughts. In one of the revised passages, he expanded the description of Stuart's reasons for leaving America, in a way that commented on his own literary reputation:

> In New York, the word that had been bandied about when he talked about his vague plans was "escapism." People said, "You're trying to turn your back on your times"—but was he? He hadn't turned his back on the twenties and had the

memory of a thousand hangovers to prove it. If he hadn't known rich people, the twenties would have turned their back on him. What were "his times"? He was alive and the world was all around him. Why not use his unearned freedom to take what he wanted from it?[30]

It is easy to hear Gordon's frustration with the American critics, who *did* accuse him of "escapism" and of being ignorant of the problems of "real" gay men. He had known plenty of "real" gay men and had written about them, yet he was constantly berated for neglecting "his times." What were "his times"?

Gordon added other self-references to *Perfect Freedom*. He changed the name of a minor character from Ernest Godet to Bernard Godet, a not-so-subtle nod to Bernard Geis, his erstwhile publisher, and added other details that signified Geis. He changed the setting from a fictional St. Martin to Saint-Tropez, making more clear the novel's origins in his life in Provence in the 1940s. He revised the Tour Engloutie, the nightclub where Toni performs, to resemble more the Lido, the Parisian nightclub where Hulse had worked in the 1950s. In other places he simply made Robbie sound more like himself, at least culturally: "He felt French, or at least a native of the small part of France that his father owned."[31]

Gordon's most personal addition to *Perfect Freedom* took the form of an homage. He devised a storyline that alluded to the two men who had most profoundly shaped his literary career. In the last section of the novel, Robbie becomes aware of his deep attraction to Maurice, his art teacher. At first Maurice is a mentor figure, nurturing Robbie's art and taking him to museums and exhibitions. After his experiences with Toni and other gay men, Robbie realizes that he has fallen in love with Maurice. He concocts an elaborate plan to seduce him. While Maurice's professionalism initially keeps him from responding to Robbie's advances, his defenses are finally melted by Robbie's sincere and candid declaration of his feelings. They become devoted lovers, and Maurice introduces Robbie to a large circle of openly gay artists: "an undisguisedly homosexual circle, writers, musicians, theater people, a painter or two, who came from Paris." Robbie understands their relationship to be a longterm commitment, a fact that is recognized by Maurice's circle of gay friends: "They were treated like a newly married couple."[32] Robbie's confidence—both as an artist and as a gay man—grows through his relationship with Maurice.

The character of Maurice was partly based on Gordon's actual teacher at Princeton, his French professor Maurice Coindreau. Coindreau had encouraged Gordon's acting talent and had given him excellent training in French, both of which had made it possible for Gordon to be an OSS agent in France and to live in France right afterward. Like the novel's Maurice, Coindreau had been a friend who had taken Gordon to theater and museums, and he had introduced him to literature that would influence his style. Gordon was evidently thinking about Coindreau as he was writing *Perfect Freedom*. When at the same time he was interviewed by Mabille, he spoke at length about Coindreau, recalling how his erstwhile mentor had helped him discover Gide, Proust, and Céline.[33]

Gordon also used the character to honor his other lifetime mentor, E. M. Forster. It was a convenient fact that Coindreau shared the same name as the title of Forster's gay novel, but Gordon added other details that suggested Forster. The novel's title comes from a passage in *The Longest Journey* (the same passage that Gordon had used for the epigraph in *Demon of Noon*). In one scene in *Perfect Freedom*, he carefully describes Robbie's artistic growth under Maurice's influence, which simultaneously causes Robbie to sense their shared sexuality: "He had been evolving some advanced and intricate techniques under the guidance of M. Monneret, his art teacher at school.... His thoughts lingered briefly on his teacher. Maurice? Possibly."[34] In another scene, Robbie shows Maurice an unusually sensual nude self-portrait; Maurice is fascinated but takes pains to hide his enchantment. Forster had not lived long enough to read *The Lord Won't Mind*, but Gordon could still playfully wonder what the older Englishman would have thought of his own personalized take on *Maurice*. One of Forster's novels actually appears earlier in the novel, in a passage that thematizes Robbie's dawning awareness of his sexuality:

> He had heard plenty of crude jokes about boys doing things together but he didn't mean anything like that.... He wanted only something he had caught hints of in an E. M. Forster novel he had read that winter, nothing explicit but something that seemed to quiver beneath the words, a sense of a deep passionate masculine love that could light life with joy, as if friendship were almost like falling in love.[35]

Although the text does not specify which Forster novel this is, it cannot be *Maurice*, which was not published until 1971. With deliberate cleverness, Gordon suggests here that Forster's "straight" novels are actually coded gay novels, whose sexual truth ("hints . . . that seemed to quiver beneath the words") are perceptible by sensitive gay readers. This was a masterstroke. In essence Gordon is reframing Forster's novels in the same way that he was reframing his own postwar novels—as "gay" novels that had not yet come out of the closet.

Gordon created other self-reflexive episodes, some of which never made it into the final published version. In an early draft of *Perfect Freedom*, Gordon wrote an episode in which Robbie befriends Eric, another student at the school where Maurice is teaching. At this point in the novel Robbie is mulling over the possibility of a romance with Maurice. He senses that Eric is interested in him, and so he uses the situation to try to understand Maurice's point of view: "He would play Maurice to Eric's Robbie. He wanted to find out if it were possible to feign convincing indifference no matter how much he might be tempted."[36] This is a strange but deceptively layered episode. In one way it dramatizes the kind of mental role-playing that gay men often had to do when trying to find each other out—a kind of double-consciousness that necessarily shaped the interactions of gay men who were not yet out to each other. From another perspective the episode figures Gordon's method as a writer. In writing gay characters, he had to do his own role-playing, imagining the perspectives of gay men different from himself—in age, background, or experience. Gordon eventually deleted the Eric storyline, perhaps because the novel was already too long or because the episode added a distracting wrinkle to the Maurice plotline. In either case, the episode shows that Gordon was thinking about his characters, and about his writing, in complex ways.

Most critics did not catch the allusions to Forster. Nor did they notice that *Perfect Freedom* was a complete overhaul of a pre-Stonewall "homosexual" novel. Predictably, most of the leading gay periodicals ignored it, and the few that didn't were acerbic, calling it "devoid of literary merit" while simultaneously predicting it a bestseller.[37] The novel was more favorably reviewed in alternative gay magazines, whose readership consisted of Gordon Merrick fans. Charles Musgrave, a San Francisco-based writer whose work often appeared in gay erotic magazines, admitted the enduring popularity of Merrick in his review for *Drummer* magazine. He also noted a strong resemblance between Robbie Cosling and *The Quirk*'s Rod McIntyre—a perceptive observation given that both characters originated in Gordon's early straight novels.[38] In *Gay Times*, a short-lived San Francisco magazine, Joe Cote took seriously Robbie's sexual and social development in the novel: "Along the way each stage of [gay] development is explored: from innocent, pre-adolescent games . . . to youthful discovery of the real thing, to overindulgence and guilt that follows the realization that one is a sick pervert, to a growing understanding of love and self-respect and worth in the world." Cote, an owner of a leather shop who had once met Tennessee Williams as a teenager, was wholly unpretentious in his assessment of *Perfect Freedom*. "Don't miss this book," he succinctly told his readers.[39]

Leslie Irons, a host of the public-access television show *Gay Morning America*, took a more polemical stance in his review for *Topman*. He used *Perfect Freedom* as an opportunity to rail against the harsh treatment of openly gay works by gay critics and activists:

> *Making Love*, a milestone in gay films, was attacked by many gay militants because it was about beautiful rich people. Well boys, there are many, many

gays who are both beautiful and rich. Films and books are put under the critical microscope because they show our seamy side. Why? Do any of you out there think we don't have a seamy side?

He then evoked Gordon as a paradigmatic example, noting that his novels are called "pure trash" despite selling over a million copies. Irons was adamant about the sheer pleasures of reading explicitly gay fiction, a phenomenon which he accused gay critics of taking for granted: "It is like reading a well written, classy, stroke book. The nice thing is you can buy it in supermarkets and drugstores. Imagine that in the 50s."[40]

As usual, the warmest reactions came from critics outside the urban centers of American gay culture. A member of the Mississippi Gay Alliance wrote a gleeful review of *Perfect Freedom* for the organization's newsletter, beginning with an enthusiastic "Welcome Home, Gordon Merrick!" Although the reviewer thought the novel's picaresque section was excessive, they deemed the characterization "beautifully executed" and the narrative "beautiful." "There are places where it will whisper to you," the reviewer promised, "and you will be left with an unforgettable after-glow."[41] In at least one way, the reviewer was far more informed than the highbrow critics: the reviewer had read *The Strumpet Wind* and noted that *Perfect Freedom* constituted a return to Merrick's postwar novel style of writing.

The Mississippi Gay Alliance reviewer clearly knew Gordon's oeuvre better than the gay literati—but also better than Gordon's publisher. Bob Wyatt had no idea that *Perfect Freedom* was a revision of an earlier novel, and he learned about it only after someone at *The Advocate* (likely Richard Hall) called to warn him about a "damning" review of *Perfect Freedom* that was going to be published in the magazine. According to the *The Advocate* source, Wallace Hamilton, a gay novelist whose works had often been overshadowed by Gordon's, was planning to "expose" the truth about *Perfect Freedom* and portray Wyatt as an incompetent editor. (For reasons that are unknown, the review was never published.) Wyatt was furious. He accused Gordon of presenting the novel to him as an entirely original work and making him look "foolish." Wyatt had just accepted a new job with Ballantine Books, but he told Gordon to stay with Avon. He had no interest in working with him again.[42]

Gordon did not feel too bad about Wyatt's embarrassment. The incident confirmed what he had likely suspected for some time—that Wyatt did not read his novels. Gordon had sent him copies of his postwar novels in the hopes of having them reissued by Avon, but Wyatt had shown no interest. If Wyatt had bothered to read even the dust jackets of these novels, he would have realized that *Demon of Noon* and *Perfect Freedom* were based on the same material. Instead, as always, he focused his energy on the marketing of

Gordon's novels. His letters to Gordon show that he was mostly concerned with timing the release of the novels to coincide with the beginning of Fire Island season.[43] Like the highbrow critics, Wyatt had a preconceived notion of a Gordon Merrick novel, regardless of the different approaches that Gordon took in his writing. It did not occur to him that Gordon had orchestrated *Perfect Freedom* as a tribute—an updated and uninhibited one—to Forster.

The rupture with Wyatt reminded Gordon of the importance of editors and agents who were willing to read his work and take him seriously as a novelist. He was reminded of his longtime agent Monica McCall, who had died the previous July, only a few months after *Perfect Freedom* appeared in print. Her health had been declining for years, and she finally passed away after a bad case of pneumonia.[44] Gordon had not worked with McCall for some time, ever since Mitch Douglas and Jeannie Sakol took over as his agents. Although McCall's effectiveness had waned in her last years due to her health, she had been a diligent advocate of Gordon's writing during the crucial years. She had certainly been pivotal for the publication of *The Lord Won't Mind*. And, importantly, she had read Gordon's work. She had helped Gordon revive his literary career at a crucial moment and become a bestselling writer, if not a critically acclaimed one.

Gordon, now sixty-six years old, was thinking deeply about the people who had influenced his writing over the years. He couldn't help but think of Bernard Geis, who had contacted Gordon a year earlier out of the blue. With his usual cheery humor, and acting as though he and Gordon had parted on good terms, he proposed collaborating again on a new book project—a "Merrick breakthrough" as he put it. He lamented that Avon was not allowing Gordon to reach his full potential, and he had several ideas to help get him back on track. For example, Gordon could write a suspense thriller, like *Raise the Titanic* or *The Taking of Pelham One Two Three*. Or still better, he could write something that combined his penchant for international intrigue with his talent for sex scenes:

> This is probably indiscreet but I do think you deserve something to prime the pump. We just received an outline for a novel in which Prince Charles, at the age of fifteen, was robbed of his seed. This was sold to six wealthy women, resulting in four bastard heirs to the throne: You can imagine the plot possibilities.[45]

Surprisingly, Gordon did not slam the metaphorical door in Geis's face. He may have been known for his temper, but he was not one to hold a grudge for years. Instead, he instructed Geis to get in touch with Bob Wyatt (who had not yet left Avon) to discuss a possible deal.

And why not? Gordon had little concern for pleasing the gay critics or getting glowing reviews in the *New York Times*. As long as he sold books he would write whatever pleased him, without apologizing for it. He was likely thinking of this when he added a certain line—one that imitates the end of Milton's *Paradise Lost*—during his revision of *Demon of Noon*: "He was alive and the world was all around him. Why not use his unearned freedom to take what he wanted from it?"[46]

NOTES

1. Charles Hulse, interview by the author.
2. Monica McCall to Gordon Merrick, 25 June 1969, GMP, box 16, folder 1; 11 September 1975, GMP, box 17, folder 1.
3. Robert Wyatt to Gordon Merrick, 29 March 1978, GMP, box 17, folder 4.
4. See for example the February 22, 1979 issue of *Gay News*.
5. "Bosie!," *Gay News*, June 12, 1980; Sigrid Nelson, review of Vincent Lardo's *China House*, *Gay Scotland*, November 1983; Frieda Fetische, "Smiths, Not Synths," *Gay Scotland*, May 1984.
6. John Hyde, "Edinburgh Festival Reviews," *Gay Scotland*, October 1989.
7. "Going Gay," *Gay News*, March 8, 1979.
8. "Two Lavender Years, Two Parties," *Gay Scotland*, November 1984.
9. "Trio Tries to Ban Books," *Daily Journal* (Franklin, Indiana), January 18, 1983; Gary Ruderman, "Gay Books: Fundamental Conflict," *Los Angeles Times*, March 6, 1983.
10. "More Customs Seizures," *Gay Scotland*, January 1985.
11. "Bookshop Prepares for Court Battle," *Gay Times*, July 1984; "'Bloomsbury Nine' Face Charges," *Gay Times*, December 1984.
12. Keith Howes, *Outspoken: Keith Howes' "Gay News" Interviews 1976–83* (London: Cassell, 1995).
13. Keith Howes, "Where Love Has Gone," *Gay News*, July 26, 1979.
14. Keith Howes, "Once A Spy . . . ," *Gay News*, August 24, 1978; Howes, "Where Love Has Gone."
15. "'Quirk' Author on the Move," *Gay News*, November 15, 1979; Howes, "Once A Spy."
16. Michel Mabille, "Ceylon to Tricqueville: The Restless Life of an American Author," *L'Éveil de Pont-Audemer*, August 27, 1981. Translation by Ann Scott.
17. Mabille, "Ceylon to Tricqueville."
18. Vincent Canby, "'Race D'Ep' Links Photography and Sexuality," *New York Times*, May 19, 1982.
19. Jean-Michel Senecal to Gordon Merrick, 23 August 1986, GMP, box 18, folder 5.
20. Christian Hym to Gordon Merrick, 27 September 1986, GMP, box 18, folder 5; Christian Hym to Gordon Merrick, 18 February 1987, GMP, box 7, folder 2; Gordon

Merrick, *Beaux À Se Damner*, trans. Michel Caignet (Paris: Éditions Entre Chiens et Loups, 1987), editor's preface.

21. Claude Sarraute, "Rose et bleu," *Le Monde*, March 11, 1987. Translation by Ann Scott.

22. Didier Lestrade, "Gordon Merrick, Le Dynastie Pédé!," *Gai Pied Hebdo*, March 7, 1987. Translation by Ann Scott.

23. Monica McCall to Gordon Merrick, 3 September 1975, GMP, box 17, folder 1.

24. Monica McCall to Gordon Merrick, 20 March 1973, GMP, box 16, folder 5.

25. Gordon Merrick, unpublished introduction to *The Strumpet Wind*, 1979, GMP, box 15, folder 13.

26. Felice Picano, *Art and Sex in Greenwich Village: Gay Literary Life after Stonewall* (New York: Carroll & Graf, 2007), 128–37.

27. Richard Hall, "Books: Reviews & Previews," *The Advocate*, June 15, 1977.

28. Gordon Merrick, *Perfect Freedom* (New York: Avon Books, 1982), 209.

29. Merrick, *Perfect Freedom*, 208, 210.

30. Merrick, *Perfect Freedom*, 11.

31. Merrick, *Perfect Freedom*, 105, 135.

32. Merrick, *Perfect Freedom*, 386.

33. Gordon Merrick to Mary Merrick, 17 November 1936; Mabille, "Ceylon to Tricqueville."

34. Merrick, *Perfect Freedom*, 270.

35. Merrick, *Perfect Freedom*, 141.

36. Gordon Merrick, working draft for *Perfect Freedom*, insert p. 255, GMP, box 12, folder 1.

37. Review of *Perfect Freedom*, source unknown, GMP, box 20, folder 7.

38. Charles R. Musgrave, "Paperback Assassins," *Drummer*, June 1982.

39. Joe Cote, review of *Perfect Freedom*, *Gay Times*, n.d., GMP, box 20, folder 7; Obituary, Joseph Louis Cote Jr., *Bay Area Reporter*, December 10, 2008.

40. Leslie Irons, "Cast 'N Irons," *Topman*, June 21, 1982.

41. Review of *Perfect Freedom*, *Mississippi Gay Alliance*, n.d., GMP, box 20, folder 7.

42. Robert Wyatt to Gordon Merrick, 1 January 1983, GMP, box 18, folder 1.

43. Robert Wyatt to Gordon Merrick, 28 October 1980, GMP, box 17, folder 6.

44. Mitch Douglas to Gordon Merrick, 5 October 1982, GMP, box 17, folder 8.

45. Bernard Geis to Gordon Merrick, 6 April 1981, GMP, box 17, folder 7.

46. Merrick, *Perfect Freedom*, 11.

Chapter Seventeen
Merrick vs. Kramer

In the end, Gordon did not write a novel about Prince Charles's stolen seed. The one he *did* write, however, was hardly more believable. *The Great Urge Downward*, his eighth gay novel, is a melodramatic sexcapade that generally lives up to the stereotypical idea of a Gordon Merrick romance. The novel, which appeared in bookstores in the fall of 1984, focuses on Lance Vanderholden, a rich, handsome American who flees to Mexico to escape the wreckage of a failed marriage. At first he seduces a naïve Mexican girl, but he is then distracted by a string of beautiful men with whom he has intense, wrenching affairs. His biggest affair is with Robbie Cosling—the same character from *Perfect Freedom*. In *Downward*, Robbie's lover Maurice has died tragically in a plane crash, and Robbie is now a world-famous painter known as "Robi." Robbie falls in love with Lance and patiently tries to help him come to terms with his sexuality. Their relationship is tested when Lance discovers in himself an inclination for exhibitionist sex and S&M. A bigger problem is Lance's mother, who arrives on the scene with a devious plan to take him back to America and put him in a psychiatric hospital to cure his homosexuality. Lance ultimately escapes this fate through Robbie's help, involving a final plot twist that would be at home in a Gilbert and Sullivan opera. It is all huge fun and utterly ridiculous.

Readers of Gordon's early novels would recognize from this summary that *Downward* is a "gay" version of *The Vallency Tradition*. As he had done in *Perfect Freedom*, Gordon recycled earlier material by adding gay storylines and explicit sex scenes. This time he at least acknowledged his use of earlier material, in an Author's Note at the beginning of the book:

> This novel—like *Perfect Freedom*, which preceded it . . . had its origins in long ago, long out-of-print work. In both cases I have dealt with characters and themes that I was unable or unwilling to explore thoroughly at the time. Over the years they remained naggingly in my mind like unfinished business or an unpaid debt. In this case, so little remains of the earlier work—a setting, a family

background, the partial outline of a plot—that it's worth noting only for the sake of an occasional reader with the gift of total recall who might be afflicted at moments with a sense of *déjà vu*. *The Great Urge Downward* is an original publication of Avon Books. It has never before appeared in book form.[1]

This was a complete lie. In truth, Gordon did much the same thing in *Downward* that he had with *Perfect Freedom*, though he added more new material this time. He changed Lance Vallency's name to Lance Vanderholden, but he left much of the earlier material practically untouched: for example, the first forty pages of *Vallency* are reproduced almost verbatim. Avon, still smarting from the embarrassment over *Perfect Freedom*, had made Gordon clarify the extent of his self-borrowing and had printed a guarantee that nothing substantial in *Downward* had been published before.[2] They did not, however, look at the earlier novel to see if this claim was accurate.

Despite the recycled material, *The Great Urge Downward* feels vastly different from *The Vallency Tradition*—and even more different from the original version of *Vallency* that was published only in French. In revising the earlier novel, Gordon added nearly three hundred pages detailing Lance's gay sexual past and introducing several gay storylines. (In *Vallency*, Lance is unequivocally heterosexual.) The gay storylines form the central plot, so that the *Vallency* material becomes a "heterosexual" phase that Lance undergoes before realizing his true desires. In the Author's Note, Gordon explained this change as the exhumation of a latent truth that he was "unable or unwilling to explore thoroughly" in 1955. This may have been true in the sense that straight characters in Gordon's postwar novels were often based on people who were gay, but the changes in *Downward* feel more like a playful experiment with *noir* fiction than an honest attempt to recover history.

In one way the new novel *did* recover an aspect of the original that had actually been repressed in the 1950s. As I showed in chapter 7, the original version of *Vallency* featured an interracial relationship between Lance and an African-American woman. Gordon was able to publish a French translation of this version, but his American publisher made him remove the interracial plot. In *Downward*, Gordon partly resurrected the interracial storyline—by writing a storyline in which Lance has an affair with Andy, an African-American who works for a legal firm that advocates for civil rights. The storyline is largely inconsequential for the main plot, and it seems primarily to have been added to make the novel appear more progressive and current. Unfortunately, the attempt largely backfires. There are some noble passages where Andy discusses the challenges of his job (which Gordon had learned from his brother Samuel, who had advocated for black labor rights as a lawyer), but too often the episode comes off as a clumsy attempt by a white man to imagine a black man's experience. At its worst moments, the character of Andy sounds like a stereotype of a black man, almost bordering on caricature. In one passage where Lance and Andy are showering together, Andy playfully jokes with Lance, "Don't come too close until I've washed. All niggers smell funny. You know that."[3] Such wince-inducing lines showed Gordon's fundamental inability to mimic black speech or write convincing black characters. The novel's reviewers, including those who were inclined to be sympathetic, noticed the problematic representation of race and quoted the offending passages as evidence of the novel's racism.[4]

Even in a screwy novel like *Downward*, Gordon managed to include moments of true self-awareness. In one episode Robbie explains to Lance that his life as a gay man has been relatively easy because of the inherent advantages of his social position:

> I fought my battles when I was so young that I forgot I was fighting for my right to be different. At first, I thought I was damned and acted accordingly. My father was eventually able to talk to me about being a decent homosexual. His making an effort at understanding made me want his approval, and Maurice was a very decent man. We were accepted as a couple in respectable society. It's different in Europe. Class, who you know, counts for more than what you are. I began to forget there was anything special about me.[5]

At sixty-eight years of age, Gordon had still not figured out how to write about women or about race, but he had realized the important role that social status had played in his life. He had seen enough of the world to realize that gay men who did not have the same economic and geographical privileges had a very different experience fitting into "straight" environments. By this point he had stopped writing the lofty anti-capitalist screeds that had defined his pre-Stonewall career and had come to understand better the complexity—what we would today call the "intersectionality"—of sexuality and class.

Gordon likely thought his recycling of *Vallency* would go unnoticed. The early novel had been out of print for decades and had garnered less attention in America than his other postwar novels. The French version had been more popular, but its readers were unlikely to be on Avon's mailing list in 1984. Sure enough, no news of the prehistory of *Downward* reached Page Cuddy, Gordon's new editor at Avon. Cuddy was an experienced publisher and former vice president at Simon & Schuster who bragged of having "pretend adversarial relationships with authors."[6] While she handled the editing of his novel in a professional manner, she did not spend any more time on it than was necessary. For their part, Gordon's loyal fans gobbled up *Downward* as they had his other gay novels, though they, too, seemed to recognize it as erotic fantasy more than genuine romance. One reader, an English professor at Bowling Green State University, wrote Gordon to tell him that he "came three times in one day reading *The Great Urge Downward*."⁷ For Gordon's adversarial critics, *Downward* provided an especially easy target. Richard Labonte, a regular book review columnist and one of the founders of A Different Light, the iconic gay bookstore chain, proclaimed *The Great Urge Downward* one of the five worst gay novels of all time, noting that "only the self-loathing symbolism of the title makes it stand out as one of Merrick's too many sucky romances."⁸

The revived interracial storyline in *Downward*, however misguided, showed that Gordon at least *heard* the complaints made by the critics, even if he professed not to understand them. One review that he read while writing *Downward* was Richard Summerbell's review of *Perfect Freedom* for *Body Politic*, a gay monthly magazine published out of Toronto. This was a very mixed review, but it came from someone who did not scoff at gay romance or explicit sex scenes (he acknowledged the value of Boyd McDonald), and whose initiation into gay literature had been profoundly shaped by Gordon's novels. Summerbell began his review by recalling his discovery of *The Lord Won't Mind*, which had been the first gay novel he ever read:

> I was eighteen, and had just initiated my coming out process about a fortnight earlier. The guy who loaned me his copy of *The Lord Won't Mind* was nineteen, a more experienced closet case—the first person I'd ever shared closet space with. He had composed a classified ad, you see, and I had written a sincere letter to an anonymous box number. The book, it turned out, had been stolen from a public library because my friend couldn't bear to take it to the librarian's desk.

This was by now a familiar story, yet Summerbell follows it with a concise cultural history of Gordon Merrick novels and a theory about their enduring appeal. The problem with the novels, Summerbell then explains, is that they are not accurate representations of "real-life romance"—a shortcoming that Summerbell realized only as an older man. This criticism was also not new, but Summerbell fleshes it out with details showing he has read all of the novels:

> His protagonists are extraordinarily attractive—so attractive that Merrick scarcely describes them at all, allowing you to conjure their exact appearances out of your own daydreams. . . . Merrick takes pains not to deviate too far from reality, and deaths and disappointments do occur—but somehow they lack any tragic impact. Passion animates everyone and everything, whether it be a boy leaping off a precipice while spattering out his last orgasm or a fiendish gigolo stealing another man's wife and son simply by fucking them both. How can there be any real pain in a world intoxicated by such stuff?

And then, of course, there are the sexist and racist streaks in the novels, which Summerbell identifies as traits of "the Ugly Gay Man": "Charlie sees American blacks as 'an army of monkey-faced servants, children, animals,' while Gerry, in *Now Let's Talk*, bemoans the featurelessness of Orientals." Unlike other critics who had quoted specific lines as evidence of the novel's racism, Summerbell acknowledges that, in context, such lines were probably intended to represent the racism of specific people or eras, not the novelist's. But, Summerbell warns, to do so is to venture into "dangerous territory": "Why extend wish-fulfillment to misogynists and racists?"[9]

These were valid criticisms (except the charge that Gordon does not describe his characters' physical appearances) and Gordon tried to address most of them in his next novel—which would turn out to be the last novel he saw to publication. *A Measure of Madness* (originally titled *Fat Tuesday* until, as usual, Gordon's editor asked him to change it) centers on Phil Renfield, a smart, sensitive gay man who works as an editor for an academic textbook publisher. He goes to Greece after a string of relationships that have left him emotionally scarred. There he meets a diverse group of characters, most of whom he has sex with, and through whom he gains a new self-image and a healthier, more realistic outlook on gay relationships. Early in the novel, he tried again to compose an interracial gay sex scene, as he had done in *Downward*, though he tried to be more careful this time. In the relevant episode, Gordon makes it clear that Phil's racist impulses are *his* problem—one that he struggles to overcome:

> Phil caught himself thinking that Lester didn't look very Negroid. His lips were seductively full but not thick, and his nose wasn't flattened. Phil decided that this was racist stuff and willed himself to be attracted without racial references. . . . Some deep-seated atavistic revulsion gripped him momentarily, but he was determined to overcome it. It had been a struggle to accept being a faggot, but he'd never forgive himself if he was a racist faggot.[10]

The intention is clearer here, but the heavy-handed approach makes it seem perfunctory. Gordon's editor rightly warned him against making Phil's thoughts about having sex with a black man *too* dramatic, since it risked making Phil's racism seem almost natural. From a certain angle this reads as autobiographical projection, as though Gordon were using Phil's response to Lester as a proxy for working through his own, deep-seated racial prejudice.

Gordon's other attempt to address Summerbell's criticism was more successful. The first sex scene in the novel does not take place between two "extraordinarily attractive" demigods, but between Phil, now in his midthirties, and Johnny Marston, a gangly English man "with oddly out-of-balance features . . . ugly but confident of his sex appeal." Still capable of wry self-irony, Gordon gestured at this departure from form in Phil and Johnny's first conversation:

> Johnny shrugged. . . . "Have you taken a look at the boys?"
> Phil felt the question in his groin but tried not to look flustered. "As a matter of fact, I have. . . . They're not what I expected, either. What became of the Greek gods?"

Moreover, sex between them does not lead to a moony romance but is rather the expression of a mature, freehearted friendship. The episode also demonstrates one of Gordon's unquestionable talents: his ability to capture the heightened consciousness that gay men experience when trying to ascertain another man's interest—the hypersensitivity to the slightest body contact or changes in demeanor, all complicated by the awareness that you are being observed as well. Gordon was nearly seventy years old at this point, but he could still reconstruct vividly the intricate mix of emotions and perceptions that attend on such a situation.

Although *Measure* had some admirable moments, it also proved again that Gordon was perfectly capable of writing potboilers. The novel is an unapologetic combination of sexual melodrama and exotic intrigue. Much of it reads like a nostalgic, hallucinogenic trip in which memories from Gordon's long life appear and take on distorted or exaggerated forms. There are characters who closely resemble his Hydra friends George Johnston and Charmian Clift, who in the novel are reimagined as sexual swingers who would have taken Gordon to bed. Leonard Cohen appears looking just like himself but now gay, English, and a drug smuggler. The specter of Bob Richardson appears in the form of a sexual sadist who has a compulsion for public sex. Gordon's first real romance, the Episcopal Academy football star who went to Yale, is here a confirmed homosexual who comes back from Yale ready to marry him. Gordon even recreated the famous masked ball in Hydra, which in the novel becomes the pretext for a grisly murder. By all appearances Gordon was simply having fun. He lovingly dedicated the novel to Hulse, who would have understood all of the autobiographical twists, calling it "an anniversary celebration" of their thirty years together. Gordon knew he had an army of loyal readers who would take whatever he gave them, and he knew that the Avon marketing machine—with the irresistible Victor Gadino covers—would ensure that his books were put in bookstores everywhere.

Or at least he thought he knew. As was typical of New York publishing firms, the editors at Avon moved around like a game of musical chairs. Page Cuddy was replaced by a new editor in chief, Susanne Jaffe, another experienced publisher who, like Cuddy, had also been a vice president at Simon & Schuster. Jaffe had a penchant for thrillers and historical romances and would go on to write several romance novels of her own. Unlike Cuddy, she had no interest in retaining Gordon as an Avon author. When Gordon sent her *A Measure of Madness*, she let the manuscript sit on her desk for several weeks before sending it back with a terse letter informing him that Avon would not publish his new novel and that Gordon should find a new publisher going forward. The Avon marketing machine would no longer be running for him.[11]

Gordon was confused and enraged. As one of Avon's bestselling authors, he expected more than an unceremonious brush-off. The steady flow of royalty checks from Avon confirmed that his novels were still selling well, and moreover Avon had just received a nice cut from the sale of Japanese language rights to Gordon's novels. He quickly wrote to Jaffe demanding an explanation in light of his strong sales figures. She responded a month later with another short letter, this time including jargon about cover prices and publishing cycles. In any case the matter was settled as far as she was concerned, and she did not write again. Gordon, with his usual irascibility and barely concealed sexism, blamed things on the notion that, after Wyatt's departure, Avon had become an "incompetent hotbed of feminism."[12] Hulse also thought Jaffe's line about sales was "spurious," but he had a different theory for her antipathy toward Gordon's novels. He had heard from Mitch Douglas that the prevalence of AIDS had made gay-themed works a dirty word in the industry.[13] Whether Jaffe was part of a larger effort at Avon to move away from gay fiction toward more "feminist" work, or whether she was reacting to a perceived backlash against gay novels remains an open question. (When I contacted Jaffe, she denied ever having had anything to do with Gordon and suggested I had confused her with another Avon editor.)

For the first time in over ten years, Gordon was again without a publisher. He turned for help to Mitch Douglas, his longtime agent at ICM. Douglas had continued to work on Gordon's accounts, but he had been somewhat sidelined once Gordon brought on Jeannie Sakol to represent him. For all of her ebullience and charm, Sakol was a terrible agent. Despite several expensive lunches with publishers and her constant assertion that she had the "inside scoop" on publishing trends, she had failed to land a single deal on Gordon's behalf. Gordon realized he had made a mistake doing business with a friend, and he went to Douglas with his proverbial hat in hand. "I'd like to take refuge again behind your efficient authority," Gordon wrote in an unusually obsequious letter, "I've collapsed on your doorstep."[14] Douglas, who had dealt with personalities far more erratic than Gordon (including Tennessee Williams and Richard Yates), was not the type to take personal offense. He considered Gordon and Hulse his friends and wanted to help. Equally important, as a gay man himself, he thought Gordon's novels deserved to be published.[15]

Gordon had turned to the right person. Within a few weeks of getting Gordon's letter, Douglas found a publisher for *A Measure of Madness*, and a few days later a contract was in the mail to Sri Lanka.[16] Douglas had known that Warner Books was willing to publish explicitly gay novels, and he knew that one of Warner's chief editors, Mario Sartori, would be especially interested in Gordon's novel. Sartori was a tall, slender, handsome man with graying hair and a mustache, who had a penchant for cultivating and mentoring gay writers. One of his discoveries, a twenty-six-year-old budding novelist named John Champagne (who would later be an English professor at Pennsylvania State University), recalled Sartori as a kind and encouraging editor who had a slightly unnerving habit of looking at people straight in the eye.[17] Sartori had been a longtime admirer of Gordon's gay novels, and he wasted no time in contracting the new book and getting started on the copyediting—though he did ask Gordon to get rid of the original title, *Fat Tuesday*. Sartori did not have time to finish copyediting the manuscript, however, since he left Warner Books only a month later to take an executive position at Lyle Stuart Books, a boutique firm based in Secaucus, New Jersey, that had a reputation for publishing controversial bestsellers.[18]

Gordon's new editor at Warner was Elmer Luke, a young energetic polyglot who would later become an important editor in the Japanese literature scene. Luke was an even bigger Gordon Merrick fan than Sartori. He had read all of Gordon's gay novels when they were published, and he had even studied *The Lord Won't Mind* in a graduate seminar at the University of Hawaii, where he had started work on a dissertation on Gore Vidal. *Lord* was one of the central texts in a graduate class on "Loners and Outcasts" taught by David Bertelson, a professor of American studies who was working on a book on cultural attitudes about sexuality in America. He was also gay, and he announced this to his graduate students when they came to Gordon's novel. Bertelson later became a friend of Luke's, who remembered the intense discussions that Bertelson had spurred about *Lord* and American sexuality in his seminar. Before moving to New York, Luke had tried his hand at a number of things, from editing law books in New Mexico to editing statistics papers at the Wharton School in Philadelphia. This range of experience made it hard for him to get a job in the New York publishing scene (which valued specialization), but in 1983 he was able to get a job as the assistant to Patrick O'Connor, a senior editor at Warner. (O'Connor had a few years earlier edited a novel by Lincoln Kirstein, whom Gordon had known during his New York days through Glenway Wescott.)[19] When Sartori left the firm, Luke eagerly took over the copyediting work that had been started, and he impressed both Gordon and Mitch Douglas with his combination of literary acumen and commercial sensibility.[20]

Gordon was thrilled. For the first time in years he felt that he had a team of agents and editors who supported him and believed in his work. When he and Hulse made a trip to New York in April that year, he had lunch with Douglas,

Sartori, and Luke. Luke was surprised to find that the man who was famous for his explicit novels was very circumspect and reserved in person—"he kept the personal personal," as Luke later put it. As an editor, Luke proved to be a scrupulous reader of Gordon's writing, and his graduate training in literature helped him temper some of Gordon's more outmoded tendencies. He immediately picked up on the awkwardness of Gordon's representation of race in *Measure of Madness*, and he suggested a number of changes to make the character of Lester seem less of a stereotype and to make Phil's thoughts about interracial sex less "overmelodramatic." He also suggested paring down the number of sex scenes, which were excessive even by Gordon's standards.[21]

Gordon complied happily with Luke's suggestions. He trusted his editorial team, and he had developed a new appreciation for the value of constructive criticism. In Sri Lanka he was now good friends with Arthur C. Clarke, who regularly shared with him his work in progress. At this time Clarke was working on *2061*, his second sequel to *2001: A Space Odyssey*, and he showed parts of the manuscript to Gordon in order to get his feedback.[22] Gordon was also helpful with *Cradle*, which Clarke was co-writing with the space engineer Gentry Lee. Clarke had struggled with the novel's explicit sex scenes, a type of writing that was "foreign" to him—but was Gordon's specialty.[23] Still, after all these years, Gordon's most important reader was Hulse, who had been working on his own autobiographical novel for some time. Gordon had been an encouraging mentor throughout the writing process, and when the novel was finished he tried to help Hulse find a publisher. He had enlisted the help of Douglas, who showed the manuscript to Jed Mattes, another gay literary agent at ICM. Mattes was already representing Ted Geisel (Dr. Seuss) and Armistead Maupin, and he would later establish his own firm where he represented a number of important gay writers, including Vito Russo and Greg Louganis. But Mattes didn't know what to do with Hulse's sensitive, coming-of-age novel; the few publishers who read the manuscript thought it genuine and well written, but they didn't think there was a commercial market for gay Southern memoirs.[24]

Gordon was an indefatigable advocate where Hulse was concerned, and he continued to explore all options. He finally hit on the idea to have Hulse send the book to Sartori at Lyle Stuart Books. Gordon had stayed on good terms with Sartori after his departure from Warner Books, and he knew that Sartori was interested in publishing new gay writers. Sartori loved Hulse's novel, and he acted quickly to issue a contract and get the manuscript into production.[25] The resulting publication was a beautiful hardcover titled *In Tall Cotton*, featuring an illustration of a devilishly smiling fifteen-year-old Hulse. In addition to being a scrupulous editor, Sartori proved to be a deft publicist as well. He secured several endorsements for the dust jacket, including breathless praise from *Publishers Weekly* and from Jane Rule, the trailblazing lesbian author of *Desert Hearts*. He also included commendations from Gordon and Hulse's friends, Leonard Cohen and the French actor Jean-Pierre Aumont. Gordon himself contributed a blurb, praising the novel for its "light comic touch" and the author's "poignant love for his characters." Hulse had waited for this moment for a long time, and in the book's dedication page he made sure to thank the two men who had meant the most to him in his life: "For GORDON MERRICK for all the reasons he knows and for my brother Larry for reasons he may suspect."[26]

Although they had not planned it, Gordon and Hulse's books came out within a few months of each other. This simultaneity provided a striking—and unexpected—study in contrast. *In Tall Cotton* was a smart-looking, hardcover book whose dustcover blurb compared it to Truman Capote's *A Christmas Memory* and John Knowles's *A Separate Piece*. It was not a bestseller, but it garnered a few warm reviews from straight and gay critics, and a year later Hulse was invited to give a reading from the novel at San Francisco's A Different Light Bookstore.[27] By most measures, it was a successful literary debut. *A Measure of Madness*, on the other hand, looked like a typical Gordon Merrick paperback. Warner's art department had somehow managed to make the book look even more "pulpy" than the Avon editions. The cover featured another Victor Gadino illustration, but unlike all the other Merrick-Gadino covers, it had no faces. The whole image was of a bronzed, muscled torso against an Aegean backdrop. The cover copy was hardly better, using language that suggested a mash-up of '50s-style gay pulp and Harlequin romance: "Desire swept him towards an island of passion, but what he needed was love."[28]

The gay press completely ignored *Measure*, not even bothering to pan it as another "sucky romance." Although this was expected, the novel's dismal sales were not. The same day the novel was released, Luke had visited A Different Light bookstore in Greenwich Village and claimed to see several gay men buying a copy. However, the next few months told the real story. Nationally, the sales figures for *Measure* were meager, outpaced even by Warner's reprints of earlier gay works like Laura Hobson's *Consenting Adult* and David Leavitt's *Family Dancing*. To add insult to injury, Gordon himself couldn't get a copy of his novel when it came out. The Customs Office in Sri Lanka confiscated Warner's shipment of copies of *Measure*, on the grounds that the books were obscene.[29]

Gordon was bewildered. He was pleased that Hulse's novel was a success, but he had not expected his own book to be a commercial dud. He knew that things could always change with a new publisher, but he had stuck to the same successful formula that had sold hundreds of thousands of books over the last seventeen years. What had changed?

The answer had a lot to do with American gay culture, which had been profoundly wracked by the ongoing AIDS epidemic. The first cases of AIDS had been detected in New York and California in 1981, and less than a year later people were talking about a lethal "gay cancer" that was spreading through gay communities in New York City and San Francisco at an alarming rate. By 1985, thousands of people had died from the disease (including the gay actor Rock Hudson), and thousands more were infected. The virulence of the epidemic, and the unforgivable reluctance of the Reagan administration and other government officials to confront or even mention AIDS, impelled gay activists in America to protest and organize and to find other ways to combat the disease. When *A Measure for Madness* hit the bookstore shelves in December 1986—three months before the March on Washington—many gay men were busy promoting safe sex and volunteering for gay health and political organizations.[30] They had little time or interest in an "escapist" gay novel whose bronzed, hale characters traipsed around the Mediterranean having spontaneous bareback sex with no health risks at all. They wanted and needed literature that could speak to them in their present time and place.

Unfortunately, Gordon never fully grasped the extent to which the pandemic had affected most gay men. He was by now a seventy-year-old man living in a monogamous relationship with his longtime partner in Sri Lanka. Though he visited New York every couple of years, he never went to gay bars or gay community centers, and so he didn't see what Andrew Holleran observed on one of his visits to New York: "The whole city has shrunk to a single fact."[31] Gordon's underestimation of the pandemic was starkly revealed in an interview he gave to *Stallion* magazine in April 1986, when he and Hulse were in New York. Brandon Judell, an ambitious and talented young journalist, had convinced Gordon to meet with him for half an hour at the apartment on East 51st Street where he and Hulse were staying. Judell was a theater enthusiast with a charismatic personality, and he had read most of Gordon's novels—well enough that he could refer to specific scenes in several of them. This combination of charm and erudition disarmed Gordon, and what had originally been planned as a half-hour interview stretched to nearly two hours. By the end of it Judell had enough material for two interviews, which he published shortly afterward in *The Advocate* and *Stallion*.[32] In the interview, Gordon let his guard down in a way he never had before, and he revealed details about his personal life (and about his friends' lives) that he had never shared with any journalist. He also did not censor himself when he talked about other gay writers.

When Judell came to the part of the interview about contemporary gay culture, Gordon gave his usual line about the perils of gay ghettoization—but then he continued talking, and he started to rant about a gay play he had just seen in London before coming to New York: "I just have a little resistance in me about making a political issue out of sex. I was really rather outraged by that Larry Kramer play that I just saw in London." The play Gordon had seen was *The Normal Heart*, Kramer's autobiographical play about AIDS that had premiered in New York the previous year. Kramer had been one of the earliest gay activists to focus attention on the AIDS crisis, having helped found the Gay Men's Health Crisis (GMHC) in 1982. Even then, Kramer had thought the GMHC was too restrained in its use of political and public pressure, and he wrote *The Normal Heart* as a polemical, emotionally wrenching indictment of "bureaucratic indifference to and gay intransigence in the face of AIDS."[33] Gordon, who didn't understand the critical role that homophobia played in the nation's response to the disease, thought Kramer was overreacting:

> Drawing an analogy with the Holocaust. To me, goddamnit, no! I mean that's really without any basis. Now if AIDS has been underfunded because the feeling was that the victims weren't worth bothering about, of course that's shocking and something should be done about it. But I'd like to hear from the scientific community if this is true. . . . Now if there hasn't been [AIDS research] here, of course you must be angry. But the scientists should be more angry than Larry Kramer, for God's sake. And I'm sure that a lot of that gay lib was very necessary. . . . I just question whether one must make declarations.

Judell tried to explain the reason why gay activists thought visibility was important, remarking that "the ideal gay life is where you don't have to [make declarations]." In effect he was gently reminding Gordon that the conditions for gay people in America were far from ideal—and far from what Gordon's own experience had been. Gordon agreed—but only in theory. He claimed that homosexuality was virtually a nonissue in France and in the other European countries where he had lived, effectively saying that the issue was all relative. Judell decided not to pursue the point, and he gracefully moved to a different topic.[34]

Judell did not editorialize Gordon's minimization of the impact of homophobia on AIDS research, but the damage was done. Kramer, who had never been a fan of Gordon's novels, eventually read the interview himself when it appeared in *Stallion*. He was outraged. As far as he was concerned, gay men like Gordon were part of the reason why so many people were dying of AIDS, and he never forgave him for his damning comments about *The Normal Heart*. Such a reaction was to be expected from Kramer, who was notorious for his acerbic responses to criticism of any kind. But the hostile divide between Gordon and Kramer was based on a much more fundamental difference in their understanding of what it meant to live as a gay man.

For all of his philosophical critiques of American bureaucracy in his protest novels, Gordon had lived his life as an assimilationist. He had thrived as an openly gay man in "straight" communities precisely by *not* rocking the boat. Kramer, by contrast, believed staunchly that gay people needed to "rebel" against the system if they hoped to avoid persecution. As David Bergman has shown, this activist approach of Kramer's was grounded in an essential analogy between the German persecution of Jews and the American response to the AIDS epidemic:

> Borrowing from Hannah Arendt's analysis of the Holocaust, Kramer argues that gay people can avoid genocide only by demanding their political rights. By capitulating to hostile authority because they trusted its essential benevolence, Jews sealed their downfall; and by believing in the responsiveness of the federal government, gays allowed AIDS services and research to be ignored, underfunded, and subjected to unconscionable delays. "Every pariah," Kramer quotes Arendt as saying, "who refused to be a rebel was partly responsible for his position."[35]

For Gordon, who had witnessed firsthand the effects of Nazi Germany, such comparisons were reckless and irresponsible. He resented Kramer pontificating about an event that he had not experienced—just as Kramer, who was on the front lines of another war, resented Gordon for criticizing a community that he was not part of.

Gordon probably did not read all of Kramer's *Faggots*, but he knew enough about it to recognize that it was a far cry from any of his gay novels. "I honestly don't know anything about people sucking cocks in toilets," he would gruffly tell Hulse when he got a review complaining that his novels didn't represent "real" gay life.[36] For Gordon, Kramer was the perfect, choleric embodiment of all the criticism he had received from gay reviewers, and he used Kramer to vent his frustrations. On the one hand, Gordon and Kramer had much in common—both Ivy-educated men from upper-middle-class backgrounds who declaimed against gay ghettoization and promiscuity (and were pilloried by gay critics for doing so). On the other hand, in their approaches to gay politics they were as far apart as two people could be. They were a generation—and a world—apart.

I didn't learn about Kramer's longstanding grudge against Gordon until 2009, more than twenty years after the *Stallion* article was published. I had met Kramer at an LGBT reunion at Yale University—the first of its kind at Yale. Kramer, who was receiving a lifetime achievement award at the reunion, was in jovial spirits at a party the night before his acceptance speech (which, true to form, would rankle members of the audience by lambasting the field of queer studies).[37] After some pleasant chit-chat I asked him what he thought about Gordon Merrick. At that point his demeanor changed instantly, and with a steely look he said simply, "I have no interest in Gordon Merrick." Thinking he had misunderstood my intention, I emailed him a few months later explaining I was writing a biography of Merrick. He responded with a curt reply, all in caps: "GORDON MERRICK DOES NOT INTEREST ME. GOOD LUCK." At the time I had not yet seen the *Stallion* interview. When I later discovered it in my research, I realized how tactless my question to Kramer had been.

NOTES

1. Gordon Merrick, *The Great Urge Downward* (New York: Avon Books, 1984).
2. Page Cuddy to Gordon Merrick, 3 March 1984, GMP, box 18, folder 2. The point about originality was also repeated on the novel's copyright page: "*The Great Urge Downward* is an original publication of Avon Books. This work has never before appeared in book form."
3. Merrick, *The Great Urge Downward*, 69.
4. Brandon Judell, "Orgasm and Organdy: Gordon Merrick, the Champion of Gay Romance," *The Advocate*, October 14, 1986.
5. Merrick, *The Great Urge Downward*, 372.
6. Page Cuddy to Gordon Merrick, 9 September 1983, GMP, box 18, folder 1.
7. Ed Daniels to Gordon Merrick, 27 August 1984, GMP, box 19, folder 7.
8. Christopher Heredia, "Gay Bookstore Founder to Lead A Different Life," *San Francisco Chronicle*, September 8, 2000, http://www.sfgate.com; Richard Labonté, "Richard Labonté's Ten Best and Five Worst Gay Books," in *The Alyson Almanac*, ed. Sasha Alyson, 103–6 (Boston: Alyson, 1993).
9. Richard Summerbell, "Success: Romantic Formulas for Hot-Blooded Best-Sellers," *Body Politic* 87 (1982): 34–35.
10. Gordon Merrick, *A Measure of Madness* (New York: Warner Books, 1986), 199, 209.
11. Susanne Jaffe to Gordon Merrick, 7 October 1985, GMP, box 18, folder 3.
12. Tom Mori to Gordon Merrick, 27 February 1985; Gordon Merrick to Mitch Douglas, 2 & 22 May 1985; Mitch Douglas to Gordon Merrick, 20 August 1985; Susanne Jaffe to Gordon Merrick, 18 December 1985; Gordon Merrick to Mitch Douglas, 31 December 1985, GMP, box 18, folder 3.
13. Charles Hulse to Jeannie Sakol, 24 October 1985, private collection.
14. Gordon Merrick to Mitch Douglas, 23 November 1985, GMP, box 18, folder 3.
15. Mitch Douglas, interview by the author.
16. Mitch Douglas to Gordon Merrick, 11 and 17 December 1985, GMP, box 18, folder 3.
17. John Gerard Champagne, email to the author.

18. Letters from Mario Sartori to Gordon Merrick, 7 and 31 January 1986, 6 February 1986, GMP, box 18, folders 3–4; John Blades, "'Gutsiest' Publisher," *Chicago Tribune*, December 20, 1988.

19. Elmer Luke, email to the author; Patrick O'Connor obituary, *Publishers Weekly*, November 7, 2012; Martin Duberman, *The Worlds of Lincoln Kirstein* (New York: Alfred A. Knopf, 2007), 639n1.

20. Elmer Luke to Gordon Merrick, 21 February 1986; Mitch Douglas to Gordon Merrick, 18 March 1986, GMP, box 18, folder 4.

21. Elmer Luke to Gordon Merrick, 21 February 1986, 4 April 1986, GMP, box 18, folder 4; Elmer Luke, email to the author.

22. Arthur C. Clarke to Gordon Merrick, notes, 10 January 1985, 17 June 1987, GMP, box 19, folder 7. The notes are accompanied by a partial draft of *2061* and part of the screenplay for *2001: A Space Odyssey*.

23. Neil McAleer, *Arthur C. Clarke: The Authorized Biography* (Chicago: Contemporary Books, 1992), 336–37.

24. Charles Hulse to Mitch Douglas, 9 September 1985, GMP, box 18, folder 3; "Pioneering Literary Agent Jed Mattes Dies," *The Advocate*, July 30, 2003, https://www.advocate.com/arts-entertainment/entertainment-news/2003/07/30/pioneering-literary-agent-jed-mattes-dies-9434.

25. Charles Hulse to Mitch Douglas, 16 May 1986; Jeannie Sakol to Gordon Merrick, 28 May 1986; Elmer Luke to Charles Hulse, 12 June 1986, GMP, box 18, folder 4.

26. Charles G. Hulse, *In Tall Cotton* (Secaucus, NJ: Lyle Stuart, 1987).

27. "Literary Guide," *San Francisco Examiner*, June 12, 1988.

28. Gordon Merrick, *A Measure of Madness* (New York: Warner Books, 1986).

29. Elmer Luke to Gordon Merrick, 4 December 1986; Mitch Douglas to Gordon Merrick, 28 May 1987; W. Dahanayake to Gordon Merrick, 24 February 1987, GMP, box 18, folders 5–6.

30. Neil Miller, *Out of the Past: Gay and Lesbian History from 1869 to the Present* (New York: Alyson Books, 2006), 409–25.

31. Andrew Holleran, *Chronicle of a Plague, Revisited: AIDS and Its Aftermath* (New York: Da Capo Press, 2008), 161.

32. Elmer Luke to Gordon Merrick, 4 December 1986.

33. Miller, *Out of the Past*, 411–13; Ray Schultz, "Larry Kramer," in *The Gay & Lesbian Theatrical Legacy*, ed. Billy J. Harbin, Kim Marra, and Robert A. Schanke (Ann Arbor: University of Michigan Press, 2007), 242.

34. Judell, "Conversation with Gordon Merrick," *Stallion*, July 1987.

35. David Bergman, *Gaiety Transfigured: Gay Self-Representation in American Literature* (Madison: University of Wisconsin Press, 1991), 137.

36. David Perry, "A Gentleman from Another Country," *Bay Area Reporter*, June 30, 1988.

37. Raymond Carlson, "First LGBT Reunion Not Controversy-Free," *Yale Daily News*, April 27, 2009.

Chapter Eighteen

Imperfect Freedom

For much of his life Gordon kept a pocket calendar which he used to keep track of appointments while he was traveling. As a result his calendars are full of plays and films that he crammed into his visits to London, Paris, and New York. There are also names of his many friends, whom he met for meals and drinks when he wasn't at the theater. In his 1988 calendar, he penned a simple entry for April 2: "Best of Friends." The entry doesn't specify who these friends are, but most likely it refers to his friends in London whom he was planning to see on an upcoming trip. If so, it was an appointment he never kept, since he died six days earlier in a hospital in Galle.

In the last years of his life Gordon had three circles of close friends, each in Sri Lanka, France, and England. In Galle he and Hulse had become regulars in Arthur C. Clarke's crowd, most of whom had connections to the film or theater industries. One of these was Gerard Raymond, a travel and arts writer who had lived in Sri Lanka before moving to New York. From New York, Raymond kept Gordon apprised of the latest theatrical events, like Kramer's *Normal Heart* ("a hysterical outburst . . . but quite powerful") and Louise Page's *Salonika*, which featured a nude Maxwell Caulfield ("the audience was salivating over his naked buns!").[1] Another friend was Steven Jongeward, a film buff who had worked for a while as Clarke's production assistant. Also part of the circle was George McDonald, an American working in Colombo. He had originally gone to Galle just to visit, but on an impulse he bought a beach house near Gordon when it unexpectedly came up for sale. All three men had read Gordon's gay novels before they met him in person in Sri Lanka, and they took an instant liking to Gordon and Hulse, often going to their "spectacular" beachside home for drinks and dinner.[2]

Being around so many film people gave Gordon the idea to test the waters again for a possible screen adaptation of *The Lord Won't Mind*. He dug around for the screenplay that Steve Warner had written years earlier. When he couldn't find it, he decided to try writing his own screenplay, based on *A Day with Leighton,* his unpublished novel from the 1960s that he had repurposed for *Forth into Light*.³ Gordon had never written a film script, so he turned to Clarke for advice; Clarke lent Gordon his copy of the screenplay for *2001* as a model.⁴ After finishing the script, Gordon sent it to Jongeward, who was now working as an associate producer at MGM Studios, to see if there might be any interest in Hollywood.⁵ Unfortunately nothing came of this latest attempt to get one of his novels on the big screen.

Gordon and Hulse had a second group of friends near their home in Tocqueville, where they continued to spend part of each year. In August 1986, Gordon and Hulse hosted a small party in Normandy for Gordon's seventieth birthday. At the party was the Italian actress Marisa Pavan, who had received an Oscar nomination for her role in the 1955 film adaptation of Tennessee Williams' *The Rose Tattoo*. Pavan had just finished a sixteen-episode stint on the American daytime soap opera *Ryan's Hope*. She was accompanied by her husband, the French actor Jean-Pierre Aumont, who had written a glowing review of Hulse's new novel for the book's dust jacket.

Gordon's closest friends were still those in London, where he now spent most of his time when he wasn't in Sri Lanka or Normandy. The April 2, 1988, entry in his calendar, "Best of Friends," probably refers to Didine and Ginette Spanier, his longtime friends whom he had first met in France in the 1940s and who were now living in London. Gordon's calendars from the 1980s are full of dates with London friends, but Didine—who appears as "Diddles," Gordon's affectionate name for her—is a constant in all his English trips. Besides Hulse, the Spaniers knew Gordon almost better than anyone else. They had followed closely his long, protean literary career, from his early postwar novels to his unexpected gay bestsellers. Through them Gordon was able to connect himself to the young romantic idealist he had once been as a thirty-year-old gay man.

Gordon's friends were especially important to him after he finished writing *A Measure of Madness*. Even before the novel was published, Gordon had begun to realize that he had exhausted the gay romance formula he had developed over the last sixteen years. Even if *Measure* had not been the commercial flop that it was, it showed that Gordon was running out of ideas for gay novels. For as long as he had been a writer, he had written about places and times that he knew well—he didn't know how to write any other way. His homes in Sri Lanka and France were comforting retreats, but they did not give him much material for a gripping story. They certainly did not provide material for the American-centered narratives that his agent and publisher were asking for. Except for his time at Princeton, his adult experience in America had been confined to a relatively short period in the 1930s and '40s, but he had already written about this period in one form or another. Elmer Luke had been strongly encouraging Gordon to write his autobiography, especially something that emphasized his experiences before and during the war. Gordon was reticent about the idea of publicizing the details of his life in such an explicit form, and he doubted whether people would even be interested in reading about them.⁶ Was there anything else he could use from his New York years that would produce an original, marketable novel?

The answer came, unsurprisingly, from his friends. During a visit to New York in April 1986 (the same visit in which he ranted about Larry Kramer to Brandon Judell), Jeannie Sakol had thrown a party for Gordon and Hulse at her apartment on East 48th Street, with several friends and acquaintances in attendance. Mitch Douglas and Elmer Luke were there, as was John Preston, a gay writer who had been an editor of *The Advocate* in the mid-'70s.⁷ Preston was now a successful writer of gay erotica and an advocate for gay sexual health; his writing was one of the earliest examples of gay erotica that depicted men having safe sex. The meeting may have been initially awkward, given how *The Advocate* had treated Gordon years earlier when Preston was at the helm. But Preston had since learned to appreciate Gordon, who had almost single-handedly brought explicit gay sex to the hardcover novel, and so he had gotten Luke to finagle an invitation for him to Sakol's party. A year later, Preston would write a literary essay for *The Advocate*, this time defending Gordon Merrick novels and other "popular" gay writers against the overly academic, "self-important" critics.⁸

At one point during the party Sakol started reminiscing about her days as a copy girl for the *New York Daily Mirror*, a sensationalist tabloid that specialized in lurid stories. One of her first assignments had been the Wayne Lonergan case, a sordid New York crime case in 1944 in which Lonergan, a handsome social climber, had been convicted for brutally killing his wife with a brass candelabra. The case had turned particularly scandalous after information surfaced that Lonergan had a secret gay past involving several affairs with older rich men—including his wife's father, William Burton. Lonergan's death in January 1986 had been all over the news and had revived the tabloid stories that had dogged the case. Sakol was considering writing a nostalgic magazine article about her memories of the trial, and she casually asked Gordon if he had heard about Wayne Lonergan. Gordon was quiet for a few seconds, and then in a quietly suggestive voice said, "Heard about him? I *knew* Wayne Lonergan."⁹

Sakol knew what he meant. Although Gordon rarely dropped the names of his sexual partners from his youth, she inferred from Gordon's response that he had gone to bed with Lonergan. The circumstances made it easy to believe. Lonergan, who was living with Burton as a "kept man" at the same time that Gordon was acting on Broadway, had a reputation for mingling with the city's elite gay men and sleeping with many of them. He was a regular at the Princeton Club and at Broadway theater premieres (and thus likely saw Gordon in *The Man Who Came to Dinner*). He was also a regular at El Morocco, the nightclub next to the apartment building where Gordon had lived for a while with Otis Bigelow and Richard Barr.[10] Photographs of Lonergan taken at the time show why he would have caught Gordon's attention. His face was strikingly similar to Gordon's, though he was taller and more athletically built. One photograph, published years later in *Vanity Fair*, shows him basking in the sun in a tight swimsuit, with smooth bronzed skin and superbly muscled features, In other words, the quintessential Gordon Merrick hero.

Sakol proposed that Gordon write his next novel about the Lonergan affair. This one would be a historical fiction novel set in New York City in the years before the war. Gordon told Sakol that he "loved the idea," though inwardly he was ambivalent. All of his novels had been autobiographical to some extent, but he had never written straightforward historical fiction. But Sakol was insistent. She suggested a working plan by which she would be in charge of collecting research about Lonergan, while Gordon would do the actual writing. She aggressively pitched the book to Douglas and Luke, who were conveniently in the same room. When Gordon later privately asked his agent for his opinion, Douglas was unequivocal in his support of the project.[11]

In many ways, a Lonergan novel seemed like the perfect opportunity for Gordon to break out of the gay romance "rut" while still drawing from his personal experiences. In fact, he wasn't the only one considering such a project. The story's gay angle, and its connections to the early New York gay scene, had prompted Christopher Isherwood to consider briefly the possibility of using it as a literary subject, and James Baldwin had said that *Giovanni's Room* was based on an earlier fictionalization of the Lonergan affair.[12] Historical novels were trending well in the publishing industry—Dominick Dunne's *The Two Mrs. Grenvilles*, about the William Woodward murder, had recently been a smash hit—and there was the real possibility that Gordon could break into the hardcover market again. Hulse also thought that Gordon should write the novel, though for different reasons. He had been increasingly concerned about Gordon's weakening health, and he thought that a new project would reinvigorate him and "shape him up."[13]

Gordon finally agreed, and Sakol wasted no time collecting materials. Shortly after Gordon and Hulse returned to France from New York, they received stacks of news clippings and magazine articles, and several historical novels (including the Dunne book), to help Gordon get started. Sakol did not refrain from offering suggestions of her own for the novel—most of them terrible. She proposed using *Citizen Kane* as a model for Lonergan, using a baseball signed by Babe Ruth as the story's "Rosebud" device. She also thought Gordon could work in his experiences as an OSS spy and perhaps even a Billie Holiday cameo. She had a penchant for conspiracy theories (she was writing her own historical novel about the "secret" truth of Alexander Hamilton's death) and suggested a version of the story in which Lonergan had actually been framed for his wife's death. Gordon graciously thanked Sakol for her ideas—and used none of them. Within a few weeks he had an outline of the novel and fifty pages of writing, and by September of that year he had drafted most of the novel, which he named *The Good Life*.[14] For the first time in his long career, his agent and editor thought that his first choice of a title was fine. Encouraged by his team, and cheered on as always by Hulse, Gordon hoped that, for the third time in his life, he would be able to reinvent himself as a novelist.

Sadly, Gordon was not able to do any work on *The Good Life* beyond a rough draft. His health problems continued to worsen, and he spent much of 1987 confined to his bed and making frequent trips to the doctor's office. His doctor had increased the dosage of his blood pressure medication, a side effect of which was weakness and fatigue.[15] But these chronic problems were minor compared to what was happening to Gordon's body. Although he may not have known it when he and Hulse returned to Sri Lanka in November 1986, Gordon had lung cancer.

The draft that Gordon *was* able to finish shows that Luke had been right about an autobiography. The most colorful and entertaining parts of the novel are the episodes that recreate Lonergan's initiation into the gay theater scene in the 1930s.[16] Here Gordon was able to give free rein to his memories of being a young handsome actor in New York, and since he was writing historical fiction he decided not to use fictionalized names for most of the people he had known. (He did use fictional names for Lonergan and Burton, though he explained in the foreword that this was only a legal practicality.) He featured his old friend Clifton Webb (and Webb's mother) as he had done in some of his earlier novels, but this time he used Webb's real name and referred to the actual shows that Webb had performed. In the novel Webb invites Perry (Lonergan) to a lavish party at his Park Avenue apartment, where he manages to sequester him in a bedroom and give him a blow job. Afterward Webb gallantly escorts Perry out of the room and thanks him with his trademark wit: "As far as I'm concerned, you're a hit. I'll give you a good review."[17]

Gordon also had Moss Hart, the playwright who had launched his brief Broadway career, appear at the same party. He gave Hart a fleeting cameo that deviously hinted at Hart's rumored affair with his actors (including himself), without writing anything that could be taken definitively:

> Rodney's playwright, Moss Hart, was there, glittering with wit and gold. Perry's ring caught his eye when they were standing near each other, and he asked to see it. . . .

"A pretty bauble," he commented, handing it back. "Do you own gold mines?"
"Only one."
"Much depleted, no doubt." Moss Hart looked at him with interest. "You're not an actor, I hope?"
"No."
"Then it's safe to talk to you. I can't blink at an actor without his thinking I've hired him."[18]

Gordon had told Hulse that he had slept with Hart during *The Man Who Came to Dinner*, but other people who had been part of the gay theater scene at the time would have also caught the sly inference in this passage. One of these people would have been Otis Bigelow, who also makes a cameo appearance in the novel:

At one party a guy named Otis approached him. He was beautiful rather than handsome, but Perry had felt something cold and calculating about him that put him off.
"I want to go to bed with you," Otis said as if he were offering Perry the answers to all his prayers. . . . . "Will you take me home with you?"
"I'd love to, but I can't. I'm staying at the Y."
"Oh. Somebody said you were a Wall Street wonder. I thought you were a bit young." He switched his seduction off like a light. "My room isn't as good as the Y. We'd both better start hustling."[19]

Hulse undoubtedly loved reading this part.

The theater scenes in *The Good Life* are an endless parade of famous figures that Gordon had seen or met in the 1930s: Cole Porter, Tallulah Bankhead, Noël Coward, Marlene Dietrich, Lucius Beebe. And, because the historical Lonergan had found his way into other gay networks in New York, Gordon was able to include his longtime friend Glenway Wescott. He had never fictionalized Wescott before in any of his novels, but the Lonergan plot gave him the excuse to present Wescott in his own person, together with his longtime partner Monroe Wheeler and the photographer George Platt Lynes, who in 1939 was still in a three-way relationship with Wescott and Wheeler. In the novel Lynes asks Perry to pose for a series of male nude photographs, an event that may have occurred with the historical Lynes and Lonergan but has not been documented. Still, Gordon gave pride of place in this section of the novel to Wescott, whom he recreated in loving detail: "He made a point of spending some time with Glenway Wescott, the first famous author he'd ever met. He was a pixieish man with great personal magnetism and a clever, lively air. Perry impressed himself for being able to converse so easily with him." This was more Gordon's impression of Wescott than Lonergan's, and it was a fitting tribute to the man who had encouraged his writing at a crucial moment in his life. Wescott would never read this tribute, since he died only a few months later in his home in New Jersey.

Gordon also gave himself a small role in the novel, although he didn't use his own name for the character. He called the younger version of himself "Rodney"—his father's name, and the name he had used for his fictionalized self in *The Vallency Tradition* three decades earlier. In the novel, Perry meets Rodney at the YMCA, where both men are staying:

> One was an actor with the improbable name of Rodney Fairfield. He looked a bit like Robert Taylor, and Rodney thought Perry looked like Tyrone Power. The two movie stars were quickly fast friends. Rodney was going to be in the new Kaufman and Hart show after Christmas starring Fredric March at the Radio City Center.[20]

Rodney becomes a helpful guide to the New York gay scene, taking Perry to private parties and teaching him how to dress for dates with rich older men. He also has sex with Perry. This would be the closest that Gordon would come to admitting in public that something had once happened between him and Lonergan.

Perhaps the experience of writing *The Good Life* would have warmed Gordon to the idea of writing a straightforward autobiography, though his ingrained sense of privacy would likely have kept him from including many personal details. As it so happened, Gordon was contacted out of the blue one day in 1987 by a thirty-year-old man named Ricardo Hunter Garcia, who was interested in writing Gordon's biography. Garcia was a literary agent in New York who would later become famous in the Los Angeles gay scene for his ubiquity in the city's gay media. He became well known for his gay news columns, his public-access television show (*The Gay Boy Ric TV Show*), and his subversive gay takes on pop/rap music, including an anti-Eminem single, "A Song for Eminem (You Don't Want to Fuck with Gay Boy)," that he performed on *The Howard Stern Show*.[21] He was also a huge Gordon Merrick fan. A military brat, he had first discovered *The Lord Won't Mind* at a military base library in Spain, where he was attending high school. He was so inspired by it that he decided to apply to Princeton, the same school that the novel's Charlie attended, and he became a member of Princeton's Class of 1979. He was also a big admirer of Hulse's *In Tall Cotton*, which he had discovered independently. He had read Hulse's novel and been "blown away" by it, and it was only afterward that he noticed the dedication page with Gordon's name. His love for Gordon's novels—and his industriousness—led him to hunt down Gordon's telephone number in Sri Lanka. Gordon was charmed by the smart, earnest young man, and he candidly talked with him about his life and writing, providing details that Garcia later used in his writings and interviews about Merrick. Gordon happily "drafted" Garcia as his "official obituary/biographer."[22]

Garcia's duties as Gordon's obituary writer were called upon earlier than he expected. On March 27, 1988, Gordon died in the main hospital in Galle, from complications from lung cancer. A month later, obituaries appeared in the *New York Times*, *New York Native*, and the *International Herald Tribune*—all the result of Garcia's persistent efforts.[23]

Hulse was devastated. He had witnessed firsthand Gordon's deteriorating health, but he was not prepared for the shock of Gordon's death. The loss was made only more painful by the hospital's medical staff, who treated Hulse like a casual acquaintance rather than Gordon's life partner. For the rest of his life, Hulse remembered how he received the news about Gordon's death. "Would that be Mr. Hulse?" a hospital staff member had asked on the telephone. When Hulse answered in the affirmative, the staff member curtly informed him, "Your patient has expired. Can you please pay the bill and pick up the remains?" Feeling a combination of grief and rage, Hulse had a quick reply: "You certainly have your priorities straight."[24] The reality of Gordon's death made clear another painful truth. For all that Gordon and Hulse had done during their thirty-two years together to establish themselves as a couple, they were not recognized as married or even as relatives of each other. Years earlier Gordon had taken care to incorporate his assets together with Hulse's, so that all of his belongings would be in Hulse's name if and when he died. This protected Hulse financially, but it did not mean that he would be treated as a spouse in other ways. When Princeton's alumni magazine printed an obituary for Gordon, Hulse's name was not included.

Hulse had many friends who understood the significance of the loss, and many of them reached out in the way that they could from the other side of the world. Leonard Cohen sent Hulse a letter containing a single sentence: "I often think of you."[25] For a while, Hulse felt the loss deeply. He missed the notes saying "I love you" that Gordon used to leave all around the house for no particular reason. He especially missed the endearments they would always say to each other ("darling," "baby"). Ironically, critics had often mocked such language in Gordon's novels as sappy and affected—when in fact it had been an accurate account of Gordon's personality in a relationship. Hulse started using such endearments for everyone he knew, since, as he put it, "there was no longer anyone to use them for."

One way that Hulse coped with the loss was by keeping busy. He flew to San Francisco in June to see his family, and while there he was asked to do a public reading and book signing for *In Tall Cotton* at A Different Light Bookstore.[26] He was also interviewed by David Perry for the *Bay Area Reporter*, the city's leading gay newspaper. Unsurprisingly, the interview became a sort of retrospective on Gordon's life and career. Hulse revealed many details about their life together, including the circumstances of their first meeting in Paris in 1956. The interview covered other topics, including Hulse's discomfort with the word "gay" (he preferred referring to himself as "queer") and the evolution of the Castro district as the city's gay center. Eventually the discussion turned to the subject of AIDS. Hulse was remarkably candid about the subject—in a way that Gordon had never been—and expressed how the epidemic had personally affected his own attitude toward gay relationships: "I've lost more friends from AIDS than I can count. . . . If any good has come from this . . . it is that people are having more serious relationships. . . . I know, it's hard sometimes. It's difficult, and it's so easy to say 'forget it.' But that's what we're all looking for, a companion. Someone to share with. So I say, when you find someone you love, hang on."[27]

Hulse also kept busy by picking up the Lonergan novel that Gordon had left unfinished, with the aim of getting it published. He got some help with the editing and revising from Sakol, and Douglas was perfectly willing to get the novel published. However, the manuscript was in need of serious editing; it was long and bloated in some places and confusingly terse in others. Gordon had been struggling with the focus of the narrative, and neither Hulse nor Sakol knew how to fix the deep structural problems in the manuscript. Douglas grew frustrated with the successive drafts that Hulse sent him, which he found unpublishable, and the situation nearly threatened to end their friendship.[28] The manuscript sat idly for nearly ten years until Hulse, who had become a shrewd businessman, struck a deal with Alyson Books, a small publishing firm that had recently started specializing in gay books. In an effort to expand their catalogue of gay titles, the firm proposed reissuing all of Gordon's gay novels, with glossy, updated new covers. Hulse agreed, with the stipulation that they print the Lonergan novel. In 1997, The Good Life appeared in gay bookstores across the country. Both Gordon and Hulse were listed as authors, and Sakol and Douglas were thanked on the dedication page.

Hulse did another thing that helped keep Gordon's legacy alive. In 1991 he contacted William L. Joyce, the librarian for Rare Books and Special Collections at Princeton University. Hulse proposed donating a collection of Gordon's letters, manuscripts, and photographs to the library for the purpose of preserving them and making them available to scholars who might be interested in studying them in the future. Joyce, who was an enthusiastic archivist, heartily welcomed the proposal, and he promptly put together an agreement by which Hulse could donate Gordon's materials without losing his legal rights to their content.[29] Hulse proceeded to gather as many of Gordon's professional letters and documents as he could find, and he contacted Avon Books to get the manuscripts of Gordon's novels.[30] He collected other "artifacts" as well, such as passports, daily calendars, news clippings, contracts,

Figure 18.1 Charles Hulse being interviewed about Gordon Merrick by the author, Galle 2012.
Source: Estate of Charles Hulse. Photo by Paul Hinkle.

Figure 18.2 Charles Hulse, March 2012.
Source: Estate of Charles Hulse. Photo by Paul Hinkle.

playbills—anything that would help flesh out the variegated, peripatetic life that Gordon had led. Hulse reasoned that, although interest in Gordon's work had cooled for the moment, a future reader might be interested in tracing the life of his longtime partner.

NOTES

1. Gerard Raymond to Gordon Merrick, 24 May 1985, GMP, box 19, folder 7.
2. Gerard Raymond, email to the author; Steven Jongeward, email to the author; George McDonald, email to the author.
3. Gordon Merrick to Mitch Douglas, 16 July 1984; Mitch Douglas to Gordon Merrick, 26 July 1984, GMP, box 18, folder 2; Charles Hulse to Gerard Raymond, January 8, 1986, private collection.
4. Arthur C. Clarke to Gordon Merrick, notes, 10 January 1985, 17 June 1987, GMP, box 19, folder 7.
5. Gerard Raymond to Gordon Merrick, 24 May 1985, GMP, box 19, folder 7.
6. Gordon Merrick, interview by Brandon Judell.
7. Mitch Douglas to Jeannie Sakol, 29 April 1986, GMP, box 18, folder 4; Elmer Luke to Gordon Merrick, 4 December 1986, GMP, box 18, folder 5.
8. John Preston, *My Life as a Pornographer & Other Indecent Acts* (New York: Masquerade Books, 1993); John Preston, "Gay Genre Writing: The Power and Politics of Our Popular Literature," *The Advocate*, May 26, 1987.
9. Dominick Dunne, "The Talented Mr. Lonergan," *Vanity Fair*, July 2000; Albin Krebs, "Wayne Lonergan, 67, Killer of Heiress Wife," *New York Times*, January 3, 1986; Jeannie Sakol, interview by the author.
10. Allan Levine, *Details Are Unprintable: Wayne Lonergan and the Sensational Café Society Murder* (Lanham, MD: Lyons Press, 2020).
11. Jeannie Sakol to Gordon Merrick, 22 May 1986, 15 June 1986; Mitch Douglas to Gordon Merrick, 30 June 1986, GMP, box 18, folder 4.
12. Jaime Harker, *Middlebrow Queer: Christopher Isherwood in America* (Minneapolis: University of Minnesota Press, 2013), 18.
13. Jeannie Sakol to Mitch Douglas, 21 June 1986; Gordon Merrick to Mitch Douglas, 21 May 1986, 8 July 1986; Mitch Douglas to Gordon Merrick, 30 June 1986, GMP, box 18, folders 4–5; Sakol, interview by the author.
14. Jeannie Sakol to Gordon Merrick, 28 May 1986, 15 June 1986, 20 and 30 July 1986; Mitch Douglas to Gordon Merrick, 31 July 1986, 19 September 1986; Gordon Merrick to Mitch Douglas, 27 October 1986, GMP, box 18, folders 4–5.
15. Trevor C. B. Stamp to Gordon Merrick, 9 April 1986, GMP, box 18, folder 4.
16. The gay literary historian Drewey Wayne Gunn, who was not otherwise a fan of Merrick's novels, finds this aspect of *The Good Life* to be what sets it apart from other Lonergan novels. "Wayne Lonergan's Long Shadow," Mysterical-E, Spring 2017, http://mystericale.com/article/wayne-lonergans-long-shadow.

17. Gordon Merrick and Charles G. Hulse, *The Good Life* (Los Angeles: Alyson Books, 1997), 103.
18. Merrick and Hulse, *The Good Life*, 100–101.
19. Merrick and Hulse, *The Good Life*, 35.
20. Merrick and Hulse, *The Good Life*, 34.
21. "Memorial: Richard H. Garcia '79," *Princeton Alumni Weekly*, January 16, 2013; "Passages: Columnist Gay Boy Ric," *Windy City Times*, February 25, 2004; Stephen Saban, "Remembering Ric," *WOW Report*, August 22, 2005, https://worldofwonder.net/remembering-ric.
22. Ricardo Hunter Garcia to the Editor of *OUT* magazine, 25 May 1996, Gordon Merrick student file.
23. "Gordon Merrick, 71, Reporter and Novelist," *New York Times*, April 23, 1988; Obituary for Gordon Merrick, *New York Native*, May 9, 1988; Obituary for Gordon Merrick, *International Herald Tribune*, April 28, 1988.
24. Charles Hulse, interview by the author. The paragraphs that follow are also taken from this interview.
25. Leonard Cohen to Charles Hulse, 3 October 1988, GMP, box 19, folder 1.
26. "Literary Guide," *San Francisco Examiner*, June 22, 1988.
27. David Perry, "A Gentleman from Another Country," *Bay Area Reporter*, June 30, 1986.
28. Letters from Mitch Douglas to Charles Hulse, 22 February 1989, 17 April 1989, 8 and 18 May 1989, 16 June 1989; Charles Hulse to Mitch Douglas, 24 March 1989, 3 May 1989, 26 June 1989, 2 August 1989, GMP, box 18, folder 7.
29. William L. Joyce to Charles Hulse, July 20, 1991, photocopy given to the author by Jeannie Sakol.
30. Charles Hulse to David Highfill (Avon Books), 11 September 1991, photocopy given to the author by Jeannie Sakol.

Afterword

GAY LITERARY CANONS

Literary canons are tricky things. They present themselves as lists of books that people *should* read, but just as often they are impassioned defenses of books that people have *already* read. I remember being a student in Harold Bloom's Shakespeare seminar at Yale at the same time his book *The Western Canon* was published. For months afterward, whenever I mentioned Bloom's class, the common reaction was an exasperated, "Oh God, *the Western canon!*" Bloom had ruffled feathers with his characteristic potshots at literary critics, but what truly riled the academy was the book's appendix: a breathtaking forty-page list of 850 writers whom he deemed "essential" reading.[1] As expected, it was the omissions that got the most attention. *How can the very first English novel not make the cut? Why are Livy and Tacitus not considered literature? So there was nothing important written between 300–1200? Where the hell is Canada?*

Gay literary canons are even trickier, since they provoke the question of what makes something a "gay" work. Moreover, since there are far fewer gay literary works than nongay ones, any significant omission can seem like a grave oversight. This is likely to be the experience of some readers of Sharon Malinowski and Christa Brelin's *Gay & Lesbian Literary Companion*, a beautifully produced volume that includes profiles of forty-five gay and lesbian writers. Malinowski and Brelin do not call their selection of writers a "canon," but they do assert that their list constitutes "a representative selection of writers of lesbian and gay literature."[2] They claim to have started with a list of over a thousand gay and lesbian writers, which an advisory board narrowed down to two hundred before the editors selected the final forty-five. (The book does not include these lists, though it's difficult to imagine a list of more than a thousand gay and lesbian writers before 1995.) Among these forty-five are many of the usual suspects (Oscar Wilde, Virginia Woolf, James Baldwin, Radclyffe Hall) as well as some lesser-known writers (May Sarton, Manuel Puig, Jewelle Gomez, Malcolm Boyd). Gordon Merrick is never mentioned in the book's six hundred pages, but neither is E. M. Forster—not even in the chapter on Christopher Isherwood, whose writing is represented solely by a short poem.

To be sure, it is unfair to criticize an anthology too harshly for its omissions. As the literary historian Gregory Woods puts it in *A History of Gay Literature*, "all canons are naturally élitist, more exclusive than they are inclusive." His book is a case in point. His observation about canons and exclusivity opens a chapter on gay male popular fiction, in which he proposes to look beyond the canonical gay texts that have "received various academic imprimaturs" and consider those works in which "homosexual men have been represented in the past by authors who were addressing large, popular audiences." This would seem the perfect setup for a discussion of Merrick, but instead the chapter focuses mostly on Dashiell Hammett and Ian Fleming—neither of whom were gay or wrote gay fiction. In the chapter's last paragraph Woods seems on the verge of mentioning Merrick when he acknowledges the value of gay writers who appropriated the romance novel genre to write about gay men. Again he dodges the opportunity: "Gay literature as a whole has been greatly enriched by such work as . . . the gay male romances of women novelists like Patricia Nell Warren and Chris Hunt."[3] Merrick's name never appears at all in the chapter or in the rest of the book's 450 pages.

In these cases the omission of Merrick starts to feel like a personal slight. After reading *A History of Gay Literature*, I did some research to see if there were any special circumstances that might explain why Woods never mentions Merrick in this book—or in his four other books on gay literature. Did Merrick write a bad review of one of Woods' books? Did Merrick caricature a friend of his in a novel? Did Merrick spill a drink on him at a party? So far nothing has emerged. In fact, Woods was very much adhering to the norm when he failed to include Merrick. Most similar studies, including some that make even bigger claims about comprehensiveness, also exclude Merrick or consign him to an appendix. In such books any mention of Merrick is actually a surprise, despite the fact that he was extremely well known among gay readers in the last three decades of the twentieth century—so much so that gay writers regularly used his name as a shorthand for comments about literature.[4]

The strangeness of this exclusion is best summarized by one of the few gay histories that *does* discuss Merrick at length. In his discerning essay on Merrick for the *Gay & Lesbian Literature* volume, Bill McCauley begins right off the bat with a stark assessment of Merrick's critical misfortunes:

Perhaps the most remarkable fact about the critical response to Gordon Merrick's novels is that there is virtually none. Despite the substantial corpus of 13 novels, one of which (*The Lord Won't Mind*) remained on *The New York Times* best seller list for 16 weeks, critics and reviewers have remained strangely silent about Merrick's work. This could be dismissed as the elitism that has long accompanied the boundary between "high" and "popular" culture, but contemporary theory has sufficiently eroded that boundary so that recent works on gay literature would be expected to deal with Merrick. Such has not been the case. Works such as *The Gay and Lesbian Literary Companion*, *The Lesbian and Gay Studies Reader*, *Gaiety Transfigured: Gay Self-Representation in American Literature*, *Gay Men's Literature in the Twentieth Century: A Queer Reader*, and *The Gay and Lesbian Literary Heritage*, all published in the 1990s, make no reference to him. When Merrick is mentioned at all, it is usually in a dismissive and pejorative fashion.[5]

To McCauley's copious list can be added *The Cambridge Companion to Gay and Lesbian Writing*, *The Encyclopedia of Contemporary LGBTQ Literature of the United States*, along with the books by Malinowski, Brelin, and Woods. Reed Woodhouse's *Unlimited Embrace: A Canon of Gay Fiction, 1945–1995* does mention Merrick briefly, but only to explain why he is not really a gay author.[6]

McCauley has a few persuasive theories as to why literary historians struggle with Merrick. One explanation is that the critics have a hard time with Merrick's refusal to follow the conventions of gay literature. Unlike gay characters in other canonical gay novels, Merrick's gay men are simultaneously inside and outside the "straight" heterosexual world that seeks to define them according to rigid (and inaccurate) categories of gender and sexuality. However, as McCauley argues, Merrick's novels appear confused about gay identity because their *characters* are confused about gay identity. They struggle to find a language, a "code of communication," through which they can comprehend their romantic and erotic feelings toward other men while still coping with the reality of their other socially defined roles (gender, age, class, family). For McCauley, the fact that Merrick represents this complex negotiation of identity shows that he was "well ahead of his time." His other explanation for Merrick's exclusion is that critics are simply put off by the sex scenes. For these readers, the graphic accounts of men having sex—of which the paperback covers are a constant reminder—automatically relegates the novels to "pulpy" romance or "soft-porn."[7] Thus there is a poignant irony in the fact that gay literary critics who raised a ruckus over the expurgation of graphic sex scenes from *Brokeback Mountain* and *God's Own Country* take a different view when gay sex is depicted in a novel.

While McCauley's theories do much to explain the critical aversion to Merrick, I think there is another reason—one that has to do with broader, more entrenched conventions of gay historiography. With few exceptions, histories of gay literature routinely draw a line between pre-Stonewall and post-Stonewall writing. According to this periodization, gay novels written before the Stonewall riots of 1969 are more covert and pessimistic, while those written afterward represent gay people more honestly and positively. One of the earliest articulations of this history was made by Robert Ferro, one of the members of the Violet Quill. In 1987 Ferro was invited to Oberlin College to speak about gay literature, and he delivered a long, thoughtful lecture on the current state of gay literature in relation to what had come before. For Ferro, Stonewall was *the* definitive event that shaped the development of gay writing:

> In 1969, a group of patrons at a New York gay bar called the Stonewall replied with thrown bottles and resistance when police, as was routine, tried for the second or third time that night to shut the place down. . . . Known now as the Stonewall Rebellion, this event marked the beginning of gay liberation, ushering in a period of unprecedented political and literary activity in the gay world. Most important, it marks a major shift in self-perception from the myth of the victim to activist. The ensuing twenty years have seen a general restructuring of the gay ethos by a growing army of writers whose work has helped to redefine the psychological, social, sexual, spiritual make up of American gay people.[8]

While this version of gay literary history has been modified over the last thirty-five years, its basic contours have proved remarkably durable. Ferro's essay appears in a book whose very subtitle, *The Emergence of Gay Writing after Stonewall*, reinforces his idea of a new "gay ethos" in literature after 1969. Other books, like Claude Summers' *Gay Fictions: Wilde to Stonewall* and Byrne Fone's *A Road to Stonewall*, likewise have titles that present as axiomatic a categorical divide between pre- and post-Stonewall gay writing.[9] Even studies that have problematized the simplistic characterization of pre-Stonewall fiction—Michael Bronski's *Pulp Friction*, Patricia Juliana Smith's *The Queer Sixties*, Drewey Wayne Gunn and Jaime Harker's *1960s Gay Pulp Fiction*—continue to use 1969 as an epochal marker and continue to refer to pre-Stonewall gay novels as "pulps."[10] Most recently, the *Oxford Research Encyclopedia of Literature* gave its own venerable imprimatur to this scheme, drawing a line between "closeted" postwar gay writers and "openly gay" post-Stonewall writers.[11]

The problem is that Merrick does not fit into these categories. In fact, his work highlights what the conventional periodization of gay literature oversimplifies or leaves out. Merrick's gay characters are neither "victims" nor "activists"—the two roles that Ferro repeatedly cites as the two sides of pre- and post-Stonewall gay fiction. Charlie and Peter, like most other gay characters in Merrick's novels who get a happy ending, manage to carve out a life as an openly gay "married" couple in a predominantly heterosexual society that has *not* been shaped by Stonewall. As I have shown in this biography, this was not a fantasy for Gordon; it was a lived reality. Even when Stonewall occurred, he was living on a Greek island that was largely unaffected by events in America. In essence, Merrick's gay novels do not seem influenced much by Stonewall because *he* was not influenced much by Stonewall. Ironically, his one gay protagonist who *does* live in a post-Stonewall America—Walter Makin in *An Idol for Others*—is also the one who has a truly tragic ending. Just as Merrick's novels show that not all gay men were outcast and miserable before Stonewall, they also show that Stonewall did not immediately change everything for everyone.

Most scholars have responded to the challenges that Merrick poses to conventional gay literary history by simply refusing to acknowledge him. Others try to cram Merrick into the Stonewall narrative, either by fudging his dates or misrepresenting his novels. For example, Felice Picano moves Merrick forward in time by nearly a decade in order to situate him "outside the canon" of serious gay literature, dating his switch from mainstream novels to gay romances in the "late 1970s."[12] Rob McDonald, on the other hand, tries to move Merrick's gay novels backward, in order to group them with the "dystopian novels" of Gore Vidal. He then faults *The Lord Won't Mind* for being unrealistic, claiming that "most of the action occurs during the Great Depression and World War II, but we see little poverty, and nobody loses anybody during the war."[13] (In fact, the entire novel takes place *between* these events.)

The most common, and perhaps the most pernicious, misrepresentation of Merrick's gay novels is that they are "soft-core pornography" or poorly written "pulp." Reviewers of gay novels who were offended by graphic sex scenes had often used the "pornography" label to criticize works by Richard Amory and John Rechy, and in Merrick they found an easy target. The "pulp" label is even more misleading. The fact is that most gay readers did not register Merrick's novels as "pulp" when they appeared in the 1970s, and his writing is perceptibly different than the works typically categorized as such.[14] Merrick had developed early in his career a concise, Fitzgeraldesque style of prose, which he maintained throughout his life. Stylistically his writing is not in the same league as Andrew Holleran or Edmund White, but it is clearly more refined than Amory or Larry Kramer. Even when Merrick's editors and publishers complained about the content of his novels, they always praised the quality of his writing. Bernard Geis, who published *The Lord Won't Mind* and its sequel, afterward revealed that, of all his writers, Merrick had saved him the most time since the polished quality of his writing meant that Geis never had to worry about line editing.[15]

Literary canons evolve, however, and over the past decade different ways of constructing gay literary history have emerged. The fiftieth anniversary of Stonewall prompted many scholars to reevaluate the conventional distinction between pre- and post-Stonewall gay culture. In a perceptive essay on gay publishing in the 1960s and '70s, the prolific gay fiction writer Victor J. Banis cautioned that "the dividing line [between pre- and post-Stonewall] does not work in the realm of gay fiction."[16] While the impulse to rethink gay periodization is more common now, such reconfigurations had already been around. No less an authority than Richard Hall warned in 1977 that the categories created by gay literary critics had little to do with what—or how— gay people were reading.[17] One of the most original gay literary "canons" appeared in 2004, as a single paragraph in *Queer Street*, James McCourt's sprawling history of twentieth-century gay life. Instead of dividing gay writers around Stonewall, McCourt sees their works rippling across the epochs. His significant writers are those who embody a distinct mode of gay representation and who, like St. Augustine, "mimicked" themselves in their work:

T. S. Eliot, W. H. Auden, Tennessee Williams, Truman Capote, Paul Bowles, Gore Vidal, James Baldwin, William Burroughs, Coleman Dowell, Alfred Chester, and later Frank O'Hara, James Schuyler, John Ashbery and James Merrill, together with Boyd McDonald (redactor of the notorious Straight-to-Hell testimonies of toilet-wall queer America), John Rechy and the amazing and anomalous literary shipwreck that was Gordon Merrick.

The placement of Merrick at the end of this list is stunning. McCourt's nautical metaphor at first seems like a slam, but in truth he is fascinated by Merrick. As he sees it, conventional gay histories or genres cannot explain the phenomenon of Merrick's novels, and so he can only document their "transgressiveness" by representing them as a dizzying mess of disparate literary influences: "The John Marquand-meets-Frank Harris, D. H. Lawrence and Oscar Wilde for-an-evening-of-pornographic-blackjack sagas of the hilarious Gordon Merrick . . . rather stirring romances [that turn] into queer pulp trash and [turn] back again."[18]

Like McCourt, Richard Drake also sees Merrick's gay novels as resisting classification. Yet it is precisely because of such strangeness that Drake gives Merrick a prominent place in *The Gay Canon*. Drake, who studied at St. John's College ("one of the Great Books schools"), takes to heart Bloom's notion of canonicity, arguing that "great"—i.e., canonical—works are those that possess "a strangeness, a mode of originality that either cannot be assimilated, or that so assimilates us that we cease to see it as strange." *The Lord Won't Mind* unquestionably fits the bill. Drake locates the novel's strangeness in its *earnestness*, its utter unapologeticness in offering "the perfectly told love story, surrendering its heroes to passion's convulsions and taking us, the readers, along with them." Further, in an interesting turn, Drake claims that the reason for the novel's canonicity and critical notoriety are one and the same: "People love to hate this book because it spurns pretensions to high art. But that's precisely how *The Lord Won't Mind* manages to leap over more ambitious works, quickly forgettable in their sameness, and remain perfectly canonical: wholly familiar, yet startlingly strange and new."[19]

As critical distance from Stonewall has grown, scholars have also been able to view more sympathetically those works that gay activists in the 1970s and '80s—who had their own reasons for making a distinction between pre- and post-Stonewall gay culture—saw as retrograde. In this new climate the complexity of Merrick's novels has been better appreciated. Ian Young, in his insightful history of gay paperback covers, gave significant attention to the Avon editions of Merrick's novels. Instead of ridiculing their sensuous Victor Gadino covers, he placed them in the larger context of twentieth-century gay paperbacks to show how innovative and progressive they really were, "dispens[ing] utterly with the Solitaries, Looming Presences and Looking Away conventions of the past."[20] In his beautifully produced, critically praised collection of essays on early gay fiction, *The Golden Age of Gay Fiction*, the literary historian Drewey Wayne Gunn included an essay devoted to Merrick's gay novels.[21] Even Picano, who had earlier kicked Merrick out of the canon, recently admitted in an interview that, had it not been for Merrick's early gay novels, "there probably still wouldn't be any gay literature today."[22]

At the same time, gay *politics* have changed over the last fifty years. While activists like Randy Wicker had made strong arguments about the radical potential of gay liberation in the 1970s, there can be little question that the "assimilationist" side of the debate was the public face of gay activism in the twenty-first century—most visibly in the fight for same-sex marriage. This development has helped Merrick's critical fortunes. One of the clearest—and most colorful—documents of this trend is William J. Mann's *Gay Pride*, a collection of vignettes that was written at the same time the same-sex marriage battle was raging in Massachusetts. Mann organizes the book around 101 "fabulous reasons" why gay men and lesbians can be proud. Included in the list are Alexander the Great, Ellen DeGeneres, ACT UP, Alan Turing, Frida Kahlo, *The Laramie Project*, Dance Music, Provincetown—and Gordon Merrick. Like so many others, Mann's first gay book was *The Lord Won't Mind*, which he discovered as a teenager at his local Waldenbooks. While he acknowledges that Merrick's novels can at times be "turgid and stereotypical," he ultimately deems them to be "affirming." As an adult, Mann read the cranky 1970 *New York Times* review of *Lord* that predicted it would "set homosexuality back at least twenty years." Mann flatly states this was wrong: "In truth, Merrick's books . . . did just the opposite." In explaining why Merrick's gay novels are on his list, he places them firmly in the gay literary canon: "At a time when homosexuality in literature was still largely treated as a closet identity that could only end in tragedy, Merrick wrote with celebration (and juicy details) about gay relationships that ended happily. His books anticipated the rise of the Violet Quill writers and a self-affirming gay literature by the end of the decade. And they made a generation of adolescents like myself giddily aware that we weren't the only ones in the world with that great urge downward—and that, ultimately, the Lord wouldn't mind."[23]

It has certainly also helped that "romance" is no longer a dirty word in academic writing about gay literature. In 2016 the prolific lesbian romance writer Len Barot wrote an essay on queer romance for *Romance Fiction and American Culture*, an academic volume of essays that took seriously the genre of romance fiction. In her essay, Barot argues that romance novels, *especially* gay ones, played a uniquely important role in "reflect[ing] the current sociopolitical nature of the community that it represents (and seeks to reach) and portends the emerging forces shaping the future direction of that same community." She singled out Merrick's novels as a vital factor in the historical struggle to normalize and affirm gay relationships: "Mainstream publishing had taken the first steps toward representing queer relationships not as clandestine affairs doomed to end in failure, but love stories culminating in emotional and physical fulfillment."[24] Since Barot's essay appeared, hundreds of LGBTQ romance novels have been published, representing an immense variety of contexts and characters. The venerable Lambda Literary Foundation has given awards in the categories of gay and lesbian romance since 2006.

In 2020, the fiftieth anniversary of the publication of *The Lord Won't Mind*, the *Gay & Lesbian Review*, arguably the preeminent periodical for reviews of LGBTQ books, featured an article on the historical background of the novel and its author.[25] It is no coincidence that the same year saw the appearance of works that, had they happened in an earlier year, might have been panned for being too much "like a Gordon Merrick novel." Mart Crowley's *Boys in the Band*, reviled by gay critics for nearly fifty years, was given a glitzy new screen treatment by Ryan Murphy for Netflix (which had followed Murphy's slightly less glitzy Broadway revival of the play in 2018). It won the GLAAD Media Award for Outstanding Film of the year. Two months after the *Boys* film, there was an unprecedented explosion of gay holiday romances—*Happiest Season, The Christmas Setup, The Christmas House, Dashing in December*—most of them with handsome, starry-eyed male actors.[26] Advertisements for these films showed images of two men gazing lovingly into each other's eyes—not unlike the paperback cover of *The Lord Won't Mind*. Depending on one's tastes, these were either wonderful or cloying. But it was hard to argue that the presentation and marketing of these films in mainstream venues was not significant. At the end of the day, one had to admit that it was probably a good thing if straight people saw two men kissing amid gently falling snow. Gordon Merrick may have "set back homosexuality twenty years" when he wrote *The Lord Won't Mind*, but he was also fifty years ahead of his time.

NOTES

1. Harold Bloom, *The Western Canon: The Books and School of the Ages* (New York: Houghton Mifflin Harcourt, 1994).
2. Sharon Malinowski and Christa Brelin, eds., *The Gay & Lesbian Literary Companion* (Detroit: Visible Ink Press, 1995), xix.
3. Gregory Woods, *A History of Gay Literature: The Male Tradition* (New Haven: Yale University Press, 1998), 237, 246.
4. To give only one example from the hundreds I found in my research, a 1995 *Advocate* article by Bruce Vilanch cites Gordon Merrick to characterize the media circus over Hugh Grant's arrest for having sex in his car with a prostitute.
5. Bill McCauley, "Gordon Merrick," in *Gay & Lesbian Literature*, vol. 2, ed. Tom Pendergast and Sara Pendergast, 255–59 (Detroit: St. James Press, 1998), 256.
6. Reed Woodhouse, *Unlimited Embrace: A Canon of Gay Fiction, 1945–1995* (Amherst: University of Massachusetts Press, 1998), 4.
7. McCauley, "Gordon Merrick," 256. McCauley's quotation of "fleshy, suggestive covers" comes from Leigh W. Rutledge, *Gay Decades* (New York: Plume, 1992). The designation of Merrick's gay fiction as "soft-porn" is from Joseph Boone, "Mappings of Male Desire in Durrell's *Alexandria Quartet*," in *Displacing Homophobia: Gay Male Perspectives in Literature and Culture*, ed. Ronald R. Butters, John M. Clum, and Michael Moon (Durham: Duke University Press, 1989), 98.
8. Robert Ferro, "Gay Literature Today," [1987], in *The Violet Quill Reader: The Emergence of Gay Writing after Stonewall*, ed. David Bergman (New York: St. Martin's Press, 1994), 389.
9. Claude J. Summers, *Gay Fictions: Wilde to Stonewall: Studies in a Male Homosexual Literary Tradition* (New York: Continuum, 1990); Byrne R. S. Fone, *A Road to Stonewall: Male Homosexuality and Homophobia in English and American Literature, 1750–1969* (New York: Twayne, 1995).
10. Michael Bronski, ed., *Pulp Friction: Uncovering the Golden Age of Gay Male Pulps* (New York: St. Martin's Griffin, 2003); Patricia Juliana Smith, ed. *The Queer Sixties* (New York: Routledge, 1999); Drewey Wayne Gunn and Jaime Harker, eds., *1960s Gay Pulp Fiction: The Misplaced Heritage* (Amherst: University of Massachusetts Press, 2013). Not surprisingly, the accounts of gay literary history in these three excellent books are often more nuanced than the titles would suggest. For example, in addition to noting that many gay "pulps" were actually paperback versions of mainstream hardcover novels, Bronski dispels the conventional, oversimplified

characterization of pre-Stonewall fiction as a myth, a "post-Stonewall invention" created to promote a specific version of gay history.

11. Edward Halsey Foster, "Gay Literature: Poetry and Prose," *Oxford Research Encyclopedia of Literature*, September 26, 2017, http://oxfordre.com/literature.

12. Felice Picano, *Art and Sex in Greenwich Village: Gay Literary Life after Stonewall* (New York: Carroll & Graf, 2007), 13.

13. Rob McDonald, "Incurably Romantic," in *The Golden Age of Gay Fiction*, ed. Drewey Wayne Gunn, 37–51 (Albion, NY: MLR Press, 2009), 48–49.

14. A good anecdotal example is Will Shank's recollection of reading Merrick's novels as a teenager: "When I was a teenager in small-town Pennsylvania in the 1960s, I worked in a bookstore on weekends and evenings. There, hidden among the straight porn section, were pulp fiction books . . . with hard-core gay sex described with a maximum of saliva on every page . . . Then came the Seventies, and suddenly there was Gordon Merrick. His novels gave blatantly gay themes a certain respectability, and they were the perfect books for the Stonewall generation." Will Shank, "Breathless," *Bay Area Reporter*, February 26, 1998.

15. Ricardo Hunter Garcia, "Gordon Merrick, Journalist, Actor and Popular Novelist, Dies at 71 in Sri Lanka," press release, 1988, Gordon Merrick student file.

16. Victor J. Banis, "The Gay Publishing Revolution," in *The Golden Age of Gay Fiction*, 113.

17. Richard Hall, "The Unnatural History of Homosexual Literature," *Village Voice*, August 22, 1977.

18. James McCourt, *Queer Street: Rise and Fall of an American Culture, 1947–1985* (New York: W. W. Norton, 2004), 8, 255, 417.

19. Robert Drake, *The Gay Canon: Great Books Every Gay Man Should Read* (New York: Doubleday, 1998), xvi, 377.

20. Ian Young, *Out in Paperback: A Visual History of Gay Pulps* (Albion, NY: MLR Press, 2012), 66.

21. Joseph M. Ortiz, "Gordon Merrick and the Writing of Romance," in *The Golden Age of Gay Fiction*, 167–76. Gunn later acknowledged in an interview that he was reluctant to include a chapter on Merrick in the book until he was persuaded by Ian Young. Despite his professed distaste for Merrick's novels, Gunn proved to be an extremely generous and insightful reader of the essay.

22. Daniel M. Jaffe, "Felice Picano: An Interview," Talking across the Table column, BiblioBuffet, https://laurensb.wordpress.com.

23. William J. Mann, *Gay Pride: A Celebration of All Things Gay and Lesbian* (New York: Citadel Press, 2004), 195–96.

24. Len Barot, "Queer Romance in Twentieth- and Twenty-First-Century America: Snapshots of a Revolution," in *Romance Fiction and American Culture: Love as the Practice of Freedom?*, ed. William A. Gleason and Eric Murphy Selinger, 389–404 (New York: Routledge, 2016), 389, 397. See also J. Todd Ormsbee, "The Tragedy and Hope of Love between Gay Men: *The Boys in the Band* and the Emotionality of Gay Love in the 1960s and 70s," in *The Boys in the Band: Flashpoints of Cinema, History, and Queer Politics*, ed. Matt Bell, 266–91 (Detroit: Wayne State University Press, 2016).

25. Joseph M. Ortiz, "*The Lord Won't Mind* at Fifty," *Gay & Lesbian Review*, March–April 2020.

26. In fact, the trend had been foreseen a year earlier by the journalist Tim Teeman, who wrote a much-shared *Daily Beast* article about a 2019 Lifetime holiday movie that featured a gay male couple. With his usual discernment, Teeman predicted, correctly, that this would be followed by holiday television movies that made the gay couple the focus rather than a subplot. Tim Teeman, "The Gay Kiss in 'Twinkle All the Way' Could Herald a Lifetime Christmas Movie Revolution," *Daily Beast*, November 30, 2019, https://www.thedailybeast.com/the-gay-kiss-in-twinkle-all-the-way-could-herald-a-lifetime-christmas-movie-revolution.

Bibliography

Archives

The Daily Princetonian, Larry DuPraz Digital Archives. http://theprince.princeton.edu.

Glenway Wescott Papers, Yale Collection of American Literature, Beinecke Rare Book & Manuscript Library, Yale University Library, New Haven, Connecticut.

George Fisher Papers, Division of Rare and Manuscript Collections, Cornell University Library, Cornell University, Ithaca, New York.

Gordon Merrick Papers (GMP), Manuscripts Division, Department of Special Collections, Princeton University Library, Princeton, New Jersey.

Gordon Merrick student file, Princeton University Archives, Seeley G. Mudd Manuscript Library, Department of Special Collections, Princeton University Library, Princeton, New Jersey.

Lesbian, Gay, Bisexual and Transgender Periodical Collection, Manuscripts and Archives Division, New York Public Library, New York, New York.

Monica McCall Collection, Howard Gotlieb Archival Research Center, Boston University Library, Boston, Massachusetts.

Personnel Files of the Office of Strategic Services (OSS), Joint Chiefs of Staff, Office of Strategic Services, National Archives, College Park, Maryland.

Redmond Frankton Wallis Papers, Alexander Turnbull Library, Wellington, New Zealand.

Theatre Intime Records, Princeton University Archives, Seeley G. Mudd Manuscript Library, Department of Special Collections, Princeton University Library, Princeton, New Jersey.

Interviews and Correspondence

Champagne, John Gerard. Email to the author. September 25, 2020.
Cosentino, Joe. Email to the author. December 17, 2020.
Douglas, Mitch. Interview by the author. June 13, 2013. Transcript.
Gadino, Victor. Email to the author. December 13, 2021.

Hulse, Charles. Interview by the author. March 15, 2012. Digital recording.
Hulse, Lawrence. Interview by the author. April 28, 2020. Transcript.
Jaffe, Daniel. Email to the author. December 2, 2021.
Jongeward, Steven. Email to the author. January 27, 2022.
Luke, Elmer. Email to the author. January 5, 2022.
McDonald, George. Email to the author. January 28, 2022.
Merrick, Eleanor. Interview by the author. July 7, 2013. Transcript.
Merrick, Gordon. Interview by Brandon Judell. April 1986. Digital recording.
Raymond, Gerard. Email to the author. January 26, 2022.
Sakol, Jeannie. Interview by the author. May 28, 2010. Digital recording.
White, Edmund. Interview by the author. October 17, 2014. Transcript.

Published Works

Aldrich, Robert. *The Seduction of the Mediterranean: Writing, Art and Homosexual Fantasy*. London: Routledge, 1993.
"An Exclusive Interview with Gordon Merrick." *Michael's Thing* 1, no. 30 (1971): 13.
Arenson, Karen W. "Princeton Honors Ex-Judge Once Turned Away for Race." *New York Times*, June 5, 2001.
Armstrong, April C. "Bruce Wright's Exclusion from Princeton University." Princeton & Slavery. Princeton University. Accessed June 1, 2020. http://slavery.princeton.edu/stories/bruce-wrights-exclusion-from-princeton-university.
Atkinson, Brooks. "Fannie Brice in the 1936 Edition of the 'Follies' under Shubert Management." *New York Times*, January 31, 1936.
———. "Fable for Our Times." *New York Times*, January 29, 1939.
———. "Moss Hart and George S. Kaufman Discuss 'The Man Who Came to Dinner.'" *New York Times*, October 17, 1939.
———. "White Owl of Lake Bomoseen." *New York Times*, October 22, 1939.
Austen, Roger. *Playing the Game: The Homosexual Novel in America*. Indianapolis: Bobbs-Merrill, 1977.
Axtell, James. *The Making of Princeton University*. Princeton: Princeton University Press, 2006.
Bach, Steven. *Dazzler: The Life and Times of Moss Hart*. New York: Da Capo Press, 2001.
Bailey, Blake. *A Tragic Honesty: The Life and Work of Richard Yates*. New York: Picador, 2003.
Banis, Victor J. "The Gay Publishing Revolution." In *The Golden Age of Gay Fiction*, edited by Drewey Wayne Gunn, 113–25. Albion, NY: MLR Press, 2009.
Barot, Len. "Queer Romance in Twentieth-and Twenty-First-Century America: Snapshots of a Revolution." In *Romance Fiction and American Culture: Love as the Practice of Freedom?*, edited by William A. Gleason and Eric Murphy Selinger, 389–404. New York: Routledge, 2016.
Bawer, Bruce. *A Place at the Table: The Gay Individual in American Society*. New York: Poseidon, 1993.

Beebe, Lucius. "Blowing Cold on 'Gone with the Wind.'" *St. Louis Post-Dispatch*, December 31, 1939.

Beeson Jr., Hugh. "Love Story with a Twist." *Boston Globe*, August 30, 1970.

Bell, Matt, ed. *The Boys in the Band: Flashpoints of Cinema, History, and Queer Politics*. Detroit: Wayne State University Press, 2016.

Bergman, David. "The Cultural Work of Sixties Gay Pulp Fiction." In *The Queer Sixties*, edited by Patricia Juliana Smith, 26–42. New York: Routledge, 1999.

———. *Gaiety Transfigured: Gay Self-Representation in American Literature*. Madison: University of Wisconsin Press, 1991.

———. *The Violet Hour: The Violet Quill and the Making of Gay Culture*. New York: Columbia University Press, 2004.

Bérubé, Allan. *Coming Out Under Fire: The History of Gay Men and Women in World War Two*. New York: The Free Press, 1990.

Blades, John. "'Gutsiest' Publisher." *Chicago Tribune*, December 20, 1988.

Bloom, Harold. *The Western Canon: The Books and School of the Ages*. New York: Houghton Mifflin Harcourt, 1994.

Boone, Joseph. "Mappings of Male Desire in Durrell's *Alexandria Quartet*." In *Displacing Homophobia: Gay Male Perspectives in Literature and Culture*, edited by Ronald R. Butters, John M. Clum, and Michael Moon, 73–106. Durham: Duke University Press, 1989.

Borgers, Edward W. "The Significance of Princeton's Theatre Intime." *Educational Theatre Journal* 4, no. 4 (1952): 308–14.

Boutell, Clip. "Soup de Gaulle or Vichyssoise." *New York Post*, February 10, 1947.

Boyd, Nan Alamilla. *Wide Open Town: A History of Queer San Francisco to 1965*. Berkeley: University of California Press, 2003.

Bradford, Barbara Taylor. "Gordon Merrick's Greek Home: Three Houses Turned into One." *Detroit Free Press*, August 14, 1971.

Bram, Christopher. *Eminent Outlaws: The Gay Writers Who Changed America*. New York: Twelve, 2012.

Bravmann, Scott. *Queer Fictions of the Past: History, Culture, and Difference*. Cambridge: Cambridge University Press, 1997.

Brinton, Mary Williams. *Their Lives and Mine*. Philadelphia: Mary Williams Brinton, 1972.

Bristow, Joseph. "'I Am with You, Little Minority Sister': Isherwood's Queer Sixties." In *The Queer Sixties*, edited by Patricia Juliana Smith, 145–63. New York: Routledge, 1999.

Bronski, Michael. *Pulp Friction: Uncovering the Golden Age of Gay Male Pulps*. New York: St. Martin's Griffin, 2003.

———. Introduction to *Song of the Loon*, by Richard Amory. Vancouver: Arsenal Pulp Press, 2005.

Brudnoy, David. "Books in Brief." *National Review*, June 16, 1971.

Burgess, George H. and Miles C. Kennedy. *Centennial History of the Pennsylvania Railroad Company 1846–1946*. Philadelphia: Pennsylvania Railroad Company, 1949.

Burns, John Horne. *The Gallery*. 1947. New York: New York Review Books, 2004.

Busch, Charles. "Guilty Pleasures." *The Advocate*, September 19, 1995.
Canby, Vincent. "'Race D'Ep' Links Photography and Sexuality." *New York Times*, May 19, 1982.
Carlson, Raymond. "First LGBT Reunion Not Controversy-Free." *Yale Daily News*, April 27, 2009.
Caver, Joseph, Jerome Ennels, and Daniel Haulmen. *The Tuskegee Airmen, An Illustrated History: 1939–1949*. Montgomery, AL: NewSouth Books, 2011.
Cervini, Eric. *The Deviant's War: The Homosexual vs. the United States of America*. New York: Farrar, Straus and Giroux, 2020.
Chauncey, George. *Gay New York: Gender, Urban Culture, and the Making of the Gay Male World, 1890–1940*. New York: Basic Books, 1994.
Chee, Alexander. "The Afterlives of E. M. Forster." *New Republic*, September 21, 2021.
———. "Paperback Writer." *The Advocate*, June 1996.
Chenier, Elise. "Gay Marriage, 1970s Style." *Gay & Lesbian Review*, March–April 2013.
Clark, Philip. "'Accept Your Essential Self': The Guild Press, Identity Formation, and Gay Male Community." In *1960s Gay Pulp Fiction*, edited by Drewey Wayne Gunn and Jaime Harker, 78–119. Amherst: University of Massachusetts Press, 2013.
Clemente, Deirdre. "Caps, Canes, and Coonskins: Princeton and the Evolution of Collegiate Clothing, 1900–1930." *Journal of American Culture* 31, no. 1 (2008): 20–33.
Cole, Rob. "Gay Marriage 'Boom': Suddenly, It's News." *The Advocate*, August 6–18, 1970.
Collins, Theresa M. *Otto Kahn: Art, Money, and Modern Time*. Chapel Hill: University of North Carolina Press, 2002.
Colton, Helen. "Reluctant Star." *New York Times*, September 4, 1949.
Cory, Donald Webster. *The Homosexual in America: A Subjective Approach*. 2nd ed. New York: Greenberg, 1959.
Coulson, Thomas. "Some Prominent Members of the Franklin Institute: 1. Samuel Vaughan Merrick, 1801–1870." *Journal of the Franklin Institute* 258 (November 1954): 335–346.
Crespy, David A. *Richard Barr: The Playwright's Producer*. Carbondale: Southern Illinois University Press, 2013.
Curzon, Daniel. "Gay Trash Driving Out the Good." *The Advocate*, April 13, 1974.
Cushman, Robert. "A Stunning *Macbeth* from the RSC." *New York Times*, February 5, 1978.
Dean, Douglas. "Fuck Books or Gay Literature?" *Vector*, May 1973.
Delpech, Jeanine. "Gordon Merrick a choisi la Provence." *Les Nouvelles Littéraires*, March 2, 1950.
D'Emilio, John. *Sexual Politics, Sexual Communities: The Making of a Homosexual Minority in the United States 1940–1970*. 2nd ed. Chicago: University of Chicago Press, 1998.

Dick, Bernard F. *The Hellenism of Mary Renault*. Carbondale: Southern Illinois University Press, 1972.

Distelberg, Brian J. "Mainstream Fiction, Gay Reviewers, and Gay Male Cultural Politics in the 1970s." *GLQ* 16, no. 3 (2010): 389–427.

Dlugos, Tim. "Rough Trade: Notes on the Book World." *Christopher Street*, March 1977.

Dowling, Linda C. *Hellenism and Homosexuality in Victorian Oxford*. Ithaca: Cornell University Press, 1994.

Drake, Robert. *The Gay Canon: Great Books Every Gay Man Should Read*. New York: Doubleday, 1998.

Duberman, Martin. *The Worlds of Lincoln Kirstein*. New York: Alfred A. Knopf, 2007.

Dunne, Dominick. "The Talented Mr. Lonergan." *Vanity Fair*, July 2000.

Eisenbach, David. *Gay Power: An American Revolution*. New York: Carroll & Graf, 2006.

Ellenzweig, Allen. *George Platt Lynes: The Daring Eye*. Oxford: Oxford University Press, 2021.

Elliott, S. James. "Homosexuality in the Crucial Decade: Three Novelists' Views." In *The Gay Academic*, edited by Louie Crew, 164–77. Palm Springs: ETC Publications, 1978.

Fearing, Kenneth. "St. Martin's Peninsula." *New York Times*, November 14, 1954.

Ferro, Robert. "Gay Literature Today" [1987]. In *The Violet Quill Reader: The Emergence of Gay Writing after Stonewall*, edited by David Bergman, 387–97. New York: St. Martin's Press, 1994.

Fetische, Frieda. "Smiths, Not Synths." *Gay Scotland*, May 1984.

Fields, Arthur C. "The War, Bandaged and Sterile." *Saturday Review of Literature*, April 5, 1947.

Fone, Byrne R. S. *A Road to Stonewall: Male Homosexuality and Homophobia in English and American Literature, 1750–1969*. New York: Twayne, 1995.

Forster, E. M. *Maurice*. 1971. New York: W. W. Norton, 2005.

———. *Selected Letters of E. M. Forster*, edited by Mary Lago and P. N. Furbank. Cambridge, MA: Harvard University Press, 1985.

———. *Two Cheers for Democracy*. New York: Harcourt, 1951.

Forster, E. M. and Christopher Isherwood. *Letters between Forster and Isherwood on Homosexuality in Literature*, edited by Richard E. Zeikowitz. New York: Palgrave Macmillan, 2008.

Forsythe, Ronald [Donn Teal]. "Why Can't 'We' Live Happily Ever After, Too?" *New York Times*, February 23, 1969.

Foster, Edward Halsey. "Gay Literature: Poetry and Prose." *Oxford Research Encyclopedia of Literature*, September 26, 2017. http://oxfordre.com/literature.

Fox, Margalit. "Martin Levin, Prolific Book Reviewer, Dies at 89." *New York Times*, May 30, 2008.

Gale, Patrick. *Armistead Maupin*. New York: Open Road Media, 2016.

Genoni, Paul and Tanya Dalziell. *Half the Perfect World: Writers, Dreamers and Drifters on Hydra, 1955–1964*. Clayton, Australia: Monash University Publishing, 2018.

Gifford, James J. *Glances Backward: An Anthology of American Homosexual Writing 1830–1920*. Peterborough, Ontario: Broadview Press, 2007.

———. "Proem: How to Read Gay Pulp Fiction." In *1960s Gay Pulp Fiction*, edited by Drewey Wayne Gunn and Jaime Harker, 29–42. Amherst: University of Massachusetts Press, 2013.

Gill, Joan. "Merrick's New Novel Has Merit." *Miami News*, March 23, 1958.

Goodwin, Daniel R. "Obituary Notice of Samuel Vaughan Merrick, Esq." *Proceedings of the American Philosophical Society* 11, no. 81 (1869): 595–96.

Gorton, Don. "*Maurice* and Gay Liberation." *Gay & Lesbian Review*, November–December 2009.

Gunn, Drewey Wayne. *Gay Novels of Britain, Ireland and the Commonwealth, 1881–1981: A Reader's Guide*. Jefferson, NC: McFarland, 2014.

———. ed. *The Golden Age of Gay Fiction*. Albion, NY: MLR Press, 2009.

Gunn, Drewey Wayne and Jaime Harker, eds. *1960s Gay Pulp Fiction*. Amherst: University of Massachusetts Press, 2013.

Hall, Richard. "Books." *The Advocate*, October 5, 1977.

———. "Is the Future of Gay Publishing a Fiction?" *The Advocate*, May 31, 1979.

———. "The Problem's Distribution." *The Advocate*, August 10, 1977.

———. "Reviews & Previews." *The Advocate*, March 9 and June 15, 1977.

———. "The Unnatural History of Homosexual Literature." *Village Voice*, August 22, 1977.

Hanshe, Rainer J. "James Purdy: Bibliography." *Hyperion* 6, no. 1 (2011): 222–26.

Harbin, Billy J. "Monty Woolley." In *The Gay & Lesbian Theatrical Legacy: A Biographical Dictionary of Major Figures in American Stage History in the Pre-Stonewall Era*, edited by Billy J. Harbin, Kim Maara, and Robert A. Schanke, 392–95. Ann Arbor: University of Michigan Press, 2007.

———. "Monty Woolley: The Public and Private Man from Saratoga Springs." In *Passing Performances: Queer Readings of Leading Players in American Theater History*, edited by Robert A. Schanke and Kim Marra, 262–79. Ann Arbor: University of Michigan Press, 1998.

Hardman, Henrietta. "By Men, For Men, About Men." *Hartford Courant*, March 2, 1947

Harker, Jaime. *Middlebrow Queer: Christopher Isherwood in America*. Minneapolis: University of Minnesota Press, 2013.

Harrity, Christopher. "Artist Spotlight: Victor Gadino." *The Advocate*, September 17, 2011.

Hart, Moss. "How A. W. Came to Dinner, and Other Stories." *New York Times*, October 29, 1939.

Hart, Moss and George S. Kaufman. *The Man Who Came to Dinner*. Bristol, RI: Hildreth Press, 1939.

Heredia, Christopher. "Gay Bookstore Founder to Lead A Different Life." *San Francisco Chronicle*, September 8, 2000. http://www.sfgate.com.

Hesthamar, Kari. *So Long, Marianne: A Love Story*, translated by Helle V. Goodman. Toronto: ECW Press, 2014.

Hibbs, Thomas S. "David Brudnoy Signs Off." *National Review*, December 10, 2004.

Hodges, Andrew. *Alan Turing: The Enigma*. Princeton: Princeton University Press, 1983.

Holleran, Andrew. *Chronicle of a Plague, Revisited: AIDS and Its Aftermath*. New York: Da Capo Press, 2008.

Holt, Thaddeus. *The Deceivers: Allied Military Deception in the Second World War*. New York: Scribner, 2004.

Howell, Frank J. Review of *The Quirk*. *Bay Area Reporter*, November 9, 1978.

Howes, Keith. "Once A Spy . . . ." *Gay News*, August 24, 1978.

———. *Outspoken: Keith Howes' "Gay News" Interviews 1976–83*. London: Cassell, 1995.

———. "Where Love Has Gone." *Gay News*, July 26, 1979.

Huhn, Rick. *Eddie Collins: A Baseball Biography*. Jefferson, NC: McFarland, 2008.

Hulse, Charles. *In Tall Cotton*. Secaucus, NJ: Lyle Stuart, 1987.

Hyde, John. "Edinburgh Festival Reviews." *Gay Scotland*, October 1989.

Irons, Leslie. "Cast 'N Irons." *Topman*, June 21, 1982.

Jackson, Joseph Henry. " A Bookman's Notebook." *San Francisco Chronicle*, January 30, 1947.

Jaffe, Daniel M. "Felice Picano: An Interview." Talking across the Table. BiblioBuffet. Accessed May 5, 2009. https://laurensb.wordpress.com.

Janes, Dominic. "The 'Curious Effects' of Acting: Homosexuality, Theatre and Female Impersonation at the University of Cambridge, 1900–1939." *Twentieth Century British History* 33, no. 1 (2022): 1–34.

Johnson, David K. *Buying Gay: How Physique Entrepreneurs Sparked a Movement*. New York: Columbia University Press, 2019.

———. *The Lavender Scare: The Cold War Persecution of Gays and Lesbians in the Federal Government*. Chicago: University of Chicago Press, 2006.

Johnson, Niel M. "George Sylvester Viereck: Poet and Propagandist." *Books at Iowa*, November 1968.

Jordan, John W. *Colonial Families of Philadelphia*. 2 vols. New York: Lewis Publishing, 1911.

Judell, Brandon. "A Conversation With Gordon Merrick." *Stallion*, January 1987.

———. "Orgasm and Organdy: Gordon Merrick, the Champion of Gay Romance." *The Advocate*, October 14, 1986.

Just, Richard. "Hidden Lives." *Princeton Alumni Weekly*, April 3, 2013.

Kaiser, Charles. *The Gay Metropolis: The Landmark History of Gay Life in America*. New York: Grove Press, 1997.

Kaplan, Fred. "The Day Obscenity Became Art." *New York Times*, July 20, 2009.

Karabel, Jerome. *The Chosen: The Hidden History of Admission and Exclusion at Harvard, Yale, and Princeton*. Boston: Houghton Mifflin, 2005.

Kauffmann, Stanley. "Homosexual Drama and Its Disguises." *New York Times*, January 23, 1966.

Kirk, Robert. "Irony Has a Field Day." *Mattachine Review*, May–June 1955.

Krebs, Albin. "Wayne Lonergan, 67, Killer of Heiress Wife." *New York Times*, January 3, 1986.
Labonté, Richard. "Richard Labonté's Ten Best and Five Worst Gay Books." In *The Alyson Almanac*, edited by Sasha Alyson, 103–6. Boston: Alyson, 1993.
Leavis, F. R. "E. M. Forster." *Scrutiny*, September 1938.
Leavitt, David and Mark Mitchell, eds. *The Penguin Book of Gay Short Stories*. New York: Viking, 1994.
Leddick, David. *Intimate Companions: A Triography of George Platt Lynes, Paul Cadmus, Lincoln Kirstein, and Their Circle*. Miami Beach: White Lake Press, 2020.
Leff, Leonard. "Becoming Clifton Webb: A Queer Star in Mid-Century Hollywood." *Cinema Journal* 47, no. 3 (2008): 3–28.
Lestrade, Didier. "Gordon Merrick, Le Dynastie Pédé!." *Gai Pied Hebdo*, March 7, 1987.
Levin, Martin. "Reader Report." *New York Times*, April 26, 1970.
Levine, Allan. *Details Are Unprintable: Wayne Lonergan and the Sensational Café Society Murder*. Lanham, MD: Lyons Press, 2020.
Lingeman, Richard R. "Homosexual Titles." *New York Times*, July 17, 1977.
Litsky, Frank. "Samuel V. Merrick, 86, Director of U.S. Olympic Yachting Team Dies." *New York Times*, April 21, 2000.
Loftin, Craig M. *Masked Voices: Gay Men and Lesbians in Cold War America*. Albany: State University of New York Press, 2012.
——— . "Unacceptable Mannerisms: Gender Anxieties, Homosexual Activism, and Swish in the United States, 1945–1965." *Journal of Social History* 40 (2007): 557–96.
Lombardi, John. "Selling Gay to the Masses." *Village Voice*, June 30, 1975.
Lomonaco, Martha Schmoyer. *Summer Stock!: An American Theatrical Phenomenon*. New York: Palgrave Macmillan, 2004.
Long, Michael G., ed. *Gay Is Good: The Life and Letters of Gay Rights Pioneer Franklin Kameny*. Syracuse: Syracuse University Press, 2014.
Loughery, John. *The Other Side of Silence: Men's Lives and Gay Identities: A Twentieth-Century History*. New York: Henry Holt, 1998.
Ludovici, L. J. *The Three of Us*. London: Marjay Books, 1993.
Mabille, Michel. "Ceylon to Tricqueville: The Restless Life of an American Author." *L'Éveil de Pont-Audemer*, August 27, 1981.
Mader, D. H. "The Greek Mirror: The Uranians and Their Use of Greece." *Journal of Homosexuality* 49, nos. 3–4 (2005): 377–420.
Malinowski, Sharon and Christa Brelin, eds. *The Gay & Lesbian Literary Companion*. Detroit: Visible Ink Press, 1995.
Mann, William J. *Gay Pride: A Celebration of All Things Gay and Lesbian*. New York: Citadel Press, 2004.
Margolick, David. *Dreadful: The Short Life and Gay Times of John Horne Burns*. New York: Other Press, 2013.
Mark, Julian [Vincent Lardo]. "Being Erotic Doesn't Make It Trash." *The Advocate*, April 24, 1974.

Marsden, George M. *The Soul of the American University*. Oxford: Oxford University Press, 1996.
Martin, Robert K. and George Piggford, eds. *Queer Forster*. Chicago: University of Chicago Press, 1997.
Maryles, Daisy and Robert Dahlin. "Books on Homosexuality: A Current Checklist." *Publishers Weekly*, August 8, 1977.
Mather, Bobby. "Tempest in a Love Rut." *Detroit Free Press*, May 10, 1970.
Matzner, Sebastian. "From Uranians to Homosexuals: Philhellenism, Greek Homoeroticism and Gay Emancipation in Germany 1835–1915." *Classical Receptions Journal* 2, no. 1 (2010): 60–91.
[Mavity, Nancy Barr] N. B. M. "Freedom's Cost: Doing What Comes Naturally Is Not So Easy as It Sounds." *Oakland Tribune*, January 16, 1955.
Mavity, Nancy Barr. "Two Novels Defy Old Notions." *Oakland Tribune*, January 15, 1956.
McAleer, Neil. *Arthur C. Clarke: The Authorized Biography*. Chicago: Contemporary Books, 1992.
McCauley, Bill. "Gordon Merrick." In *Gay & Lesbian Literature, Volume 2*, edited by Tom Pendergast and Sara Pendergast, 255–59. Detroit: St. James Press, 1998.
McConnell, Michael and Jack Baker. *The Wedding Heard 'Round the World: America's First Gay Marriage*. Minneapolis: University of Minnesota Press, 2016.
McCourt, James. *Queer Street: Rise and Fall of an American Culture, 1947–1985*. New York: W. W. Norton, 2004.
McDonald, Rob. "Incurably Romantic." In *The Golden Age of Gay Fiction*, edited by Drewey Wayne Gunn, 37–51. Albion, NY: MLR Press, 2009.
McGrory, Mary. "Tragic Wartime Dilemma Is Theme of Fine First Novel." *Boston Traveler*, February 26, 1947.
Meeker, Martin. "Behind the Mask of Respectability: Reconsidering the Mattachine Society and Male Homophile Practice, 1950s and 1960s." *Journal of the History of Sexuality* 10, no. 1 (2001): 78–116.
Mensforth, Charlotte. "Wine Dark Sea." In *When We Were Almost Young: Remembering Hydra through War and Bohemians*, edited by Helle V. Goldman, 69–89. Tromsø, Norway: Tipota Press, 2018.
Merrick, Gordon. "The Case for the Blob." *New Republic*, July 13, 1959.
———. *The Demon of Noon*. New York: Julian Messner, 1954.
———. *Forth into Light*. New York: Avon Books, 1974.
———. "The Frenchman and the American Merged—And Merrick Had a Novel." *San Francisco Chronicle*, March 30, 1958.
———. *The Great Urge Downward*. New York: Avon Books, 1984.
———. "The Home of the Phonus Balonus." *New Republic*, February 23, 1959.
———. *The Hot Season*. New York: William Morrow, 1958.
———. "How to Write Lying Down." *New Republic*, December 8, 1958.
———. *An Idol for Others*. New York. Avon Books, 1977.
———. *L'amour est un commencement*. Translated by Hélène Claireau. Flammarion, 1955.

———. *Lancelot 5ème Avenue*. Translated by Therese Aubray. Paris: Flammarion, 1950.

———. *La Rafale Amoureuse*. Translated by Denise Meunier. Paris: Flammarion, 1951.

———. *The Lord Won't Mind*. New York: Bernard Geis, 1970.

———. *A Measure of Madness*. New York: Warner Books, 1986.

———. "No Laughing Matter." *New Republic*, September 7, 1959.

———. *Now Let's Talk about Music*. New York: Avon Books, 1981.

———. *One for the Gods*. New York: Bernard Geis, 1971.

———. *Perfect Freedom*. New York: Avon Books, 1982.

———. *The Quirk*. New York: Avon Books, 1978.

———. *The Strumpet Wind*. New York: William Morrow, 1947.

———. *The Vallency Tradition*. New York: Julian Messner, 1955.

Merrick, Gordon and Charles G. Hulse. *The Good Life*. Los Angeles: Alyson Books, 1997.

Miller, Laurence. "The 'Golden Age' of Gay and Lesbian Literature in Mainstream Mass-Market Paperbacks." *Paperback Parade* 47 (February 1997): 37–66.

Miller, Neil. *Out of the Past: Gay and Lesbian History from 1869 to the Present*. New York: Alyson Books, 2006.

Mintler, Catherine. "From Aesthete to Gangster: The Dandy Figure in the Novels of F. Scott Fitzgerald." *F. Scott Fitzgerald Review* 8 (2010): 104–29.

Moffat, Wendy. *A Great Unrecorded History: A New Life of E. M. Forster*. New York: Farrar, Straus and Giroux, 2010.

Morgenthau III, Henry. *Mostly Morgenthaus: A Family History*. New York: Ticknor & Fields, 1991.

Morton, Hortense. "Theater School Planned by Straw Hat Group." *San Francisco Examiner*, August 15, 1954.

Mullin, Michael. "Stage and Screen: The Trevor Nunn *Macbeth*." *Shakespeare Quarterly* 38, no. 3 (1987): 350–59.

Musgrave, Charles R. "Paperback Assassins." *Drummer*, June 1982.

Nail, Robert. *Time of Their Lives*. In *The Nassau Literary Magazine* 91, no. 5 (May 1933).

The National Cyclopædia of American Biography: Being the History of the United States. New York: James T. White, 1906. s.vv. "Samuel Vaughan Merrick."

Nelson, Sigrid. Review of Vincent Lardo's *China House*. *Gay Scotland*, November 1983.

Norman, Tom. *American Gay Erotic Paperbacks: A Bibliography*. Burbank: Tom Norman, 1994.

O'Connor, Garry. *Ian McKellen: A Biography*. New York: St. Martin's Press, 2019.

Ogren, Peter. "The Lord Won't Mind: The Reader Won't Care." *Gay*, April 20, 1970.

Ormsbee, J. Todd. "The Tragedy and Hope of Love between Gay Men: *The Boys in the Band* and the Emotionality of Gay Love in the 1960s and 70s." In *The Boys in the Band: Flashpoints of Cinema, History, and Queer Politics*, edited by Matt Bell, 266–91. Detroit: Wayne State University Press, 2016.

Ortiz, Joseph M. "Gordon Merrick and the Writing of Romance." In *The Golden Age of Gay Fiction*, edited by Drewey Wayne Gunn, 167–76. Albion, NY: MLR Press, 2009.

———. "*The Lord Won't Mind* at Fifty." *Gay & Lesbian Review*, March–April 2020.

———. "'The World Won't Mind': The Accidental Success of Gordon Merrick." *Princeton University Library Chronicle* 67, no. 3 (Spring 2007): 611–26.

Ortiz, Ricardo L. "L.A. Women: Jim Morrison with John Rechy." In *The Queer Sixties*, edited by Patricia Juliana Smith, 164–86. New York: Routledge, 1999.

Paris, Orlando. Review of *The Lord Won't Mind*. *Queens Quarterly*, Summer 1970.

Perry, David. "A Gentleman from Another Country." *Bay Area Reporter*, June 30, 1988.

Perry, Imani. *Looking for Lorraine: The Radiant and Radical Life of Lorraine Hansberry*. Boston: Beacon Press, 2018.

Picano, Felice. *Art and Sex in Greenwich Village: Gay Literary Life after Stonewall*. New York: Carroll & Graf, 2007.

Pinckard, H. R. "Lean, Rent and Beggar'd by *The Strumpet Wind* of Fate." *West Virginia Advertiser*, February 22, 1947

Pitts, David. *Jack & Lem: John F. Kennedy and Lem Billings: The Untold Story of an Extraordinary Friendship*. New York: Carroll & Graf, 2007.

Preston, John. "Gay Genre Writing: The Power and Politics of Our Popular Literature." *The Advocate*, May 26, 1987.

———. *My Life as a Pornographer & Other Indecent Acts*. New York: Masquerade Books, 1993.

Quin-Harkin, Janet. "Like Reading Lady Chatterley at Age 14." *Pacific Sun*, May 6, 1970.

Rader, Dotson. "The Gay Militants." *New York Times*, October 3, 1971.

Raymont, Henry. "Bankruptcy Step Is Taken by Geis." *New York Times*, November 13, 1971.

Richlin, Amy. "Eros Underground: Greece and Rome in Gay Print Culture, 1953–65." *Journal of Homosexuality* 49, nos. 3–4 (2005): 421–61.

Riding, Alan. *And the Show Went On: Cultural Life in Nazi-Occupied Paris*. New York: Vintage Books, 2010.

Roditi, Georges. "Gordon Merrick: Lancelot Cinquième Avenue." *Flammes: Bulletin D'Information des Éditions Flammarion*, February 1950.

Romero, Anthony D. "Public Service in a Self-Interested Age." *Princeton Alumni Weekly*, April 8, 2020.

Rosco, Jerry. *Glenway Wescott Personally: A Biography*. Madison: University of Wisconsin Press, 2002.

Ruderman, Gary. "Gay Books: Fundamental Conflict." *Los Angeles Times*, March 6, 1983.

Rutledge, Leigh W. *The Gay Decades: From Stonewall to the Present: The People and Events that Shaped Gay Lives*. New York: Plume, 1992.

Sarraute, Claude. "Rose et bleu." *Le Monde*, March 11, 1987.

Schultz, Ray. "Larry Kramer." In *The Gay & Lesbian Theatrical Legacy*, edited by Billy J. Harbin, Kim Marra, and Robert A. Schanke, 240–43. Ann Arbor: University of Michigan Press, 2007.

Schwartz, Michael. "David Leavitt's Inner Child." *Harvard Gay & Lesbian Review* 2, no. 1 (Winter 1995): 1, 40–44.

Seaman, Barbara. *Lovely Me: The Life of Jacqueline Susann*. New York: Seven Stories Press, 1996.

Shank, Will. "Breathless." *Bay Area Reporter*, February 26, 1998.

Sidaway, Valerie Lloyd. "Hydra Reflections." In *When We Were Almost Young: Remembering Hydra through War and Bohemians*, edited by Helle V. Goldman, 115–35. Tromsø, Norway: Tipota Press, 2018.

Solomon, Jeff. *So Famous and So Gay: The Fabulous Potency of Truman Capote and Gertrude Stein*. Minneapolis: University of Minnesota Press, 2017.

Somerville, Siobhan. "Queer." In *Keywords for American Cultural Studies*, edited by Bruce Burgett and Glenn Hendler, 203–7. New York: New York University Press, 2014.

Spanier, Ginette. *And Now It's Sables*. London: Robert Hale, 1970.

———. *It Isn't All Mink*. London: Collins, 1959.

Spooner, John D. "What Young Writers Can Learn from a Publishing Pioneer." *Cognoscenti*, July 5, 2013. https://www.wbur.org/cognoscenti/2013/07/05/monica-mccall-john-d-spooner.

Spring, Justin *Secret Historian: The Life and Times of Samuel Steward, Professor, Tattoo Artist, and Sexual Renegade*. New York: Farrar, Straus and Giroux, 2010.

Stein, Marc. "Canonizing Homophile Sexual Respectability: Archives, History, and Memory." *Radical History Review*, no. 120 (Fall 2014): 53–73.

Stephens, John Russell. *Emlyn Williams: The Making of A Dramatist*. Wales: Seren, 2000).

Strong, Lester Q. "Josephine Baker's Hungry Heart." *Gay & Lesbian Review*, September/October 2006.

Stillinger, Jack. *Multiple Authorship and the Myth of Solitary Genius*. New York: Oxford University Press, 1991.

Strub, Whitney. "Historicizing Pulp: Gay Male Pulp and the Narrativization of Queer Cultural History." In *1960s Gay Pulp Fiction*, edited by Drewey Wayne Gunn and Jaime Harker, 43–77. Amherst: University of Massachusetts Press, 2013.

Stryker, Susan. *Queer Pulp: Perverted Passions from the Golden Age of the Paperback*. San Francisco: Chronicle Books, 2001.

Sullivan, Andrew. "Buckley and the Gays," *Atlantic*, February 28, 2008.

Summerbell, Richard. "Success: Romantic Formulas for Hot-Blooded Best-Sellers." *Body Politic* 87 (1982): 34–35.

Summers, Claude J. *Gay Fictions: Wilde to Stonewall: Studies in a Male Homosexual Literary Tradition*. New York: Continuum, 1990.

Teeman, Tim. *In Bed with Gore Vidal: Hustlers, Hollywood, and the Private World of an American Master*. Bronx: Magnus Books, 2013.

———. "The Gay Kiss in 'Twinkle all the Way' Could Herald a Lifetime Christmas Movie Revolution." *The Daily Beast*, November 30, 2019. https://www

.thedailybeast.com/the-gay-kiss-in-twinkle-all-the-way-could-herald-a-lifetime-christmas-movie-revolution.

Terry, C. V. "The Passive Fascist." *New York Times*, March 2, 1947.

Townsend, Larry. "Who Gauges Market Correctly, Publishers or Writers?" *The Advocate*, August 19–September 1, 1970.

Trilling, Lionel. *E. M. Forster*. 1943. New York: Harcourt, 1964.

Tuller, Roger H. "'A Subject of Absorbing Interest to Mankind': U.S. Supreme Court Obscenity Rulings, 1934–1977." In *The Golden Age of Gay Fiction*, edited by Drewey Wayne Gunn, 135–40. Albion, NY: MLR Press, 2009.

Viereck, George Sylvester. "Sex Is a Demon." *Good Times* 2, no. 15 (1954): 56–64.

Wald, Alan M. *Exiles from a Future Time: The Forging of the Mid-Twentieth-Century Literary Left*. Chapel Hill: University of North Carolina Press, 2002.

Waller, Douglas. *Wild Bill Donovan: The Spymaster Who Created the OSS and Modern American Espionage*. New York: Free Press, 2011.

Watters, Jim. "Ruth Ford & Dotson Rader: A December Mistress-Muse to May." *People*, March 24, 1975

Weir, Marion E. "Between Book Ends: Love Is the Beginning." *St. Louis Post-Dispatch*, February 10, 1955.

Wescott, Glenway. *Apartment in Athens*. Introduction by David Leavitt. New York: New York Review of Books, 2004.

———. *"A Visit to Priapus" and Other Stories*, edited by Jerry Rosco. Madison: University of Wisconsin Press, 2013.

———. *Continual Lessons: The Journals of Glenway Wescott 1937–1955*, edited by Robert Phelps and Jerry Rosco. New York: Farrar Straus Giroux, 1990.

White, Edmund. "Out of the Closet, onto the Bookshelf." *New York Times*, June 16, 1991.

Whitmore, George. "Beer, Baloney, and Champagne." *Body Politic*. Review Supplement, September 1978.

———. "The Gay Novel Now." *Gaysweek*, October 9, 1978.

———. "Out of the Closet and onto the Shelves." *Washington Post*, January 8, 1978.

Wickramasinghe, Nira. *Sri Lanka in the Modern Age: A History*. Oxford: Oxford University Press, 2014.

Wilbur, Ray. "Clash of Duty and Principle." *Philadelphia Inquirer*, February 23, 1947.

Will, Barbara. "The Strange Politics of Gertrude Stein." *Humanities* 33, no. 2 (2012): 25–49.

———. *Unlikely Collaboration: Gertrude Stein, Bernard Faÿ, and the Vichy Dilemma*. New York: Columbia University Press, 2011.

Williams, Tennessee. *Memoirs*. 1972. New York: New Directions Books, 2006.

Winks, Robin W. *Cloak & Gown: Scholars in the Secret War 1939–1961*. 2nd ed. New Haven: Yale University Press, 1987.

Woodhouse, Reed. *Unlimited Embrace: A Canon of Gay Fiction, 1945–1995*. Amherst: University of Massachusetts Press, 1998.

Woods, Gregory. *A History of Gay Literature: The Male Tradition*. New Haven: Yale University Press, 1998.

———. *Homintern: How Gay Culture Liberated the Modern World*. New Haven: Yale University Press, 2016.

———. "No Source of Pride." *Times Literary Supplement*, May 5, 2017.

Wright, William. *Harvard's Secret Court: The Savage 1920 Purge of Campus Homosexuals*. New York: St. Martin's Press, 2005.

Young, Ian. *Out in Paperback: A Visual History of Gay Pulps*. Albion, NY: MLR Press, 2012.

———. "The Paperback Explosion: How Gay Paperbacks Changed America." In *The Golden Age of Gay Fiction*, ed. Drewey Wayne Gunn, 3–12. Albion, NY: MLR Press, 2009.

Zilboorg, Caroline. *The Masks of Mary Renault: A Literary Biography*. Columbia: University of Missouri Press, 2001.

Index

2001: A Space Odyssey, 297, 306

Abbott, Cary, 57
Academy Awards, 41
Aciman, André, 9
Ackerley, J. R., 109
ACT UP, 277, 323
Addinsell, Richard, 107
Advocate, The, 7, 182, 206, 228, 232, 249, 251, 260–61, 263, 266–68, 273, 279, 284, 299, 307
After Dark (periodical), 232
Aida, 179
Albee, Edward, 33, 169, 197, 240
Albion, Robert, 41
Alchemist, The, 241
Alexander the Great, 323
Alvarez, Mark, 210
Alyson Books, 313
Americana Corporation, 61
American Army Service Editions, 107
American Civil Liberties Union (ACLU), 27
American Field Service, 60–61, 66, 71–72, 78
American Philosophical Society, 12
American Way, The (play), 55
Amory, Richard, 9, 181, 204–6, 217, 227–28, 321

Anderson, John, 31
Annie Get Your Gun, 109
Another Country, 204
Another World (TV series), 211
Apartment in Athens, 87, 278
Apple of the Eye, The, 64
Arbor House (publisher), 230
Arms, Russell, 60
Armstrong, April, 27
Artaud, Antonin, 119
Ascent of F6, The, 64
Ashbery, John, 3, 322
Astaire, Fred, 138
Atkinson, Brooks, 31, 55, 58
Atwater, Edith, 55
Aubray, Therese, 119
Auden, W. H., 33, 64, 109, 322
Aumont, Jean-Pierre, 107, 298, 306
Austen, Jane, 181
Austen, Roger, 3
Australian Broadcasting Corporation, 202
Autobiography of Alice B. Toklas, The, 102–3
Avon Books, 194, 220, 230–34, 248–51, 268, 284–85, 290–91, 294–95, 323
Ayers, Lemuel (Lem), 31, 43, 50, 53–54, 61, 74, 118, 246–47, 273

Babe Ruth, 308
Bacall, Lauren, 137
Bach, Stephen, 57
Bailey, Blake, 189
Baker, Josephine, 36, 180
Bala Cynwyd, PA. *See* Villanova, PA
Baldwin, James, 3, 125, 168, 182, 204–5, 308, 318, 322
Ballantine Books, 284
Baltimore Evening Sun, 62
Banis, Victor, 322
Bankhead, Tallulah, 310
Barot, Len, 324
Barr, James, 182
Barr (Baer), Richard, *32*, 32–33, 42, 44, 50, 53, 55, 61, 64, 170, 240, 308
Bates, H.E., 81
Bawer, Bruce, 266
Bay Area Reporter, The, 312
Bay Head, NJ, 21
Beaton, Cecil, 63
Beaux' Stratagem, The, 44
Beebe, Lucius, 310
Beeson, Hugh Jr., 207–8
Benson, Randolph, 221
Bent (play), 211
Berger, Helmut, 264–65
Bergman, David, 260, 300
Bernhardt, Sarah, 22
Bernstein, Carl, 248
Bertelson, David, 296
Bérubé, Allan, 75
Best Little Boy in the World, The, 218
Bigelow, Otis, 7, 50, *51–52*, 53–55, 57, 61, 65, 137, 139, 171, 180, 196, 244, 308, 310
Billings, Kirk LeMoyne (Lem), 28
Billups, Clarice (Marston), 21–22, 24, 36–37, 54–55, 61, 64, 66, 123–24, 171–72
Billups, Melvin, 21, 24, 124, 239
Bismarck, Countess Mona von, 77
Bloom, Harold, 317
Blueboy, 261
Body Politic (periodical), 259–60, 292

Bohlen, Arndt von, 264–65
Boles, Jack, 209
Book of Job, The (play), 30
Borzage, Frank, 36
Boston Globe, The, 207–8
Bowles, Paul, 63, 255, 322
Bowling Green State University, 291
Boy on a Dolphin (film), 153, 164
Boyd, Malcolm, 318
Boys in the Band, The, 33, 170, 175, 179, 193, 203, 240, 324
Brave New World Revisited, 120
Breakfast at Tiffany's (book), 146
Brelin, Christa, 317, 319
Brideshead Revisited, 34, 271
British Broadcasting Corporation (BBC), 21, 108, 202
British Secret Intelligence Service (MI6), 75
Britten, Benjamin, 113
Broadway (theater), 6–7, 31, 33, 39, 42, 49–50, 53, 55–60, 136–37, 162, 177, 195, 244, 246, 248, 273, 307
Brohier, Nesta, 264
Brokeback Mountain, 9, 319
Bronski, Michael, 169, 320
Brooklyn Record, 201
Brown, Geoff, 190
Brown, Hunt, 71
Bruce, Bobby ("Bouncy"), 137
Brudnoy, David, 202–3
Bryant, Anita, 248
Brynner, Yul, 63, 136–37
Buckingham, Robert (Bob), 108–9, 113
Buckley, William F., 202
Bullock, John, 221
Burke, James, 151–52
Burns, David, 55
Burns, John Horne, 96–97, 143, 278–79
Burroughs, William S., 227, 322
Burton, Richard, 203
Burton, William, 307

Cadmus, Paul, 63–65, 109, 112
Cage, John, 157

Calder, Alexander, 63
Callas, Maria, 153
Cambridge University, 108, 110–112
Campbell, Joseph, 109
Camus, Albert, 120
Cannes Film Festival, 104
Capote, Truman, 146–47, 160, 298, 322
Carmer, Carl, 17
Carnegie family, 120
Carsey, Keith, 239
Cartwright, Brad, 137, 139
Cather, Willa, 21
Caulfield, Maxwell, 305
Céline, Louis-Ferdinand, 282
Celle, Henri de la, 133, 135
Central Intelligence Agency (CIA), 72
Cervantes, Miguel de, 17
Champagne, John, 296
Chauncey, George, 37, 50
Chee, Alexander, 182
Chester, Alfred, 322
Chevalier, Maurice, 82, 106
Child, Julia, 73
Children of Darkness, 30
Choate Academy, 28
Chodorov, Edward, 39
Christmas Memory, A, 298
Christopher and His Kind, 250, 266
Christopher Street, 7, 232, 243, 252, 261
Citizen Kane, 308
City and the Pillar, The, 95–97, 125, 191, 213, 229, 260
City of Night, 168
Clarke, Arthur C., 7, 255, 297, 305–6
Clean Straw for Nothing, 161
"Clear Conscience, A," 160
Clift, Charmian, 153–54, 157–58, 161, 164, 294
Closer to the Sun, 161
Cocteau, Jean, 104, 265
Cohen, Leonard, 7, 156–57, 160, 163, 294, 298, 312
Coindreau, Maurice, 29–30, 39, 41, 44, 74, 281–82

Colbert, Claudette, 133
Cold War, 144–45
Coley, Thomas, 109
College Board, The, 20
Collins, Eddie Jr., 18–19, 35–36
Columbia Studios, 49
Columbia University, 266
Coming Out, 250
Connelly, Marc, 55
Conrad, Joseph, 265
Consenting Adult, 298
Cooke, George, 31
Cooper, Gary, 36
Copacabana (nightclub), 136
Cornell University, 126
Corso, Gregory, 152–53
Cosentino, Joe, 211
Cotugno, Victor, 212
Coward, Noël, 107, 240, 265, 310
Cox, Christopher, 260
Crawford, Joan, 16, 206
Craxton, John, 153
Crowley, Mart, 33, 170, 175, 179, 203, 324
Cuddy, Page, 291, 294–95
Cummings, Curtiss, 29
Cunningham, Merce, 157
Cure, The (play), 240
Curzon, Daniel, 260

DaCosta, Morton, 153–54, *154*
Dahl, Roald, 243
Daily Princetonian, The, 30–31, 36–37, 40–41, 44, 58, 244
Dalziell, Tanya, 157, 163
Damned, The (Die Verdammten), 264
Dancer from the Dance, 259–61, 274
Dassin, Jules, 153–54, *155*
David (periodical), 206–7
David Kopay Story, The, 250
David McKay (publisher), 190, 230
Day With Leighton, A (The Day the Dog Talked), 163–64, 167, 190, 223–24, 277, 305–6
Dean, Hazell, 272

Deceivers, The (Holt), 79
DeGeneres, Ellen, 323
Delacorte-Dell (publisher), 190, 230
Delpech, Jeanine, 120–21
D'Emilio, John, 65
Demon of Noon, The, 112, 121–27, 146–47, 168, 277–80, 282, 284, 286; French translation of, 127, 278; "gay" revision of, 277–80, 284, 286
Dench, Judi, 241
Denneny, Michael, 211
Desert Hearts, 298
Designing Woman (film), 137
Desire (film), 36
Detroit Free Press, The, 201
Dietrich, Marlene, 36, 63, 107, 280, 310
Die Walküre, 194
Different Light Bookstore, A (CA), 292, 298, 312
Disney, Walt, 36
Distelberg, Brian, 3, 206, 261
Dlugos, Tim, 251
Dodds, Harold, 29
Dog Beneath the Skin, The, 33
Dollar Book Club, The, 107
Donaghe, Ronald, 9
Donen, Stanley, 138
Donovan, William ("Wild Bill"), 72–73, 75, 87
Dostoevsky, Fyodor, 229
Douglas, Mitch, 285, 295–97, 306, 308, 313
Douskos (Hydra), 154
Dowell, Coleman, 322
Downes, Donald, 75
Dr. Joyce Brothers Show, 198, 228–29
Draguignan (France). *See* Provence
Drake, Richard, 322–23
Dreis, D. David, 251
Drew, Richard, 239–40
Drummer (periodical), 283
Duke, Patty, 190
Dunne, Dominick, 308
Dyer, Richard, 203

Edinburgh Arts Festival (Fringe Festival), 272
Ekstrom, Arne, 79–80
El Morocco (nightclub), 50, 176, 308
Eliot, T. S., 322
Embry, Norris, 153
Eminem, 311
Encyclopedia Americana, 61
Engstand, Stuart, 191
Episcopal Academy, The (PA), 13, 17–19, 221, 294
Esquire, 243
Evans, Maurice, 42
Everage, Dame Edna, 273
Everard Baths (NY), 261
Everywhere I Roam (play), 55
Exhibitionist, The, 190, 193

Faerie Queene, The, 4
Faggots (novel), 211, 259, 301
Fair Stood the Wind for France, 81
Fairbanks, Douglas, 153
Family Dancing, 298
fan mail. *See* Merrick, Gordon
Farber, Jackie, 192–94, 249
Farquhar, George, 44
Farragut Playhouse, 49
Fearing, Kenneth, 126
Federal Bureau of Investigation (FBI), 72
Ferber, Edna, 50
Ferrer, José, 41
Ferrer, Mel (Melchior), 7, *32*, 33–34, 38–39, 41, 55, 139
Ferro, Robert, 260, 320
Feuchtwanger, Lion, 81
Final Days, The, 248
Finch College, 44
Finch, Peter, 153
Finistére, 226
Fire From Heaven, 221
Fire Island (NY), 231, 261, 285
Fisher, Eddie, 153
Fiske, Dwight, 37

Fitzgerald, F. Scott, 19, 37, 64, 91, 119, 124, 144, 172, 184, 191, 233, 321
Fitzgerald, Zelda, 172
Fitzpatrick, Ena, 133
Flammarion (publisher), 119–20
Fleet's In, The (painting), 65
Fleming, Ian, 318
Fonda, Henry, 153
Fone, Bryne, 320
Ford, Charles Henri, 63, 278–79
Ford, John, 73
Forster, E. M., 7, 9, 17, 64, 87, 108–14, 119, 163–64, 168–69, 172–73, 181–82, 195–96, 221, 227, 231, 265, 282–83, 285, 318
Forth into Light, 223–27, 230–32, 248–49, 271, 277, 306; revisions of, 224–25
Fouchet, Max-Pol, 120
Franklin, Benjamin, 12
Franklin Institute, 12
French, Jared, 63, 65
French, Margaret, 65
French Secret Service, 145
Friedkin, William, 33, 193
Front Runner, The, 229, 260, 271–72
Fullmer, Richard (Dirk Vanden), 217, 228
Funny Face, 138–40
Funnyhouse of a Negro, 33

Gadino, Victor, 232–33, 249, 262, 294, 298, 323
Gai Pied Hebdo (periodical), 277
Galle. *See* Sri Lanka
Galleria Umberto Primo (Naples), 96
Gallery, The, 96–97, 143, 278
Garbo, Greta, 16, 280
Garcia, Rick (GayBoyRic), 5, 311–12
Garland, Judy, 142
Garland, Rodney, 124
Gay (periodical), 204, 206, 228
Gay & Lesbian Review, The, 324
gay beauty pageants, 206
gay bookstores, 227, 250

gay civil rights movement, 182–83, 197, 204–6, 213, 220, 245, 248, 262–63, 266, 272–74, 277, 299–300, 320–21, 323; backlash against, 248, 262; March on Washington, 299; response to AIDS epidemic, 299–300
gay literature: debates over, 3, 206, 228, 260, 263, 283–84; Hellenism in, 221–22, 264; histories of, 317–22; impact of AIDS on, 295, 299; readers of, 7; tragic convention in, 182–83, 191–92, 226
Gay Men's Health Crisis (GMHC), 300
Gay Morning America (TV show), 283
Gay News (UK), 257, 271–72
gay romance films, 324–25
Gay Times (CA), 283
Gay Times (UK), 265, 272
gays in the military. *See* World War II
Gay's The Word bookstore (UK), 272
Gaysweek, 260
Geis, Bernard, 190–98, 201, 203, 210, 212, 222, 228–31, 239, 249, 271, 281, 285, 321
Geisel, Ted (Dr. Seuss), 297
Gendell, Jay, 197
Genet, Jean, 227, 272
Genoni, Paul, 157, 163
Gere, Richard, 211
Gershe, Leonard, 138
Gershwin, George, 179
Gide, André, 172, 227, 282
Gielgud, John, 36, 244
Gilbert and Sullivan operas, 194
Ginsberg, Allen, 153
Ginsberg, Harvey, 230–31
Giovanni's Room, 125, 168, 205, 308
GLAAD, 324
God's Own Country, 319
Gomez, Jewelle, 318
Gone With the Wind, 30
Good Life, The, 308–11, 313
Good Times (periodical), 125–26
Goodman, Dean (Douglas Dean), 227
Goodner, Carol, 55

Goodwin, Daniel, 19
Gordon, William Cartwright, 16, 24
Gordon Merrick Papers (Princeton), 5
Goschen, Angela, 157–58
Goschen, David, 157–59
Grant, David Marshall, 211
Great Urge Downward, The, 59, 289–93
Grecian Guild Pictorial, 211
Greene, Graham, 189
Greenleaf Press, 169
Greenwich Village, 53, 61, 64–65, 239–40, 298
Greenwood Cemetery (NJ), 141, 162
Grenaud, Pierre, 127
Griffiss Air Force Base, 136
Grosvenor Hotel, The, 21
Grove Press, 168
Grumley, Michael, 260
Guild Press, 169
Guilleminault, Gilbert, 120
Gunn, Drewey Wayne, 203, 320, 323
Gypsy (musical), 239

Hair (musical), 195
Hall, Radclyffe, 182, 318
Hall, Richard, 249–50, 279, 284, 322
Halsey, Cortland Van Rensselaer, 24
Hamilton, Alexander, 309
Hamilton, Patrick, 32
Hamilton, Wallace, 250, 284
Hamilton College, 55, 65
Hamlet, 36, 42, 244
Hammerstein, Oscar II, 136
Hammett, Dashiell, 73, 318
Hansberry, Lorraine, 7
Hare, Humphrey, 79
Harker, Jaime, 320
Harlem, NY, 53
Harrington, Patrick, 158
Harris, Frank, 322
Harris, Sam, 55
Harrison, Rex, 203
Hart, Moss, 7, 55, 57–58, 60, 309–10
Hartford Courant, The, 94
Hartley, Jesse, 18

Hartley, Marsden, 63
Harvard Gay and Lesbian Review, 4. *See also Gay & Lesbian Review*
Harvard University, 20, 28, 35, 97
Haslam, Greville, 17, 20
Hearst Publishing, 232
Hecht, Ben, 81, 87
Heermance, Radcliffe, 24, 27–28
Hellenism. *See* gay literature
Hemingway, Ernest, 17, 91, 94, 191
Henry II, 11, 135
Hensley Field (Texas), 89
Hepburn, Audrey, 33, 138–39, 153
Herald Tribune, The, 32
Herviou, Lucian, 80, 91, 103
Highland Hospital (NC), 172
Hilton, James, 17
Hirschfield, Magnus, 275
Hobson, Laura, 298
Hochberg, Alexander, 133
Hockney, David, 273
Hockney, May, 108
Holleran, Andrew, 9, 259–61, 273–74, 277, 321
Holliday, Billie, 309
Hollinghurst, Alan, 8–9
Holocaust. *See* Nazism.
Holt, Thaddeus, 79–80, 91
Homosexual Novel in America, The, 3
homosexuality: internalized homophobia, 267; terms for, 7, 18, 245, 313
Hoover, J. Edgar, 72
Horton, Rip Jr., 28
Hot Season, The, 143–45
House of Balmain, 104
House Un-American Activities Committee, 117, 126, 245
Houseman, John, 31–32, 42, 55
Howard, Leslie, 36
Howard, Sidney, 30
Howard Stern Show, The, 311
Howe, Arthur, 72
Howes, Keith, 272–74
Hoysradt (Hoyt), John, 55

Hudson, Rock, 299
Hulse, Charles, 3, 5, 7, 107, 109,
　135–43, *138*, 147–48, 151–54, *154*,
　157–60, 162–64, 167, 171, 175–76,
　183, 229, 239, 242, 252, 256, 274,
　294–98, 301, 305–6, 308–15, *314*
Hulse, Clarence, 135
Hulse, Lawrence (Larry), 135–36,
　159, 252, 356
Hunt, Chris, 318
Huxley, Aldous, 120
Hydra (Greece), 141, 151–64, 173, 217,
　223, 255–56, 271–72, 294
Hym, Christian, 275

I Want What I Want (novel), 190
Ibsen, Henrik, 31
Idol for Others, An, 49, 75, 142,
　243–52, 259, 261–62, 264, 267,
　271, 273, 320
Ihlen, Marianne, 157, 160
*Importance of Being Earnest,
　The*, 31–32
In Tall Cotton, 135–36, 297–98,
　306, 311–12
International Herald Tribune, 312
intersectionality, 291
Irons, Leslie, 283–84
Isherwood, Christopher, 6, 33, 63–64,
　109, 112–14, 146, 169, 182, 210,
　227, 250, 265–66, 268, 279, 308, 318
Island of Love (film), 153–54, *155*
Islas, Arturo, 9

Jacobi, Derek, 273
Jaffe, Stanley, 229
Jaffe, Susanne, 294–95
James, Henry, 119
Jarman, Derek, 273
Jensen, Axel, 157
Jensen, Axel Joachim, 158
Johnson, David K., 206
Johnston, George, *154*, 157–58, 161,
　163–64, 294
Johnston, Martin, 164

Jongeward, Steven, 305–6
Jonson, Ben, 41, 241
Joyce, William, 313
Judell, Brandon, 75, 79, 299–300, 307
Julian Messner (publisher), 124–25,
　127, 190, 193
Just, Richard, 35

Kahlo, Frida, 323
Kahn, Otto, 177, 179
Kaiser, Charles, 54, 65
Kalki (novel), 251, 259
Karabel, Jerome, 20, 37
Katsikas (Hydra), 154, 158
Kauffmann, Stanley, 169–70
Kaufman, George, 50, 55, 58
Keegan, Mel, 9
Keller, Patricia and Dale, 156
Kelly, Grace, 107
Kennedy, Adrienne, 33
Kennedy, Jacqueline, 154, 156, *156*, 255
Kennedy, John F., 28, 156
Kind Lady (play), 39
King And I, The, 136–37, 139, 142
King Lear, 242–43
Kinsey, Alfred C., 109, 173; sexual
　scale of, 126
Kirk, Robert, 124–25
Kirstein, Lincoln, 64, 296
Kite, Clement, 40
Kitt, Eartha, 273
Knowles, John, 298
Kopay, David, 250
Korean War, 136
Kramer, Lawrence (Larry), 211, 231,
　259, 273, 300–302, 305, 307, 321

Labonte, Richard, 292
Ladd, Alan, 153
Lady Chatterley's Lover, 168–69, 202
Lambda Literary Foundation, 324
Lambda Rising (DC), 227
Lanner, Paul, 211
Lansbury, Angela, 239
Laramie Project, The, 323

Lardo, Vincent, 260
Last of the Wine, The, 221
Lavender Menace Bookshop (Scotland), 272
Lavender Scare, The. *See* McCarthyism
Lawrence, D. H., 112, 119, 168, 202, 322
Lawrence, T. E., 108
Lawrence of Arabia, 108
Le Carrousel (nightclub), 139
Le Monde, 277
Leavis, F. R., 111
Leavitt, David, 4, 298
L'Echo D'Alger (periodical), 127
Lee, Gentry, 297
Lehmann, John, 109
Lessey, George, 55
Lestrade, Didier, 277
Levin, Martin, 203–4
Lewis, Sinclair, 17
Liberace, 273
Library of Congress, 1, 73
Lido, The (nightclub), 135, 137–42, 281
Life (magazine), 103, 151
Life and Death of Sir John Falstaff, The, 43
Lincoln University, 28
Lingeman, Richard, 250
Loftin, Craig, 222
Lombardi, John, 249
Lonergan, Wayne, 180, 307–11
Longest Journey, The, 64, 112, 282
"Lord May Barf, The," 260
Lord Won't Mind, The, 2, 18, 21–22, 34–36, 50, 55–57, 141, 170–85, 189–98, 201–13, 217–18, 225, 227–32, 239–40, 243, 247–48, 259, 272–73, 275–77, 285, 292, 296, 305, 321–25; adaptations of, 229–30, 239–40, 248; bestselling status of, 1–3, 198, 217, 227; marketing of, 197–98, 201, 231–34, 271; publication of, 190–98; racism in, 4–5, 178–80, 195–96, 293; realism of, 197, 207–10; revisions of, 173–75, 194–96; sexual explicitness in, 173–76, 297; translations of, 213, 275–77, 295. *See also* Merrick, Gordon: critical reception of; reader responses to
Loren, Sophia, 153, 164
Lotus Wing (entertainer), 137
Louganis, Greg, 297
Loughery, John, 212–13
Louis XIV, 21, 118
Lovers: The Story of Two (novel), 211
Loving v. Virginia, 127
Luke, Elmer, 296–98, 306–8
Lyle Stuart Books, 296–97
Lynes, George Platt, 63, 65, 310

Mabille, Michel, 274–75, 282
Macbeth, 241
MacLeish, Alexander, 73–74
Mailer, Norman, 197
Making Love (film), 283
male physique magazines, 206, 221
Malinowski, Sharon, 317, 319
Malraux, André, 73
Man Who Came to Dinner, The, 55–60, 59, 109, 118, 308, 310
Manchester College (Indiana), 275
Mann, William J., 323–24
Marcel, Gabriel, 119
Marquand, John, 322
Marsden, George, 29
Marston, John, 21
Martin, David, 189
Marx, Harpo, 242
Mathau, Walter, 153
Mather, Bobby, 201
Matisse, Henri, 104
Mattachine Review, The, 124–26
Mattachine Society, The, 125, 147
Mattachine Times, The, 205, 227
Mattes, Jed, 297
Maugham, Somerset, 63, 81, 87, 227, 265
Maupin, Armistead, 231, 259, 297
Maurice, 112–14, 168–69, 181–82, 195, 221, 227, 231, 282

Mavity, Nancy Barr, 126–27
Mayer, Edwin Justus, 30
Mayer, Peter, 231, 249
Mayon, Charles (Chizzie), 42
McCall, Monica, 189–90, 192–94, 229–31, 239–43, 248–49, 261–62, 271, 285
McCarter Theatre, 31, 44
McCarthyism, 111, 117, 119, 168, 245, 248, 275
McCauley, Bill, 318–19
McClymonds, Terry, 251
McCourt, James, 322
McDonald, Boyd, 277, 292, 322
McDonald, George, 305
McDonald, Rob, 321
McKellen, Ian, 7, 17, 241–43, 274
Measure of Madness, A, 293–99, 306; representation of race in, 297
Merchant of Venice, The, 93, 159
Mercouri, Melina, 153–54, *154*
Mercury Theatre, 31–33, 42, 55, 65
Merrick, Eleanor (Perry), 8, 15, 104
Merrick, Gordon: awards won by, 250–51; censorship of, 272, 298; critical reception of, 4, 7, 94–95, 110–11, 119–21, 124–27, 201–8, 212, 222, 227–28, 247, 250–52, 258–64, 266–68, 273–74, 283–84, 291–93, 298, 312, 318–24; reader responses to, 6–7, 208–13, 222, 251, 271–72; French reception of, 5–6, 22, 119–21, 127, 180, 274–77; health problems of, 16, 255, 308–9, 312; journalism career of, 7, 61–63, 72; unpublished works, 145–46, 160–61; World War II service, 7, 71–83
Merrick, John and Rebecca (Maine), 11
Merrick, John Vaughan (b. 1828), 12, 18
Merrick, John Vaughan (b. 1864), 18–19
Merrick, Leonard (novelist), 126
Merrick, Mary (Cartwright Gordon), 12–16, 21–22, 33, 37–38, 40–41, 43, 60, 77–78, 81–82, 87, 102, 104, 124, 141, 162–63, 183–84; Catholicism of, 13–15, 82, 162
Merrick, Rodney King, 12–13, 16, 19, 41, 43, 104, 124, 141, 162, 311
Merrick, Samuel Vaughan (b. 1801), 11–12, 19; Reconstruction efforts of, 12
Merrick, Samuel Vaughan (b. 1856), 12
Merrick, Samuel Vaughan III (b. 1914), 12–13, 16, 19, 24, 53, 60, 81, 104, 118, 159, 162, 249, 290
Merrick, Sarah Otis, 12
Merrick, William Henry (b. 1831), 12
Merrill, James, 322
Messner, Kathryn, 124–25
Metropolitan Opera, The, 177, 179–80
Meunier, Denise, 120
MGM Studios, 306
Miami News, 249
Michael's Thing (periodical), 171, 175, 229
Midler, Bette, 273
Midnight Cowboy, 229
Miller, Hugh, 272
Milton, John, 286
Miracle in the Rain, 81
Mississippi Gay Alliance, 284
Moffat, Wendy, 108
Monette, Paul, 259
Moreau, Jeanne, 153
Morgan, Junius, 73
Morgenthau, Henry III, 28–29, 38
Munro, Maureen, 210, 277
Munson, Louise, 88, 118
Murphy, Ryan, 324
Murray Theatre (Princeton), 43
Museum of Modern Art, 63
Musgrave, Charles, 283
Music Box Theatre (New York), 58
My Brother Jack, 161

Nail, Richard, 39
Nassau Literary Magazine, 30, 37
Nathan, Robert, 81
National Archives, The, 76

National Council for Civil
   Liberties (UK), 272
National Labor Relations Board,
   22, 118, 290
National Review, The, 202
Nazism, 300–301
Nephew, The, 167
Netflix, 324
New American Library, 167
New Oriental Hotel (Galle), 256, 264
New Republic, The, 13, 146–
   47, 169, 182
New York, gay scene in, 36–37, 50,
   52–53, 61–64, 173, 245. See also
   Harlem, Greenwich Village
New York Daily Mirror, 307
New York Drama Critics Circle, 31
New York Herald, The, 30
New York Herald Tribune, The, 44, 169
*New York Journal and
   American, The*, 44
New York Native, 312
New York Post, The, 62–63, 72, 95
New York State Supreme Court, 28
New York Times, The, 1–2, 5, 31, 41, 55,
   58, 95, 107, 111, 117, 126, 128, 169,
   182–83, 190, 198, 202–3, 206, 217,
   222–23, 227, 233–34, 241, 247, 250,
   260, 285, 312, 323
New York Zoological Society, 54
New Yorker, The, 243
Newley, Patrick, 240
Newman, Paul, 229
Niehoff, Richard, 44
Nixon, Richard, 5, 248
Nobel Prize in Literature, 108
Nocturnes for the King of Naples, 259
Nolan, Sidney, 153
Normal Heart, The, 300, 305
Now Let's Talk About Music,
   263–66, 293
Nunn, Trevor, 241

Oakland Tribune, 126
Oberlin College, 320

O'Connor, Patrick, 296
Office of Strategic Services (OSS), 4,
   60, 72–82, 87–93, 95, 101–3, 117,
   124–25, 145, 162, 273, 281, 308
Ogren, Peter, 204–5
O'Hara, Frank, 3, 322
Olivier, Laurence, 133
Onassis, Aristotle, 153
One (periodical), 206
One for the Gods, 34, 62, 71, 107, 159,
   217–23, 228–33, 272
Orientalism, 264–65, 293
Orton, Joe, 271
Osborn, Shirley (Ayers), 54
Oscar Wilde Bookshop (NY), 227
Our Town, 109
Outward Bound, 50
*Oxford Research Encyclopedia of
   Literature*, 320
Oxford University, 108, 221

Pacific Sun, The, 202
Page, Louise, 305
Pallas, Laura, 272
Palmerton, Guy, 61
Paradise Lost, 286
Paramount Pictures, 229
Paris, Orlando, 206
Passage to E. M. Forster, A, 109
Passage to India, A, 108, 112, 163
Patch, Alexander, 76–77
Patten, Dick Van, 55
Patton, George, 78
Pavan, Marisa, 306
Peck, Gregory, 137
Peel Me A Lotus, 153, 161
Peer Gynt (play), 31–32
*Penguin Book of Gay Short
   Stories, The*, 4
Pennsylvania Railroad Company, 11
Pennsylvania State University, 296
Perfect Freedom, 2, 112, 277–85,
   289–90, 292
Perkins, Anthony, 153
Perkins, Maxwell, 191

Perry, David, 312
Perry, Imani, 7
Peters, Fritz, 226
Phaedra (film), 153
Philadelphia Evening Bulletin, 61
Philadelphia Inquirer, The, 94
Philadelphia Zoological Society, 12
Phillips Exeter Academy, 50
Picano, Felice, 213, 231, 260, 321, 323
Picasso, Pablo, 280
Pilchard, Frances, 39
Pilgrim Hawk, The, 63–64
Pinckard, H. R., 94
Place at the Table, A, 266
Plato, 221
Playboy, 243
Pledge of Allegiance, 160
Pollinger, Murray, 243
Porgy and Bess, 179
Porter, Cole, 39, 55, 57–58, 310
Porter, Katherine Anne, 64
Portnoy's Complaint, 192
Portsmouth Herald, 50
postwar novels, 87, 93–97, 117, 278, 284
Pratt Institute (NY), 232
Preston, Don, 190–94, 210
Preston, John, 307
Preston, Robert, 153
Pride and Prejudice, 182
Priestley, J. B., 17
Princeton Alumni Weekly, 58, 312
Princeton Club (NY), 307
Princeton Stories, 19
Princeton University, 5, 7, 16, 18–22, 24, 27–44, 53–54, 58, 62, 72–74, 82, 90, 95, 139, 156, 162, 170, 172, 177, 221, 232, 246, 281, 306, 311; admissions practices of, 20, 27–28; eating clubs of, 37–38; gay life in, 35, 43, 173; reputation of, 19, 29; university library, 73, 160, 172, 208, 313. *See also* Terrace Club, Theatre Intime, *Daily Princetonian*
protest novels, 122–24, 226

Proust, Marcel, 79, 282
Provence (France), 80, 101–4, 133
Publishers Weekly, 250, 298
Puig, Manuel, 318
Pulitzer Prize, 55
Purdy, James, 167
Putnam's (publisher), 190, 230, 248

Queens Quarterly (NY), 206
Queer Street, 322
Querelle, 272
Quin-Harken, Janet, 202
Quinn, William, 76
Quirk, The, 43, 211, 257–63, 273, 283

Race D'Ep (film), 275
racial segregation, 248
Radcliffe College, 104
Rader, Dotson, 223, 225
Randall, Tony, 153–54, *155*
Raymond, Gerard, 305
Reagan, Ronald, 5, 299
Rechy, John, 9, 168–69, 227, 250, 321–22
Reed, Carl, 42
Renault, Mary, 6, 9, 182, 210, 221, 227
Reuben, David, 190
Richard II, 42
Richardson, Marcia, 209
Richardson, Mary Hilburger, 88
Richardson, Newton, 88
Richardson, Robert B., 66, 88–89, 94, 101–2, *105–6*, 113, 133, 135, 139, 143, 148, 162, 164, 167, 171, 183, 294
Rivers, Joan, 2, 278
RKO Palace Theatre, 142
Robinson, William G., 41
Rockefeller family, 120
Rockwood, Irene, 211–13
Rodgers, Richard, 136
Roerick, William, 109
Rogers, Rosemary, 251
Romeo and Juliet, 241
Romero, Anthony, 27

Roosevelt, Franklin D., 5, 13, 28–29, 72
Rope's End, 32
Rosco, Jerry, 63
Rose Tattoo, The, 306
Rosenberg, Edgar, 278
Roth, Philip, 192
Royal Shakespeare Company (RSC), 241–43
Rukeyser, Muriel, 189
Rule, Jane, 298
Russo, Vito, 297
Ryan's Hope (TV series), 306
Rye, Bjorn, 266–67, 273

Safran, Sheri, 228
Sagarin, Edward (Donald Webster Cory), 125
Saint-Tropez (France), 104, 121, 281
Sakol, Jeannie, 158, 285, 295, 307–8, 313
Salonika, 305
same-sex marriage, 220–21, 323. *See also* gay liberation movement
San Francisco Chronicle, The, 94, 143, 145, 220
San Francisco City College, 136
Santorini (Greece), 222
Sarraute, Claude, 277
Sarton, May, 318
Sartori, Mario, 296–97
Saturday Review of Literature, The, 97, 127
Sausalito (CA), 142, 147
Schuyler, James, 322
Schwartz, Michael, 4–5
Schwartz, Peter, 40
Selassie, Haile, 31
Senecal, Jean-Michel, 275
Separate Peace, A, 298
Sexual Behavior in the Human Male, 109
Sexual Outlaw, 250
Shakespeare, William, 5, 31, 93, 159, 241–43, 317
Shan, Molly, 240

Shelley, Percy Bysshe, 159
Simon & Schuster, 291, 294
Singer, Winnaretta, 265
Single Man, A, 169
Slaughterhouse 5, 190
Slavitt, David, 190
Sling and the Arrow, The, 191
Smith, Patricia Juliana, 320
Smith, Robert Hardy Jr., 171–72
Snow White and the Seven Dwarfs, 36
Society for Individual Rights (CA), 206, 228
Sondheim, Stephen, 33, 273
Song of the Loon trilogy, 181, 204–6, 217, 228
Southern Railway Company, 21
Spanier, Didine, 183, 306
Spanier, Ginette, 104, 106–7, 133, 158, 160, 175–76, 306
Sparsholt Affair, The, 8
Spartacus travel guides, 271
Spender, Stephen, 109
Spenser, Edmund, 4
Splinters Company (NY), 239–40
Sri Lanka, 3, 255–57, 263–64, 298, 305–6, 311; expatriate community in, 255–56; political situation in, 256, 274
Stage Door (play), 50
Staircase, 203
Stallion (periodical), 212, 299–302
St. Augustine, 8, 322
St. John's College, 322
St. Louis Post-Dispatch, The, 126
St. Martin's Press, 268
Star Trek, 3
Stein, Gertrude, 64, 102–3, 128–29
Steward, Samuel (Phil Andros), 205, 228
Stiebel, Victor, 107
Stonewall Riots. *See* gay liberation movement
Strachey, Lytton, 108
Stranger's Child, The, 8
Stratford (UK), 241

Stritch, Elaine, 239
Strumpet Wind, The, 76, 80, 89–97, 101, 103, 107, 110–13, 117–19, 124, 141, 143, 167–68, 196, 273, 278, 284; French translation of, 120
Strumpet Wind, The (boat), 159, 167
summer stock theater, 38–39, 49–50, 59, 61
Summerbell, Richard, 292–93
Summers, Claude, 320
Sundgaard, Arnold, 55
Susann, Jacqueline, 190–91
Sweeney Todd, 33

Taking Care of Mrs. Carroll, 259
Tales of the City, 231, 259
Talk of the Town, The, 30, 39
Taylor, Brian ("Brodie"), 242
Taylor, Elizabeth, 153
Taylor, Holland, 211
Tchelitchew, Pavel, 63
Teal, Donn (Ronald Forsythe), 182–83, 198, 202
Teddy Boys, 127
Teeman, Tim, 96
Tempest, The, 31–32
Tenney, Del, 278
Tenth Floor (nightclub), 261
Terrace Club (Princeton), 37–38, 73–74
Terry, C. V., 94–95
Theatre Intime (Princeton), 30–35, 39–41, 43–44
This Side of Paradise, 19
Thompson, Kay, 139
Thomson, Virgil, 63
Time (magazine), 58
Time of Their Lives, 39–41, 44
Tobias, Andrew, 218–19
Tocqueville (France), 271, 274, 306
Tolkien, J. R. R., 6, 210
Tonight Show, The, 2
Townsend, Larry, 228
To Wong Foo, Thanks for Everything! Julie Newmar, 8
Topman (periodical), 283

Trainer, Paul, 272
Trenet, Charles, 93
Triangle Club (Princeton), 34
Trilling, Lionel, 111
Troubled Midnight, The, 124
Turing, Alan, 35, 323
Two Mrs. Grenvilles, The, 308
Tyler, Parker, 278

Undiscovered Country (play), 41–42
United Service Organizations (USO) shows, 136
United States v. Windsor, 220
University of Hawaii, 296
University of Iowa, 53
University of Pennsylvania, 12, 16, 19–20, 24
University of Texas at El Paso, 88
University of Tulsa, 231
University of Virginia, 211
Unyielding Memory, The, 161
Uranian poetry, 125
U.S. Air Force, 65–66, 71, 76, 88, 136
U.S. Army, 66, 78, 104
U.S. Civil War, 12
U.S. Olympic yachting team, 16, 159
U.S. Quartermaster Corps, 88
Ustinov, Peter, 153

Vallency Tradition, The, 56, 60, 88, 113, 117–21, 124, 127–29, 170–71, 179, 225, 289–91, 311; French translation of, 5, 119–21, 180, 290–91; interracial relationship in, 118–20, 290
Valley Forge Military Academy, 16
Valley of the Dolls, 190–91, 193
Valliére, Louise de La, 21, 118
Vallone, Raf, 153
Vanderbilt family, 120
Vane, Sutton, 50
Vector (periodical), 205–6, 227
Verdi, Giuseppe, 179

Vidal, Gore, 95–96, 113, 125, 182, 191, 197, 213, 227, 229, 251, 259–60, 279, 296, 321–22
Viereck, George Sylvester, 125–26
Vietnam War, 189, 264
Village Voice, The, 113, 212, 228, 232, 249
Villanova, PA, 13, 87–88
Violet Quill, The, 260, 320, 324
Visconti, Luchino, 264–65
Volpone, 41
Vonnegut, Kurt, 190

Wagner, Richard, 194
Waldenbooks, 1–2, 323
Walker, Alice, 189
Walker, Stanley, 30
Wallis, Redmond, 157–58, 161, 173
Wallis, Robyn, 157
War and Peace (film), 33
Warner Books, 296–98
Warner Brothers, 60
Warner, Stephen, 229, 305
Warnke, Richard, 208–9
Warren, Patricia Nell, 6, 210, 227, 229, 260, 271–72, 318
Washington Evening Star, The, 62
Washington Post, The, 259
Washington Post Magazine, The, 35
Watergate scandal, 248
Waugh, Evelyn, 34, 271
Weaver, Neal, 240
Webb, Clifton, 60, 74, 265, 309
Webb, Joyce, 209
Welles, Orson, 31, 33, 42, 55, 61
Werfel, Franz, 13
Wescott, Glenway, 7, 63–66, 87, 93, 109–110, 112–14, 133, 135, 143, 169, 173, 265, 278, 296, 310–11
West Coast Review of Books, 250–51
West Point (U.S. Military Academy), 171–72
West Virginia Advertiser, The, 94
What I Believe, 110
Wharton School (PA), 296

Wheeler, Monroe, 63–65, 109, 310
White, Edmund, 213, 259–60, 321
Whitmore, George, 213, 259–60
Who's Afraid of Virginia Woolf?, 33, 169
Wicker, Randy, 204, 323
Wilbur, Ray, 94
Wilde, Oscar, 6, 31, 210, 227, 318, 322
Wilde, Percival, 30
Wilder, Clinton, 33
Wilder, Thornton, 17
William Morrow (publisher), 93–94, 119, 124, 141, 143, 190, 193, 230, 248–49
Williams, Emlyn, 7, 240, 243
Williams, Jesse Lynch, 19
Williams, Tennessee, 3, 53–54, 113, 273, 283, 295, 306, 322
Wilmington News Journal, The, 127
Wilson, Woodrow, 27, 29, 37
Windham, James B., 88
Winter's Tale, The, 241
Wolf, Tom, 30
Wooddell, Barbara, *59*
Woodhouse, Reed, 319
Woods, Gregory, 318–19
Woodward, Bob, 248
Woodward, William, 308
Woolf, Leonard, 108
Woolf, Virginia, 108, 112, 318
Woollcott, Alexander, 56, 58
Woolley, Monty, 7, 55–58, *59*
World War I, 82, 108, 125
World War II, 4, 7, 63, 65, 71–83, 102–3, 109, 125, 128–29, 203, 217, 265, 273; Abwehr agents, 76–77, 79–81, 95, 103; American Seventh Army, 76–78; D-Day landings, 76, 90; French Resistance fighters, 82, 89, 133, 135, 145; gay soldiers in, 65, 74–75, 78–79, 92–93, 278; Nazi persecution of homosexuals, 126; Operation Dragoon (Anvil), 76; Operation Overlord, 76; Vichy government, 89–90, 95, 103; Victory Day, 82

Wright, Bruce, 27–28
Wyatt, Robert (Bob), 231–32, 249–50, 252, 261–62, 271, 284–85, 295

Yale University, 4, 18–20, 35, 40, 57, 90, 294, 301, 317
Yates, Richard, 189, 295
You Can't Take It With You (play), 55
You Never Know (play), 55
Young, Ian, 232, 323
Young and the Evil, The, 278

zazous, 127
Ziegfeld Follies, 36

About the Author

Joseph M. Ortiz is associate professor of English at the University of Texas at El Paso, where he teaches Renaissance and comparative literature. He studied at Yale University and Princeton University, and he has held residential fellowships at Cornell University's Society for the Humanities and the Folger Shakespeare Library in Washington, DC. He is the author of *Broken Harmony: Shakespeare and the Politics of Music* and the editor of *Shakespeare and the Culture of Romanticism*. He has published articles and reviews on Renaissance literature and music, LGBT literature and history, and opera. He lives with his husband in La Union, New Mexico.

www.ingramcontent.com/pod-product-compliance
Lightning Source LLC
Chambersburg PA
CBHW021339300426
44114CB00012B/1005